THE NEW ALCHEMISTS

THE NEW
ALCHEMISTS

Silicon Valley and the
Microelectronics
Revolution

DIRK HANSON

LITTLE, BROWN AND COMPANY   *Boston ◇ Toronto*

FIRST EDITION

Portions of Chapter Seven first appeared in *New West*, July 28, 1980.

Library of Congress Cataloging in Publication Data

Hanson, Dirk.
  The new alchemists.

  Includes index.
  1. Microelectronics industry — California —
History. I. Title.
HD9696.A3U5546 1982 338.4'76213817'097946 82–8964
ISBN 0-316-34342-0   AACR2

MV

*Published simultaneously in Canada
by Little, Brown & Company (Canada) Limited*

PRINTED IN THE UNITED STATES OF AMERICA

For Kathryn

Those who are able to harness science itself, and direct it to their own ends, have gained considerable advantage. For them, the competitive task of anticipating the future has become easier since they now have the means for determining the future themselves. So it was with the alchemists of the late nineteenth century, and their successors of the twentieth, who undertook to transform science into gold and, in the process, gave rise to modern science-based industry.

— David Noble, *America by Design*

Acknowledgments

A number of personal friends and professional acquaintances provided valuable help during the research and writing that culminated in this book. For assisting my entry into the world of high-technology electronics, I thank Jim Lydon, Martin Gold, Howard Raphael, Bob Harrington, Tom Skornia, Ken McKenzie, Gary Summers, Roy Twitty, Paul Plansky, Walt Matthews, Joe Clark, Elliott Sopkin, Keith Parsons, and dozens of others, all of who gave unstintingly of their time, answered my incessant questions, and returned my phone calls.

I am particularly indebted to those who reviewed the entire manuscript, among them Dr. Robert Noyce, Tom Hinkleman, Dan Kennedy, Roger Donald, and Michael Mattil.

A special thanks to Susan Benson, for her wise and generous editorial assistance, and to Craig Zarley, a friend and fellow journalist whose apt suggestions helped keep me from losing sight of the forest for all the trees.

The Grid

"Plastics," a well-meaning elder whispered to young Benjamin in *The Graduate*. It was sound enough financial advice, but "silicon" would have been closer to the mark. Forty miles south of San Francisco, in a place known as Silicon Valley, the blueprints of the technological future are being etched on tiny slivers of crystalline silicon. Microelectronics — the science of creating thousands of solid-state electronic elements on a silicon chip — is the hidden foundation of modern technology, and it is changing how we live, work and interact with others in ways even the architects of the transformation do not fully understand.

As the nerve center of the microelectronics revolution for the past twenty-five years, Silicon Valley has gained a well-deserved reputation as the Florence of the information age. It houses perhaps the densest concentration of high-technology brainpower in the world; a heady mix of digital circuit and computer manufacturers, Nobel Prize winners, maverick scientists, university researchers, electronic warfare specialists and high-octane investors. From silicon, nature's most abundant element after oxygen, the science-based corporations headquartered there have created and refined an inexpensive "universal machine," — the microprocessor or, as it is commonly known, the computer on a silicon chip. This tiny device, one of this century's key technological advancements, is opening up new vistas, new possibilities and new threats in almost every field of human endeavor. In the few short years since the invention of the microprocessor and related microelectronic circuits, Silicon Valley and its outposts worldwide have mapped a grand marketing strategy which, if successful, ultimately will add every scientific field, every industry, every man, woman and child in America to its growing customer list.

Even today, microelectronics has become indispensable to the practice of modern science and industry. Moreover, it has transformed the American electronics industry into the "compunications" industry, a blend of communication and computer companies which is destined to play a crucial and controversial role in industrial society as the electronic age unfolds.

In the century that has passed since the inventions of men like Thomas Edison and Nikola Tesla launched the electrical industry, electricity has been shaped into an invisible grid that in some way affects the lives of all four billion inhabitants of the planet. Fashioned from electromagnetic waves, the grid is a man-made spiderweb of information and energy. Its transmission hardware includes such tools as radio, television, telephones, computers and communication satellites. The technology that makes it possible was created by the electronics industry. And the software that makes it all go is the human mind.

The electronic grid began with the light bulb, the telegraph and the vacuum tube, and its use has changed the lives of consumers, the architecture of cities and even the meaning of work and leisure. The industry that spawned it has established itself, unwittingly or not, as the fundamental agent of technological change in the world today. Alter the grid, and almost everything else will be altered in the process. This unique industry has been responsible for two major societal revolutions. In the late 1800s electrical power was the means by which the United States shifted from an agricultural society to an industrial society. Today a similar "post-industrial" revolution is taking place. Since World War II the electronics industry has been altering the way electricity is put to work. The transistor and the electronic computer, by-products of war research on radar and cybernetics, shifted the focus of electronics to information processing and laid the groundwork for microelectronics. The integrated circuit and the microprocessor which followed sparked an explosion of electronic applications, from hand-held calculators to hunter-killer spy satellites, from home computers to bionic limbs for the handicapped, "from making steel to making Big Macs," in the words of one industry executive.

"Microprocessors are getting into everything," according to Arthur C. Clarke. "We won't be able to pick up a single piece of equipment in the near future, except maybe a broom, that hasn't got a microprocessor in it."

Dr. Robert Noyce, co-inventor of the integrated circuit and vice-chairman of Intel, the company that developed the first computer on a chip, claims "A true revolution: A qualitative change in technology, the integrated microelectronic circuit, has given rise to a qualitative change in human capabilities."

The list of applications is long and impressive, so much so that it can obscure the enormous and controversial impact of microelectronics on consumers and workers. (In West Germany, the microprocessor has been dubbed the "job killer" because of its role in automation.) The new information environment made possible by microelectronics is still in its infancy, but already almost half the U.S. work force, by many estimates, is employed in the collection, manipulation and transmission of information.

"Just as the physical environment determines what the source of food and exertions of labor shall be," writes Neil Postman of New York University, "the information environment gives specific direction to the kinds of ideas, social attitudes, definitions of knowledge and intellectual capacities that will emerge." And further, "when there occurs a radical shift in the structure of that environment, this must be followed by changes in social organization, intellectual predispositions and a sense of what is real and valuable. . . . We might say that the most potent revolutionaries are those people who invent new media of communication, although typically they are not aware of what they are doing."

In fact, the revolutionaries of Silicon Valley *cannot* be fully aware of what they are doing because they can never foresee all the ways in which each new generation of digital devices will be put to work by creative users. The first microprocessor was intended for use in a Japanese calculator, nothing more. By 1980 the industry had delivered more than ten million microprocessors, and a complete listing of all the ways in which they are used would fill a telephone book. This explosion of applications was neither intended nor expected, but one aspect of the microelectronics revolution has been clear since the beginning: inventing new media of communication is a profitable business. Silicon Valley is the reason why the top fifty electronic firms racked up $88.4 billion in sales in 1978, or about four percent of that year's total GNP.

Until recently, the profitable practices of the microelectronics industry were of concern mainly to its trio of top-drawer customers — government, big business and the military. But now the industry has turned its attention to the consumer. Calculators, digital watches and video games are only the opening forays into customer electronics. Plans call for a home computer in every living room and dozens of microprocessors controlling the operation of every automobile. Because the microprocessor is so cheap and its applications so pervasive, there is little doubt that this transition will come to pass. However, like any advanced technology, microelectronics is a double-edged sword, so it is not surprising that two competing visions of the computer future have grown up around it.

One argument holds that there are too many computers about already. In the mythical dialogue between man and the computer of the future, man might ask, "What is love?" and the computer would answer, "That does not compute." According to this view, computers and microelectronic technology are worms in the apple; symptoms of a misguided technological high road that can lead only to the total estrangement of man from his environment, and possibly from himself. Holders of this view are often suspicious of engineers and technology in general. For them, the microprocessor is just a machine that has put more people out of work in less time than any other machine ever built. Attempting to solve human problems with electronic technology, it is argued, is a particularly dangerous example of the myth of the imminent technological fix; the kind of gimmickry, like the space program, that keeps people from getting on with the real work at hand. In short, the microcomputer revolution is really the Age of Dehumanization, the triumph of machine over man, the consolidation of control over human destiny in the hands of a technological elite. Dr. Joseph Weizenbaum of MIT, himself a widely respected computer scientist, recently told a conference: "People can still pull the computer's plug. However, we may have to work hard to even maintain that privilege." In Boston, a young man cut the connection between his house and the local electrical utility. "I wasn't using electricity," he told the authorities, "electricity was using me."

Opposing this pull-the-plug scenario is a view as relentlessly optimistic as the first one is dire. When man asks the computer of the future, "What is love?" the computer answers the question. Correctly. This computer of the future can *think*. It has been endowed by its creators with the power of reason. In fact, silicon-based electronics just may be in the evolutionary scheme of things. "I don't think that life in the cosmos, more than a fraction of it, is some distorted replica of our chemistry," says Dr. Robert Jastrow of NASA. "I would put my money on the silicon memory bank as an immortal form of life and on the disembodied form as the ultimate."

Less cosmic, but equally drastic, are the claims made for the simplest computing unit of all, the microprocessor. According to some, the microprocessor will have the singular effect of increasing human intelligence. "It has often been said," writes Dr. Robert Noyce in *Scientific American,* "that just as the Industrial Revolution enabled man to apply and control greater physical power than his own muscle could provide, so electronics has extended his intellectual power."

The verdict is still out, and the outcome of the microelectronics revolution is far from ordained. Surely the companies that sparked this revolution deserve the same scrutiny that is attached to the activities of the oil and automobile industries, the more so since the microprocessor has become an integral part of the operation of almost every business and industry in America. The choices these companies make or choose not to make and the mistakes they avoid or fall victim to will affect everyone.

If chemists and physicists are the modern inheritors of the alchemistic tradition, then the marriage of those two disciplines in the science of microelectronics is the new alchemy of the twentieth century. The ancient alchemists held as their goal the transformation of man as well as the elements. The new alchemists, in the process of transmuting silicon into digitized information, are affecting social changes as profound as those which followed the discovery of the wheel, the steam engine and the automobile.

Dr. Noyce once said that Silicon Valley "holds the keys to the kingdom." This book is an attempt to discover where this new electronic priesthood came from, and exactly what manner of kingdom they have in mind.

CONTENTS

THE NEW ALCHEMISTS

CHAPTER ONE

Why Is Thomas Edison Frying Dogs?

*In fact, I've come to the conclusion that I
never did know anything about it.*
— THOMAS EDISON, *on electricity*

"The Logos in the Lightning"

On March 27, 1899, an invisible message flashed across the English channel from Boulogne to Dover. By "signalling through space without wires," a young scientist named Guglielmo Marconi had successfully connected England and France.

Bridging one body of water with his crude transmitters led Marconi to wonder whether they were capable of yet another, more formidable, task: sending a message across the Atlantic Ocean. For this he would have to make some improvements. His thoughts turned to some rather unusual experiments on the phenomenon of electrical resonance performed by an eccentric European inventor now working in America. Perhaps Nikola Tesla's giant transformers might shed some light on the problem. . . .

That same year, Nikola Tesla arrived in Colorado Springs at the invitation of his patent attorney. One of the foremost electrical investigators of the age, Tesla was not greatly awed by the accomplishments of Marconi, Edison or anyone else, for Tesla believed that he alone was destined to discover the true secret of electricity. His recent victory over Edison in a bitter dispute about the direction of the electrical industry, coupled with an impressive record of invention, had earned him a reputation as an ingenious but highly unorthodox inventor. Tesla brought with him to Colorado a grand dream: to unite the world through the wireless broadcast of "intelligence and power" to every corner of the globe.

Tesla intended to prove the truth of his vision by performing a singular experiment. In the center of his laboratory stood the instrument by which, in the space of a few years, he intended to send electricity around the world. It was a curious form of an electrical current transformer known as a Tesla Coil, consisting of two circular wooden frames wrapped with wire and positioned one inside the other. By arranging the two frames so that they vibrated at the same electrical frequency when connected to a power source, Tesla had managed to generate powerful electrical oscillations on smaller models. In New York, these prototypes had produced millions of volts; more power than any other machine of the age was capable of producing. And now that he had constructed the largest Tesla Coil ever built, neither Tesla nor his lab assistant, Kolman Czito, knew exactly what would happen when they switched on the power.

On the eve of the Colorado experiment, Tesla was excited, but Czito feared that the giant machine might kill them both. Electrocution, he knew, was an occupational hazard in this line of work. To make matters worse, Tesla intended to play the role of Prometheus in reverse. Attached to the inner frame of the Tesla Coil was a copper wire supported by a wooden mast. The mast extended through a hole in the ceiling and was capped two hundred feet above the ground with a large copper ball. It looked something like a giant lightning rod and no doubt would have behaved as one, except that Tesla hoped to *create* lightning instead. If his theory was sound, a series of lightning bolts would erupt from the copper ball atop the mast.

When all was ready, Tesla walked out into the yard and stood where he could see the mast. He was wearing his usual midnight lab attire — silk shirt, cutaway coat, suede gloves and special shoes with inch-thick rubber insulating soles. Upon hearing the appropriate signal, Czito threw the switch. Inside the lab, a series of snaps and pops emanated from the equipment, followed by a rumble, and then a series of rifle-shot explosions. Czito huddled near the switch and watched as an eerie blue glow suffused the lab. The coils shook furiously and spat fire as peals of thunder broke across the room. Little hairs of flame danced on the walls and the lab smelled of ozone. Czito couldn't hear above the roar and it occurred to him, as sparks began to stab his own fingers, that Tesla could not call upon him to end this holocaust because Tesla had no doubt been killed.

But Tesla, dancing and clapping outside the lab, was very much alive. He watched with joy as jagged streamers of lightning, more than a hundred feet long and thick as a man's arm, burst from the copper ball like God's own sneezes.

After only a few minutes, the tremendous voltage of the coils blew out the main generator at the Colorado Springs Electric Company. Overload. The experiment was over.

Nikola Tesla's artificial lightning was an attempt to prove a theory that is now a daily fact of life: the worldwide transmission of information by electrical means. According to Tesla, the lightning was merely a spontaneous discharge resulting from the powerful electrical oscillations his coils produced. He pictured these vibrating waves rippling around the earth, like waves caused by a rock dropped into a pool of still water, and believed that electrical energy or coded messages could be drawn from them at any point on the planet with a properly grounded antenna. Tesla was a man both ahead of and behind the times. His plan for world broadcasting failed, but his realization that mankind would come to depend almost totally upon electricity as a source of power and information was remarkably prescient. Even Thomas Edison, who played a central role in the domestication of electricity, did not foresee the pervasive role it would play in shaping the direction of twentieth-century society.

To the men who created and ran the electrical industry at the beginning of the twentieth century, electricity symbolized power and wealth. But for centuries it stood for mystery; an unseen force, its effects puzzling, its essence unknown. The early physicists who called themselves "electricians" suspected that this mysterious force harbored occult powers of healing and destruction. Their instincts were sound even when their theories were not, for electricity, together with the force of magnetism, is known today as electromagnetism, one of the four basic forces in nature. Electricity's fundamental attribute is charge, a term physicists use to describe how subatomic particles react to each other. Charge comes in two forms — positive and negative. Oppositely charged particles attract, particles with like charges repel and chargeless particles remain neutral. This phenomenon of attraction and repulsion is the glue that holds living things together by allowing atoms to combine in the form of molecules. When we walk, the electrical potential of our bones changes. When we think, the electrical potential of the synapses alters as the neurons fire, generating a current that can be measured with electrodes on the scalp.

Of course, the early electricians knew nothing of this. Nor did they know that lightning is actually electricity in a spectacularly visible form. But it is clear that lightning has fascinated scientists and philosophers throughout history. Nikola Tesla was not the first to see this manifestation of natural forces as a symbol for intelligence and power. "It is the thunderbolt," wrote Heraclitus, a Greek philosopher of the sixth century B.C., "which steers the course of all things."

Zeus had lightning in his arsenal, as did the early Mesopotamian gods. One of the thunderbolt's devastating effects is fire which, strictly speaking, is a chemical reaction. And fire had much to do with the woes of Prometheus. Wisest of the Titans and, according to one legend, creator of the human race, Prometheus learned various "useful arts" from Athena and thoughtfully passed them on to mankind. But the fire in the lightning was another matter; a secret Zeus did not wish to share. When Prometheus stole fire for the benefit of mankind, pandemonium broke loose in heaven, human civilization began and Prometheus lost his liver for it — several times.

For the early researchers who called electricity "rational fire," the Promethean myth must have seemed an apt metaphor, for it was not long before they too discovered that attempting to steal its secret could prove hazardous, if not fatal.

One of the earliest electrical experiments was the Leyden Jar, named not after a person, but a place. The Leyden Jar consisted of a glass container lined inside and out with tinfoil. Based on earlier experiments, scientists suspected that electricity was a fluid, or possibly several fluids, that somehow flowed through some objects like amber and metal, but not through others like glass. If electricity was a fluid, albeit a rather unusual one, then perhaps it could be captured and bottled. The jar took a relatively weak charge of static electricity and temporarily stored the spark. Whatever electricity was, the scientists seemed to have bottled it. The device was the first crude capacitor — two metal plates separated by an insulator.

The magical Leyden Jar fascinated everyone. Eighteenth-century electricians didn't understand how it worked, but they ran all manner of colorful experiments to see what it could do. Electricity and magnetism, which seemed to be linked in some strange way, became the rage in polite society on both sides of the Atlantic. For the amusement of Louis XV, king of France, the Abbé Nollet arranged a hand-holding train of 180 gendarmes, all linked to a series of jars. "It is singular," he noted, "to see the multitude of different gestures, and to hear the instantaneous exclamation of those surprised by the shock." Bizarre theatrics ensued across the continent: electrified boys hanging from silk threads, holes blasted in cardboard, liquor set blazing and small animals destroyed. Upon dissecting birds he had electrocuted, Nollet found that the ruptures and discoloration looked very much like the internal mayhem that resulted when creatures were struck dead by lightning. But he did not read the meaning of the clue.

The Leyden Jar also fascinated Benjamin Franklin who was, among his many other talents, one of the premier electricians of the age. Franklin took a profound view of electricity as a fundamental and understandable force of nature. He suspected that it was one thing, not several fluids, and had a strong hunch that lightning was actually electricity in disguise: nothing more or less than a spark from a Leyden Jar.

Other electricians began to suspect as much, but Franklin put theory to practice, as was his habit, in one of the best-known — and most dangerous — experiments in the history of science. In 1752 he threaded a metal key onto the string of a kite and flew the kite during a thunderstorm. A small electric charge ran down the moist string to the key, and a spark jumped from the key to his knuckles. Franklin was not only a good early scientist; he was an extremely lucky man. Some of his European colleagues were not. A few were killed attempting to perform similar experiments. The lightning rod, a practical result of his experiment, killed a few others.

Having proven the unity of lightning and electricity, Franklin was now convinced that electricity was a single force and further, that it had "positive" and "negative" attributes. He began to concentrate on the concepts of charge and current. His theories spread, and although they did not account for all known effects, the days of trying to bottle the electrical fluid came to an end as electricians began opening up new areas of research.

Science historian Thomas Kuhn calls this process of new theory formation a "paradigm shift." Writes Kuhn in *The Structure of Scientific Revolutions* (1962), "Sometime between 1740 and 1780, electricians were for the first time enabled to take the foundations of their field for granted. From that point they pushed on to more concrete and recondite problems, and increasingly they then reported their results in articles addressed to other electricians rather than in books addressed to the learned world at large."

The Little Engine That Could

By the early 1800s electricians had amassed a wealth of facts about electricity, and experimentation had matured into a systematic process. Still, the power of the thunderbolt had not been harnessed to practical application; as yet, no reliable machines existed that could put electrical current to use. Electricity and magnetism remained the dominant concerns for physicists of the period and Michael Faraday, a self-taught physicist and former bookbinder's apprentice, was no exception. In 1821 Faraday pieced together a crude forerunner of the electric motor — a magnet that caused a wire to move when connected to a battery. In 1831, at the Royal Society in London, Faraday set out to prove that the principle he had discovered could be used to produce a sustained electrical current. The Faraday disk dynamo, as the apparatus he built there became known, converted mechanical energy (a rotating disk) into electricity, while the electric motor converted electricity into mechanical power.

Up until Faraday began investigating what was later called electromagnetic induction, the steam engine was the king of nineteenth-century industry. When Matthew Boulton teamed up with James Watt to build an improved steam machine, he claimed, "I sell here, sir, what all the world desires to have — power." But now Faraday's work seemed to hint at a new method of supplying power. Shortly after his famous demonstration of the disk dynamo, Faraday had received an anonymous letter suggesting that his discovery might be put to use in the creation of giant and powerful machines. Faraday did not pursue the suggestion, but others did, and the giant and powerful machines — electric motors, generators and dynamos — were not long in coming.

In short, Faraday's disk dynamo quickly became the little engine that could. The reversibility of electrical and mechanical power caught the attention of both practical tinkerers and men of industry. Electricity carried by wires seemed to hold immense potential advantages over the direct use of coal or compressed steam for powering industrial equipment. In theory, electricity was steadier, more reliable and most important of all, cheaper. Perhaps these new generators and dynamos could be used to convert coal and steam, the mainstays of the

Industrial Revolution, into electric current, while motors might be used to turn lathes, drive pulleys or run other industrial machines.

This was the beginning of what Lewis Mumford calls the "neotechnic" period, "marked, to begin with, by the conquest of a new form of energy: electricity." During the Industrial Revolution, or "paleotechnic," iron had been the primary raw material, but now the emphasis began to shift to a new set of raw materials, "the new alloys, the rare earths and the lighter metals" — all useful elements in the generation and transmission of electricity.

By the time President Grover Cleveland took office in 1885, the practical results of the domestication of electricity were becoming evident. Giant thousand-horsepower Corliss steam engines still belched and hissed, but the dynamo hum of electric locomotives had joined the chorus. Gas still lit most ovens and lamps in America but Edison's incandescent light was changing that too. For citizens of the day there were even more obvious signs of change. All one had to do was gaze upon the magnificent Brooklyn Bridge or the first skyscrapers cutting the urban skyline or the great steelworks of Pittsburgh. Something big was happening in the late nineteenth century, courtesy of a relatively new class of wonder workers, the engineers. Whitman and Kipling sang praises to their work, and Henry Adams returned again and again to the machinery exhibit at the Universal Exposition in Paris, drawn by the "occult mechanism" of the dynamo; this presentation of a new aesthetic. Only a few years after Adams's epiphany, Marcel Duchamp turned to a friend at another machinery exhibit and said: "Painting has come to an end. Who can do anything better than this propeller?"

It was the Golden Age of Engineering. Earlier in the century Auguste Comte had written that the engineers constituted "the direct and necessary instrument of coalition by which alone the new social order can commence." A generation later Comte's prediction was proven true by an industry whose charter was the practical application of the new electrical machines. From the outset, the electrical industry brought together two distinct types: inventors and industrialists. A product of this marriage was the electrical engineer, who was to play a major role in setting the tone for twentieth-century industrial development and the pervasive social changes that accompanied it. David Noble, Mellon Fellow in Humanities and Engineering at MIT, writes of this period:

> . . . between 1880 and 1920 the first and second generations of men who created and ran the modern electrical industry formed the vanguard of science-based industrial development in the United States. These were the people who first successfully combined the discoveries of physical science with the mechanical know-how of the workshop to produce the much-heralded electrical revolution in power generation, lighting, transportation, and communication; who forged the great companies which manufactured that revolution and the countless electric utilities, electric railways and telephone companies which carried it across the nation. At the same time, it was they who introduced the now familiar features characteristic of modern science-based industry: systematic patent procedures, organized industrial-research laboratories, and extensive technical training programs.

The result, according to Noble, was "the transformation of science itself into capital."* The electrical industry changed the nature of invention itself and with it the role of the individual inventor. Electrical invention was to become a much more systematic and controlled process as the independent inventor became the corporate employee. The story of Thomas Edison and his rival, Nikola Tesla, affords an excellent view of how this transformation came about.

---

* The electrical and chemical industries actually developed in tandem as the nation's first science-based industries. They both depended upon basic scientific advances for their technological products and they both sold those products to almost every other industry. If the electronics industry is the story of taming the free electron, then the chemical industry is the story of taming the organic molecule. The former leads to computers and electrical engineering. The latter leads to cloning and genetic engineering — another story altogether.

Thomas Edison and the War of the Currents

The life of Thomas Edison (1847–1931) illustrates one of two very different attitudes toward invention that began to divide the American and European scientific communities of the late 1800s. Edison insisted on calling himself an inventor, not a scientist, and the distinction was not idle. Scientists of the European tradition tended to view invention as mere mechanics, even though European inventors held a commanding lead over their American counterparts in the creation of potentially profitable electrical machines. Faraday had never commercialized any of his discoveries, preferring instead to pursue what the European science academies considered the far nobler calling of "pure" science. But to a practical man like Edison, nothing seemed more ludicrous than spending endless hours in the abstract world of theory.

As an inventor, Edison was nothing if not prolific. At one point, Edison set up a laboratory with the intention of making "a minor invention every ten days, and a big one every six months or so." He received more than a thousand patents in his lifetime, a record unequaled by any other inventor in history. Like Faraday, Edison was short on mathematics. Unlike Faraday, he was proud of it, an attitude that did not help his case abroad in the early years of his career. "Oh these mathematicians make me tired!" he once said, only half in jest. "When you ask them to work out a sum they take a piece of paper, cover it with rows of A's, B's, and X's, Y's . . . scatter a mess of flyspecks over them, and then give you an answer that's all wrong." Nonetheless, he added many prominent scientists and mathematicians to his lab staff as the job of electrical invention grew more complex.

Edison became an international celebrity on the basis of his contributions to telegraphy, telephony, electrical power and lighting, recorded sound, moving pictures and other fields. However, not all of Edison's contemporaries considered him a charming man. Robert Conot, his most recent biographer, called Edison "a lusty, crusty, hard-driving and occasionally ruthless Midwesterner" with a "Bunyanesque ambition for wealth." The Wizard of Menlo Park, as he came to be known at his lab near the Menlo Park train station in New Jersey, did not move gracefully through the social circles to which fame gave him access. Edison suffered from the classic Victorian aversion to the bath and clung to his personal theory that removing one's clothing altered the body chemistry, causing a host of unpleasant diseases. He often slipped into bed fully clothed, to the disgust of both his first and second wives. Just as often he did not slip into bed at all. "A man don't need any sleep," he announced, after perfecting the art of the catnap.

Edison is best remembered for two related inventions — the first commercial incandescent lamp and his direct current system of supplying the lamp with power. Commercial electric lighting began with arc light — a continuous spark between two carbon rods — and various arc lighting systems had appeared throughout Europe. Gas light still prevailed, but by 1879, the year Edison perfected his lamp, Charles Brush was marketing an improved arc lighting system in America. However, arc lighting had serious limitations. It emitted noxious gases, required frequent maintenance and tended to give off too much light for domestic use. The concept of incandescent light — a single carbon rod enclosed in a partially evacuated glass tube — was an attempt to get around these problems. An electric current sent into the lamp would heat the rod until it glowed, or at least that was the idea. After fifty years of experiment the results had not been promising. In England, Joseph Swan had better luck than most using a thick, low-resistance carbon rod, but even his lamps burned out almost immediately. Many researchers had simply given up on the project, convinced that for all its potential advantages carbon rod incandescence could never compete with arc or gas light.

They underestimated the Wizard of Menlo Park. Edison chose to enter the market for electric light only after a great deal of prior homework convinced him he stood to make more money in lighting than in the telephone or telegraph markets — providing he could devise a suitable incandescent *sys-tem*. This was the key to his success. Rather than begin work on the lamp itself, Edison concentrated his initial efforts on developing a new system of distributing electricity. "I saw the thing had not gone so far but that I had a chance. . . . It suddenly came to me, like the secret of the speaking phonograph. . . . The subdivision of light is all right. . . ." Edison wanted to subdivide the arc light overkill, parceling it out in reasonable amounts that could be metered and sold. After a thorough study of the gas industry, with its distribution system of central gas houses and gas mains connected to a network of branching pipes, he came up with a plan: a central power station linked by wires to the homes and businesses of America. "From the very outset of his work," writes an early Edison biographer, "Edison was guided by his overarching concept of a *whole electric distribution system* of which all the parts must be fitted into place. In contrast to other inventors, who searched only for some magical incandescing substance, he worked out all the supporting structure of his system: its power supply, conductors and circuit, and then came back to determine what kind of light would be demanded by it."

"It was necessary to invent everything," said Edison. "Dynamos, regulators, meters, switches, fuses, fixtures, underground conductors with their necessary connecting boxes, and a host of other detail parts, even down to insulating tape." It was clear to him, once the details of distribution had been worked out, that his dynamos required a thin, high-resistance filament so that the lights would glow with relatively small amounts of current. Only in this way would his system become a commercial reality. Scarcely had he begun work on the lamp itself when a group of backers, including one of J. P. Morgan's banking partners, joined with him to form the Edison Electric Light Company on the faith that Edison could deliver the incandescent light he envisioned. Morgan, the invisible man with the money behind Edison's success story, in effect was supporting a *research program,* marking a new phase in the relationship between business and invention.

Once Edison and his lab staff had worked out a proper vacuum for the lamp, the search began for a suitable high resistance filament. Edison tried everything from human hair to marijuana but soon returned to carbon. One night late in 1879, he inserted a filament of carbonized cotton thread into a bulb and turned on the power. It glowed . . . and when the dawn came it was still glowing. With a few more refinements he had what he needed. "To all appearances Mr. Edison has got the lamp he has so long been searching for," announced the January 1880 edition of *Scientific American*. "The light produced is perfect; the lamp inexpensive and apparently durable; the economy of the general system in which it is used is tolerably clear, and all its details seem to have been worked out with Mr. Edison's usual cleverness and practical skill." Three years later the Edison Electric Light Company opened the Pearl Street Power Station in New York. J. P. Morgan, not too surprisingly, became one of the first residents of the city to illuminate his home with an Edison power plant. By 1884 wires connected Pearl Street's steam-powered dynamos to more than five hundred homes. The era of domestic electrical power — and electricity bills — had begun.

A few years after Edison's triumph, an immigrant from present-day Yugoslavia arrived in New York carrying a few pennies, some poems he had written and a letter of introduction to the great Thomas Edison. The letter, from an executive at an Edison subsidiary firm in Paris, read, "I know of two great men and you are one of them; the other is this young man." Thirty years after his arrival, the immigrant received the coveted Edison Medal of the American Institute of Electrical Engineers, complete with this homage:

> Were we to seize and to eliminate from our industrial world the results of [his] work, the wheels of industry would cease to turn, our electrical cars and trains would stop, our towns would be dark, our mills would be dead and idle. Yea, so far-reaching is this work that it has become the warp and woof of industry.

The recipient was Nikola Tesla, whose turn-of-the-century exploits in Colorado have already been described.

Tesla is almost a forgotten figure in the history of electrical research, but it was his system of generating and distributing electrical power, and not the Edison system, that ultimately became the workhorse of industry and kicked the new Electrical Age into high gear. His personal eccentricities and extravagant boasts have proved to be a bit of a problem for historians. What are they to make of his various claims — that he was working on a "death ray" capable of killing thousands; that his "teleautomatic" robots should fight wars for men; that he could vibrate the entire planet; or that he once received intelligent signals from outer space? In all the annals of invention, Tesla's story is one of the strangest.

As a youthful engineering student at the Polytechnic School in Graz, Austria, Tesla became acquainted with a form of dynamo called a Gramme machine. Like Edison's dynamos, the Gramme machine produced electrical energy in the form of direct current (DC), which moves in only one direction, like water through a pipe. These machines, however, generated electricity in the initial form of alternating current (AC), which needed to be converted into DC, considered the more usable form. As the name suggests, alternating current reverses direction at regular intervals. One back-and-forth wave motion is called a cycle. To convert AC into DC, a device called a commutator had been introduced into the design of some electrical machines.

Direct current made sense in the Edison system because it was most efficient at shipping the low voltages required to light his incandescent lamps. At higher voltages the commutator tended to burn out and more current was lost to the wires in the form of heat. Although a few crude forms of AC machines had appeared, Tesla's professor at Graz held firmly to the prevailing opinion that an electric motor or dynamo was impossible without a commutator; in other words, that a true AC motor could not be built. But Tesla thought otherwise. Five years later, walking in a Budapest city park with a friend, the answer came to him in an unusual burst of creative vision. Tesla paused to drink in the sunset and, educated man that he was, commemorated the moment by quoting a few lines from Faust:

"The glow retreats, done is the day of toil;
It yonder hastes, new fields of life exploring;
Ah, that no wing can lift me from the soil;
Upon its track to follow, follow soaring. . . ."

As I spoke the last words, plunged in thought and marvelling at the power of the poet, the idea came to me like a lightning flash. In an instant I saw it all, and I drew with a stick in the sand the diagrams which were illustrated in my fundamental patents of May 1888. . . .

"The diagrams" outlined a method of drawing AC directly from electrical machines by means of a rotating magnetic field, completely eliminating the need for a commutator. They formed the basis for Tesla's revolutionary "polyphase" system of generating alternating current, and they were much on his mind when he arrived in America. Having failed to enlist any European backers, Tesla had been unable to build any prototypes of his AC machines. Now, in America, Tesla hoped Thomas Edison would prove to be more open-minded.

Thanks to his letter of introduction, Tesla landed his first job as an Edison lab assistant. The two men respected each other's inventive talent, but Tesla immediately began singing the praises of alternating current, a concept which Edison, whose inventions required direct current, wasn't greatly interested in hearing about. Tesla considered himself an electrical genius on a level far above that of the ordinary lab assistant and his employer found this arrogance extremely irksome. In a sense, Tesla was everything Edison was not. Edison had little use for mathematicians or poets and Tesla, the product of Europe's finest universities, was both. This visionary Eastern European was just too foreign to Edison's Midwestern Horatio Alger heart. Tesla spoke eight languages and enjoyed dressing to the teeth for dinner at Delmonico's. He suffered from a germ phobia and bought new ties and gloves on a weekly basis. Edison, however, was hard put to master the intricacies of English and damaged his health by subsisting mostly on pie and coffee. He favored ratty Prince Albert coats and a soiled handkerchief in place of a cravat. The board of General Electric, as the Edison companies became known, later voted him "$75 a month for personal expenses so he could buy a decent suit, pay off his small accounts and not be an embarrassment to Wall Street." Tesla, without doubt, would have made the more scintillating dinner companion.

Their inventive styles clashed even more seriously. Edison surrounded himself with talented lab assistants, though he never gave them much credit, and measured everything he did "by the size of the silver dollar." He preferred the trial-and-error method, documented his work meticulously and attempted to work out the commercial requirements of his inventions before inventing them. Tesla scoffed at this approach and once told a *New York Times* reporter: "If he [Edison] had a needle to find in a haystack, he would not stop to reason where it was most likely to be, but would proceed at once with the feverish diligence of the bee to examine straw after straw until he found the object of his search. . . . I was almost a sorry witness of his doings, knowing that just a little theory and calculation would have saved him 90 per cent of his labor." Tesla's inventions came to him in completed bursts, the diagrams of the finished machines dancing in his head, as he demonstrated so vividly in Budapest. He rarely built any machine, or scratched a single diagram on paper, until he had mentally built it, run it, repaired it and run it again, while simultaneously performing the required mathematical calculations. Little of what he did, with the exception of patent diagrams, was ever written down. And he worked best alone.

With this in mind, it comes as no surprise that Tesla, "the poet of science" as Edison sneeringly referred to him, left after only a year in Edison's employ, claiming he had been cheated out of a promised bonus. He spent the next year digging ditches. But when he finally found backers for his own New

York lab, he quickly built and patented the generators, motors, transformers and other machines that had come to him in Budapest. They worked beautifully. Besides eliminating the commutator, the Tesla system could operate on three or more alternating currents at once (polyphase), which greatly increased the flexibility of AC machines. The system had great range because a very high voltage could be sent out over the lines and then stepped down via transformers for domestic or industrial use. Moreover, Tesla's machines were lighter and simpler to build than many DC machines.

If J. P. Morgan was the financial man of the hour for Edison, Tesla's guardian angel was George Westinghouse, inventor of the air brake and founder of the Westinghouse Company. Westinghouse entered the market for electric light and power by way of automatic switching devices for electric railways. Recognizing the significance of Tesla's patents was perhaps the shrewdest thing George Westinghouse ever did. Coupled with William Stanley's earlier patents on AC machines (which Edison also turned down), the Tesla patents gave Westinghouse an early dominant position in the alternating current market.

Thomas Edison could see what the Tesla system meant for him and his subsidiary companies. It meant bad business. Now that alternating current and Tesla and Westinghouse had all combined to pose a direct competitive threat, Edison embarked on a smear campaign designed to discredit AC on grounds that it was hazardous to one's health. He sought to portray AC as cold and lethal; DC as warm, friendly and safe. The real reason for the campaign was the growing rivalry between Westinghouse and the Edison companies, although many prominent European scientists agreed that high-voltage transmission made possible by AC could be dangerous.

The campaign kicked off with a series of grisly press conferences. Before a throng of reporters, Edison's assistants nudged stray dogs onto a sheet of tin wired to a power source and then zapped the animals with a thousand volts of alternating current. Predictably, they died. (One dog that miraculously walked away intact after a jolt of 1,400 volts was dubbed Ajax by the lab crew, "for having survived the thunderbolt.") Edison himself used to amaze his co-workers at Western Union by rigging a tinfoil device that electrocuted any cockroaches foolish enough to go for his lunchbox, but in this case he stayed in the background, turning the actual dirty work over to "Professor" Brown, a lab assistant. Brown helped convince the New York State Prison System that electrocutions, courtesy of alternating current, were more in keeping with modern times than hanging. They would also, Brown suggested, serve to illustrate the "humane" use of alternating current. Edison even suggested that the appropriate term for such an execution would be "to Westinghouse."

The stage was set, but prison officials feared that AC electrocutions had not been proven on larger animals. Brown and his helpers cheerfully complied by killing first a calf, then a horse, and finally, an elephant.

George Westinghouse was outraged when he heard of the plan, quickly pointing out that DC could be every bit as deadly as AC. But high voltage was indeed AC's domain and prison officials hired Brown to wire up three Westinghouse AC generators for the first state-sanctioned human electrocution in history. On August 7, 1890, Thomas Edison inadvertently became the father of the electric chair. Playing the part of the stray dog was William Kemmler, condemned murderer. But a grievous miscalculation took place — the voltage that had popped the eyes out of a dog scarcely rolled poor Kemmler's. This AC was a new thing under the sun and would take some getting used to. The next morning, the *New York Times* read:

FAR WORSE THAN HANGING
Kemmler's Death Proves an Awful Spectacle. The Electric Current Had to be Turned on Twice Before the Deed was Fully Accomplished.

Or, as George Westinghouse put it, "They could have done it better with an ax." Later, they almost did. Reports surfaced that prison officials were sawing off the top of prisoners' heads and removing the brain after electrocution to assure that the Deed had been Fully Accomplished. It was the culmination of Edison's public relation campaign but it failed to stem the tide of alternating current. It became clear that AC was the most practical form of electrical power in the majority of cases, and three years after the first electrocution, Westinghouse and alternating current powered the lights of the Chicago World's Fair. That same year, the big prize — the taming of Niagara Falls — was awarded to AC-based designs offered by the Westinghouse interests. Industry was crying for AC to replace steam engines and run heavy electrical equipment. Reluctantly, Edison General was forced to enter the market for AC and the war of the currents was over.

The Edison-Westinghouse rivalry produced another form of competition that might be called the War of the Patents and something of its flavor still lingers in Silicon Valley today. Early on, Edison's backers had suggested that the problem of "fierce competition and low prices" caused by the patents of another competitor, Thomson–Houston, could be solved through a merger. Thomson–Houston had taken most of the arc lighting market away from Charles Brush and now was gaining on the Edison companies in incandescent lighting. The idea of a merger appalled Edison but secret negotiations began anyway as his influence in management decisions waned. While Edison's assistants were frying dogs, negotiations with Thomson–Houston continued and in 1892 J. P. Morgan gave the go-ahead for the merger. Edison felt, not without reason, that his company had been sold right out from under him. The new consolidation was known simply as the General Electric Company and J. P. Morgan was now an official member of the board.

But the impasse with Westinghouse continued. GE had Westinghouse checkmated on incandescent lighting and also held key patents on electric railway equipment. Westinghouse in turn had GE in a headlock over rights to Tesla's AC machines and even filed a countersuit over Edison's light bulb on the basis of some incandescent patents it also held. Edison's costly but successful defense of his patents, coupled with GE's good fortune in the incandescent market, served notice to other companies that the patent could be used as a potent weapon in the battle for the marketplace. By squeezing as many basic patents as possible out of a single invention, a company holding the rights could make it difficult if not impossible for another company legally to enter the market with a competitive product. And since every new generation of electrical inventions posed new and untested questions for the patent courts, it behooved companies to sue first and work out the merits of the lawsuit, if any, at a later date; tactics known today as "nuisance suits."

By 1896 there were more than three hundred patent suits pending between GE and Westinghouse. GE executives went to the bargaining table with Westinghouse, as they had done with Thomas–Houston, seeking a mutually agreeable end to the practice of hobbling each other's growth. The solution they arrived at avoided the necessity of a merger. The two companies formed a Joint Board of Patent Control to oversee the pooling of their respective patents. The firms remained separate but now had access to most of each other's patents without fear of legal reprisal. A related practice in the modern microelectronics industry is called "second sourcing," in which one company acquires microelectronic circuit designs, which of themselves cannot be patented, from another company. The deal may involve either cash or an exchange of one set of designs for another, or both. Certain profitable designs attract several second sources and in the case of the microcomputer, various companies have grouped together in this way to form factions within the industry, each faction supporting its own competing "family" of devices. But such designs are often pirated and copied in the absence of a license to second source, resulting in a great deal of legal squabbling and effort to convince Congress that copyright protection should extend to the design of microcomputer chips (see Chapter Seven).

Curiously, the electrical industry's patent imbroglio began with what may have been Edison's most significant invention of all, and one for which he could never have hoped to receive a patent. According to Norbert Wiener, one of the founders of cybernetic theory (see Chapter Two), "Edison's greatest invention was that of the industrial research laboratory." Edison and his assistants at Menlo Park — a group George Bernard Shaw once described as "sensitive, cheerful and profane; liars, braggarts and hustlers" — were the first research and development lab in history. Edison called the concept an "invention factory," and it was one of the distinctive features setting the electrical and chemical industries apart from other industries.

Alternating current brought with it the need for a higher order of mathematical analysis. Men like Tesla and GE's Charles Steinmetz, the hunchbacked German scientist who became one of America's leading electrical engineers, rose to the fore on the basis of their thorough knowledge of higher mathematics. To GE and Westinghouse, these developments meant that a well-funded, systematic team approach to invention was the most sensible way to proceed. By assigning different inventors to different parts of a problem, corporations saw to it that any resulting invention belonged to no single engineer. Now that inventors were on the payroll, team invention became an inseparable part of the industrial process, while patent ownership began to shift from the individual to the corporation as a whole. GE began by offering employee-inventors a dollar bonus for patentable work but soon discontinued the practice, fearing it would foster the illusion of inventing for personal gain rather than for the overall good of the corporation. This was not exactly what the designers of the patent system had had in mind.

For Edison, patents came to mean nothing more than "an invitation to a lawsuit." When GE asked Edison's approval for another in the seemingly endless series of suits and countersuits over his incandescent lamp, Edison shot back: "Say I have lost all faith in patents, judges and everything relating to patents. Don't care if the whole system was squelched."

Toward the end of his life he claimed that "My electric light inventions have brought me no profits, only forty years of litigation," adding that he had spent as much money defending his patents as he had securing them. But Edison was to die a very rich man, and that is more than can be said for Nikola Tesla, who left Westinghouse after only a year to pursue a new and exciting theory about electricity; one he hoped would unlock its final secret.

The Wardencliff Vision

By 1900 Edison was busy with motion pictures and ideas for an improved storage battery, while defending his many patents from would-be usurpers. Tesla, true to form, wanted to get on with the Next Big Thing. Psychologically unfit for service in an invention factory and unconcerned with the fate of his parents, Tesla cared only that he had enough money to continue his research — alone. He became obsessed with a vibratory phenomenon called electrical resonance and built a series of oscillators and transformers, including the Tesla Coils, in order to study it. In much the same way that soldiers marching in cadence across a bridge can set up resonant vibrations powerful enough to crack its foundations, Tesla's new machines could produce impressive effects. Once, in New York, Tesla's friend Mark Twain stopped by to see what unusual experiments Tesla might have planned for the evening. (Tesla worked best at night.) Twain decided to try out a vibrating platform Tesla had hooked to some of his equipment. He found the humming platform quite soothing. Positively therapeutic. Tesla warned him repeatedly to climb down but Twain lingered, enjoying the massage, feeling his body relax . . . and soon he began to feel the tingle of gentle contractions . . . his bowels began to uncork . . . and Mr. Clemens was off the platform and headed for the bathroom in a desperate race to save his trousers.

Tesla left New York briefly to experiment with his coils in Colorado and returned convinced he could now fire electricity around the world as easily as he shot lightning back into the sky. J. P. Morgan saw that if Tesla was right, it could lead to a monopoly on a world power source. As an alternative he could acquire rights to the system and then sit on the whole project if that proved the more prudent market procedure. Morgan gave Tesla about $150,000 and sat back to see what would happen. At Wardencliff, a real-estate development in New York, Tesla used the money to build a broadcast tower and lay plans for a power station at Niagara Falls. The Wardencliff Project was to be the culmination of his grandest dreams about electricity; his gift to mankind. But that is as far as he got. Morgan had second thoughts, the money ran out and Tesla was forced to close down Wardencliff in 1905. Because of his autocratic nature, nobody knew precisely what Tesla was up to at Wardencliff, and his whole scheme was widely considered impossible. However, Tesla did write down what he had *intended* to accomplish, and called it:

THE WARDENCLIFF VISION

The first World System power plant can be put into operation in nine months. With this power plant it will be practical to attain electrical activities up to ten million horsepower and it is designed to serve for as many technical achievements as are possible without undue expense. Among these may be mentioned:
 1. Interconnection of the existing telegraph exchanges of offices all over the world;
 2. Establishment of a secret and non-interferable government telegraph service;
 3. Interconnection of all the present telephone exchanges or offices all over the Globe;
 4. Universal distribution of general news, by telegraph or telephone, in connection with the Press;
 5. Establishment of a World System of intelligence transmission for exclusive private use;

6. Interconnection and operation of all stock tickers of the world;
7. Establishment of a World System of musical distribution, etc.;
8. Universal registration of time by cheap clocks indicating the time with astronomical precision and requiring no attention whatever;
9. Facsimile transmission of typed or handwritten characters, letters, checks, etc.;
10. Establishment of a universal marine service enabling navigation of all ships to steer perfectly without compass, to determine the exact location, hour and speed, to prevent collisions and disasters, etc.;
11. Inauguration of a system of world printing on land and sea;
12. Reproduction anywhere in the world of photographic pictures and all kinds of drawings or records.

It is an impressive document, and almost all of it has come to pass. But Tesla did not foresee the means by which his predictions would be fulfilled. The transformation of the patent system had all but sidelined individual inventors like Tesla. While GE and Westinghouse held firm control over the electrical manufacturing industry, the various Bell interests had become American Telephone and Telegraph, with an equally dominant position in electrical communication. Tesla died penniless and forgotten in a New York hotel room, but not before making one last "astounding discovery": "We are automata entirely controlled by the forces of the medium, being tossed about like corks on the surface of the water, but mistaking the resultant impulses from the outside for free will."

The modern electrical revolution which has proven the truth of his predictions is not powered by ever higher voltages, more power and bigger machines. The heart of the information age can be found in tiny electrical devices powered by smaller and smaller amounts of power; a mere fraction of what Tesla had worked with. Millivolts, not megavolts, power the modern integrated circuit.

The Grid Comes Alive

By the early 1900s the first layer of the coming electronic grid was in place. Increasingly, electrical power was the motive force behind the expansion of American industry and the wiring up of American homes. When the electric sparks met gasoline, the internal combustion automobile was born. And as Tesla envisioned, electrical power was becoming inextricably linked with electrical communication. Alexander Graham Bell's magnetic telephone was very practical evidence that sound and voice, as well as raw power, could be transmitted over wires. Moreover, the successes of Marconi and others in "signalling through space without wires" hinted at new, wireless layers of the electronic grid, made possible by the harnessing of previously untapped portions of the electromagnetic spectrum.

While Marconi telegraph companies had sprouted in Europe and America, and the Bell Companies had established commercial short-distance telephone service, radio, the most ambitious form of electrical communication, was still more amateur craft than exacting commercial science. In a sense, radio was an attempt to combine the best of both worlds — electrical voice and sound communication without wires. Radio began with the discovery of the tuned circuit — a means of tuning a receiving device so that it "recognizes," or detects, only signals of a specific wave frequency emanating from the sending device.

By far the weakest link in the early radio systems was the means of detection at the receiving end, so a host of inventors set to work on the problem. In doing so, they returned to a curious phenomenon Thomas Edison had discovered in the process of perfecting his light bulb. It was known as the "Edison effect," and historians generally consider it to be Edison's one major discovery of "pure" science. By inserting a metal plate into an ordinary light bulb, Edison was able to detect a measurable electric current streaming through the vacuum from the heated filament to the plate. The inventor patented his Edison effect lamp solely as a tool for measuring current in lighting circuits, but John Ambrose Fleming, an Englishman, set out to discover what applications the Edison effect lamp might have as a detector of radio signals. After some tinkering with the metal plate inside the glass bulb, Fleming was pleased to discover that the device could be configured so as to detect and convert high-frequency radio signals. The device, however, could not amplify, or boost, the signal, a factor which severely limited the efficiency and the distance of wireless transmission. Nonetheless, the Edison light bulb had evolved into the two-element Fleming "diode." It was left for Lee De Forest, an American mathematician and engineer, to insert a third crucial element into the bulb, yielding the triode, or three-element vacuum tube.

The De Forest vacuum tube was the invention that broke open the embryonic field of electrical communication. Improved markedly by later inventors, a fact De Forest was loath to admit, the vacuum tube was the technical advancement that put radio, radio telephony, wireless telegraphy and long-distance telephone service on a sound commercial footing. With the tube, the electrical industry became the electronics industry as wired and wireless communication joined the roster of industry concerns — electrical power, light and manufacturing. It also served as a springboard for a raging battle over electrical communication among AT&T, GE, Westinghouse and scores of others. Global electronic communication, while still not exactly what Nikola Tesla had had in mind, was soon to be established in a stunning variety of forms. No single person could have made it all possible, but Lee De Forest, the self-styled "father of radio," strove mightily to convince the world that he had done just that.

De Forest's inspiration — the third element inside the glass bulb — was called a control grid. In the form of either a wire bent into a zigzag shape or a thin metal plate shot through with holes, it acted on the current in the vacuum in such a way as to make the tube a far more sensitive and reliable detector of wireless signals. And although De Forest did not immediately recognize it, when the control grid was properly connected to a signal source it amplified the incoming signal considerably. De Forest patented his device as the De Forest "Audion" and started the De Forest Radio Telephone Company in New York.

As a businessman, De Forest proved to be somewhat less than shrewd. His choice of backers and associates also proved ill-advised, and by 1911 his venture, then known simply as the Radio Telephone Company, was on the verge of collapse, audion or no audion. Broke, he gratefully accepted a job with the Federal Telegraph Company of Palo Alto, California, and moved West. Federal Telegraph was one of the earliest radio companies in America, and while it might seem that most of the activity in the electrical field stemmed from the East Coast, the San Francisco area was a hotbed of radio experimentation in the early years of the century.

While working for Federal Telegraph, De Forest confirmed that the vacuum tube could be made to amplify electrical signals. At a small lab on Emerson Street in Palo Alto, De Forest and his associates tried hooking up a few tubes in series, and connecting them to a magnetic phonograph in various ways. De Forest, periodically running out into the street, found that the tubes made it possible to hear the phonograph record as much as two blocks away. With headphones, he was even able to hear the scuttling of a housefly on paper. This improved amplification was made possible by a process known as negative feedback. At roughly the same time, however, Edwin Armstrong was working with the De Forest vacuum tube at Columbia University and saw considerable room for improvement. Independently, Armstrong worked on the negative feedback principle and described its effects on amplification in much more detail than had De Forest. Since De Forest's original patents had not covered the circuitry required to make the audion tube a true amplifier, both he and Armstrong raced to file patents on the vacuum tube as an amplifier. The battle over primacy of invention between De Forest and Armstrong (who sold his patents to Westinghouse) raged in the courts for nineteen years until the Supreme Court decided that the winner was De Forest.

Shortly after his successful amplification experiments in Palo Alto, De Forest, always pressed for cash, set his sights on selling the patent rights to his audion amplifier. The logical and most lucrative candidate was American Telephone and Telegraph.

AT&T's story began in 1877 with Alexander Graham Bell and his patent on a "talking machine," or magnetic telephone. Bell's early experiments were financed in part by his father-in-law, but when the money ran out Bell embarked on a frustrating search for funds with which to bring his telephone to commercial fruition. Bell offered his patent to Western Union for $100,000, but the company turned him down. A group of wealthy Boston financiers eventually came to his rescue, but the price for their largesse was high. Bell managed to lose all control over his patents in only two years, even faster than Edison had lost control of his. The Boston directors of the new Bell Telephone Company voted themselves two votes for each share of stock, compared to a single vote per share for Bell and his associates. When the Boston group reorganized into the National Bell Telephone Company, Alexander Graham Bell was listed on the company roster simply as "electrician." When the Boston financiers found themselves in need of additional capital, AT&T quietly floated a noncompetitive bond issue, purchased exclusively by J. P. Morgan and Company for $150 million. From then on, Morgan and his associates held the reins of AT&T.

Under Morgan, AT&T pursued a policy of cost-cutting, standardization and the by then well-tested strategy of tying up competitors with patent-infringement claims. However, the fiscal strategy also included trimming staff and making patent acquisitions at the expense of in-house development. By 1906 the company was somewhat thin on the engineering bench, and AT&T's chief engineer reported to the company's president that "no one is employed who, as an inventor, is capable of originating new apparatus of novel design." And this at a time when the company was waking up to the possibilities of wireless. "Whoever can supply and control the necessary telephone repeater," read an AT&T memorandum, "will exert a dominating influence in the art of wireless telephony when it is developed."

The necessary repeater appeared in the form of the De Forest vacuum tube amplifier, the patent rights to which AT&T subsequently purchased. In 1915, the excited De Forest was back in business with his own company, and had come to San Francisco for a demonstration of his device at the Panama-Pacific International Exposition. The booth reserved for De Forest's company was a modest affair; modest compared to American Telephone and Telegraph's lavish display nearby. AT&T was feeling its oats that year, and Lee De Forest knew why. De Forest sauntered over to the AT&T booth to bask in the glory he so richly deserved. De Forest had a high, prominent forehead, bushy eyebrows, a Charlie Chaplin mustache and an exceedingly large ego. A lover of recognition and public acclaim, he stood before the AT&T exhibit in San Francisco with the rest of the fairgoers, listening to the lecture and watching the company men demonstrate long-distance telephone service to New York via headsets. He listened to the company men sing the praises of the Pupin loading coil and other acquired patents. But there was nothing, not a word, about De Forest or his audion. And it was the same when he leafed through AT&T's promotional booklet. Nothing. It was as if the audion, arguably the best long-distance telephone repeater in the world, had never existed. De Forest felt like a spectator at his own oblivion, bought off and canceled right out of the history books.

Ranting, he left the fair with a copy of the AT&T booklet. He stayed up all night in his room at the St. Francis Hotel. By morning he had rewritten it to his satisfaction, including the title.

AT&T's version:

THE STORY OF A GREAT ACHIEVEMENT
Telephone Communication from Coast to Coast

In De Forest's hands, this became:

THE STORY OF A GREAT ACHIEVEMENT
Which Made Telephone Communication
from Coast to Coast Possible

In the morning, while his co-workers handed out copies of his booklet to fairgoers and AT&T men alike, De Forest, to drive the point home, strung a ten-foot banner over his display: "THE DE FOREST AUDION AMPLIFIER LICENSED TO THE AMERICAN TELEPHONE AND TELEGRAPH COMPANY AS A TELEPHONE RELAY MADE THE TRANSCONTINENTAL TELEPHONE SERVICE POSSIBLE."

And what did AT&T have to say about that? "In all the 3,400 miles of line," an AT&T pitch man told his audience that day, "there is no one spot where a man may point his finger and say, 'here is the secret of the transcontinental line; here is what makes it possible to telephone from New York to San Francisco.' " It was true.

The Wireless War

While the vacuum tube proved central to the development of long-distance telephone communication over wires, improved versions of the tube led directly to the rapid expansion of wireless radio as well. During World War I, this new form of electronic communication over the airwaves found immediate practical application as a weapon of war. Historians generally regard World War I, in a scientific sense, as the war of the chemists, with gas as their weapon. But the physicists and engineers who were a part of the electronics industry played no less a role in this period than they played in the Second World War, in which their role was largely overshadowed by the activities of the atomic physicists. Nonetheless, starting with

World War I, electronics began to exert a profound and lasting effect on military strategy, the overall fortunes of war, the advancement of science in general and the direction of industrial research. With the advent of the vacuum tube and commercial wireless, the focus of this book shifts to the "electronics" industry, parting company with the public and private power transmission enterprises that make up the "electrical" industry.

"War," said the astronomer George Ellery Hale, onetime head of the National Research Council, "should mean research." And it did. And if World War I proved to be a boon for both American business and American science, then it was bound to prove doubly true for the electronics industry, which was both. Wireless went to war as scientists and technicians struggled to apply the young science to the problem of detecting German submarines. So pressing was this need that the British even considered the idea of training sea lions as submarine bloodhounds. The Navy undertook sub detection research at the New London, Connecticut, research station. Thomas Edison was pressed into service — mainly for publicity purposes — as an adviser to the Naval Consulting Board, along with Willis Whitney of GE, Frank Sprague of electric trolley fame, and Elmer Sperry of Sperry Gyroscope. Edison fashioned dozens of electrical devices for the war effort ("all perfectly good," he claimed) but the Navy vetoed all of them. The board also received thousands of ideas from the public, most of them useless. "There is no known method of 'charging the sea with electricity,' " the board replied to one such spirited suggestion.

While radar did not develop in full until World War II, a few crude wireless detection systems were used against subs in the English Channel. The same research applied to early techniques of airborne photography, electronic signaling and signal detection. Wireless was also the basis for a new branch of study — "traffic analysis," or cryptography, the practice of reaching into the airwaves to capture and decode wireless orders issued by the enemy.

In addition to the first forays into radar and cryptography, the science of ballistics came to the fore. Initially the domain of the mathematician and the mechanic, ballistics is a special case of classic Newtonian physics dealing with the flight of projectiles through space. Strictly speaking, this definition would even include Newton and his apple, but in a practical sense it means the study of the trajectory of war weapons, from bullets to cannonballs to rockets. A shell from "Big Bertha," the nine-inch-caliber gun the Germans fired on Paris early in the First World War, carried twice as far as the ballistics charts predicted. It was due to the thinner air at higher altitudes, which spurred efforts to update the ancient study of ballistics to meet the needs of the day. A formidable list of variables conspire to make the calculation of artillery shell trajectories quite mathematically top-heavy, requiring calculations covering size and velocity of shell, air speed, wind speed, air temperature and density as a function of altitude, drag coefficients, and so on. Ballistics became a world of differential equations, and murderously difficult ones at that.

The application of electronics to the needs of the military did not end with the war. The United States, Great Britain and Germany in particular raced ahead with war-related research on radio, other forms of wireless, radar, coded electronic signals and ballistics. Thanks in part to support from the U.S. military, major electrical research centers existed by war's end at AT&T, GE, Harvard, and MIT, as well as within the armed forces research agencies.

The common thread running through all these avenues of post-war research was that the mathematical equations involved had simply gotten out of hand. Mathematics, it seemed, had outrun the human ability to calculate the numbers with the necessary degree of speed and accuracy. The problem was to be solved, with revolutionary consequences, in the next war.

After World War I, the battle for control of commercial electronic communications resumed, with the same result as the earlier GE–Westinghouse showdown over power transmission — stalemate. Move and countermove, patent-infringement claim and counterclaim. Once again, the answer proved to be patent pooling. The radio patent pool agreement of 1920 divided the warriors into a telephone group (AT&T and Western Electric) and a radio group (GE, RCA, Westinghouse and others). The telephone group gained access to any pertinent telephone patents held by the radio group, and vice versa. In reality, it was not nearly that clear-cut, and as disputes over interpretation arose the government entered the picture as a referee, in the same way it had undertaken to regulate utilities, banks and railroads earlier. The end result was the establishment of the Federal Communications Commission in 1934, at which point AT&T became a legal, regulated monopoly rather than a de facto monopoly. While patent pooling did not end the internecine warfare between the giants by any means, it did work effectively against smaller companies who were not members of the club and against individual inventors outside the corporations. In fact, patent control had become so potent a tool for market control that AT&T's Frank Jewett was able to announce, presumably with tongue nowhere near cheek, that the benefits of science "reach practically all industries, and in proportion to the size and importance of each."

One Nation, Electrified

During the "electrifying" twenties, the benefits of science began to reach the American consumer in novel ways. Radio brought the nation together as a single, vast audience; one that could be addressed intimately yet simultaneously. Language as communication was no longer limited by the range of the human voice or the dictates of the printed word. Radio and telephone broke down geographic barriers, cut across time zones, and loosened the isolation of small towns and communities. Companies like GE and Westinghouse brought forth the first commercial electrical appliances — toasters, iceboxes, irons, stoves, washing machines, all widely heralded as an electronic emancipation for women. Television, or "sending pictures by radio," was in an early experimental stage by the late twenties, using light-sensitive vacuum tubes.

The Saturday Evening Post, marveling at these new electronic wonders, remarked that "Science is not a thing apart. It is the bedrock of business." *The Nation* proclaimed, "A sentence which begins, 'Science says,' will generally be found to settle any argument in a social gathering or sell any article from tooth-paste to refrigerators."

But the Great Depression brought graphic evidence that science-based business could have its devastating social effects as well. The Bell system, then the nation's largest private employer, began converting its central office telephone stations to the dial system, knocking some twenty thousand workers off the payroll during the worst days of the Depression. Automation had reared its controversial head, and it helped spark a drive for corporate reform. A number of socialist and anarchist movements sprang to life in the thirties with the aim of trimming the excesses of corporate capitalism. One of the most curious of these movements was Technocracy, which called for a seizure of power by a "soviet of engineers" who would lead the working class toward a new and more humane — but still technological — society. The movement, which took for its logo the ancient yin-yang symbol, to signify a harmony between man and machine, dwindled quickly, but the reasons for its brief popularity were aptly summarized in 1933 by the dean of the Case School of Applied Science: "John Doe isn't quite so cock-sure as he used to be that all this science is a good thing. This business of getting more bread with less sweat is all right in a way, but when it begins to destroy jobs, to produce more than folks can buy and to make your wife's relatives dependent on you for a living, it is getting a little too thick."

Other critics homed in on science itself. G. K. Chesterton, far from being mesmerized by the occult mechanism of the dynamo, as Henry Adams had been, wrote in "A Plea That Science Now Halt" (1930): "There is nothing wrong with electricity; nothing is wrong except that modern man is not a god who holds the thunderbolts but a savage who is struck by lightning."

Artists grappled with the impact of new technology, in some cases using the technology itself to do so, and the future did not look good. In *Metropolis,* Fritz Lang's 1927 film about an automated industrial future where workers toil abjectly under the command of a giant dynamo, a scientist fashions a svelte female robot and proclaims, "I have created a machine in the image of man, that never tires or makes a mistake. Now we have no further use for living workers." Charlie Chaplin parodied the excesses of the standardized machine age in his 1936 film, *Modern Times.*

Even radio, that marvel of the airwaves, came under fire between the wars, most stridently from its putative father, De Forest himself. De Forest saw radio and, later, television as vehicles for what he might have called the intellectual enrichment of the masses. It soon became clear that radio (and, later, television) had been harnessed to quite another master altogether. A few years before his death, in a letter to the *Chicago Tribune* entitled "A Father Mourns his Child," De Forest spelled out his misgivings:

> What have you gentlemen done with my child? He was conceived as a potent instrumentality for culture, fine music, the uplifting of America's mass intelligence. You have debased this child, you have sent him out in the streets . . . to collect money from all and sundry, for hubba hubba and audio jitterbug. You have made of him a laughing stock to the intelligence, surely a stench in the nostrils of the gods of the ionosphere; you have cut time into tiny parcels called spots (more rightly "stains") wherewith the occasional fine program is periodically smeared with impudent insistence to buy or try. . . .
>
> Some day the program director will attain the intelligent skill of the engineers who erected his towers and built the marvel which he now so ineptly uses.

De Forest never forgave the corporate owners of radio and television for adopting electronic advertising, but in this he simply refused to recognize the business logic of a straightforward, profit-making decision. By turning to easily digestible entertainment as content, the broadcasting industry assured itself the broadest possible audience and thus the maximum potential return from electronic advertising. In *Understanding Media* Marshall McLuhan writes: "The early stages by which information itself became the basic economic commodity of the electric age was obscured by the ways in which advertising and entertainment put people off the track." In the same way, the early stages by which microcomputer-based distributed intelligence systems become a primary means of information processing are obscured by such things as video pong games and triple-X-rated home video cassettes.

By the eve of World War II the electronics industry was a powerful, expanding and inventive industry dependent on basic advances in science for its product line. It was also an industry which had emerged only recently from the Darwinian jungle of unregulated robber baron capitalism. Its primary products (electrical power, light and heavy equipment excluded) were tools for enhancing man's innate capability to do physical work and to communicate. But the coming war would reveal even greater potential from the electron in the form of the electronic computer: a machine that enhanced brainpower. The advent of the computer grafted an unprecedented branch onto the electronics industry family tree. The computer and postwar solid-state electronics directed the study of electricity toward the study of intelligence and control. The search for the keys to the kingdom began in earnest during World War II.

CHAPTER TWO

World War II and the Universal Machine

"I propose to consider the question, Can Machines Think?"
— ALAN TURING

The Zero and the One

Electronics, in the modern sense, emerged from the smoke and madness of World War II as the result of an explosion of classified research from 1940 to 1945. Behind a wall of secrecy, a remarkable aggregation of physicists, mathematicians and electronics experts gave birth to the computer age. In doing so, they laid the foundations for a new industry which was as different from the industry of De Forest's day as the electronic computer was unlike the mechanical adding machine. The tangled trail of events culminating in the invention of ENIAC (Electronic Numerical Integrator and Computer), America's first fully realized electronic computer, can only be hinted at here, but the work of an unlikely group of drafted amateur intelligence agents closeted in total secrecy at Bletchley Park, a Victorian mansion near London, serves aptly as both a starting point and a portent of things to come.

The work at Bletchley was a part of Project ULTRA, a top-secret British intelligence effort headed up by William Stephenson, code name INTREPID. Stephenson, an expert in radio communication, a friend of GE's Charles Steinmetz and many other prominent electrical engineers, had dropped from sight in 1935 to work behind the scenes for British intelligence as the Nazi buildup gathered momentum. In early 1940 he helped assemble this peculiar group — scientists, engineers,

39

mathematicians, a wide array of brilliant and eccentric thinkers. There were university professors of literature and Merchant Navy radio operators. There was the former cryptographer to the czars of Russia. And there was twenty-eight-year-old Alan Turing, an awesomely talented mathematician with a strong interest in calculating machines.

The task before the group was to crack ENIGMA, a top-secret German cipher machine with which the Nazi high command issued coded orders to its field commanders. One of the mechanisms had been smuggled out of Poland and was now at Bletchley. About the size of a typewriter, it consisted of a keyboard attached to a box full of mechanical wheels and drums. When the user typed in a message, electrical relays spun the drums and coded the message into a stream of nonsense letters. The receiving machine, with its drums set in the same sequence as the sending machine, decoded the message. The arrangement of the drums permitted an almost unlimited number of permutations. ENIGMA allowed the Nazis the luxury of using a code once, then shifting the drums to a new one, playing fox with an endless list of codes, to the baffled hounds of Bletchley.

All manner of Nazi tactical information passed through the ENIGMA machines. The British, hopelessly outclassed, or so it seemed, in men and war materiel, knew that if they could crack ENIGMA, their fortunes would take a dramatic upturn. But even with a copy of the machine in their hands, the task looked impossible, beyond the capabilities of the best cryptographers and mathematicians in the world.

Alan Turing, with a "shrill stammer and crowing laugh which told upon the nerves even of his friends" (as his mother frankly put it) must have cut a memorable figure as he bicycled about Bletchley, now and then donning his gas mask to mitigate acute bouts of hay fever. Tall and powerfully built, a sloppy dresser, a lover of long-distance running, chess and children's stories, Turing was a bold and original numbers theorist with a Tesla-like ability to calculate in his head. A colleague once described him as "The rough prototype of the coming age of Science and Machines."

Prior to joining the war effort at Bletchley, Alan Turing had written a remarkable paper on mathematical logic in which he had described a theoretical universal computing machine. The Turing Machine was an imaginary apparatus through which passed a paper tape. The tape was marked off in squares, each square either marked with a symbol or left blank. The machine could move the tape in either direction one square at a time. It could also print a symbol in a blank square or erase a symbol in a marked square and print a new one in its place. On the surface of it, that was about all the mechanical Turing Machine could do. As humble as these capabilities may seem, Turing argued that his conceptual machine would be able to mimic the function of any other computing or calculating machine: that it could in fact solve a variety of complicated mathematical and logical problems, when given instructions coded into a deceptively simple form of mathematical logic — Boolean algebra, the binary language of the zero and the one. Years after Turing's ground-breaking paper of 1936 one of his colleagues wrote of it: "It is difficult today to realize how bold an innovation it was to introduce talk about paper tapes and patterns punched in them into discussions of the foundations of mathematics." Turing also wondered whether his imaginary universal computing machine actually could be built, and at Bletchley he was to get his chance.

The result of the collective effort at Bletchley was COLOSSUS, an early hardware embodiment of Turing's computing theories and a foretaste of the mathematical principles later incorporated in ENIAC. A huge array of vacuum tubes and photoelectric paper tape readers, COLOSSUS effectively mimicked the operation of the ENIGMA cipher machine by performing the same numerical permutations, enabling British cryptographers to decode German messages plucked from the airwaves. ENIGMA was broken, thanks to one of the earliest digital electronic computers powered by vacuum tubes. "I won't say what Turing did made us win the war," observed I. J. Good, a mathematician who served as Turing's statistical clerk at Bletchley, "but I daresay we might have lost it without him." (Similarly, the Americans eventually broke related Japanese codes by building mechanical copies of the rotor-operated machines which produced the codes.)

It was Boolean algebra, a key mathematical insight set down almost a hundred years before World War II, that made the dream of a universal machine into a crude but fully electronic reality during the war years.

In 1854 the English mathematician George Boole published a paper known as *The Laws of Thought* in which he proposed to construct no less than a "mathematics of the human intellect." His stated purpose was to "investigate the fundamental laws of those operations of the mind by which reasoning is performed: to give expression to them in the symbolical language of a Calculus."

Boole's presumptuous intent had precedent. The quest to discover and map out the "mechanics" of rational thought has deep roots in science and philosophy. It is at least as old as the ancient Greeks, who explored the nature of truth, the systematic patterns of logic and the connections between language and mathematics. This controversial quest for the rules of rational thought, or the laws of logic, can be seen in Descartes's yearning for a "universal language of logic," in the rise of Rationalism in Europe and, later, in the symbolic mathematics of Russell and Whitehead and the logical positivists.

Perhaps the most zealous early proponent of the notion that thinking is nothing more or less than calculation by explicable rules was Gottfried Wilhelm Leibnitz, a seventeenth-century mathematician-philosopher. Leibnitz undertook a search for what he called a "universal calculus," a grand mathematical sweep which would result in "a kind of alphabet of human thoughts" by which all truths of the reason could be unambiguously expressed in numbers. He had no doubt that this could be accomplished: "If someone would doubt my results, I would say to him: 'Let us calculate, Sir,' and thus by taking pen and ink, we should settle the question." Leibnitz and others like the Frenchman Julien de la Mettrie, who wrote *Man, the Machine* in 1747, were mechanists who believed that all natural processes, including the workings of the human mind, obey discoverable physical principles. It follows, then, that Leibnitz was also a mathematician entranced by, even obsessed with, the power of numbers.

The power of numbers is not limited to the decimal system, which some historians suggest was adopted as the primary language of mathematics for no other reason than that humans come equipped with ten fingers as handy markers for counting. Leibnitz was fascinated by the peculiar properties of *binary* number systems, in which all numbers are represented in strings composed of only two, rather than ten or some other number of symbols.

Doing binary arithmetic is quite straightforward when the two symbols used are zero and one. The four basic arithmetical operations — addition, subtraction, multiplication and division — can all be accomplished by manipulating the zero-one strings in certain specified ways and then adding sums. Arithmetic, then, boils down to addition in this binary system, an operation which machines had been performing, with varying degrees of success, even in Leibnitz's time. General binary systems of notation, however, can represent more than just numbers. Morse code is a familiar example — a two-symbol code (dots and dashes) which represents the alphabet.

Leibnitz did not find his binary universal calculus, but about one hundred and fifty years later George Boole took a giant stride in the direction of fulfilling the quest. In *The Laws of Thought,* Boole discovered that the general principles of "pure" logic could be expressed symbolically in a binary system of zeros and ones.

Boole's contribution was to extend the power of binary theory beyond the mere symbolic representation of numbers and alphabets as strings of two symbols. In Boole's hands, the zero-one binary system became a concise and graphic shorthand for representing the various patterns of formal logic as well, whether expressed in words or in numbers. The Boolean system, commonly encountered in the form of "truth tables" where statements of logic are represented as a one if true or as a zero if false and then manipulated according to a finite set of rules, was a rigorous mathematical procedure which made no sharp distinction between the mechanics of numerical logic (math) and the mechanics of non-numerical logic (reasoning via language). In short, Boolean algebra proved to be a verifiable, universal language for expressing formal logic symbolically.

The connection between Boole's contribution to mathematics and the search for the universal computing machine took a while to develop. However, one early stab at it deserves mention. A few years before the turn of the century Charles Sanders Pierce, who worked for the U.S. Coastal Survey but whose real love was philosophy and logic, wrote to a friend: ". . . it is by no means hopeless to expect to make a machine for really very difficult mathematical problems. But you would have to proceed step-by-step. I think electricity would be the best thing to rely on." It was left for Claude Shannon of MIT to prove this prediction correct just before World War II, by pinning down the link between Boolean logic and the study of electronics.

Shannon, a young electrical engineer, studied the behavior of electronic switching circuits composed of electromechanical relays. A relay, consisting of an electromagnet, a movable electrical contact and spring, and a stationary electrical contact, worked much like a telegraph key. When the movable contact was drawn into the stationary contact by the electromagnet, it turned on an electrical circuit. When the electromagnet was de-energized, the spring pulled the movable contact away from the stationary one, blocking the current and turning off the circuit. Thus a relay had only two states — on or off — although technically this is a bit of an exaggeration. Complicating this rather simple picture is the fact that, in reality, relays and switching circuits such as those typically used in direct-dialing phone systems were composed of many relays and wires all linked together in various combinations and operating all at once, rather like a wire maze connected by gates in series or parallel arrays. All of this made the analysis of complicated switching systems of great interest to AT&T.

Given the two-state effect of any individual relay, Shannon wondered whether some form of mathematical logic might not apply to the matter of describing the overall behavior of many electrical circuits all hooked together by wires and operating at once. He realized that there was: the algebra that perfectly described the behavior of electronic circuitry was the same algebra Boole had discovered; the "algebra of thought." Boole's binary system not only described the operations of numbers and logic, but the nature of electronic circuitry as well.

Since the relays that make up circuits are two-state devices, they may be likened to little electronic traffic stations called gates. A relay in its on state can stand for a Boolean one, meaning true. The same relay in its off state represents by analogy a zero, or false. Thus, in Boolean terms, the state of an individual relay represents either a zero or a one at any given moment. Used appropriately, the state of the relay gate can represent a single *b*inary dig*it*, or "bit" of information — the basic binary notation of computer theory.

All of the rules for doing logic in the Boolean zero-one system could be represented as a set of simple combinatory rules. Electrical engineers now had a mathematical shortcut for describing the behavior of an electrical system composed of relays. But since this was the same shorthand with which Boole represented the mechanics of logic, they had much more than that. By configuring relays into logic gates, they had a way of designing electrical systems that could perform not just operations of arithmetic, but operations of logic. Shannon's discovery was a stunning breakthrough when one considers that heretofore electromechanical systems could transmit and receive information, but not act upon, or "use" it. It hinted very strongly at the possibility that an electronic machine, designed according to Boolean rules, could express logic as well as add numbers.

It worked both ways. Boolean algebra could represent the

operation of electronic circuits, and electronic circuits could express the operation of Boolean logic. It was logic itself to take this thinking one step farther. If circuits could express logic, and be used to test for mathematical truth, was this just a roundabout way of saying that electronic circuits harbored the power of reason? That electronic circuits might be able to express logical *thought*? Or, as Turing simply and provocatively put the question, "Can Machines Think?"

Boolean algebra, together with the refinements offered by Turing and Shannon, pointed the way toward electronic machines that could perform logic and math in a basic binary language. It formed the cornerstone of modern electronics, computer science and artificial intelligence. It was the secret of Turing's imaginary machine and the very real prototypes which followed. COLOSSUS and the other early electronic computers were the hardware realizations of Boolean logic; testaments to the power of the zero and the one. In the hands of the wartime computing pioneers, the Boolean binary system was to be shaped into something very much like what Leibnitz had been after — a universal calculus and a universal machine operating according to its principles. Electronics sparked the fusion.

The Logic of Gravity's Rainbow

The dream of a universal calculating machine actually began long before World War II and the work of Turing and Shannon. Mechanical adding machines had existed as commercial products since before the turn of the century, and the term "computer" had been used even longer, although it referred to a clerk who performed calculations by hand. In fact, the French philosopher Blaise Pascal built, in 1642, a mechanical adding machine not much different in principle from early twentieth-century versions. Turning numbered wheels caused a series of gears to rotate in a prescribed sequence, performing additions and subtractions and displaying the results on another wheel. But it operated in decimal, not binary, fashion.

Thirty years later in Germany Leibnitz built a similar machine called the Leibnitz Wheel, feeling that "it is unworthy of excellent men to lose hours like slaves in the labor of calculation which could safely be relegated to anyone else if machines were used." Peter the Great sent one of these machines to the emperor of China as an example of the technical wonders of the West. Considering the efficiency with which the Chinese for centuries had been using the abacus for the same purpose, one wonders if the emperor was not a touch underwhelmed.

The true patron saint of the modern computer, in the mechanical sense, was Charles Babbage, an irascible British engineer who began work on an automatic calculator, the Difference Engine, in 1822. As an engineer, Babbage was all over the map. He drew up the first actuarial tables for the insurance industry, invented both the cowcatcher and the speedometer for the railroads and even hinted at a future of mass production based on "universally interchangeable parts." Babbage was a strict and unwavering mechanist, and in the course of his research on statistics he calculated the odds on Biblical miracles. Rising from the dead rated a chance of one in 10^{12}.

Babbage's contribution to computer history was strictly theoretical — not that he did not try to make it concrete. Fully a century ahead of his time, Babbage's curse was to conceive and design all-purpose calculating machines — the Difference Engine and the even grander Analytical Engine — that were such intricate collections of steam-powered cranks, gears, pulleys and levers that no mechanic or group of mechanics of the day could ever have built them. The parts tolerances he required were beyond the capabilities of even the best machinists and metallurgists of the period. But the need for such machines was real — hand-calculated astronomical charts and navigational tables of the day were a horror, as were the shipwrecks caused by errors endlessly copied and recopied. Babbage hoped to use a series of punched cards, like the cards that controlled the workings of the Jacquard weaving loom, as a means of feeding numerical quantities into his machine — a very early stab at a concept later embodied in the term "programming." He stressed the need for designing an arithmetic-processing unit and a memory unit, with some means of transferring data between them and some way of printing out the results of the calculation. At his death, the rooms of his house were strewn with half-completed models of the Analytical Engine, and it was not until the eve of World War II and the switch to electrical means of computation that Babbage was vindicated.

The U.S. Census of 1890 marked the first major commercial use of calculating machines in America. Herman Hollerith designed and built a system of tabulating the population data. The Hollerith machine, which operated on punch cards and recorded the data on counter wheels, made use of something Babbage did not have the luxury of — electromechanical relays. At each hole in the card an electrical circuit was completed, which tripped a relay and added a number to the appropriate counter wheel. It was a more efficient means of tabulation than the usual array of axles, gears and wheels, but it could not perform complicated equations. With the Hollerith machine, tabulation of the 1890 census took only a month, compared to several years for the prior census. The machine worked so well that census clerks sabotaged it every now and then in order to gain a respite.

Hollerith also sold versions of his machine to the railroads for tabulating timetables and ticket sales, and his Tabulating Machine Company eventually became the International Business Machine Company (IBM) in 1924 under the leadership of Thomas Watson. Still another census shop engineer built a competitive punch card tabulator and his Powers Tabulating Machine Company of 1911 merged with Remington Rand and later with Sperry Gyroscope to become Sperry Rand, IBM's principal early competitor. IBM's Watson, who exhorted his salesmen with such aphorisms as "Think," "Men–Minutes–Money" and "You grow a business when you begin growing men," learned in 1929 of a report that only two percent of

U.S. accounting needs were being handled by machines. "Think of that!" said Watson, according to the story. "I haven't been able to get that out of my mind since I read it. Two per cent! Think of the field we have to work upon."

While ten-key punch card tabulators and various mechanical calculators met with some commercial success in the early years of the century, they were little more than giant adding and sorting machines. But it quickly became apparent that even these machines could handle a wide range of cost and accounting chores beyond the abilities of hundreds of human clerks. In steel mills, department stores, equipment factories and government statistical bureaus, the mechanical calculator soon became a staple piece of office equipment, and the number of companies that manufactured them grew. However, none of these machines was of much use for solving equations describing the parabola of an artillery shell, or later a rocket, in flight. In 1930, with $25,000 and a small army of assistants, Vannevar Bush, the dean of engineering at MIT who had worked on submarine detectors during World War I under the sponsorship of a J. P. Morgan company, attacked the problem of calculating more formidible equations by building a mechanical computer, the Differential Analyzer. The only electrical parts were the motors used to drive the intricate assemblage of gears and shafts. The electric motor activated a shaft which turned a gear which pushed a rod which engaged a cog . . . and so on, the calculation carried out by brute force, so to speak, as metal clanked against metal until the machine had run its cycle and the equation was solved. Obtaining the answer was a matter of measuring curves and machine part positions, though later versions incorporated punch card and paper tape systems. The analyzer looked like it had been built from a giant erector set, but it could solve differential equations — an impressive feat of mechanics. In order for it to do other things with numbers, however, it had to be torn apart and laboriously reconnected in a new mechanical configuration.

The Bush machines had two immediate and related applications in the thirties. The kinds of equations they were designed to solve were those frequently encountered in both ballistics research and electronic circuit theory, so analyzers were built for both the Moore School of Electrical Engineering at the University of Pennsylvania and the Ballistic Research Laboratory at Aberdeen, Maryland.

The analyzers brought Bush fame, which he in turn parlayed into political clout. "In a scientific war," said Bush, "the scientists should aid in making the plans." When Bush, as the first chairman of the National Defense Research Committee in 1940, found that the body did not have the authority to push new military weapons into production, he successfully lobbied for a new agency, the Office of Scientific Research and Development (OSRD) and ran it as undisputed "czar of research" by executive order. When the Joint Chiefs of Staff set up a Joint Committee on New Weapons and Equipment in 1942, there was Bush again, sitting as a member along with a rear admiral and a brigadier general.

Ingenious as they were, Bush's mechanical machines were special-purpose constructions. They would have been no match for the German ENIGMA, and they were not going to make real the Leibnitz–Babbage dream of universal machines operating on a universal calculus in which one could express everything from the whole of mathematics to the step-by-step process of logical thought — let alone the very practical logic of the ballistics arc. As the war progressed, stunning new weapons appeared — rockets, proximity fuses, automated antiaircraft guns, "smart bombs" and guidance control mechanisms, the black boxes that could "see" under water and into the night through a process called radar, electronic cryptography, electronic espionage, electronic propaganda, electronic computers and, finally, the atomic bomb. At Princeton, Harvard, MIT, Berkeley, Bell Labs as well as in Europe and the United Kingdom, a web of influential scientists, mathematicians and engineers laid the foundation of what came to be known broadly as the information sciences.

One particularly intriguing branch of information theory tied scientists and the war effort not only to electronic technology but also directly to the quest for the universal machine: "Besides the electrical engineering theory of the transmission of messages, there is a larger field which includes not only the study of language but the study of messages as a means of controlling machinery and society, the development of computing machines and other such automata, certain reflection upon psychology and the nervous system, and a tentative new theory of scientific method."

This was Norbert Wiener's ambitious definition of *cybernetics* (from the Greek *kybernetes*, for steersman, governor). Wiener, a child prodigy who took a Ph.D. in mathematical logic at Harvard when he was nineteen, joined the MIT faculty in 1919 and remained there until shortly before his death in 1964. He coined the term to encompass a wealth of his own insights and others from the work of Claude Shannon, Vannevar Bush, Turing in England and a number of America's foremost mathematicians, among them John von Neumann, Warren McCulloch and Warren Weaver. Although a popular history of cybernetics is beyond the scope of this book, the whole history of microelectronics and computer systems is in a sense the tale of cybernetics in action. In brief, cybernetics is the study of the twin processes of *communication* and *control* in humans, in machines, and in systems comprised of either or both. As Boolean logic had made no great distinction between the logic of numbers and the logic of words, so cybernetics offered no clear-cut division between communication processes in humans and in machines. That was in fact one of the aims of cybernetic theory — to create a theory of messages scientifically rigorous enough to include *all* forms of information transmission, from the cellular level of the brain to radio broadcasting to communication between electronic machines. "The theory of control in engineering," as Wiener put it, "whether human or animal or mechanical, is a chapter in the theory of messages."

Cybernetics, in practice, evolved as a solution to the problems associated with the growing complexities of ballistics. As Wiener explained it:

> At the beginning of World War II, the comparative inefficiency of anti-aircraft fire made it necessary to introduce apparatus which would follow the position of an airplane, compute its distance, determine the length of time before a shell could reach it, and figure out where it would be at the end of that time. . . . All the figuring must be built into the gun control itself. . . . The problem of determining the flight statistics of a plane from the actual observation of its flight, and then of transforming these into rules for controlling the gun, is itself a definite and mathematical one. . . . The adjustment of the general plan of pointing and firing the gun according to the particular system of motions which the target has made is essentially an act of learning. It is a change in the *taping* of the gun's computing mechanism, which alters not so much the numerical data, as the process by which they are interpreted. It is, in fact, a very general sort of feedback, affecting the whole method of behavior of the instrument.

Here is not only a plan for better artillery, but a very pragmatic discourse on the notion of seemingly "intelligent" machinery and the seeds of a semantic tangle over defining the ability of a machine to modify its behavior from information it "learns" about its environment. By feedback, Wiener did not mean the technical circuitry of the vacuum tube. In the cybernetic sense, feedback meant a means of controlling automatic machinery by feeding the actual results of its past performance back into the machine so that the machine could modify its performance in order to accomplish a specific task. In the broadest sense, feedback is a simple mechanical principle, as old as the rudder of a ship. When a steersman (*kybernetes*) pushes the rudder to the right, the ship tacks to the left, and vice versa. Steering a straight course involves repeated left-right rudder movements. The extent to which the ship veers slightly in one direction is feedback: it tells the steersman how far to move the rudder in the opposite direction to correct the ship's course. The feedback principle of controlling future performance on the basis of past performance was the principle behind the gyroscopically controlled torpedos of World War I. Like a little spinning oarsman inside the torpedo, the gyroscope detected changes in course and was hooked to the movable fins of the weapon in such a way as to correct its course in the usual series of back-and-forth wave motions toward the target. Airplanes and ships used gyro stabilizers and other automatic guidance systems as well.

In the case of Wiener's plans for better artillery, feedback came in the form of information about the target's speed and direction, fed to the gun's computing mechanism by means of automatic sensing devices. For feedback to have any meaning, the information fed back would have to be taped, or programmed, in a form the machine had been designed to manipulate. Between input and output, modification of the machine's behavior would result from a conversation of sorts between machine parts, in machine language. Language, as Wiener insisted, "is not exclusively an attribute of living beings but one which they may share to a certain degree with the machines man has constructed." Finally, the computing mechanism would use the feedback information to calculate the optimum firing angle, and mechanical control mechanisms would position the gun accordingly.

Wiener and his colleague Julian Bigelow felt that in the design of any such automatic antiaircraft gun, human operators could be treated as just one more component of the overall system, "as if they were pieces of feedback apparatus." Wiener meant no ill in this — the idea was to shoot down the target, not to attack the pleasure of handcraft. As he further observed, "A series of operations of the same structure can be carried out through electrical and even vacuum tube means. . . . What the feedback and the vacuum tube have accomplished is not the sporadic design of individual automatic mechanisms, but a general policy for the construction of automatic mechanisms of the most varied type. In this they have been reinforced by our new theoretical treatment of communication, which takes full cognizance of the possibilities of communication between machine and machine. It is this conjunction of circumstances which now renders possible the new automatic age," including the massive automation of American industry which was to follow at the close of the war.

Wiener drew up the plans for his gun in 1941, but they were never realized. In 1942, however, a group of researchers at the Bell Telephone Laboratories used similar principles to build the M-9 90mm gun director, which was used to defend London against German V-1 "flying bomb" raids. Radar plotted the bomb's incoming position. The information was translated into a corresponding series of varying voltages, and these were fed into a computing mechanism built from special vacuum tubes. Servomechanisms pointed and fired the gun automatically. The M-9 scored heavily against V-1 bombs again in the 1944 Allied defense of Antwerp.*

The cyberneticists began with ballistics, mechanical machines and message theory: How can a gun fire automatically not at the target, but at the point in space where the target *will* be? How can a bomb be made to explode only in the vicinity of its intended target? How can a machine "learn" to alter its operation on the basis of information about its past performance? But they quickly found themselves drawn into a wider arc of inquiry which included the realms of biology and sociology: What are the mechanisms of communication and control at the level of the human brain? How can the behavior of large bodies of men and equipment be predicted mathematically (a discipline known as operations analysis)? The connecting link was electronics, and the almost mystical fit between mathematical logic and the behavior of electronic cir-

---

* Behavioral psychologist B. F. Skinner had his own novel plan for retaliating in kind with American automatic flying bombs. He trained pigeons to peck at the image of a ship whenever it appeared on the screen. He then mounted a lens in the nose of the bomb which reflected an image of the ship toward which the bomb was hurled. When the kamikaze pigeon, jacketed inside the bomb, pecked frantically at the approaching target, the pecking action tilted the screen, and since the screen was hooked to the bomb's adjustable steering fins, this avian feedback had the effect of steering the bomb toward its intended target. The military, however, declined to implement "Project Pigeon."

cuits. The thrust of the new information sciences was to precisely define and measure "information" in mathematical terms; to add information to the list of fundamental definitions basic to science — matter, energy, electric charge and the like.

The early information theorists did not present the world with a unified, tidy scientific discipline, but rather an outline of possibilities and avenues of investigation. Many prominent theorists took little interest in the machine side of information theory. But those who did laid the theoretical ground work for computer science and the commercial computer industry by focusing on the analysis of information flow through machines composed of electrical circuits. What gave the research a relentlessly practical turn, as Wiener made clear, was wartime ballistics. All of the discoveries, insights and hunches thus far discussed could be taken as hints that properly designed machines might take the burden of ballistic computation off the backs of humans. Such universal machines, later in the war, might even take the measure of "Gravity's Rainbow," novelist Thomas Pynchon's graphic symbol for the parabolic arc of the V-2 pulse-jet rockets that shot the study of ballistics, quite literally and urgently, into the stratosphere. "All the rest will happen according to the laws of ballistics," wrote Pynchon in his novel of wartime England. "The rocket is helpless in it. Something else has taken over. Something beyond what was designed in."

The Unknown Race and a Quest Fulfilled; How Many Computers Is Enough?

The covert race between the Germans and the Allies to map out the principles of rocketry and the atomic bomb is the stuff of spy thrillers, both real and imagined. But there was another covert race, this one to build a fully electronic, digital, programmable computer, and Turing's COLOSSUS was only one entry. It was a race made all the more remarkable by the fact that the participants, under the cloak of wartime secrecy, did not know with any certainty that the race was on. Nor did they know for certain that the result would be a machine lacking any firm theoretical limits on the uses to which it could be put — the universal machine.

Project COLOSSUS, that vacuum tube and paper tape wonder that cracked ENIGMA, was built for code-breaking, not ballistics, but the bag of tricks was the same in either case: electronic circuits, paper tape, Boolean logic, information theory and a hardworking team of electrical and mechanical engineers. What Alan Turing and the rest of the ULTRA group did not know was that a German named, incredibly enough, Zuse, had begun work on electronic computers as early as 1934. Conrad Zuse, a student of Babbage's ideas, toyed with the idea of using vacuum tubes as the basic switching circuits, but tubes were risky and untested in such applications and Zuse ultimately chose to work with electromagnetic telephone relays. After a few early prototypes, some of which he built in his parents' living room in Berlin, Zuse designed the Z3 electronic computer with the help of the German Aircraft Research Institute. The Germans were quick to use its successor, the Z4, in the development of flying aircraft bombs and other ballistics research because it proved to be an able "cruncher" of complex mathematical equations. The Z4 used old movie film in place of punched paper tape. Hitler, without knowing it, was well on his way to becoming the patron of the electronic computer. "It has frequently been said that Britain's secret code-cracking computer . . . ensured victory for the Allies," Christopher Evans, the late British computer expert, wrote in *The Micro Millennium.* "Might not the possession of a fully operational machine in German hands at an early stage of the war have had the reverse effect?" If Zuse had chosen to work with vacuum tubes instead of telephone relays, the world might have found out.

Then again, probably not. Most of Zuse's machines were themselves destroyed by bombs during a 1944 air raid on Berlin, though he managed to salvage a few parts of his Z4. A crucial year for the war and a nice piece of luck for the Allies — electronic computers could solve equations related to the development of the atomic bomb just as handily as any other kind. And who could say what other forms of machine logic were in the offing? Zuse was captured near the end of the war and brought to London for an interrogation at the hands of an official of the British Tabulating Machine Company. However, the official spoke no German and Zuse no English. The import of Zuse's work, not widely known until much later, did not survive the translation.

In wartime America, work on computers was no less urgent and highly classified than abroad. Howard Aiken of Harvard began laying plans for an electronic computer at roughly the same time as Turing proposed his Turing machine and Zuse built his first computer. Aiken chose to work with electromagnetic relays rather than vacuum tubes, and the Harvard Mark I, as the finished product was called, began operation in late 1943. After the war and the secrecy ended it would receive considerable publicity as America's first "electronic brain." It solved equations according to the two-state Boolean dictates of circuitry. It is difficult to picture the aggregate interactions and permutations of all these thousands of relays as each individual relay flips on or off according to binary instructions coded on punched paper tape.

Aiken's computers had the expected applications to ballistics research, and caught the attention of the Navy and the Air Force, but his machines were obsolete as quickly as they were installed — by late 1945, ENIAC had arrived, a far more awesome and sophisticated American computer, the designers of which had shunned the telephone relay for the power — and the engineering headaches — of De Forest's vacuum tube. ENIAC, with vacuum tubes, was five hundred times faster in operation than the relay-rigged Mark I. It was much more complex than the then-unknown COLOSSUS. It could add five hundred numbers in exactly one second. It could multiply two 23-digit numbers in less than five seconds. For the War Department's ballistics people, who had been shepherding the project all along under the shadow of German advances in rocketry and atomic physics, those were very compelling skills indeed.

ENIAC had its genesis in the rumors about Aiken's work which leaked into the scientific and engineering communities at Pennsylvania's Moore School of Electrical Engineering, at Princeton, Harvard, MIT, Bell Labs — and at Iowa State College, now Iowa State University. There, physics professor John Vincent Atanasoff and his colleague Clifford Berry built a crude prototype of a vacuum tube computer. It was an ad hoc, special-purpose array of only three hundred vacuum tubes, designed to solve linear equations. It was nothing like the holy grail of the computing quest, the universal machine, and far less potent a number cruncher than the larger Mark I, but it did use tubes.

The next year, after joining the staff of the Moore School in Pennsylvania, John W. Mauchly wrote a memorandum proposing the construction of a larger and more general purpose electronic computer, to be implemented with vacuum tubes. The proposal excited no great enthusiasm until Herman Goldstine of the Army Ordnance Corps got wind of the project. In 1943 the highly secret project began with a $400,000 contract from Army Ordnance. The purpose: to develop and build a very fast computer, the fastest ever built, for calculating gunnery tables and rocket trajectories at Aberdeen Proving Ground. Heading the project was Mauchly and J. Presper Eckert, Jr., an electrical engineer. During work on ENIAC, other scientists and information theorists involved in the war effort made trips to the Moore School. The National Defense Research Committee came, as did representatives of the Theoretical Physics Division at Los Alamos.

From an engineering standpoint, the problem facing the Moore School team was the performance of the vacuum tube. A tube, like an electrical relay, can be operated so that it has two distinctly recognizable states — on and off. In Boolean terms, one and zero. It was therefore logical to propose that tubes could perform Boolean logic just as relays did. But the tube, having no moving parts, could switch states far more quickly than relays — in a few millionths of a second — which meant that a computer built of vacuum tubes should be able to perform far more difficult calculations than any other kind of computer. As every operation the computer performed had to be broken down into its Boolean constituents, a tube switching on-off a million times a second could work through the steps much more quickly. The faster the computer could operate, the more complex the operations it could perform. Making all this a reality meant building a computer out of thousands and thousands of vacuum tubes. Vacuum tubes generated tremendous amounts of heat, and if it wasn't dissipated in some way the combined thermal power of all those tubes blinking on and off clearly was going to cause large numbers of them to blow. Reliability was a problem with the vacuum tube anyway — they blew with distressing regularity even when they weren't stacked together like little bowling pins. The Moore School proposed to use eighteen thousand of them in ENIAC.

That ENIAC worked at all is high tribute to the engineering wizardry of Mauchly and Eckert. The common legend, no doubt apocryphal but nonetheless telling, is that the lights of Philadelphia dimmed when ENIAC was switched on. For ENIAC was truly an electronic monster, an engineer's nightmare that was more a room than a machine. It was indisputably the most sophisticated electronic machine in the world. While COLOSSUS had employed two thousand tubes and Atanasoff's machine only three hundred, ENIAC had eighteen thousand tubes, seventy thousand resistors, ten thousand capacitors, six thousand assorted switches and a maze of connecting wires. It measured one hundred feet long, ten feet high and three feet deep, and weighed in at thirty tons. It sucked power like a locomotive but in the space of thirty seconds — half the duration of the incoming weapon's flight — it could rattle off a trajectory calculation that would take a human working with a mechanical computer some twenty hours to finish.

Tube reliability, however, proved to be every bit as difficult a business as the engineers had figured. They rigged all manner of fans and blowers to carry off the tremendous heat generated by eighteen thousand vacuum tubes crammed in behind the metal panels, and still the temperature in the ENIAC room soared to 120 degrees F. Search-and-replace teams combed the machine for blown tubes while other engineers scurried about rewiring major portions of ENIAC to conform to the dictates of each new trial run.

Early on, von Neumann recognized that the abilities of ENIAC might be brought to bear on equations relating to atomic bomb research, and to Los Alamos went the honor of supplying ENIAC's first formal test problem, a sort of official unveiling, in 1945. ENIAC passed with flying colors, as it did in subsequent runs on ballistics problems, weather forecasts and wind-tunnel simulations.

In retrospect, ENIAC was about as big as it possibly could have been. There was no real solution to the heat problem; engineers unleashed the full power of ENIAC's postwar descendents not because they learned how to string more and more tubes together, but because of John von Neumann's "stored program" concept (which Eckert claims as well).* The *stored* program was a way of prewiring certain basic logical operations and programmed instructions into the circuitry of the computer itself, and it eliminated much of the rewiring that took place at the outset of each new problem. It was also a major step toward machine memory: a stored program computer could retrieve, from its own repository of information, the answer to a given "chunk," or subset of the overall problem. It was a shortcut; in human terms, something like taking the value of pi to ten digits from a table and substituting that value into an equation, rather than taking time to calculate pi from scratch whenever it appears in the problem. This meant that computers could handle instructions just as they handled the usual numerical data. No longer were computer operators

---

* A computer program, also known as computer software in order to distinguish it from the computer's "hard-wired" circuitry, is a set of instructions that have been coded into a binary language, upon which the computer can act.

required to punch in each and every instruction needed for a problem. The computer could retrieve certain blocks of the instructions stored in its memory as numerical data. This, in turn, enabled the computer to choose the optimum order of operations by which to execute the instructions without outside help, and resulted in the now-common flow chart diagrams used to program computers. The ability to store the rules for logical operations was the twist that made postwar computers faster and less specialized and therefore far more powerful than ENIAC.

When the war ended, the military's interest in computers did not. The BINAC and UNIVAC projects — ENIAC's stored program successors — got off the ground with preliminary contracts from Northrop (a designer of the new intercontinental ballistic missiles), the Army and the Air Force. And yet, the computer as a weapon of war — certainly its first practical application — was not entirely what Leibnitz, Babbage and the rest of the computer forefathers had in mind when they contemplated the wonders of a universal machine. Von Neumann in particular saw the computer as a general problem-solver and not simply as a master calculator of military codes and ballistics tables. Nonetheless, the prototypes of today's automated battlefields had been established, along with the first hardware in the vast servomechanism known today as military computer-based "C³": Command, Control and Communications (see Chapter Twelve). Unlike the controversy surrounding the obvious and dramatic dangers posed by the atomic bomb, the adoption of the computer as the automated central nervous system of military operations and weapons proceeded apace with little public debate over what the consequences of such a decision might be, or whether that decision very shortly might begin to look irreversible. It was enough to know that ENIAC had given the U.S. a flying head start in computer technology.

The computer emerged from the war as a weapon and as a powerful if still undeveloped tool for mathematical logic. With

ENIAC, all the threads had come together: the calculus of Leibnitz and the dreams of Babbage, Boole's algebra and Turing wizardry of the ENIAC crew. In post-war England, Alan and Lee De Forest's vacuum tube, the cybernetic ideas of Wiener and von Neumann and, finally, the practical engineering wizardry of the ENIAC crew. In postwar England, Alan Turing went on to design stored program machines for Ferranti, an early British computer company, and for Manchester University. He vigorously explored the possibilities of machine intelligence until his mysterious death in 1954 at the age of forty-two. His mother claimed the death was accidental, but others have suggested that Turing was a homosexual and that he had been discovered and threatened with public exposure, meaning, in those repressive days, the loss of his job, his friends and practically everything else. The coroner's verdict was suicide by poison; a spoon coated with traces of cyanide had been discovered in his lab.

In Germany, Conrad Zuse was back in business as the head of a new computer company which he eventually sold to Siemens, the giant West Germany electronics conglomerate. No one knew what the Russians were up to, but in America Mauchly was busy writing up patent applications for ENIAC. As work at the Moore School had turned toward stored program successors to ENIAC, Mauchly and Eckert began to find themselves at odds with the university over the issue of patents. And as the importance of ENIAC began to come clear, the two men resigned and founded their own commercial enterprise, the Electronic Control Company, with the aim of making the electronic computer a viable commercial product. "It was time," as Herman Lukoff, one engineer who left the Moore School to join them, put it, "for business to exploit this modern miracle."

The idea was to build a stored program universal automatic computer, not just for the military, but for commercial use, a concept which culminated in UNIVAC. Short of cash, a condition that seems to come with the territory when the territory is electronic invention, the two inventors embarked on a search for funds after Northrop's support fizzled out. IBM, preoccupied with the number-knitting of the Aiken machines and the world of the punch card, showed interest but didn't back it up with money. Mauchly and Eckert finally found a buyer for their company in 1950, and it turned out to be Remington Rand (later Sperry Rand), IBM's main competitor in the office equipment market.

On the commercial front, calculating machines were chewing up more than ten thousand tons of punch cards a year by the late forties. Henry Ford's methods of standardizing industrial production, coupled with the automatic machinery of the war years, guaranteed an acceleration of the trend toward "automation," a term first coined in the late forties. (By 1960, the term would be replaced by "cybernation," to indicate the effect of adding the electronic computer to the mix.)

UNIVAC offered superior performance and substituted programmed instructions on magnetic tape for the older punch cards. Operators typed in the instructions as before, but they became a series of magnetized dots on the tape caused by electrical pulses, rather than holes punched in cards. Though few women traditionally pick electrical engineering as a profession, women played a major role in pioneering the techniques of computer programming. Adele Goldstine, the wife of Captain Herman Goldstine, wrote the first programs for ENIAC. Grace Hopper did much of the early program writing for the Harvard Mark I, and as senior mathematician with the Eckert–Mauchly Corporation she was a central figure in the development of new computer languages such as COBOL. Charles Babbage would have been lost without his wife, the daughter of the poet Lord Byron. Ada Lovelace, a skilled mathematician, seemed far more adept at explaining what her husband had in mind than he was.

Nonetheless, the sales picture looked grim. "The UNIVAC I was clearly a technical success," wrote Lukoff, "but would it be a financial success? The first three systems had been sold to the government in 1948. Our marketing department was active, attempting to sell further UNIVAC I systems but no further sales had been made. Commercial companies Prudential and A. C. Nielsen, interested earlier, had dropped out. Was this it, three sales to the government? There had been an early forecast that five systems would be sold. I had even heard some wild speculation that this country could support eight or ten systems . . . the future was certainly unclear."

Further clouding the future was the limbo state of Mauchly and Eckert's ENIAC patents. The mammoth document, containing 148 claims relating to the fundamentals of digital computing, had been filed in June of 1947, and was quickly followed by a long list of interference claims.

Jumping ahead of the story for a moment, it was not until 1964 that the two inventors finally received their patents. In 1971, twenty-six years after ENIAC was switched on, the patents were the subject of a landmark computer case in Minnesota. Honeywell, claiming the patents were invalid, filed suit for violations of the Sherman Act. Sperry Rand, holder of the patents, charged infringement in return. Two years later the court turned the ENIAC saga upside down, ruling Mauchly and Eckert's patents invalid and declaring the winner to be John Vincent Atanasoff of Iowa State and his $650 three-hundred-tube equation solver. Atanasoff, who was not even widely known to have been in the running, had been declared the legal father of the computer. In Mauchly's view, "Because I visited J. V. Atanasoff for just two or three days in 1941, the 1974 decision of Judge Larsen was that I derived all my notions about building electronic computers from Atanasoff. . . ." For Sperry Rand and the members of the original ENIAC crew, it was as if Edison's patents on the light bulb had been invalidated because others before him had placed carbon rods in glass tubes.

In 1951 the Eckert–Mauchly Division of Remington Rand finally sold another UNIVAC I to the U.S. Bureau of Census. In 1952, as part of the CBS network's election eve coverage, a Remington Rand UNIVAC I successfully predicted Eisenhower's victory over Stevenson on the basis of early returns from the East. The Remington Rand division continued to land the odd government contract. A descendant of ENIAC which carried the eerie name of MANIAC went to Los Alamos under the aegis of the Atomic Energy Commission for work on thermonuclear equations. Scientists there also used it for some early runs at teaching a computer to play chess, an avenue of inquiry that proved central to the development of artificial intelligence.

In 1954 the commercial future of the computer cleared considerably when General Electric purchased a UNIVAC exclusively for business data processing. It was a big break, and it signaled that more than just warfare, atomic physics and the U.S. Census had grown too complex, or so it seemed, for human calculation. American business was growing in both size and complexity as well, a tempting if uncertain target for computer sales. Universities were showing some interest in computer science, and electronic equipment and machine companies like Burroughs, Philco and IBM were testing the waters. Electronic computers were poised on the brink of a commercial breakthrough, but no one could say how the flowering would unfold.

In *Faster Than Thought* (1953) British computer expert B. V. Bowden offered this wry speculation:

> It will be interesting to see if these machines play in the next decade the part of the cyclotrons and high voltage generators of the "thirties." In those days every university had to have a cyclotron on the campus; they were mysterious and expensive and they gave tone to the place. . . . There is much to be said for digital computers as research projects for the time being; they are not so expensive as cyclotrons, they are much less messy, they are even more incomprehensible, and perhaps before very long they too will have to be taken over by the big firms.

Wiener, in *The Human Use of Human Beings* (1950) took a less bemused view: "We have a good deal of experience as to how the industrialists regard a new industrial potential. . . .

Industry will be flooded with the new tools to the extent that they appear to yield immediate profits, irrespective of what long-time damage they can do."

And again: "It is perfectly clear that [automatic machines] will produce an unemployment situation, in comparison with which the present recession and even the depression of the thirties will seem a pleasant joke."

And finally: "Our papers have been making a great deal of American 'know-how' ever since we had the misfortune to discover the atomic bomb. There is one quality more important than 'know-how' and we cannot accuse the United States of any undue amount of it. This is 'know-what' by which we determine not only how to accomplish our purposes, but what our purposes are to be."

With the vacuum tube, electricity had become electronics, and its focus had shifted from power to information transmission. But in the computer, free electrons streaming through the vacuum tube, processing logic in digital form, took on another role — manipulators, not just carriers, of information. Radio and TV, which look like rather brute artifacts of one-way information transmission compared to the computer, cannot use the information they transmit. Computers, even with the vacuum tube as the active element — a positively primordial approach compared to today's micro methods — quite obviously were the most powerful and versatile tool mankind had yet managed to invent. The power of symbolic logic, if nothing else, would have guaranteed that. The computer was an aid to mankind's intelligence, not just his muscle, and that was only the power of the computer at its most evident level. It was "better" than the brain, if the measure of the brain is taken to be its aptitude for computation — except for the occasional walking miracle like the legendary Mr. Dase, who could multiply two 100-digit numbers in his head, and did just that for European governments in the mid-eighteenth century. Just as a colony of termites can build an arch, though no individual termite understands "arch" or even "termite," so free electrons in the aggregate, channeled through the on-off gates of an electronic computer, can solve complicated problems which whole teams of mathematicians and scientists might spend years solving, if they managed it at all. It would make no difference, only a few short years after the war, whether the logic performed by the computer pertained to the path of a missile through space or the state of a patient during surgery or even the statistical probability of rain tomorrow. That was the boggling thing about the electronic computer — the lack of firm theoretical limitations on what it could be programmed to do. It could do math, certainly, but it was also a meta-machine that could mimic the functions of other machines and, just possibly, the brain itself.

Thus began a seductive, one-to-one mapping of computer theory to brain theory. As the events of this chapter reveal, the study of electronics and the study of human intelligence became joined in several important ways. New discoveries in biology, cross-fertilized with the tentative insights of cybernetic theory and the practicality of digital computers, led to the suggestion that the human brain, with its billions of neurons firing on and off in all-or-none, two-state fashion, might be performing logic very much as the computer did. If the computer was an analog of the brain, or in press terms, a "giant electronic brain," then the brain itself was some form of organic computer and it would not be heresy to suggest, as artificial intelligence researchers later did, that the human animal is, in essence, a "meat machine." Despite Norbert Wiener's warning that "If we insist too strongly on the brain as a glorified digital machine, we shall be subject to some very just criticism," the computer did present striking parallels with the brain. "I believe that at the end of the century," wrote Turing, "the use of words and general educated opinion will have altered so much that one will be able to speak of machines thinking without expecting to be contradicted." Here lie the seeds of a formidable semantic revolution, and others did not wait until anywhere near the end of the century to declare the birth of the thinking machine. What role computers and machine logic would play in the world was unclear from the beginning. But it was not hard to offer some intriguing speculation. A programmable computer with memory and a means of modifying its behavior on the basis of new information might be said to be capable of something very much like learning. Even thinking. And furthermore, if one was willing to speculate a bit, perhaps computers could someday be programmed to build and program other computers. Any machine that can think and replicate its own kind might reasonably be viewed as a species of sorts. In the end, if one shrugged off the belief that intelligence was the exclusive property of a certain configuration of carbon, hydrogen, oxygen and nitrogen atoms, the computer could be posited as an analog not only of brain, but of mind. At the least, computers ought to be capable of mustering a passable game of chess. (The matter of artificial intelligence and the brain–computer connection will be taken up again in later chapters.)

But the computer might have remained little more than a lab curiosity, a number cruncher for the military, a piece of accounting equipment for business and an intriguing focal point for scientific speculation, if not for a far-reaching postwar transformation of electronics as a whole. A new means of building basic electronic devices would ultimately consign the vacuum tube, save for certain specialized applications, to the status of a museum piece.

In the late forties, microelectronics was only one paradigm shift away.

CHAPTER THREE

The Solid State

The transistor in 1949 didn't seem like any-thing very revolutionary to me. It just seemed like another one of those crummy jobs that re-quired one hell of a lot of overtime and a lot of guff from my wife. . . .
— A WESTINGHOUSE EMPLOYEE

Out of the Vacuum

On July 1, 1948, readers of the *New York Times* who perused the "News of Radio" section would have encountered a number of intriguing possibilities for the holiday weekend. Mel Torme in a "situation comedy with musical overtones" was slated to replace the Dinah Shore–Harry James program Tuesdays at 8:00 on NBC. Fordham University was celebrating the first year of its FM radio station complete with "a critical discussion of present-day radio." Station WOR was adding a new game show, *On Your Mark*, to its offerings. The day's baseball broadcasts would begin with the Giants at Boston.

If the reader was diligent enough to scan the section clear through to the end, he or she would have discovered, buried beneath the news that NBC would air *Waltz Time* on Friday nights, the following four-inch blurb:

A device called a transistor, which has several applications in radio where a vacuum tube ordinarily is employed, was dem-onstrated for the first time yesterday at Bell Telephone Labora-tories, 463 West Street, where it was invented.

The device was demonstrated in a radio receiver, which contained none of the conventional tubes . . . the transistor was employed as an amplifier, although it is claimed that it also can be used as an oscillator in that it will create and send radio waves.

In the shape of a small metal cylinder about a half-inch long, the transistor contains no vacuum, grid, plate or glass envelope to keep the air away. Its action is instantaneous, there being no warm-up delay since no heat is developed as in a vacuum tube.

The working parts of the device consist solely of two fine wires that run down to a pinhead of solid semi-conductive material soldered to a metal base. The substance on the metal base amplifies the current carried to it by one wire and the other wire carries away the amplified current.

There is something unusual about this terse description. It does not list the names of any individual inventors. The gist of it seems to be that an entity known as Bell Labs invented the transistor. In a sense, the *Times* missed the boat: three physicists would receive the Nobel Prize for the transistor. But in a larger sense the *Times*, perhaps inadvertently, was right on the mark. Journalists, in the main, are prone to the single-inventor theory, fond as they are of determining who did it first, last, worst, most or best. A writer laboring through the thicket of science history that is electronics pinpoints specific inventors at his own risk. While the processes of science and invention often look linear, they almost never are, and picking the winners can be a tricky and altogether misleading business for several reasons.

First, the complexities of scientific practice and the success of the corporate invention factory conspire heavily against the "father of" approach to inventions and discoveries of science. Today, it is out of the question. In 1979 an international team of physicists cranked up a West German particle accelerator to fifteen billion electron volts, smashed electrons and positrons together, and got solid evidence for the existence of a subatomic particle called a gluon. There were two hundred and fifty scientists intimately involved in the project. If that discovery proves worthy of a Nobel Prize, who gets it?

There is also the matter of distinguishing between discoveries, which Thomas Kuhn calls novelties of fact, and inventions, or novelties of theory. The former would seem to be the province of the scientist and the latter the engineer, but of course many prominent workers, it should be clear, have combined the roles quite successfully. Lewis Mumford has argued that Joseph Henry invented the telegraph, not Morse; that Faraday invented the dynamo, not Siemens; that Maxwell and Hertz invented radio, not Marconi and De Forest. In that light, one could go on to argue that Alan Turing and John von Neumann invented the electronic computer, not Eckert or Mauchly or Zuse. But even if one manages to make that distinction, it is a safe bet that for every invention credited to specific workers, somebody else somewhere else thought of it first, and probably built it.

The idea of a paradigm shift — a fundamentally new way of looking at an old field — means that the history of invention can never be as tidy as writers would have it. The transistor is a good case in point, and if the science writers at first greeted it with a yawn, not bothering to inquire after the names of the scientists/inventors who discovered/invented it, they were not alone. The device Bell Labs billed as the answer to "the old dream of a control valve for electrons flowing in solids" was no obvious commercial breakthrough. The idea of a superior replacement for the vacuum tube consisting of a peculiar little slab of metal and a couple of fine wires — no moving parts, no glass, no vacuum, almost no heat — was just as foreign to most electrical engineers.

The transistor in reality inaugurated the age of the microchip. It was a piece of extraordinary science that shifted the story of the electronics industry directly to Silicon Valley, California, but manufacturers did not start throwing away their vacuum tubes with the announcement of it. The idea of the transistor was so foreign, so unrelated to all the accumulated knowledge about the vacuum tube, that even the technical journals moved slowly in praising it. It was not at all clear in the beginning whether there was anything very practical about it at all. The first transistors were miserable performers compared to today's ultraminiature versions and the idea of manufacturing large working batches of them, as companies were doing with the tube for 75 cents apiece, did not look immediately promising.

The computer was not the only scientific marvel pressed home by the demands of war. Radar, for Radio Detection and Ranging, was the result of a multidisciplinary research effort in Great Britain and the United States, and it drew heavily on basic discoveries in quantum physics. Many scientists held to the wisdom that "the atomic bomb only ended the war. Radar won it." In addition to all its other uses, radar was an important key to the automatic weaponry Wiener had envisioned. Radar was the province of "solid-state" physics, a branch which deals with the properties of solid matter.

The war had been a financial shot in the arm for physics in general. Some 40 percent of war-related government research and development contracts had gone to only ten large corporations; fully 90 percent of the Office of Scientific Research and Development's money went to only eight universities and 35 percent of that ended up at MIT's Radiation Laboratory for radar research. Moreover, the contractors were allowed to keep any patents that resulted from this outpouring of public funds. The trend continued after the war and by 1949 the Department of Defense and the Atomic Energy Commission were spending 96 percent of the total federal research money handed out to universities for research in the physical sciences.

It was the beginning of what came to be immortalized as the military-industrial complex. More and more scientists chose industry over university after the war. Industry, quite simply, paid better, and practiced plenty of good science, providing that the ambitious scientist joined the right company. Social critics began to wonder just who would end up controlling all the new scientific wonders after the war, and the migration of scientists to industry hinted at the answer.

Science already was a big business. It had been thus ever

since Edison's first industrial research laboratory, the most robust descendant of which was the mighty Bell Telephone Laboratories. Established by AT&T in 1924 as the research and patents counterpart to its Western Electric manufacturing subsidiary, the labs are by definition a practical think tank where the disciplined group method of invention has been the approach all along; employees numbered 3,600 a year after the labs began operation. "Pure" research did flow from there, and some of the best physicists of the century were a part of it. Up until the Second World War it had a larger basic research budget than any single university in the country.

A great deal of radar research everywhere had centered on the properties of a curious class of elements known as semiconductors, so named because they conduct electricity more readily than an insulator, such as glass, but not as freely as a conductor, such as copper. In relatively pure crystalline form, these substances, such as germanium and silicon, showed great promise as signal detectors in radar — a throwback to the early days of crystal radio. The efficacy of solid-state detectors in radar brought the research full circle, and sparked the search for a solid device that could do the work of the vacuum tube. Purdue and MIT had done considerable wartime work on germanium and silicon, but the massive Bell Labs were better equipped and more traditionally inclined to pursue an avenue of research that might yield new switches and amplifiers for the phone system.

The new theories of physics afforded a foundation for explaining the behavior of electrical current when it moves (or, in the case of insulators, doesn't move) through a solid. The electrons of an atom have specific energy levels, or bands. A conductor, like copper, is a material in which the bands of highest energy, where the attraction holding the electrons to the atom are the weakest, admit of new electrons rather freely. Therefore, electrical current can "flow" through a conductor. An insulator, like glass, does not conduct electricity well because its electrons are tightly bound to the atomic lattice. Moving a current through an insulator requires more energy than a normal electrical force can deliver. A semiconductor, like silicon, however, is an amalgam of the two extremes. The composition of semiconductors offered a particularly promising way of altering the current-carrying properties of solids. Semiconductors also offered new hope for the dream of a solid-state replacement for the vacuum tube.

In 1945, with the aid of a wealth of new information about semiconductors gleaned from the radar research effort, Bell Labs assembled a meeting of its semiconductor researchers to discuss work on germanium crystals. The labs had enough practical experience with the vacuum tube to realize that the tube suffered some serious performance limitations in the newer and faster telephone switching systems. In the summer of 1945, officials drew up an "Authorization for Work" on solid-state materials, which said in part:

> The research carried out under this case has as its purpose the obtaining of new knowledge that can be used in the development of completely new and improved components and apparatus elements of communication systems. . . . There are great possibilities of producing new and useful properties by finding physical and chemical methods of controlling the arrangement and behavior of the atoms and electrons which compose solids.

Bell Labs was about to turn its resources loose in pursuit of a solid-state alternative to the versatile vacuum tube, and it would take only two years for the effort to bear its first fruit.

Bell Lowers the Drawbridge

Bell's talented staff included two physicists well qualified to head up a post-war coordinated hunt for a solid-state amplifier: Walter Brattain and William Shockley. Brattain had taken a Ph.D. from the University of Minnesota, where Erwin Shrödinger, Arnold Sommerfeld and other leading lights of quantum physics had served as guest lecturers. After joining Bell Labs in 1929 he spent some time researching the vacuum tube and then began working with solid-state materials. Shockley, with a Ph.D. in physics from MIT, joined the labs in 1936 and also served a stint in the vacuum tube department under Clinton Davidson, a Nobel laureate. Because of Shockley's interest in solid-state physics he soon joined with Brattain in researching semiconductors.

Meanwhile, a Bell team of chemists and metallurgists had been investigating the properties of another semiconductor about which much had been learned during the war — silicon. In combination with oxygen and other elements, silicon occurs almost everywhere in the earth's crust as silica and silicate. It is nature's most abundant element except for oxygen, and it is the basic ingredient in sand, quartz, glass, bricks and concrete. In the form of a relatively pure metallic-gray crystalline slab, silicon, like germanium, had proven an excellent semiconductor for radar detection.

As with other semiconductors, the electrical properties of silicon and germanium could be readily altered. As completely pure crystals, however, silicon and germanium were very poor conductors. A semiconductor crystal must be slightly "dirty," in a chemical sense, if it is to do its electronic work. The presence of trace amounts of foreign elements in the crystal — often no more than a few atoms of another substance — alters its electrical characteristics.

The atomic rules governing this process were by no means well understood when Bell began its semiconductor research. The Bell chemists had learned to pull relatively pure ingots of silicon and germanium from a melt by "growing" them from scratch — melting silicon, for example, in a vacuum and then drawing it out slowly as it cooled. The chemists knew that the silicon obtained in this way was not completely pure, but the trace contamination was so small as to defy analysis. Still, these minute impurities affected the performance of silicon as a semiconductor.

Through painstaking chemical analysis, Bell researchers discovered how to deliberately "dope" small pieces of silicon and germanium with trace amounts of other elements. This working glimpse of the mysteries of doping allowed investigators to enhance and control the electrical properties of semiconductors in a much more systematic way. Researchers also discovered two basic kinds of doped semiconductors, dubbed "n-type" and "p-type," and much work began to center on the electrical behavior produced when the two types were sandwiched together to form a "junction."

Under Shockley's direction, the solid-state group of 1945 concentrated all of its efforts on silicon and germanium. They were soon joined by John Bardeen, a solid-state physicist from Princeton, another hotbed of radar research, who had worked on sub detection devices at the Naval Ordnance Laboratory during the war. The three men — Bardeen the theorist, Brattain the practical experimenter and Shockley, team leader and a bit of both — formed a troika at the apex of a pyramid of Bell's best talent. But they were stuck, and their early attempts at a solid-state amplifier failed.

It was John Bardeen who finally broke the impasse. Something unusual, he decided, was taking place at the surface of the semiconductor whenever a voltage was applied. Bardeen's theory of surface states warranted a closer look, and by late 1947 the work suggested to Bardeen and Brattain that they try attaching two thin wires as close together as possible on the same side of a tiny slab of suitably prepared germanium. The two scientists decided to see what would happen when they spaced the two contacts only two-thousandths of an inch apart — a difficult feat, since the finest wire then available to them was twice that thick to begin with. Brattain jerry-rigged an ingenious solution to the problem by covering a polystyrene triangle with gold foil and then splitting the foil slightly with a razor at one point of the triangle. When that point of the triangle was placed against a slab of germanium and wiggled about to make a good contact, Bardeen and Brattain were delighted to discover that the device could receive and amplify electrical signals. On December 23, 1947, Bardeen and Brattain demonstrated their little germanium-and-wire device to the rest of the Bell team, and used it successfully to amplify voice.

This modest piece of apparatus, lacking any moving parts or relays or vacuum or grid or glowing elements or anything else directly connected to the mainstream world of electronics, was a true solid-state amplifier, crude but workable. Moreover, Bardeen and Brattain had discovered it after turning away from the direct attempt to develop such a device. A Bell colleague telescoped the term "transfer resistance" into "transistor," and the name stuck. Specifically, the Bardeen–Brattain device was called a point-contact transistor. Here, at least in theory, was the solid-state replacement for the vacuum tube in telephone switching systems and equipment. In addition, the transistor was a hundred times smaller than the vacuum tube.

The invention of the transistor caught Bell Labs and AT&T by surprise, and it presented Bell management with a number of problems as well as opportunities. The transistor had popped up so unexpectedly from the surface state investigations that the solid-state group hardly knew enough about its workings to file a comprehensive patent. They did know, however, that a team at Purdue University was close behind them. Secondly, the military would have to be given a look to see whether transistor work should be classified, as the early computer work had been. In addition, while team leader Shockley had contributed greatly to the research, none of his calculations had predicted the Bardeen–Brattain point-contact transistor. A final problem facing Bell was to dog the new transistor industry for years: It was one thing to invent the transistor, and quite another to find a way of manufacturing it reliably and profitably.

Bell's first order of business was to clamp a lid of secrecy on the project while undertaking a three-month crash research program in order to glean enough information for a patent application. This was done, and the patent quickly granted, but the names on the first transistor patent were Bardeen and Brattain — not Shockley. After the military chose not to classify the work, the transistor went public seven months after its invention, at a press conference on June 30, 1948. To this day, Bell likes to present the transistor troika as the keystone example of Edison's legacy, the invention factory. In *Revolution in Miniature,* from which a portion of this discussion has been taken, Ernest Braun and Stuart MacDonald write: "There are grounds for being severely skeptical of any claim that the invention of the transistor was the product of scientists allowed the freedom of loose reins. Industrial research organizations do not work that way — not even Bell Laboratories."

The transistor age had arrived, but the point-contact transistor, by itself, would not have ushered in the age of solid-state electronics any more than the De Forest audion, without significant improvements, would have ushered in the age of radio, TV and long-distance telephony. Each point-contact transistor seemed to have slightly different electrical characteristics than the last one. It was not as if one could simply yank out a vacuum tube from a radio, for example, and insert a transistor in its place. The design parameters, specifications and equations were completely different — a new and untested form of electronics. For his part, Shockley remained convinced that there were better ways to make a transistor, and his vindication came in 1950 when he succeeded in building a precisely doped "p-n-p junction" transistor, again with germanium. Shockley's junction transistor was a much more reliable, high-performance form of solid-state device than the Bardeen–Brattain point-contact transistor, and it was to be a major commercial success for solid-state electronics.

Manufacturing problems aside, AT&T now found itself in much the same position as it had enjoyed with the vacuum tube — it was in control. AT&T's historical successes had stemmed from a policy of acquiring and controlling as many patents as possible, while zealously tripping up less fortunate competitors with infringement suits. But with the transistor, the company executed a precedent-shattering about-face. In a series of famous seminars in the early fifties, Bell Labs gave away the secrets of the transistor — for a price, to be sure, but a reasonable one — thus guaranteeing that any company, domestic or foreign, would be allowed to manufacture and use the transistor without fear of reprisal. At the first public seminar in 1952 (an earlier one the year before had been restricted to government and military officials) twenty-five American companies and ten foreign firms laid out $25,000 apiece as a down payment on a license. Inside the gates, Bell researchers revealed everything they had discovered about building the point-contact transistor — already beginning to appear in telephone systems — and also made known what they had learned about the far more difficult process of manufacturing Shockley's superior junction transistor.

Braun and MacDonald suggest several practical reasons for AT&T's break with tradition, and they are worth noting because of the tone they set for the future semiconductor industry. One incentive for Bell's largesse may have been the fact that the Justice Department had brought an antitrust suit against AT&T in 1949. Considering that what Justice sought was no less than the divestiture of Western Electric, AT&T had no wish to play Goliath against a host of smaller Davids anxious to learn of semiconductor developments. In the wake of the transistor, some of Bell's solid-state workers were leaving the fold for other opportunities, and it was a good guess that other electronics companies would be willing to risk infringement of Bell's patents if the transistor took hold. A flurry of well-publicized lawsuits by Bell in an attempt to hold the fort would not, in all likelihood, sit well with Justice Department officials. In addition, Bell announced in 1954 that it would not require licenses for transistors meant for use in hearing aids, "as a memorial to Alexander Graham Bell and to his interest in the deaf." In the consent decree of 1956, which got Justice off AT&T's back for a time, AT&T agreed not to sell transistors or computers in the open market, while retaining Western Electric and remaining free to produce such products for its own use and for military contracts.

There were other sound reasons for the Bell policy. Setting up future licensees through the seminar program guaranteed for Bell a substantial income from its transistor patents. As an option, companies could cross-license for the patents, meaning that Bell would gain access to important semiconductor developments down the road that were, in industry jargon, NIH — Not Invented Here. Finally, though the electronics industry was slowly warming to semiconductors, the transistor in the early fifties was still not recognized as any sort of trailblazing commercial triumph. From circuit design to production, the transistor meant a whole new way of thinking. Electrical engineers *understood* the tube and the behavior of free electrons in a vacuum. But solid-state was a new ballgame, and it posed a direct threat to the livelihood of vacuum tube engineers, whose jobs and training were at stake. Therefore, the more companies Bell could bring into the transistor world, the better the likelihood that semiconductor electronics would be here to stay. The more firms in the business, the better the chances of exploiting any new discoveries that went beyond simple tube replacement. This latter reasoning was the tack *Electronics* magazine took when it became a transistor booster in 1953:

> As we enter the age of transistors, it is important that engineers open their eyes wide to the potentialities of these new devices that are like tubes and yet are not like tubes. Circuits can be developed by thinking of transistors as substitutes for tubes. But more important circuits will come in the harnessing of characteristics that are peculiar to transistors themselves.

A New Industry

"The transistor was not simply a new sort of amplifier, but the harbinger of an entirely new sort of electronics with the capacity not just to influence an industry or a scientific discipline, but to change a culture." That judgment, written in 1978 by Braun and MacDonald, had the benefit of considerable hindsight. Still, by 1956, the year Shockley, Bardeen and

Brattain won the Nobel Prize in physics for discovering the transistor effect, no less than twenty-six companies were manufacturing transistors under Bell license, and semiconductors were on their way to becoming a robust subset of the electronics industry. Almost as many companies were building vacuum tube computers by this time as well. The licensed transistor firms fell into three categories: established electronics firms with vacuum tube experience, existing firms which had never been in the electronics business before, and new firms formed wholly for the purpose of making transistors. While Bell had invented the transistor with its own money, military R&D funds began to flow to transistor makers shortly after the 1952 seminar, the lion's share of it ending up with the established tube suppliers. In 1952 the Department of Defense added a Subpanel on Semiconductor Devices to its Panel on Electron Tubes and awarded $5 million in transistor research contracts to the Big Four vacuum tube makers — General Electric, Raytheon, Sylvania and RCA. It also purchased almost all of the ninety thousand transistors manufactured that year by Western Electric. There was good reason — tube failures in military equipment ran distressingly high.

Raytheon took the first stab at commercial consumer applications of the transistor by cornering the hearing-aid market, a use which was soon to be followed by "transistorized" radios. A new company called Germanium Products popped up in Jersey City to chase Raytheon in the hearing-aid market, its president prophetically declaring, "Trouble with the big companies is too many long-haired boys and not enough practical horse sense. . . . We expect to chase the vacuum tube price to hell and gone." Old-liners Philco and Motorola were in, and so was a rowdy young Texas manufacturer of geophysical equipment for the oil industry — Texas Instruments. TI, as it is known, had never manufactured tubes or any other electronic device, but its management had decided that there was money to be made in the nascent transistor business. TI took two things from Bell's solid-state program: a license to manufacture transistors, and Gordon Teal, a Bell scientist. By late 1953

TI was manufacturing a modest number of transistors in a new semiconductor division headed by Teal, and the group was assigned the task of building a silicon version of the germanium junction transistor. Bell's initial successes had come from germanium transistors, but Teal knew that silicon had a number of potential advantages, not least of which was a melting point of 1,420 degrees C. That made silicon a good bet for transistors for use in what the military calls "high-stress environments," meaning rockets and missiles. And the military, through its funding, was demonstrating that it held a definite interest in the transistor — its experience with ballistics, radar, cryptography and computers had established a link between the Defense Department and the electronics industry which has never been broken.

Military willingness to pay premium prices for new kinds of transistors, even when they were not altogether reliable, was used to advantage by Texas Instruments. Teal and his group succeeded in building the first silicon version of the junction transistor in 1954, and TI and the military have maintained a mutual love affair ever since. The company, eyeing the successes other firms were having with hearing aids, was also looking to establish itself with a major commercial sale. It did so, in league with the IDEA Corporation, by offering a transistor radio called the Regency. Even though silicon showed every sign of being a better bet than germanium for rugged, high-frequency transistors, TI managed to hold exclusive title to the silicon transistor market for three years — an unheard-of lead in today's semiconductor components market.

Tubes were still the main order of business in the electronic computer industries during the fifties, but in addition to government funding, the influence of solid-state thinking was becoming evident in other ways. Scientific papers on solid-state physics ran a close second in number to papers on atomic physics, and the few scientists and engineers who understood semiconductor electronics found themselves caught up in a heady battle for their talents. In general, Bell opted to follow the same laissez-faire approach to talent raids that it was taking toward transistor patent infringement. In both cases, the wounds were far from mortal. No longer could an electronics company — AT&T or any other — afford to adopt the approach of not employing inventors "capable of generating novel designs." There was nothing very standard about transistor manufacturing processes, and simply buying the patent was not enough. A company in the transistor business needed individual brainpower of a new sort that could not be found among the ranks of the tube men. While the transistor drew upon previous experience in crystal radio and radar, it was a sharp departure from both, and it did not evolve logically as the tube had evolved from Edison's light bulb.

Industrial resistance to new techniques is far more formidable than might be supposed, given the swift pace of change in this century. At first, the financial arguments for sticking with the tube were persuasive, and tube engineers could readily temper the enthusiasm of the solid-state people with the weight of experience. Maybe the transistor was not going to be such a big deal after all the early fuss died down. For one thing, the manufacturing methods were completely ad hoc and seat-of-the-pants. Controlling electricity by rearranging the *atoms* of a solid crystal was a nice practice in theory but not quite so awe-inspiring when it came to the production line, where almost anything could go wrong and frequently did. It was like trying to do surgery on the head of a pin, as a Bell researcher later put it. It was wondrous that transistors worked at all, and quite often they didn't. Those that did varied widely in performance, and it was sometimes easier to test the things after production and, on that basis, find out what kind of electronic component they had turned out to be. If they failed, it could have been due to any number of undesirable impurities that had sneaked into the doping process. It was as if the Ford Motor Company was running a production line so uncontrollable that it had to test the finished product in order to find out if it was a truck, a convertible or a sedan.

Despite the problems, it did not take too much foresight on the part of tube engineers to see what lay down the road if the transistor took hold. They would have to learn a new business or go out of business, if all the grand promises about transistors replacing tubes in everything from radios to TVs to computers came true. Where were they to learn the new rules? Shockley had written virtually the only solid-state textbook in existence, and if the cutting edge of electronics did indeed shift from the behavior of electrons in a vacuum to the behavior of electrons in and on the surface of solids, then an entire generation of electrical engineers was going to find itself on the sidelines. And that is precisely what happened.

The Department of Defense helped establish solid-state electronics by paying premium prices for transistors throughout the Korean war (making it easier for transistor makers to bring production costs down), while simultaneously spurring on the already established vacuum tube computer business. IBM entered the commercial computer field with the mass-produced 701 electronic computer, and again, the military was the prime customer. But IBM planned to sell the 701 computers to American business as well. With its keen sense of marketing, salesmanship and timing of new product entries, IBM cut deeply into Remington Rand's early lead in commercial computers. In the pre-UNIVAC days, businesses kept track of their operations with huge "tab rooms" filled with noisy electromechanical punch card calculators tended by dozens of employees. In the early fifties, IBM, Remington Rand and Burroughs' salespeople began to call on business customers to propose a different approach. When an IBM salesman called on, say, the vice-president of a manufacturing company, to propose the new system, he had a ready listener. Not only did the vice-president have a partially automated manufacturing process to keep track of, he also had perhaps several thousand employees and sales records and inventory tallies and tax files and numbers, numbers, numbers. More punch card machines would help, but the IBM man wasn't selling more punch cards; he was selling a vacuum tube computer that was far faster and would pay for itself in layoffs alone. It was also, the IBM man might well have hinted, the wave of the future and something of a high-ticket prestige item. No business of note could afford to be without one in the coming years, and if the vice-president demurred, might that not serve as a reflection on the future health and growth of his business?

The situation was much the same for banks, large manufacturing concerns, insurance companies and government agencies, and IBM doggedly took advantage of the situation through the mid-fifties. But IBM had little inkling that semiconductor electronics very rapidly would change *everything* about computers — how they were built, how they were used and how they were sold.

CHAPTER FOUR

The Silicon Priesthood

Back then you could make lots of transistors on one large slice of silicon. But then you had to cut them apart and put them in packages and finally wire them all together again. It just seemed horribly inefficient to do that.
— ROBERT NOYCE

The Lure of the Valley

Nineteen fifty-five was a memorable year for the transistor. It was then that IBM first began seriously to consider what the transistor might portend for the design of future computers. It was also the year of William Shockley's celebrated return to his former home of Palo Alto, California. As a youth, Shockley and his family had lived there for a time, occupying a home not far from the former home of Lee De Forest. When Shockley parted company with Bell Labs in 1954 to found his own company and pursue his own ideas about the transistor, he came back.

Palo Alto was a logical site for another reason. It was the home of Stanford University and Frederick Terman. Terman, whose father had developed the controversial Stanford–Binet IQ tests, taught radio engineering at Stanford before the war and had set out to marry the needs of university research to the needs of science-based industry. The American electronics industry already had a history of close cooperation between scientists in the industrial labs and scientists in the universities, and electrical industry executives had played a major role in the rise of industrial education early in the century. Training employees for industry had become an accepted part of academics, though earlier it had been the subject of a bitter debate amid fears that the trend spelled the death of universities as centers of higher learning. In 1946 William Wickenden had presaged what would happen around Stanford in his commencement address to the General Motors Institute, a technical training school:

> The very word university comes from the Latin word for corporation and the college dormitory is simply a continuation of the plan of the guilds by which the master workmen not only trained their apprentices but took them into their households to live. That is where our circle began but as it swung out on its wide arc, the world of education drew further and further away from the world of industry. . . . The Sorbonne and Oxford scarcely knew of the world of science and for the world of industry they had only disdain. But the two circles went swinging on, bringing industry and education ever closer and closer, until tonight they are closing back once more at the point of origin where industry and education are one; where corporation and university again mean the same thing.

This trend was most abundantly evident in the vicinity of Boston's Route 128, where a spate of post-war high-technology firms had bloomed in the shadow of Harvard and MIT. Route 128 had become a metaphor for an impressive blend of scientific, industrial and academic talent represented by the Los Alamos generation of physicists and the older computer companies. But it was Terman who encouraged his students to forgo the usual pilgrimage back East in search of post-graduation jobs and stay in the Stanford area to start their own companies. Many of them did, such as William Hewlett and David Packard, who began making electronic equipment in Packard's garage and soon formed Hewlett–Packard Company, now one of the world's largest electronic equipment manufacturers. When Terman returned to Stanford after the war he continued to push the idea of a business community in close proximity to the intellectual community of the university, an idea made concrete in the form of Stanford Industrial Park, where Stanford graduates could build their own companies. What others had done for the science and technology of electronics, Terman was determined to do for the business of electronics. And he was determined to do it in California.

Shockley Semiconductor Laboratories fit well with this plan, and when Shockley's first handpicked employees began arriving in Palo Alto, they found a closely knit community of scientists in the shadow of Stanford University who were grappling with the new challenge of semiconductor electronics. The broad brown run of the valley to the south was filled with fruit trees, and nearby Santa Clara and San Jose were better known for orchards than for electronic sorcery. Still, something new was quite evidently in the air. Hewlett–Packard and Varian Associates were going concerns, and Admiral, General Electric and Sylvania all had opened new divisions in the area. Moreover, a group of IBM scientists had been transferred from the East to staff a new research center in San Jose. Shockley Semiconductor Laboratories, established as a subsidiary of an electronics firm called Beckman Instruments, was the first semiconductor company among the existing electronics concerns in the Palo Alto–Santa Clara area south of San Francisco. It was research-oriented, with close ties to Stanford, but it was also intended to be a profitable manufacturing firm. As such, it would face stiff competition from Texas Instruments, "the Alger boys from Texas," as *Fortune* magazine once called them.

Shockley's reputation as the father of the transistor gave him an edge when it came to recruiting young semiconductor talent, and he soon surrounded himself with a corps of bright engineers and physicists. In the meantime, Texas Instruments was hammering away at silicon transistors and the military was interested in further "microminiaturization" of solid-state electronic circuits. There was a market awaiting the engineers who found a way to make smaller and cheaper transistors, but this meant straightening out the vagaries of the production process and seeing to it that transistors and other semiconductor components worked reliably — especially in missiles. Making transistors, at Shockley and everywhere else, was turning into a monumental headache. Here was a frightfully advanced and supposedly exacting new method of building electronic devices, opening up all manner of novel possibilities, but what it boiled down to was roomfuls of young women cutting and sorting the finished devices with tweezers, dropping or otherwise misplacing no small number of the little slabs. It was ludicrous. Assembly techniques were reminiscent of nineteenth-century woolen mills. The military accepted such conditions because it had no choice, but it had its own research programs in the offing.

Shortly after Shockley's company began, Bell Labs held another symposium to reveal a powerful new way of building transistors, discovered by Bell and GE scientists. It was called diffusion, and it was ten times more accurate than doping germanium with pellets of impurities to produce transistors. Diffusion was like baking cookies — time and temperature were the key parameters. In a furnace at high temperature and high pressure, impurities in a gaseous state could be added to the germanium. The extent of atomic bonding between the germanium and the gaseous impurities depended upon the amount of time the mix was in the furnace. But in the end, wires still had to be attached to the active areas of the transistor.

Diffusion hinted that the immediate future of solid-state miniaturization would be found not so much by inventing new devices as in discovering new *processes* of manufacture. Perfecting reliable, repeatable manufacturing processes had been the hallmark of American technology ever since the Model Ts began rolling off the assembly line. However, manufacturing problems and the lack of reliable, repeatable fabrication procedures continued to plague the emerging transistor business. Shockley's Nobel Prize established him as a prominent figure in the world of solid-state physics, but it did not necessarily ensure a successful commercial future for those ambitious young physicists and engineers who worked under him.

The relationship between Shockley and a number of his young employees began to deteriorate. "The Shockley organization just wasn't going well," in the opinion of one. "Finally, a terribly frustrated splinter group formed. They had talked to Shockley, and they had talked to Beckman, saying, hey, it just isn't working with management. In the end they gave up on that and decided to seek financing so that they could go off and do something else by themselves."

When in 1957 seven of Shockley's employees decided to defect in order to pursue semiconductor process improvements on their own, they headed to the East Coast with a business plan, hoping someone there would be willing to put up the cash for a new West Coast semiconductor company. One of the investment firms they called upon was Hayden Stone, and it was a fortunate choice. Hayden Stone was involved with an East Coast company called Fairchild Camera and Instrument whose president, John Carter, had been the youngest vice-president in the history of Corning Glass Company until Sherman Fairchild lured him away. Carter had been on a number of government boards during the war, and he was familiar with many of the breakthroughs stemming from the war research. Carter had asked the investment firm for assistance in helping Fairchild buy into the new solid-state transistor world, and at this point the Shockley dissidents arrived with a very solid business plan for a new semiconductor manufacturing enterprise. All the talk about new-process technologies and a shift from germanium to silicon transistors made sense, especially since many electronic products were rapidly becoming transistorized and the military's interest in better miniaturization was, if anything, on the increase. But good ideas were a dime a dozen; the investors also wanted evidence that the group could take charge in a management sense, and serve as articulate spokesmen in the business and financial community. To bolster their case, the seven scientists set out to recruit the perfect candidate — Robert Noyce, a physicist and a reasonably mild-mannered team player still in Shockley's good graces.

The son of an Iowa minister, Noyce grew up in small Iowa

towns and early on showed a proclivity for tinkering with gadgets. Like others in the rural Midwest, where schoolboys learn to drive cars and tractors at the age of twelve or thirteen, Noyce loved to tear apart and rebuild Model Ts. The practical workings of things delighted him, and when he enrolled at Iowa's Grinnell College in 1946 he retained his engineering instincts while pursuing a degree in physics. At Grinnell in 1948, Noyce met up with a strange new device, the solid-state transistor. He was fascinated by it, and it seemed to offer an outlet for combining his love of science, his down-to-earth engineering bent, and his strong desire to better himself. He became avidly interested in semiconductor theory, and after a Ph.D. at MIT and a brief stint with the transistor division of Philco, the soft-spoken, sharp-featured Noyce accepted the invitation to join Shockley in 1955.

People naturally gravitated toward Noyce. He had an effortless way of taking charge that marked him as a competent future manager, but Noyce had not joined the seven dissidents straightaway. Still, he was keenly interested in the potential advantages of silicon over germanium. "Shockley was concentrating on four-layer germanium diodes," Noyce recalled, "at a time when there seemed to be a swing in the semiconductor community from germanium to silicon. Most of the real start-up opportunities are when there's a shift going on somewhere. The people traditionally in the business are so committed to the previous course of action that they don't really get on with the new thing."

Noyce finally joined the dissidents, the financing clicked, and Fairchild Semiconductor opened shop a few miles away from Palo Alto in Mountain View, with parent Fairchild Camera and Instrument retaining an option to buy out its new start-up if all went well. The year was 1957, and Bob Noyce was twenty-nine. "It was the beginning of an entrepreneurial flourish in this valley. Suddenly it became apparent to people like myself, who had always assumed they would be working for a salary for the rest of their lives, that they could get some equity in a start-up company. That was a great revelation — and a great motivation too."

The "traitorous eight," as Shockley reportedly referred to them, were about to spark an industrial explosion that would transform the orchards of Santa Clara County into Silicon Valley.

The Sputnik Jitters

In late 1957, the year Fairchild Semiconductor began hiring the best semiconductor talent it could find, a Soviet rocket launched Sputnik, the world's first earth-orbiting satellite. Millions of Americans stood in their backyards under the night sky of winter and watched the artificial star blink across the horizon. U.S. military brass, however, were alarmed. It would still be a few years before the terms "space age" and "space race" entered the popular lexicon, but the Russians, as the military saw it, had thrown down the technological gauntlet. Sputnik's technical predecessor, they knew, was the German V-2 rocket, and America's first response to the Russian challenge was a Navy Vanguard rocket which blew up on the launch pad.

Sputnik put the spurs to the Cold War, and sharpened the military's efforts at electronic miniaturization. As Noyce recalled, "It was the beginning of the space age and the missile crisis and size, weight and power were crucial in the electronic circuits that were used. It was very expensive to get that stuff into space. There were several military programs aimed at miniaturization, so the idea of making an integrated piece of solid-state electronics to do a job was not new. The question was to find the most practical way of doing it."

As far back as 1952, while the transistor was still slowly emerging from its status as a laboratory curiosity, a British radar expert, G. W. A. Dummer, presented a paper on radar reliability to a symposium in Washington, D.C., in which he predicted the answer:

With the advent of the transistor, and the work in semiconductors generally, it seems now possible to envisage electronic equipment *in a solid block with no connecting wires* [italics added]. The block may consist of layers of insulating, conducting, rectifying and amplifying materials, the electrical functions being connected directly by cutting out areas of the various layers.

This prediction proved to be completely accurate, but it was not to be Dummer's countrymen who seized upon it. Writing in 1970, with Silicon Valley well in mind, Dummer concluded, "In the United Kingdom and Europe a war-weariness prevented exploitation of electronic applications and it was probably not realized how important electronics was to become." Not so in America, where three branches of the military were competing against each other with separate programs to further miniaturize not just transistors, but *all* electronic devices. After Sputnik, these research efforts received a healthy boost, but no one in the semiconductor community knew which, if any, of the military approaches would win out.

The culmination of these early efforts at miniaturization was the integrated circuit concept, commonly known as the microchip, an idea born at Texas Instruments and at Fairchild Semiconductor. Fairchild was determined to go its own way, without the benefit — or the hindrance — of direct military R&D support. "I think the maximum we ever got to in direct military support at Fairchild was four percent of our research and development budget," said Noyce. "From my point of view, it was largely because I had worked on military projects before at Philco and I felt that it was a waste of the asset. The direction of the research was being determined by people less competent in seeing where it ought to go, and a lot of time of the researchers themselves was spent communicating with military people through progress reports or visits or whatever. At the time I remember saying that selling R&D to the government was like taking your venture capital and putting it into a savings account — you're not going to make any substantial gain from it. Venturing is venturing; you want to take the risk and have the potential gains out of it. Our basic desire was to be out there venturing, and frankly, not to be beholden to other people that you don't have that much trust in. There was plenty of commercial motivation for doing it."

Despite Noyce's perceived managerial abilities, his technical prowess led to his being named director of research and development at Fairchild Semiconductor in 1959. Fairchild started out by making silicon transistors, but Noyce and the rest of the researchers soon began to focus their efforts on finding a process that would eliminate the "horribly inefficient" business of wiring together arrays of transistors by hand after production. Noyce began working closely with co-founder Gordon Moore, a gifted chemical physicist who had the bespectacled, crew-cut look of the engineer's engineer. The two began trading ideas about ways of connecting transistors together "in a solid block with no connecting wires."

If a single transistor, requiring no moving parts, could be created with a few fine wires on a tiny piece of doped silicon, why not dozens of *smaller* transistors, plus resistors and other electronic circuit elements, forming whole electronic subsystems, all crammed on the *same* "chip" of silicon? For Noyce, "the conceptual jump was from wiring together arrays of transistors to the realization that you could put all the other electronic functions on silicon as well." To do so, however, meant finding a way to make transistors even smaller.

Noyce scribbled these insights in his lab notebook, but much the same thinking already had taken place the preceding summer at Texas Instruments under the direction of Jack Kilby. Kilby, like Noyce, was a product of the Midwest. After high school in Great Bend, Kansas, a low score on a math entrance exam short-circuited his dream of attending MIT. He settled instead for the University of Illinois. In 1947, Kilby went to work for the Centralab Division of Globe–Union. In 1952 he attended the Bell Labs transistor seminar and went to work on germanium transistors for hearing aids at Centralab. Like Noyce, Kilby came to believe that silicon, not germanium, was the wave of the future, and Centralab was rather heavily invested in germanium. In 1958, after eleven years with the company, Kilby started looking for a new opportunity.

Kilby, however, was simply looking for a new employer, not a new business start-up. The Fairchild group had leaped foursquare into the world of the entrepreneur, running their own company, venturing, taking risks, scrambling for capital and trying to be innovative scientists all at the same time. Kilby, more traditionally inclined, sent out a stack of résumés, stressing silicon and his interest in miniaturized circuits, and soon found a new job. Texas Instruments, then deeply into silicon transistors and the military programs, hired him, and he never left.

"In those days, TI had a mass vacation policy; that is, they just shut down tight during the first few weeks of July, and anybody who had any vacation time coming took it then. Since I had just started and had no vacation time, I was left pretty much in a deserted plant. . . . I began to cast around for alternates — and the [integrated circuit] concept really occurred during that two week vacation period."

For Kilby, who once described himself as an inventor who "gets a picture and then proceeds doggedly to implement that picture," there were "three key features of the invention: recognition that all of the required circuit elements could be made from a single material; electrical isolation of these circuit elements so that they could operate independently; and all of the circuit elements constructed in or near one main surface of the semiconductor wafer, so as to take advantage of advancing semiconductor technology, and permitting their interconnection."

The electronic device sought by Kilby and Noyce was defined at the outset by the realities of corporate economics and the commercial marketplace, and the integrated circuit that resulted from their efforts was as far from invention by luck or accident as any invention could be. It was a logical and *evolutionary* extension of the solid-state transistor, born of the marketplace and the dictates of production costs. And yet, as a finished product, the integrated circuit proved to be a completely *revolutionary* extension of electronics in general.

Kilby's approach to miniaturization called for a cost-effective form of automatic batch processing and the elimination, so far as was possible, of handwork. In order to integrate many electronic components on the same substrate, the connections between the circuit elements would have to be on or near only one side of the semiconductor wafer, and they would have to be part of the manufacturing process itself, rather than an expensive manual wiring process. This effort was aided, in addition, by new semiconductor advances like diffusion and photolithographic techniques for reproducing very tiny geometric patterns on germanium and silicon.

Unlike less-fortunate inventors in history, Jack Kilby had no trouble selling his idea to his bosses. Management could see that this was no hare-brained scheme; Kilby was thinking costs and production and he was gunning for a commercial, profitable invention rather than a research breakthrough which someone else would have to bring to the manufacturing stage. On the basis of Kilby's lab notebooks describing a means of miniaturizing many electrical circuits, TI gave him the go-ahead for building a few crude prototypes of the kind of electrical circuit he was describing. The tiny slices of germanium (later silicon) contained even tinier resistors, transistors and capacitors, three basic building blocks of common electrical circuitry. They were not yet refined enough for mass production, but by February of 1959 Kilby and TI were confident enough about the integrated circuit to file a patent for "Miniaturized Electronic Circuits."

The active elements on Kilby's first integrated circuits, or ICs, were connected with gold wires, but his patent petition also included the phrase, "electrically conducting material such as gold may then be laid down on the insulating material to make the necessary electrical circuit connections." TI went public with the IC soon after, announcing "the development of a semiconductor solid circuit no larger than a match head," at the Institute of Radio Engineers Show in March and selling the devices at $450 each. Texas Instruments had none of Fairchild's misgivings about the military looking over its shoulder, and the Air Force soon jumped in with contract and development money.

News of the announcement quickly reached Fairchild, galvanizing the independent effort under way there. Noyce, looking for the best way of interconnecting several tiny transistors and other components on silicon as an integral part of the manufacturing process itself, found the answer in a neat technological twist discovered by physicist Jean Hoerni, another of Fairchild's original founders. Hoerni's "planar" process was a method of oxidation and heat diffusion which formed a perfectly smooth insulating layer across the surface of a silicon chip. (Planar worked better with silicon than with germanium.) "With planar," said Noyce, "you had a bunch of transistors and other circuit elements embedded in silicon, and you could isolate these circuits electrically through the insulating layer, rather than cutting them apart physically and wiring the pieces back together again." Kilby's crude integrated circuits were the first ever built, but the planar method perfected at Fairchild proved to be the commercial breakthrough which opened the door to the assembly-line manufacture of silicon chips. In this sense, Kilby played the part of De Forest in the vacuum tube saga, with Noyce playing the Armstrong who improved the device and made it a commercial reality.

On July 30, 1959, Noyce filed a patent for a semiconductor integrated circuit based on the planar process. As for the all-important connections between the circuit elements on the chip, the Noyce patent referred to "deposited . . . metal strips extending over and adherent to the insulating oxide layer for making electrical connections to and between various regions of the semiconductor body."

In 1962 TI filed a lawsuit for patent interference, and for most of the sixties a bitter debate raged between TI and Fairchild over ownership of the IC concept — a debate that continues unabated to this day. To the U.S. Court of Customs and

Patent Appeals fell the task of deciding whether Kilby's "laid down" meant the same thing as Noyce's "adherent to," as far as circuit interconnections were concerned. In 1969 the court upheld Noyce's claims on interconnection techniques, but the dispute had no real effect on the spread of the IC concept. In general, other semiconductor companies that wished to make the IC needed both a license from TI for the basic integrated circuit structure, and a license from Fairchild covering the planar process and Noyce's interconnection techniques. The two companies resolved the impasse by licensing rather than suing the new entrants. This had the further effect of spreading the word about the IC through the electronics community and, in any event, cash up front was far more useful to young, growing companies than protracted and costly lawsuits. (The semiconductor industry at large solved the TI–Fairchild matter simply by informally referring to Kilby, who built the first working integrated circuit, and Noyce, who improved it for industrial purposes, as co-inventors of the IC. Kilby was later inducted into the National Inventors Hall of Fame as the inventor of the IC.)

As the two companies began turning out the first commercial integrated circuits in the early sixties, they also started scouting for a big commercial sale; something that would kick off the IC with a splash. The young engineering managers at Fairchild and TI knew what they had: a new and extremely versatile electronic device that could conceivably replace vacuum tubes and solid-state transistors, solder, and yards and yards of wiring in all things electronic. All provided, however, that they successfully snared some sizable bugs in the IC production process, about which more later.

Planar gave Fairchild an early lead in manufacturing ICs and a built-in source of future royalties. It was the best answer to the riddle of how to mass-manufacture solid-state transistors and other semiconductor devices without resorting to a microscope-and-tweezers approach at several points along the production line. Regardless of their approach to military funding, when it came time to seek out a good first sale to prove that the IC was not just a gimmick, the Fairchild founders knew where to look.

IC Evangelism

The Minuteman project, an early intercontinental ballistic missile (ICBM) program, was part of the post-Sputnik expansion of space and defense projects in the early sixties. The older germanium transistors were designed into the guidance control system of the Minuteman I ballistic missile from the start, and that changed the manner in which the electronics industry did business with the military. "Before, the big thing had been airplane mainframes," said Marshall Cox, one of the early Fairchild sales managers. "You made twelve million F-86s and then all of a sudden the world changed in the early sixties from making thousands of jets to making, you know, hundreds of missiles. That's when all the subcontractors doing military work started to abandon the airplane business and tried like hell to get into guidance systems and satellites."

Fairchild was only too happy to assist in the transition. A company called Autonetics was building Minuteman guidance packages for Boeing, which integrated the packages into the overall missile design as a Department of Defense subcontractor. Fairchild started at the bottom of the chain by submitting to Autonetics a proposal calling for building the guidance system with planar transistors and integrated circuits, in place of the older, bulkier variety of transistor. As one Fairchilder summed it up with a grin, "The proposal was, 'Hey, using this new technology we can make this new widget which is only one-tenth the size of the old widget and uses one-tenth of the power and will last for a million years.' " Shortly thereafter, Minuteman II project planners accepted the idea of integrated circuits. "The Minuteman program," said Ben Anixter, then with the company, "gave Fairchild the liftoff."

And that was only Fairchild's piece of the action. The new emphasis on space and defense meant that there was plenty of money to go around, and a portion of the new weapons contracts provided by the military found its way to Texas as well. But as Fairchild poured on the basic research, Texas Instruments remained more cautious in its cost accounting, often at the expense of R&D. As with the transistor, older, established electronics firms and newer, smaller start-ups began learning the business of building integrated circuits, either under license or striking off in other directions on their own — a new industry and another surge of business at the patent courts. The military, by nature, tended to favor the larger firms, but such largesse did not always prove beneficial. As one case in point, RCA got off to a very slow start in the integrated circuit market due to its prior involvement with an ill-fated Army Signal Corps miniaturization scheme.

By 1963, though integrated circuits represented only about 10 percent of the total number of electronic circuits produced in the U.S., and almost all of those for the military or subcontractors, Fairchild and Texas Instruments were making waves in the business and industrial community. Parent company Fairchild Camera and Instrument in New York exercised its buy-out option the same year Noyce patented his planar integrated circuit, and when that happened Noyce and the other founders garnered more than a quarter-million dollars each. Promoted to general manager of the Fairchild Semiconductor division, Noyce found himself swept up in the world of big business as the company swiftly grew into a $150-million-a-year enterprise. Noyce the physicist had not set out with the idea of becoming a financial success in business, but with the integrated circuit, that is what he quickly became. For Noyce, "Fairchild was the first time that the scientists and technologists really got themselves in the position of controlling the operation, with high financial rewards for successful experimentation. We had a policy of spreading those rewards through the ranks and pretty soon Fairchild became the premier semiconductor laboratory in the world. It trained a hell of a lot of people in this new technology." Money was beginning to flood the Santa Clara valley; silicon was turning to gold. It did not go unnoticed.

The first official Fairchild spin-out was Rheem Semiconductor, founded by Fairchild's former general manager, who had the bad fortune to leave just as Jean Hoerni was perfecting the planar process. Rheem never really flew, and it became Raytheon Semiconductor in 1961. Also in 1961, four other ex–Fairchild employees started Signetics Corporation nearby. The same year, four of the original eight Fairchild scientists, including Jean Hoerni, left to found their own company, Amelco, later Teledyne Semiconductor. And a year later, Richard Lee, ex–Texas Instruments, and William Hugle, ex–Westinghouse, started Siliconix with no direct Fairchild ties at all. A few other Fairchilders hooked up with a Marine Corps general to found General Microelectronics in Cupertino. Technically, Fairchild's planar process was called a "bipolar" process, but there were other possible variants on the planar theme, and General Micro tackled one of them. Metal–Oxide–Semiconductor (MOS) technology had several potential advantages. It was cheaper to use and the finished ICs consumed much less power, but MOS chips were slower and not well tested in actual practice. The fast switching speed of bipolar circuits was one reason the military liked them so much in missile control systems, and in the space program. Although with future tinkering MOS would become the process of choice for making commercial microchips, General Micro's pioneering efforts met with financial and technical problems. Philco-Ford bought them out in 1966 and General Micro's founders became, according to one insider, "if not millionaires, then owners of very large chunks of cash."

By 1965 Fairchild Semiconductor had field sales offices around the country, as well as a few remote production plants, including one in Portland, Maine. It ran an overseas assembly operation in Hong Kong in order to avail itself of cheaper off-shore labor for the final, and still heavily manual, step in the IC production process — bonding the finished chips into plastic packages or tiny metal cans less than an inch square. Some twenty-five foreign and domestic firms were in the IC business by 1965, and competition was becoming keen and cutthroat. The competition for brainy engineers was no less intense. At the 1966 Institute of Electrical and Electronic Engineers (IEEE) meeting in New York, officials specifically outlawed recruiting during the proceedings. But as *Electronics* magazine described it, "One company official summed up the intensity of the talent search when he said: 'The show was a success. Our company lost only three men.'

"Outside the Coliseum a shouting match took place between recruiters and IEEE officials who tried to move the recruiters away from the entrance to the show. In hotels nearby, engineers awoke to find job offers stuffed under their doors."

Overall engineering employment in the U.S., spurred by the growth of science-based industry, rose 80 percent to roughly one million from 1950 to 1966. While the total U.S. work force increased by 50 percent between 1930 and 1965, the number of engineers shot up by 370 percent, and the number of scientists by 930 percent.

Shortly before Christmas of 1965, Fairchild transferred four of its field salesmen from around the country to the company's headquarters in Mountain View. Their job was to oversee the promotion of chip sales in the four broad markets the company defined for the IC: the military market, the industrial market, the computer market and the "consumer" market.

As the new marketing manager for industrial accounts, Jim Martin, in from New York, had working for him the fact that many of his customers were engineers who could understand the size and cost advantages of solid-state. By 1950 engineers could pack about a thousand vacuum tubes in the space of a cubic foot. By 1956 a cubic foot held ten thousand solid-state transistors and by 1958 a million. The integrated circuit promised circuit densities far beyond that, opening the door to even more complex electronic machinery. Moreover, the smaller the circuit, the better it performed, and the less it cost (see Chapter Six). Some companies tended to scoff at these exercises in arithmetic, but the aerospace contractors and electronic equipment manufacturers and atomic energy researchers did not.

For military accounts, Fairchild imported Jerry Sanders III from Chicago, by way of Hollywood. Sanders, an electrical engineer turned technology salesman, started out with Motorola, where his panache, aggressiveness and prototypical salesman's verve came to Fairchild's attention. From a tough Chicago neighborhood, ambitious, with photogenic good looks and a show-business flair for staging himself and his work, Sanders had a habit of winning Fairchild customers over to Motorola's transistors. As a long-time associate of his put it, "The Fairchild folks promised him what every young man like Sanders wants in life — a chance to live in southern California." Sanders, who didn't plan to become just another peddler from Riverside, moved into Hollywood, but was quickly transferred, with promotion, to the main office up north.

The computer market under Marshall Cox and the consumer market under Bernard Marren were in many ways the most untested areas for integrated circuit sales. "Computer" was a common household term by the mid-sixties, and IBM and Burroughs computers made possible astronaut Gordon Cooper's twenty-two-orbit flight in 1963. The space and missile races meant that it was no longer a question of selling a few hundred computers. IBM and scores of other companies in the booming "mainframe" computer business had several dozen models to choose from on the market, covering a wide range of cost and computing power and complexity. This proved to be both a boon and a problem, because each computer was a unique design, and what worked for one in terms of programming and problem-solving did not work precisely the same for any of the others. It was confusing and costly and it called for standardization in the spirit of Edison and Ford. In 1963 the IBM 360 line, the first *family* of computers, rendered virtually every earlier computer, including IBM's own, obsolete in a single stroke. Computers in the 360 line, ranging widely in price, size and power, all had basically the same inside architecture and a standardized method of input, information storage and instruction coding. IBM sold some thirty thousand of them in the sixties to government, business, industry and universities. Coding the computer's instructions via functional programs — software — was rapidly becoming a costly part of the computer business, and the 360 line helped alleviate the problem temporarily, spreading an acceptance of standardized programming languages like FORTRAN and COBOL. Finally, the 360 was a big step toward computer time-sharing, a procedure in which a mainframe computer solves many problems simultaneously for several operators.

From a hardware standpoint, IBM played it safe with the 360. Many up-to-date computers had solid-state transistors as portions of the logic circuitry, and computer memory had evolved into "magnetic core" — tiny rings of easily magnetized ferrite material threaded together like beads on thin wires. When magnetized by an electrical signal, a bead stood for "*on,*" or a "one" bit. Unmagnetized, it represented "*off,*" or "zero." For the 360, IBM adopted a middle-of-the-road approach called "hybrid" circuits, which meant soldering individual transistors, diodes and other solid-state circuits onto a ceramic base. It also meant performing many of the "horribly inefficient" hand connections the IC was designed to get around. For memory, IBM stuck with magnetic core.

Robert Lloyd, then working with solid-state technology at IBM's Silicon Valley outpost, the Advanced Computing Systems Division, recalled: "There was a lot of work on semiconductor memory at IBM, and a small group inside the company saying that integrated circuits were the wave of the future, but I wasn't one of them at the time. I became a believer later. There were projections saying it would take all the sand in the world to supply enough semiconductor circuits for computer memory in order to satisfy IBM's needs so many years out. IBM later became the first computer company to make the commitment to build memories with integrated circuits, but as for building *logic* circuits with ICs, there were simply too many unknowns. It was just too great a risk to commit the total corporation to integrated circuits for computer logic. In hindsight, you could say it was a bad decision, considering that the semi-conductor companies soon got rather heavily into the computer people's business. But at the time it was very justifiable. The selling point with the IC was low cost, and IBM didn't necessarily have to have the lowest cost. IBM sold on the basis of service and performance.''

Marshall Cox, Fairchild's new field sales manager for the computer industry, sent out sales teams to convince computer manufacturers otherwise. All across the country, dozens of semiconductor companies old and new were doing the same. Cox, a tanned, stocky native of Los Angeles, studied business and chemistry at UCLA and flirted briefly with a career in acting before joining Fairchild as a salesman. Selling the idea of silicon chips to computer companies was not always an easy task, in part because the IC concept meant that suddenly the designers of semiconductor devices would have a major say in how computer systems themselves were designed and built from the ground up. With vacuum tubes and solid-state transistors, whether computer makers bought them or built their own, they had essentially a set of raw parts, like the pieces of a tinker toy set, from which to build any sort of computer they could manage, depending upon how they interconnected the individual circuits. But the IC was different. A very large chunk of the interconnections between logic circuits was already in place and couldn't be changed, and while that saved money for computer designers it also restricted some of the things they could do. With the ICs the tinker toy pieces were not only incredibly tiny, but already connected in tiny blocks, or subsystems. Therefore, even though the IC chip meant less wiring of interconnections in computers and corresponding savings in cabinets, cables and cooling requirements, it also meant that chip designers would become computer designers to a degree. There was no good reason to assume that semi-conductor engineers were qualified to usurp that function. In the computer community, there was no good reason to assume that the semiconductor people knew *anything* about computer design. The semiconductor industry was a very technical adjunct of the industry at large, and for ideas about computers, one looked to IBM, Bell Labs, Sperry, Burroughs, Control Data. According to Cox, "Fairchild was showing up at all the early computer shows with new ideas about logic design. Computer engineers often looked at integrated circuits as a way of putting them out of business."

Computer makers tested the waters with special orders; a few custom chips made to order for a specific application. But small custom projects were anathema to the semiconductor industry. Fairchild and the other chip makers wanted to produce only very high volumes of standardized IC chips because high volume was what whipped production and sales costs down so quickly. The more chips a company could crank out, the more likely the chances of underpricing competitors. One could argue about the integrated circuit on technical grounds, but one could not argue about the cost.

Finally, there was the consumer market. Or rather, there *wasn't* any. While everyone from schoolchildren to farmers on tractors had taken to the transistor radio, television, the best-selling electronic consumer product and an even more potent medium of cultural change than radio or the automobile, was still firmly the domain of the vacuum tube. Fairchild's consumer marketing manager, Bernard Marren, recalled that "There was an attitude on the part of the television makers that if the integrated circuit was such a hot new product, why hadn't it come from the research at RCA, or GE, or even CBS? Fairchild, and Texas Instruments, were out West and just not that well known yet."

The government, Marren claims today, put Fairchild partway into the consumer electronic business without knowing it. "Early in the sixties a law was passed which said that every TV set sold in the U.S. would have to receive UHF channels as well as VHF, in order to expand the range of TV beyond twelve-channel VHF. UHF cost more and the set performance was inferior at first, so to make sure it was successful the FCC ordered TV manufacturers to build this all-channel capability into their sets. When the TV manufacturers began designing UHF tuners with vacuum tubes, they found that the tubes failed a lot at higher UHF frequencies. UHF tuners are very complicated to shield from TV radiation, so when the tube blew you couldn't just reach into the back of the set and yank it out. It was a major service problem, and the TV makers were scared stiff about the reliability problems they faced in meeting the new law. So when we started selling them transistors instead of tubes, we had a major advantage. The tube just didn't work."

It was a nice wedge, and it got many people in the consumer electronic business thinking solid-state. "Fairchild did a demonstration TV set for virtually every TV manufacturer in the U.S. Took their chassis and turned it into solid-state to show what we could do. It was all done in a very secret place in the back of the Fairchild building, where you had to hit a buzzer and identify yourself and go through all kinds of precautions to get in. For competitive reasons, we didn't want just anybody to know what we were doing. But we were doing it to sell silicon chips, not TV sets." (Earlier, Texas Instruments built a prototype solid-state computer, vastly smaller than any on the market, not in the beginning to sell computers, but to sell silicon chips.)

In all the potential markets, the Fairchild salesmen pushed the integrated circuit as if it were some sort of silicon template of the future. At times, potential customers were highly dubious — almost every new technology is a questionable "alternative" technology in its early stages of development. For Marren, "The thing that amazed you in 1965 was that I had just turned 30, and Jerry Sanders was 29, and Cox was 30 and Jim Martin was 31. Noyce was 37 and he was among the oldest guys at Fairchild Semiconductor. It was amazing, I'd never gone into a large company before where nobody was old. Nobody was even forty, and the girls on the production line were about the same age as the managers of the company. People worked unbelievable hours. Fairchild did about six million dollars in their first full year of business, as a matter of fact."

"There was this kind of obsession with the greatness of Fairchild as a new corporation," Marshall Cox added. "We were absolutely programmed — we programmed ourselves. It wasn't a sleepy firm."

The Birth of the Gamesmen

Of course, the sixties were not all Telstar satellites, moon walks and missile launchings. The Vietnam war abroad and the campus wars at home pitted the "counterculture" against "the establishment," but to the Silicon Valley community, enthralled with the successes of high technology in space and defense and industry at large, it was often known as the "anti-technology" movement, because the sixties youth movement ran distinctly counter to everything that had conspired to make Santa Clara's and San Jose's former fruit orchards the best place for raising a far more profitable crop. When astronaut Neil Armstrong set foot on the moon in 1969, it was the most stunning example to date of what the powerful integrated circuit really could do. The moon walk represented millions and millions of specific electronic circuit applications with humans as just another link in the electronic feedback chain of the system, and there was some occasional grumbling among Silicon Valley engineers about press coverage which made it seem as if everything from soup to nuts, including microelectronics, was spinning out of the high-technology space program, when in fact it was the other way around. It was easy to see the space program and the aerospace industry as particularly striking examples of industries growing up overnight under the golden spell of the semiconductor wand. The smaller and cheaper the silicon chips, the more the semiconductor industry's customers would prosper in their own line of work, or so it seemed. For the "military-industrial complex," the IC had the potential of becoming the basic building block of every piece of electronic equipment, as well as the cheapest known way to perform electronic logic, if costs continued to plummet.

Fairchild Semiconductor, it has been said, represented "the power of commercial motivation over scientific. . . ." There was plenty of basic research, to be sure, and record-setting levels of R&D, but Fairchild also showed a flair for salesmanship that, if not unique to the electronics industry, was certainly zealous for an industry solely in the business of electronic device manufacture, and not in the business of manufacturing TVs, computers or electric guitars. The semiconductor industry was not oriented toward "end product." It just built the electronic pieces. The old marketing wisdom of pinpointing a need and then building a product to fill it was giving way to a new approach — building a product so universal in application as to fulfill a rainbow of needs, many of them unforeseen by its designers. Of course, it was possible to do both, and become "vertically integrated," and many companies did. AT&T and IBM, for example, make their own chips, but buy other chips outside from time to time. But in Silicon Valley there was still no awareness that companies there soon would be selling calculators, digital watches, video games and home computers directly to consumers in competition with, and often losing out to, other electronic companies from all over the world.

With the integrated circuit, the electronics industry fragmented even more markedly into an old school and a new school. In 1961, twenty-nine major old-line electrical equipment manufacturers were found guilty of fixing prices and rigging bids on a $1.75 billion market for electronic products "from tiny $2 insulators to multi-million dollar turbine generators." In handing out prison sentences and $2 million in fines under the Sherman Act, the presiding judge said: "What is really at stake here is the survival of the kind of economy under which this country has grown great, the free-enterprise system." What had happened to GE and the others was a symptom of the newer, smaller companies bursting on the industrial scene with new products and new processes. In the early fifties GE's watchwords had become "security, complacency and mediocrity," in the candid words of the then company president. According to *Fortune* magazine, "One of the great business scandals of modern times was rooted in an industry's overcapacity, pressure on its executives to 'perform,' and their own belief that it wasn't really unethical to fix prices."

Price-fixing was the farthest thing from the minds of the IC evangelists. While the marketplace and the corporate boardroom became as natural a home to these new engineering manager/inventors as the cluttered laboratory had been to the electrical inventors of the preceding generation, the semiconductor industry was ruled by price-cutting, not price-fixing, and had been ever since the opening gun in 1959, for reasons discussed in more detail later. Thomas Hinkleman, who planned the first transistors sold by GE in the mid-fifties and who now serves as director of the Semiconductor Industry Association, recalled that "when it got into semiconductors, GE, like other large firms, attempted to build the business on old company traditions. Companies like RCA and Sylvania were the models. Everything you did was conditioned by the prevailing conceptions of the vacuum tube industry. In semiconductors, it turned out that it was better to have a new industry filled with young people who didn't know much about how you were *supposed* to do business."

Throughout the sixties, bright young engineers spun out of Fairchild Semiconductor like so many enterprising Minervas from the head of Zeus. New start-ups abounded: three new chip makers in 1966, another three in 1967, thirteen in 1968, eight more in 1969; their names a seemingly endless set of permutations on a few basic syllables — tech, tronic, inter, micro, ics, tron, etc. The engineers running these new companies were a far cry from the safe, gray image of the company man in the Eisenhower years; an image which had rubbed off on science-based industry as well. "No geniuses here," a group of white-coated scientists assured new recruits in a Monsanto training film of the fifties, "just a bunch of average Americans working together." That image did not fit the semiconductor companies which grew up in the sixties. The managers of these fast-growing operations didn't wear gray flannel suits or white lab coats. Nor did they make a habit of playing it safe. They seemed to understand precisely what President John F. Kennedy meant when he answered the question, "Why go to the moon?" by replying, "Why does Rice play Texas?" A spirit of intense and often ruthless competition marked the high-technology companies of the sixties — IBM, Xerox, Control Data, Fairchild, Texas Instruments and scores of others.

The home of microelectronics was the San Francisco peninsula, and bright young electrical engineers knew it. Slowly at first, engineering talent migrated to Silicon Valley, where the opportunities for individual success and status seemed unlimited. It was the era of the go-go corporation — exponential growth, wild sales, flashy marketing, all followed in many cases by a resounding crash. But with the integrated circuit, the semiconductor industry had latched onto a product which seemed ripe for use anywhere electricity was used, and an esoteric manufacturing process run by a cadre very much like Technocracy's "soviet of technicians," though with none of the former's slate of socialist programs.

CHAPTER FIVE

The Computer on a Chip

What do you do for an encore?
— MARCIAN E. "TED" HOFF,
Intel Corporation

Gutting Fairchild

The Golden Age of the entrepreneurial engineer struck Silicon Valley much more forcibly than other American strongholds of electronics expertise. Boston's Route 128 certainly prospered after the war, as did the Texas–Arizona Sun Belt where the semiconductor industry was anchored by Motorola Semiconductor in Phoenix and the Texas Instruments juggernaut in Dallas and Houston. TI eventually grew to become the single largest producer of microchips in the world, but the pattern of spin-out company after spin-out company was far more evident in Silicon Valley than anywhere else. Why Silicon Valley?

Semiconductor people do not lack for explanations, and in truth there is no single answer. De Forest, Shockley and Stanford University broke the ground and helped establish the area as a place where electronic research and industry thrived in tandem. In the fifties and sixties the prestige of Robert Noyce, Gordon Moore and others at Fairchild centered attention on Silicon Valley. The California climate, as mundane an explanation as it seems, was a factor as well. Fairchild recruited many engineers from electronics firms on Long Island and other outposts in the Snow Belt. Engineering talent, once honed in the labs of Silicon Valley, tended to stay in the area for new jobs and new opportunities. A technical clique had formed, and practically everybody in it had worked for or with everybody else at one time or another. The magic circle for successful silicon chip companies, so the joke went, was the shadow of Stanford University's Hoover Tower. As one engineer described the job-hopping syndrome endemic to the valley, "If you left Texas Instruments for another job, it was a major psychological move, all the way to one coast or the other, or at least as far as Phoenix. Out here, it wasn't that big a catastrophe to quit your job on Friday and have another job on Monday, and this was just as true for company executives. You didn't necessarily even have to tell your wife. You just drove off in another direction on Monday morning. You didn't have to sell your house, and your kids didn't have to change schools."

If any single ingredient guaranteed the success of Silicon Valley, it was the presence of venture capitalists eager to gamble on the growth potential of high-technology electronics. To the new and adventuresome money men of the sixties, an engineer with a Fairchild pedigree was a tempting bet. Defection after defection stung Fairchild as the new companies sprouted, but one departure more than any other signaled that there might well be more Fairchild talent *outside* Fairchild than in. In early 1967 Charles Sporck, a no-nonsense, hard-driving manufacturing wizard whose efforts had been central to making good on the commercial promise of planar integrated circuits, left Fairchild to become president of another new firm, National Semiconductor. Sporck, who had been general manager of Fairchild at one time, was lured away by Peter Sprague, a colorful venture capitalist. Young Sprague had inherited some $400,000 from Sprague Electric, the family firm, and set about buying worthy but financially ailing firms. After a number of successful money-making ventures, including a chicken hatchery in Iran, Sprague came across National Semiconductor, with headquarters in Danbury, Connecticut. In Silicon Valley, National owned a stalled Fairchild spin-out called Molectro. Sprague installed Sporck, and the engineers Sporck brought with him, as the head of the new, revitalized National Semiconductor in Santa Clara. National went on to become one of the valley's largest and fastest-growing companies, and Peter Sprague went on to rescue other companies, run unsuccessfully for Congress, and pull England's Aston Martin company out of the financial fire in 1975.

Said one Fairchild manager, of Sporck's departure, "That one shook the whole place. We couldn't believe it. Sporck and all the manufacturing talent just blew out of there." The talent continued to leak out, and a rift grew between Fairchild Semiconductor and its parent corporation back East. Robert Noyce stayed on, but he was no stranger to the activities he was witnessing. "The people from Fairchild were very attractive to the venture capital community because they could clearly take the newest and latest technology along with them. On the one side, you had the beginning of frustrations at Fairchild, and on the other side there was this beautiful new horizon with all sorts of money available to go ahead and try whatever you wanted to try. So it's not surprising that there was such a proliferation of companies coming from Fairchild."

To make matters worse, Noyce, Gordon Moore and others knew only too well that major semiconductor innovations had a habit of stemming from the newer, smaller companies. And as Fairchild Semiconductor grew, the parent corporation placed more and more restraints on the division in order to spread semiconductor profits throughout the company. For Noyce and other research-oriented managers, "that was very frustrating. Management styles had become different on the East Coast and the West Coast." Taking orders from senior management on the East Coast was not what the semiconductor industry did best. Gordon Moore began talking up the idea of starting up a new, small company and striking out all over again, with the idea of specializing in integrated circuits for computer memory. "I must admit," Noyce later said, "that as I began to see how successful some of the spin-offs were in starting up in new specialized areas, it looked very attractive to go out and do that again." In June of 1968, Noyce resigned.

By 1968 Fairchild's talented staff had been badly gutted as

venture capital flowed into the valley. "It got to the point," recalled a veteran of the early silicon wars, "where people were practically driving trucks over to Fairchild Semiconductor and loading up with employees." Fairchild Camera and Instrument's board of directors reacted with the best-known talent raid in the semiconductor industry's history. "All of a sudden," said another Fairchilder, "in walk eight or ten guys with great suntans." The suntanned engineers were from Motorola in Phoenix, and they represented the best and the brightest semiconductor production talent that company once had to offer. When C. Lester Hogan left Motorola to join Fairchild, he took virtually the entire senior echelon of Motorola's semiconductor operation with him. The mass defection prompted a long, bitter, and rather inconclusive lawsuit, but "Hogan's heroes," as the team became known, was already in place with the charter of restoring Fairchild Semiconductor. Hogan's $120,000 salary, 10,000 shares of Fairchild stock and $5 million loan for options on an additional 90,000 shares prompted whimsical engineers to measure subsequent job transfers in units of Hogan.

Two final defections, then, spelled the end of the Fairchild Semiconductor dynasty in Silicon Valley. Jerry Sanders, salesman extraordinaire, was denied a promotion, exited the company with a year's salary as compensation, and, in typical Sanders fashion, moved to Malibu with his family and sat down to contemplate his future. At about the same time, Robert Noyce, joined by Gordon Moore and Andrew Grove, formed a new company to begin the semiconductor cycle all over again from scratch.

Intel, for Short

For Noyce, Moore and Grove, financing did not prove to be a problem. Some $2 million in start-up funds was quickly secured, in part from Arthur Rock, an astute and seasoned venture capitalist who knew less about electronics technology than he did about the character of successful managers. "It may shock a lot of people to find this out," Noyce later told the *Harvard Business Review*, "but we never wrote a business plan, never wrote a prospectus. We just said, we're going into business; would you like to support it?"

With less than a dozen employees and Arthur Rock's backing, Noyce and his associates founded Intel, short for *Inte*grated *Electronics* (as well as *Intel*ligence), and began operation on the site of a former pear orchard in Santa Clara. A huge replacement market loomed for the designers who standardized a form of integrated circuit they could sell cheaply enough to replace the older core type of computer memory. But Intel was not the only new company with this idea. A firm called *Advanced Memory Systems* was beginning to offer semiconductor memories, and similar experiments were under way elsewhere, so innovation would have to come swiftly.

Intel abandoned the bread-and-butter silicon transistor business to concentrate on semiconductor memories, and the gamble paid off. The properties of silicon, the new MOS process, the push for large-scale integration (LSI) and the laws of binary computer theory turned out to be an almost perfect fit in this respect. Intel pioneered the commercial recognition of the fact that bits of information — the ones and zeroes of computer language — could be stored very cheaply on a microchip as the presence or absence of electrons at microscopic sites on the chip. In 1970, Intel caught the attention of the computer world, and Honeywell in particular, with its announcement of the 1103 random access computer memory chip (RAM). The Intel 1103 stored more than one thousand bits of binary computer data, and it pointed the way toward the possibility of building computers that were far smaller and much more powerful than the large, IBM-style mainframes, or even the newer, smaller "minicomputers" being offered by such firms as Digital Equipment Corporation and Data General. The 1103 and the more powerful memory chips that followed put Intel on the map and the magnetic core memory industry on the decline. Silicon Valley's assault on the computer market was only beginning, and if the semiconductor industry was good at anything, it was good at putting other people out of business.

But semiconductor memories represented only the opening salvo in a fourth revolution in computer design that would have an even greater impact than the vacuum tube or the transistor or the standard integrated circuit. Even as Intel struggled with reliability problems in the memory-chip production process, researchers there were designing yet another new kind of integrated circuit, and one which is today well on its way to becoming the most pervasive technological invention of this century — the microprocessor. The invention of this tiny calculating microchip was both a culmination of the integrated circuit concept and a final validation of the counter-trend toward smaller, cheaper and more flexible computers. "In the same sense that the integrated circuit came along about 1960 to give Fairchild a real boost," said Noyce, "the microprocessor and the microcomputer concept came along in 1970 to give Intel a real boost. It was the kind of major innovation that obviously you can't plan, but we had created the kind of environment in which it could occur."

The path to the microprocessor, or computer on a chip, was charted by an Intel design team under the direction of Ted Hoff, a Stanford standout hired during Intel's initial staffing campaign. Grads like Hoff had the older generation of electrical engineers shaking their heads in wonder. The integrated circuit was to solder-and-wire circuitry as quantum theory was to Newtonian physics, and integrated circuit diagrams were bewildering rat's mazes charting the course of electrons scuttling through tiny channels etched on a silicon chip. Hoff was eager "to get out into the commercial world to see if my ideas maybe didn't have some commercial value." Some of Hoff's ideas pertained to the matter of miniaturizing computer logic circuitry, so he was placed in charge of a tough engineering contract brought to Intel by a group of Japanese desk-top calculator manufacturers. The problem was to design a new commercial calculator with integrated circuits, but to do it by cramming all the required circuitry on only eleven chips of silicon. Since the circuitry didn't seem to fit on the allotted silicon real estate, Intel switched the design to only three slightly larger chips. That still did not solve the impasse, however, until Hoff came up with a clever sidestep. Why not try crowding all of the calculator's arithmetic and logic processing circuits on the *same* chip, thereby simplifying the task of fitting all the remaining circuits on the other two? Together, math and logic circuitry is called a computer's central processing unit, or CPU. With the help of designer Federico Faggin, Intel's attempt to get all of this on a single chip proved successful. What Intel now had was a complete CPU — the very heart of a full-fledged computer — on a single silicon chip measuring one-eighth by one-sixth of an inch. In all, 2,250 individual circuit elements, barely visible to the naked eye. Intel dubbed it a microprocessor, or MPU. "The actual invention of the microprocessor," insists Hoff, another engineer's engineer, "wasn't as important as simply appreciating that there was a market for such a thing."

The "computer on a chip" moniker with which Intel tagged the device was not entirely accurate. It was Boolean zero-one electronic logic on a chip, to be sure, but like a car engine without a car, the microprocessor by itself really couldn't do anything until it was hooked to other circuitry that told it what to do in binary language. That meant connecting the microprocessor to other chips containing memory and programs, and still others containing input-output circuits. With these additions, plus a clock mechanism to synchronize operations, the microprocessor became a tiny computer. By placing all these chips on a single plastic board about the size of a recipe card, it was possible to make a functioning microcomputer, as the assemblage is known, with as few as five chips. However, the tiny microcomputer packed as much potential computing power as the huge mainstays of the mid-fifties computer world. As Noyce began to realize, "Ted's idea was to say, let's build a standardized small computer that simulates any kind of logic, instead of doing a separate, custom-designed chip for every use. Then if somebody wants to program it as a calculator, that's fine, you can do that. And if somebody wants to make it into something else, that's fine, you can do that too. The real contribution was in having one standardized design for many, many electronic logic applications."

The microprocessor upset the usual timetable for adopting new electronic devices, and as Hoff remembered, "There were questions as to whether Intel should even offer it as a product." New means of working with electricity usually have been forged in the crucible of military necessity. Often, however, the carrot held out by the military has not been so much in the form of direct funding, although there has been plenty of that, but in the form of a first market for untested, still-expensive devices considered too risky for the commercial market. For the computer, the transistor and the IC, the military served as first customer, followed by government bureaus, business, industry, and, finally, a broad range of commercial and consumer applications. With the microprocessor, however, semiconductor developments began unfolding so rapidly that the military found it hard to keep up.

Ted Hoff: "My general impression about the military is that they are generally off in some area which very seldom becomes practical. Military electronics people would come to us and say, 'We've got to have this special program because we want a certain high performance electronic part and the other commercial sons of bitches won't build it for us.' But what usually happened was that the military's plans for a custom exotic device had about an extra two or three years' delay added in because of all the extra negotiations, the paperwork, and the qualification process. By the time the military gets what it asked for, the part they wanted is usually at least two years behind the times because the commercial guys just keep right on moving."

Since the military did not look to be the appropriate first market for the microprocessor, it took a while for Intel to decide just what manner of product it had, and what should be done with it. As Hoff summarized it, "Intel's business was semiconductor memories for computers, and the MPU represented a big departure. There were questions as to whether there was really a market for the microcomputer. I had people come to me and say, hey, look, the total market for the smallest computers around is maybe twenty thousand machines a year. If you're lucky, as a latecomer to the business, you get maybe ten percent of that. A few thousand chips a year is just not an interesting business."

Intel had to decide whether it wanted to become a computer company of sorts, selling a new form of tiny computer that nobody knew much about yet. Noyce, Moore and other Intel managers "had a number of well-justified fears," said Hoff. "How could Intel do computer software and support sales? You'd have to hire computer programmers, and at the time, you *couldn't* hire a computer programmer — not at a semiconductor house. Those were the days of big computers, and if a computer programmer did walk into Intel, he'd always ask, 'What size IBM 360 do you have?' We'd say, 'We don't have a 360; that's not what we're doing here,' and the guy would walk out. This was the era of big, powerful computers, and little computers just weren't that interesting. . . . Besides," Hoff added, "we were far too young and naive, and the concept was so new, that we just didn't see the evidence that the MPU would revolutionize the computer and electronics industry."

In the end, Intel took the plunge, aware that other semiconductor firms, TI included, also were experimenting with single-chip logic for simple computer functions. "Announcing a new era of integrated electronics," read Intel's advertisement for the 4004, the first widely available microprocessor for general-purpose applications, "a microprogrammable computer on a chip." * The five-chip microcomputer set based on

* It should be noted that Texas Instruments strenuously objects to this account of the microprocessor's genesis. In a geographical rivalry dating back a quarter of a century, TI claims exclusive ownership of the invention of the integrated circuit, the microprocessor and the microcomputer.

the 4004 was offered as the MCS-4. Ted Hoff was thirty-four years old.

"What the Hell's It Good For?"

Intel soon knew that the microprocessor and the microcomputer were more than just the answer to the Japanese calculator puzzle, because early buyers of the MPU tended to use it in novel applications no one at Intel had expected. For example, some of Intel's first microprocessors were purchased by a small Monterey electronics firm. Designers there first built a digital clock around the MPU, but by switching only the memory chips attached to it, and adding a loudspeaker, they converted the microcomputer clock into a microcomputer phonograph which played the theme song from *The Sting.* Hooked to still other memory chips, the same MPU mimicked the sound of an electric piano. Hoff remembered that "some of the other stuff seemed really weird to us at that time. We were surprised when people came to us with ideas for slot machines, and some other people wanted to use our microcomputers to automate cows. They wanted to automatically record how many times the cows drank water, or something like that, and correlate it with milk production."

Intel had not set out to design a chip capable of mimicking an electric piano or automating cows, but the microprocessor could do it nonetheless. The MPU could perform logical operations on *any* string of binary instructions stored in associated memory chips. It didn't make any difference what kind of work the binary instructions were designed to accomplish. The MPU didn't care. It was master traffic controller in almost any electronic application. It was in fact the tiniest universal machine ever built, and by the end of the seventies it would be selling for less than five dollars.

Other uses for the MPU soon came to mind: controlling industrial processes such as making steel. The usual procedure was to monitor the rate of making ingots with electronic sensing equipment, compare the inputs to some chosen production level, and make automatic adjustments. Before the microprocessor, this sort of feedback could be accomplished only by connecting the sensing equipment to a large master computer which then performed the calculations and indicated the necessary adjustments. But big computers cost big money, and now comes a little device called an MPU, and by building microprocessors into each piece of sensing equipment and connecting all of the equipment together, suddenly there was no need for a master computer at all. The equipment itself had become "intelligent," rather than simply automated.

The possibilities opened up by the MPU led Noyce, Moore and Grove to a radically different view of the nature of computers. Up until the microprocessor, computers had been looked upon as large, complicated tools with which an elite cadre of insiders were able to store information and process logic. The computers of the fifties and sixties were "Big Brother" computers, or so they were often viewed, as social critics warned that the inherently centralized nature of computers and the work they performed would lead straight to the totalitarian nightmare of *1984.* Lending credence to this argument was the hardware evolution of the computer — ever larger, more costly, more powerful and more abstruse. In terms of operating costs, it was usually cheaper to use one large computer rather than a dozen smaller, less-powerful ones to accomplish the same amount of work. But with the microprocessor, electronic enthusiasts were beginning to theorize that 1984 might never arrive. Potentially, the MPU looked to be a radical new way of siphoning off the power of the mainframe computer.

Championing the microcomputer concept throughout the early seventies, Noyce ran into opposition from established computer makers and users for his belief that the microprocessor would prove to be the "fractional horsepower motor" of the electronics age, and that its potential applications were "almost unlimited." In 1973, Noyce undoubtedly furrowed some brows at IBM headquarters when he announced to *Business Week* that "The future is obviously in *decentralizing* computer power," by distributing smaller microcomputers wherever they could be used. With microprocessors in a remote terminal, a computer user could solve many of his tasks without recourse to the central computer at all. "As it turns out," Noyce later explained, "many of the problems addressed by computers are not really big problems at all, but rather lots of little, simpler problems. The difference between a computer and a microprocessor is like the difference between a jet airplane and an automobile. The airplane carries a hundred times as many people and it carries them ten times as fast, but ninety percent of the transportation in this country is done by automobile, because it's the simplest way to get from here to there, and the same is true of the microprocessor. Today, you wouldn't think of designing a computer system without considering the microprocessor."

The microprocessor tied in neatly with Intel's earlier breakthrough in semiconductor memories, but even so, the company first saw it commercially as a way of controlling simple electronic logic functions in such products as calculators, vending machines and electronic cash registers. In 1974 Intel introduced an improved microprocessor, the 8080, which quickly became one of the best-received pieces of integrated electronics in history. It was an eight-bit device, so called because it was designed to accept data in "words," or binary strings, of eight bits in length, and thus was more powerful than the four-bit 4004, the first MPU. The 8080 spread the microcomputer concept across the country, and it became a de facto standard of the new microcomputer business, as the IBM 360 had been the standard for the big computer business. Its architecture was particularly well suited to the job of controlling relatively simple electronic equipment such as traffic lights and hand-held calculators. But when speed of computation was not a compelling consideration, it could also control the workings of a computer terminal or part of a missile's guidance mechanism. As with the original universal machines, there did not seem to be any firm limits on what the microprocessor could do.

And yet, the semiconductor industry's initial reaction to the Intel microprocessor was mixed. As Robert Lloyd put it, "I spent a lot of my career wrestling with the question of how to implement electronic logic economically, but my first reaction to the microprocessor was, what the hell's it good for? Where does it fit into the computer business? Since most of the people in the computer industry had been focusing on large mainframe computers, the idea of a microcomputer caught everybody by surprise." Nonetheless, the advent of cheap, mass-produced microprocessors sparked an explosion in computer usage as designers found new ways to computerize functions previously performed by "hard-wired" electromechanical relays and discrete transistors.

By 1975, however, there were at least twenty other microprocessors on the market as semiconductor companies both here and abroad raced to follow Intel's lead. Among them was Advanced Micro Devices, formed shortly after Intel by former Fairchild marketing director Jerry Sanders. Sanders billed his new company, of which he was president, as Intel's "leading follower" in microprocessors, and it quickly gained a reputation for building all of its integrated circuits, regardless of use, to the most stringent of military specifications. Fairchild Semiconductor, Signetics, American Micro Systems and other Silicon Valley companies followed Intel and Advanced Micro Devices into the microcomputer business. So did Rockwell, RCA and other mainstream electronics and aerospace firms. Motorola followed suit, as did Texas Instruments and its single major spin-out, Mostek Corporation of Carrollton, Texas. Five Japanese firms soon entered the new market, plus Siemens and Philips, two giant European electronics firms. Even Exxon entered the microcomputer fray by funding a new Silicon Valley start-up in 1974. Beginning with "low-end" markets, these companies pressed home the MPU explosion in such applications as calculators, intelligent computer terminals, video games, oven timers and industrial control processes. Throughout it all, the semiconductor companies of Silicon Valley gained a commanding lead, and with it came the ability to offer newer and better versions of the microcomputer at cheaper prices, just as competitors were mastering the older versions. By 1975 a typical microcomputer "card" could perform more than a hundred thousand discrete logical operations per second, using only five volts of power. The microprocessor itself took up less than one square inch of space on the card. As the cost of the microprocessor and related circuits plummeted, it began to seem like there was no piece of electronic apparatus, no matter how simple, that could not be made "intelligent."

Due to the nature of the semiconductor manufacturing process, and the "learning curve" economics which govern it, it was possible to crank out millions of microprocessors at a fraction of the cost of designing and building the first ones. Intel's Andrew Grove, a garrulous immigrant from Hungary who favors an open shirt and gold chains over a suit and tie, added the necessary no-nonsense production touch, coining the term "high technology jelly beans" for the millions of integrated circuits which rolled off the production lines during the seventies. It was Grove who added a leavening shot of good old-fashioned American assembly-line expertise to the microcomputer business (as Sporck had at Fairchild and National Semiconductor), taking his cue from what he called "a maker of medium technology jelly beans" — McDonald's. Once Intel learned how to make a particular microcomputer circuit burger, the idea was to make as many of them as possible. With Grove in charge of production, the company picked up the nickname "McIntel." Grove realized that "the wild-eyed, bushy-haired boy geniuses that dominate the think tanks and the solely technology-oriented companies will never take that technology to the jelly bean stage. Likewise, the other stereotype — the straight-laced, crew-cut, sideburn-and-mustache-free manufacturing operators of conventional industry — will never generate the technology in the first place."

There was still one market — the biggest of all — that chip makers simply did not see coming, and it was the consumer market. In the early stages, it was limited mainly to calculators and digital watches (see Chapter Eight). As Noyce admits, "The whole consumer business was an area we just didn't see in the beginning. It just seemed impossible that this phenomenal level of electronic sophistication represented by the microprocessor could ever be reduced enough in cost so that simple consumer requirements could be met. Doorlocks, for example. There are many microprocessor-controlled doorlocks today, but then, it just didn't seem possible to ever get the costs of these sophisticated electronic devices down to the point where you could do the job, compared to the price of a simple mechanical doorlock. The home and hobby microcomputer market was an area we really didn't see in the beginning either, and so was the whole field of electronic games."

"At one point our people estimated that there were at least 25,000 different applications for the microcomputer, so it was clear that we couldn't follow up on all of them." Or, as Hoff capsulized it, "Intel has tended from the start to specialize in the industrial realm. We finally agreed that we could only directly support the needs of a few customers for the MPU, and the rest were sort of warned that they were on their own."

In the early days of the computer, a dozen sales was considered an optimistic estimate. Some thirty years later, in 1974, there were more than 200,000 computers in use worldwide. That year, Intel's Gordon Moore predicted that by 1984, a year laden with considerable emotional freight, there would be more than 20,000,000 computers in operation. With his typical flair for understatement, the soft-spoken Moore told a conference, "A world with 20 million computers will be greatly different from the present one with only 200,000." And, it goes without saying, vastly different from a world with only a dozen.

If there were only 200,000 computers in use worldwide in 1974, what was going to happen when the semiconductor industry delivered almost a million of the newer microcomputers in 1975? Who would buy them all? As a manager at Fairchild put it, "These systems will be sold to many people who aren't accustomed to programming. These people are completely lost and have to be educated."

In a technical sense, the microprocessor broke a bottleneck in the integrated circuit industry. At times, the IC was *too* successful. Cost-cutting, new and aggressive companies in the market, and the general ups and downs of the post-Vietnam economy resulted in an oversupply of integrated circuits and sometimes heavy losses. Specialized IC applications proliferated as designers fiddled with the newer chips. The microprocessor offered standardized, mass-produced microblocks of electronic logic on silicon chips. Semiconductor designers could fashion new microprocessors without any specific knowledge of how these little fractional-horsepower computation motors on silicon would be used. That was up to the buyer.

What had emerged by the mid-seventies was a new kind of corporation, a new kind of managerial elite, a new kind of product, and a market for it which seemed to include just about every activity humans engaged in. In short, wherever logic was used or memory was needed or electrical communication was employed. "All electric forms whatsoever," Marshall McLuhan asserted in *Understanding Media,* "have a decentralizing effect, cutting across the older mechanical patterns like a bagpipe in a symphony." The semiconductor industry was in possession of a set of tools with which to remake the culture, but the overriding concerns were purely technical — how to put more transistors and other basic circuit elements on a chip, how to advance the distributed processing concept by streamlining the way microchips "talk" to each other and exchange information, and how to spread computing power throughout the electronic grid. Microprocessors represented the advance guerrilla troops in a new technological colonization process, and their appearance inside cheap hand-held calculators, pong games, and the dashboards of cars was only an opening salvo of gimcracks in a broader and more serious consumer electronics revolution.

In 1969, the microprocessor did not exist. By the mid-seventies there were some 750,000 used mostly in calculators and industrial applications. By 1984 there will be somewhere between 20,000,000 and 100,000,000 of them, depending upon how one distinguishes between chips, chip sets and larger computers. There are common predictions of a billion by 1990.

How are they all being put to work?

No field of human endeavor has proven wholly immune to the effects of the microchip. Microelectronics has become an indispensable part of the practice of modern science, and in medicine the microcomputer controls complex diagnostic and critical care equipment. Communications systems for the speechless and seeing-eye microcomputer systems for the blind are only two of the promising avenues being explored.

Microelectronics has greatly accelerated the "computerization" of government, industry and business. In the burgeoning field of telecommunications, the microchip is forging a link between the telephone, the computer and the television. Sears, AT&T, Associated Press, IBM, Mattel, Exxon, Intel, Apple Computer, Radio Shack and hundreds of other companies will all play a part in shaping home electronic information systems as Congress struggles to rewrite communication and copyright law with microelectronics in mind. The home microcomputer, the culmination of events which began with the digital watch, the calculator and the TV game, is an example of an industry built entirely around the possibilities of the microprocessor.

The arts are not immune: electronic music and composition are commonplace, while visual artists explore, and sometimes fret over, computer-generated graphics and electronic three-dimensional sketch pads.

Nor is education: microcomputers are common classroom teaching tools. Scholars poring over ancient manuscripts routinely make use of computer systems for deciphering.

The microchip will play an important role in efforts to conserve energy. As Robert Noyce sees it, "It's just going to make a lot of things possible that are not possible right now. Simple things like the automatic time-of-day setback thermostat, controlled by a microprocessor, will make significant savings in home energy use. The microcomputer-controlled automotive engine will make possible similar savings in that field." But examples like these are only a first-case approximation. Noyce, given a few moments of free time in his modest office at Intel's Santa Clara headquarters, is willing to explain quite succinctly what else is involved.

"Let's go a little further than that. Any piece of paper that conveys information is a potential candidate. Like this memo on my desk. In terms of total energy use in our society, it's far cheaper to send some impulses over a wire than to produce that piece of paper. But let's carry this thinking even further. If you look out the window at the freeway there, you might ask yourself, now what are most of those automobiles doing? They're *not* carrying goods; most of them are carrying information in the form of brains from one place to another. If you want to get a little speculative, you could ask yourself, what earthly reason is there for carrying those brains around and burning all that gasoline? I think it's because we don't yet trust the computer-telephone linkup; our electronic information technology is not perfect enough yet. There's just no need for all those cars. There's no need for a high percentage of our working population to be *here* to work, because they're only handling information."

What this suggests is a society becoming increasingly dependent on microelectronic technology, a dependence which brings with it massive changes in life-style and attitudes. This transition to what is commonly referred to as an information or postindustrial society, and the accompanying rise of the "compunications" or "electromagnetic spectrum" industries, has sparked a sometimes bitter debate over the effects of electronic automation and control. "Intelligent" equipment is replacing human labor everywhere, and the resulting disruptions in employment patterns have been widely criticized. Noyce responds to such criticism by saying that "from the social and cultural point of view, there is always some fear of change. The development of this technology, to put it simply, causes arguments between the people who would like to have things change and the people who would like to have things stay the same. It's true, quite frankly, that microelectronics is going to throw a lot of people out of work, if you will, but it will put them into some other kind of employment. Already [1980], less than 40 percent of the population is out there making the goods that we use. The rest of the population is working with information of one sort or another. Microelectronics will continue this trend by displacing jobs from one segment of the society to another." And, Noyce is convinced, by creating new ones as well.

There are those who think otherwise. "It would seem," Marshall McLuhan observed, "that the logic of success in this matter is the ultimate retirement of the work force from the scene of toil . . ." at which point he adds slyly, ". . . it does not follow that we are prepared to accept the consequences." Nor does it follow that the microchip revolution leaves no important work for human hands. As with the much-heralded "green revolution" in agriculture, there are certain hidden costs associated with the microelectronics revolution, to be discussed later.

By 1975 the commercial success of the microprocessor was assured, and the first pieces of the coming microelectronic grid were in place. On the strength of the microprocessor, a chip of silicon against which the computing power of ENIAC looks frail indeed, the grid underwent a metamorphosis. It expanded and diffused until it touched every level of human activity. How the new microelectronic grid will be made to fit with human needs and wants is an important part of the technological agenda for the last quarter of this century. But before venturing a more detailed look at the impact of the microchip in specific applications — home computers, telecommunications, automation, electronic warfare and artificial intelligence — a brief dive into the economics of the chip production process is in order. There is no way to understand fully the explosion of microelectronics technology, or the changes it has wrought on the American electronics industry, without a look at the underlying technical and economic facts of life in Silicon Valley — and its outposts worldwide. Beginning in the mid-seventies, through a series of mergers, outside equity investments and outright takeovers, the U.S. semiconductor industry became a much more exclusive club with a decidedly international flavor. America's firm hold on microelectronics technology had been broken by 1980. The technology itself was a large part of the reason for it.

CHAPTER SIX

Angstrom Economics

Any sufficiently advanced technology is indistinguishable from magic.
— ARTHUR C. CLARKE

Magic is simply technology one doesn't understand.
— A BANKING VICE-PRESIDENT

Faster, Smaller, Cheaper, or Logic for Free

After watching a huddle of circuit designers brooding over one of the complex mandalas of their hermetic art and white-gowned technicians sliding racks of silicon wafers into the glowing cruciblelike diffusion furnace, it does not seem to strain the metaphor overmuch to think of these men and women as modern alchemists. Paracelsus, the prince of alchemists and a forerunner of the modern scientist, hadn't the luxury of trade-secret protection for his brand of sorcery, but there was secrecy all the same, and there is secrecy still. This time, the lore and the recipes have been entrusted to the young as a set of rituals and incantations for producing an invisible electron maze on a sliver of silicon — an integrated circuit. Like their historical brethren, members of the silicon priesthood stand jealous guard against other adepts of the inner circle by signing binding oaths of fealty, but there are always insurgents and mercenaries and infighting to be wary of. Some will succeed in etching encrypted symbols on silicon of their own, lawfully, and offer them in the public market. But woe to those who seek such knowledge by deception or by cunning. . . .

Even *Science* magazine, the prestigious journal of the American Association for the Advancement of Science, concluded that "The pure white gowns and caps of production line workers might as well be covered with moons and stars of the type that bedeck the robes of a conjurer," and that at times in the chip production process, "art overtakes science." Intel's Andrew Grove, commenting on large-scale integration (and the coming very large scale integration [VLSI]), noted that "The technology involved, judging by most laymen's reactions, is something bordering on science fiction." That is an apt description of the world in which microchips are manufactured; a world in which the operative units of measurement are the micron and the nanosecond.

"Don't worry about getting all of this straight," a National Semiconductor official once cheerfully advised his visitors on a tour of the firm's production facilities. "Even the top technical gurus don't understand *all* of it."

The chip production process begins with raw monocrystalline silicon, typically grown to order by other firms and purchased by the semiconductor industry — one of many examples of the ancillary industries essential to the semiconductor production process. The silicon is delivered in cylinders about the size of a flashlight and then sliced into wafers. Each round silicon wafer, typically three, four or five inches in diameter and less than half a millimeter thick, is now ready to become hundreds of individual integrated circuits, each circuit in turn containing thousands and thousands of individual miniaturized transistors and other electronic components. But for that to happen, there must be a master blueprint of the circuit which can serve as a stencil for guiding the chemical process of etching and diffusing the circuits on silicon.

Design teams composed of electrical engineers and programmers begin by fashioning a large blown-up version of the finished circuit on drafting paper. Increasingly, much of the initial design process is partially automated through an advance known as computer-aided design, or CAD. Since a finished microchip is composed of up to eight or ten separate layers of circuitry etched one layer at a time on silicon, the design process is repeated for each layer. At this point the shrinking process, called "mask making," begins. "Step-and-repeat" camera work reduces the size of the diagram and re-produces many copies of it on a silicon-wafer-sized glass plate — the mask. A finished mask is rather like a glass litho-graph composed of a repeated motif of tiny squares, each square containing all the circuit pathways of the single, "life-size" design on paper.

The production process itself is a matter of bringing together raw silicon wafers and glass masks through the marriage of photography and lithography known aptly enough as photo-lithography. First, workers diffuse a uniform layer of silicon dioxide across the surface of the wafer in a 2,000 degree F. oven. This smooth insulating layer, much thinner than a human hair, is the heart of the planar diffusion process and the reason why almost all microchips are made from silicon. A second layer of photosensitive emulsion completes the prepa-ration of the wafer. The coated wafer is analogous to an unex-posed sheet of photographic print paper, and the glass mask represents the transparent negative containing the image. The "enlarger," though it does no such thing, is a machine called a contact printer. When the mask and the wafer have been properly aligned and secured in an optical jig of the highest precision, the printer emits a beam of ultraviolet light, causing a chemical reaction which hardens the surface of the chip wherever it strikes. These hardened areas form the outline and final dimensions of one layer of the chip's active circuitry, and to bring out the pattern the exposed wafer must be "devel-oped," or etched in an acid bath. The unexposed areas wash away, leaving a collection of three-dimensional cell-like struc-tures only a few microns high.

The wafer now enters the furnace again so that the exposed areas can be diffused with more of the appropriate impurities. Finally, in yet another trip to the furnace, the metal intercon-nections between the transistors and other elements of each integrated circuit are formed by coating the wafer with a layer of aluminum evaporate. This eliminates the need for wiring together transistors by hand, which, given the size of today's transistors, is impossible anyway.

The steps described above represent only one masking cycle in the complete process. The finished wafer — exposed, etched, washed, doped and baked many times — contains as many as five hundred finished and identical integrated circuits, or chips, each of which contains, in turn, thousands of invisible transistors. An automatic scribing machine cuts the wafer into its individual chips and a computerized probe tests each one of them. Those that fail are rejected and crushed as scrap. For a new chip in its first production run, a yield of 10 percent working chips is considered good. After scribing and sorting, a finished chip can be examined on the tip of one's finger. There is nothing much to see — it looks a bit like a fleck of mica, dull at certain angles to the light and shiny at others. None of the layering, channeling and etching is apparent. Christopher Evans writes of the time he enthusiastically showed some friends a new microprocessor chip, only to have it escape from his tweezers and fall to his cluttered desk top, never to be seen again.

After production and testing, the chips still cannot function until they have been bonded into packages and plugged into circuit boards. The tiny rectangular package that is bonded around the chip both protects the chip and connects it to the outside world by means of rows of metallic pins, rather like the legs of a caterpillar. For economic reasons, packaging, which is mostly hand work, is usually done at overseas assembly plants. Once the chips return from overseas, they are tested again, at which point they are ready to sell.

The inhabitants of the semiconductor world live in a dimension akin to the subatomic world of the high-energy physicist, with its own arcane vocabulary and methods of visualizing problems. But there is nothing esoteric about the basic economies of chip production and the rapid decline of production costs. The falling cost of the microchip is in fact the heart of the microelectronic revolution — the basic reason for its widespread proliferation. Angstrom economics can be summed up in a widely known semiconductor industry motto called Gelbach's Law: "Any integrated circuit you can get into a single plastic package will eventually sell for five dollars, unless it sells for less." Robert Noyce explained the meaning of that insight in his introduction to the September 1977 edition of *Scientific American* devoted to microelectronics: "Today's microcomputer, at a cost of perhaps $300, has more computing capacity than the first large electronic computer, ENIAC. It is twenty times faster, has a larger memory, is thousands of times more reliable, consumes the power of a light bulb rather than that of a locomotive, occupies 1/30,000 the volume and costs 1/10,000 as much. It is available by mail order or at your local hobby shop." In the semiconductor industry, smaller is better and less is more.

Among the many traits Thomas Edison and his good friend Henry Ford had in common was the ability to define new technological products in terms of the economic costs of the *system* the products would require for widespread use, while bearing in mind the powerful production economies afforded by standardization and mass production. To make the light bulb a commercial product, Edison studied the gas business. The results were the electrical industry and domestic electrical power. To assure the success of the automobile, Henry Ford studied the mass-production methods of the munitions industry and the transportation system of the railroads. The result was the Model T, a new industry, and the highway system.

The contributions of Robert Noyce, Jack Kilby and others fall very neatly into this Edison–Ford tradition. Noyce and Kilby began by defining a needed product in terms of both support system economics and production costs, with an eye to the economic realities of the vacuum tube and solid-state transistor business. The result was the integrated circuit, the microelectronics industry and, ultimately, the computer on a chip.

And yet, there is a difference. However pervasive the changes symbolized by the light bulb, the automobile and other seminal twentieth-century inventions, the microchip is not simply one more addition to the list. With the microchip, it is possible to reach back, so to speak, and change *everything* about how the earlier inventions are put to use, by rendering them "intelligent." Before the microchip, electronic logic had little to do with the design of cars; computers did not talk over the telephone nor double as televisions. The *micro*electronic grid, powered by the microchip, has proven to be a far more radically explosive and seemingly unstoppable technological infrastructure than the electronic grid, and for this reason: for the past twenty years the microelectronics industry has been a textbook example of a capitalist production engine tuned and running to near-perfection, with fundamental research innovation serving as the fuel. As *Time* magazine observed, "It has been a long time since the inflation-battered American economy has seen a better example of how prices are supposed to behave in a free market." It has been equally long since the American economy has seen such a breathless free market diffusion unfolding without recourse to monopolistic practices or accusations thereof, price collusion, bribery scandals or incessant recalls.

In part, the success of the microchip is a function of the chip production process itself, because microchips are uniquely suited to the mass-production efficiencies and performance improvements which accrue from what economists call the "learning curve." For most manufacturing industries, the higher the volume of production, the lower the costs of production per product. This is so because the manufacturers become more efficient, in theory, as they gain experience. Learning, in this sense, can be anything from eliminating bugs in the production process to improving the productivity of line employees. The learning curve, then, functions as a yardstick for measuring the extent to which production costs, in constant dollars, are likely to fall as manufacturing volume increases over time — the ever-cheaper Model T serving as a prime example.

The learning curve, semiconductor style, is aptly if hyperbolically expressed in the well-known Silicon Valley production adage which holds that "The first chip costs a million, and the second chip costs a nickel." (Bearing in mind that the first chip will not *sell* for a million any more than the next one will sell for a nickel.) In reality, chip production costs fall roughly 30 percent each time cumulative output (experience) doubles through the typical six-or seven-year life cycle of the chip — a very greased slide down the learning curve indeed. Since the yield of good chips to bad can be as low as 10 or 20 percent on an initial production run, there is plenty of room for the learning curve to function as manufacturers fine-tune the chip recipe.

However, there is more to the dramatic cost reductions of the microchip than simple learning-curve efficiencies. As manufacturers lower costs by fine-tuning the production process with experience, they are simultaneously finding ways to shrink, or scale, the active elements on the chip. In 1964, Dr. Gordon Moore, then with Fairchild, made an astute observation about the semiconductor shrinking process: The number of individual circuits that could be crammed onto a single silicon chip was *doubling* each year, even though the chip itself was growing only marginally larger. And naturally, the more circuits per chip, the more electronic performance per chip. Dr. Moore saw no compelling technical reason why this annual density doubling would not continue for some time, and he said so. He was right: from 1960 to 1980, there was no significant deviation from what became known as Moore's Law.

Taken together, Moore's Law and the learning curve go a long way toward explaining how the cost of integrated circuitry can fall even as the chips become more complex and powerful. Moreover, the selling price, as opposed to production costs, of a given chip fall just as dramatically, because in the semiconductor industry, price is only marginally affected by such things as marketing outlets, advertising, style, brand name, and so on. Chip sales are relentlessly technical sales, made on the basis of price and performance, and large buyers typically buy large orders, or none at all. At what point they decide to buy a particular chip is governed by learning-curve pricing, as illustrated by the "cost-per-bit" graph, a staple of semiconductor industry trade presentations. For example, in 1971 a typical random access memory (RAM) chip held 256 bits of information at a cost of about two cents per bit. In 1973 the same kind of chip held more than 1,000 bits at a cost of about 0.5 cent per bit. By 1975 RAM chips held more than 4,000 bits at a cost per bit of roughly 0.24 cents, and by the eighties the cost of such memory chips holding more than 16,000 bits of information had fallen to about 0.03 cents per bit. Microprocessors, though not measurable in the same terms, have fallen just as dramatically in price. It is sufficient to note that the Intel 8080 microprocessor sold for about $360 in 1975, but by early 1980 improved versions were available for under five dollars. If the price of automobiles had followed a similar course over the past twenty years, Cadillacs would be retailing for well under ten dollars.

In the chip business, then, the smaller the individual circuits and the higher the production volume, the less the chip costs and the more it can do — more memory capacity, more logic processing, more electronic problem-solving, and all the other technical advantages of the scaling process. Smaller has proven to be better, and usually cheaper. And smaller also means ever-increasing sales: in the past twenty years the number of integrated circuits in use worldwide has doubled eleven times. All of this is indisputable evidence of what makes microelectronics go, in an economic sense. What it adds up to is more and more electronic performance at less and less cost — the driving force behind the technological upheavals which fall under the broad rubric of the postindustrial age of electronics and computers.

This brief look at semiconductor production economics suggests the overriding importance, from a competitive point of view, of being the first one to arrive at the party. A company that invents a new chip (or improves an old one), while managing to bring that chip rapidly into high-volume production, will enjoy substantial pricing advantages over latecoming competitors. As with companies, so with nations: the learning curve is the primary reason why the American lead in semi-conductor innovation and production has remained unassailed from the outset — until the recent Japanese invasion (see Chapter Seven). By inventing new devices and "ramping up" production as less experienced nations struggle along at the costly front-end of the learning curve, American chip makers have been able to outsell foreign competitors on foreign soil (the Japanese excepted), thereby garnering the lion's share of the world market for microchips.

In actual practice, there are entwined and overlapping semiconductor learning curves for individual products, companies and families of device types, as well as for the industry at large. But in all cases, the lesson of the learning curve is the same: a head start in production is a competitive advantage which is extremely difficult to overcome. The learning curve dictates a very risky brand of industrial gamesmanship and an absolute obsession with getting to the market first. One semi-conductor executive told *Business Week,* "The competition in this business is frightening. If you're not first, or a very fast second or third, you're in trouble." Innovation serves as a means of leap-frogging a late start on an established learning curve by creating a new one. Although the price of the new chip will be higher than the old one, buyers are quite willing to line up for purchases in anticipation of the price declines to come. This creates, in effect, a form of futures bidding for new chips. Chip makers, knowing their own learning curve history and the improvements that can be expected in production by virtue of it, are willing to bid against each other, at prices well below current market values, for future deliveries of chips that they have not yet even built, except in limited quantities. It is all done on the gamble that the learning curve will function smoothly as usual; everything about the production process for a new chip will go right.

But occasionally, everything does not go right at all. A number of unforeseen developments can derail the ride down the learning curve, and no semiconductor company, however advanced, has proven wholly immune to the bane of production glitches. Suddenly, a problem develops on the production line, the chips don't work, yields plummet, delivery schedules fall apart, and by the time the glitch is corrected, through an even higher and more expensive set of alchemistic incantations, much blood usually has been spilled on the company's quarterly statements. Alternately, risking it all on a new chip or a new process which turns out to be a technological dead-end can be the innovation gamble that goes awry. It takes millions of dollars and thousands of hours of engineering to design and produce a new chip, and the whole investment can go right out the window if a fast-moving competitor manages to render the chip instantly obsolete with the announcement of a superior version. And naturally, the fortunes of customers are tied intimately to the fortunes of their sources of supply. In the midst of an otherwise relentlessly technical listing of definitions in Charles J. Sippl's *Microcomputer Dictionary and Guide,* one finds the following entry for "electronics industry:"

> From its earliest beginnings, the electronic industry has developed a unique reputation as the most price cutting, device copying, yield busting, market puffing, people robbing, no-house-loyalty feeling, process spying, and in some cases, money losing business that one can possibly imagine. And this crazy industry reached a volume of over $5 billion — $2.5 billion of it in the U.S. in 1975.

And there are some who would even argue that Mr. Sippl has understated the case.

Falling cost, increasing performance and the fierce competition to innovate and take risks are the key factors behind the semiconductor success story. The sheer number of microchips in use today tells part of the story, but another way to view chip economics in action is to consider the effect of the ever-cheaper microchip on the history of computer design and usage.

In the 1950s there were no more than a thousand computers operating in the U.S., most of them owned and operated by the government and large corporations. Computer science was a relatively small and friendly neighborhood. By 1976, spurred by the falling cost of the microprocessor and related chips, there was roughly one computer in use for every thousand people, according to figures compiled by Ruth Davis for *Science* magazine. The federal government's ownership of conventional computers had shrunk to less than 4 percent, and computer science had blossomed into a field employing some 2.5 million designers, programmers, analysts and operators. Most striking of all, the actual number of computer *users* had become anybody's guess. As Davis wrote, "With microprocessors, the customers are potentially everyone . . . we can no longer know who is using computers and what they are computing. Indeed, when anyone with a telephone and between $25 to $50 per month or $2 to $5 per hour can rent a computer terminal and have access to a computer, the number of users is realistically indeterminate."

A final example: In 1977 Creative Strategies, a San Jose electronics consulting firm, estimated that by 1980 there would be more than 440 million telephones in use worldwide, and about 60 million microcomputers. What is striking about this comparison, as the firm point outs, is that "It will have taken over 100 years to reach the level of 440 million telephones, and *seven years* [italics added] for the microcomputer to reach the 60 million level."

The reason for this, of course, is cost. "By 1980 the cost of the microcomputer will be so low that processing power will essentially be free," meaning that "from the end of 1976 on, the cost of the microprocessor will cease to play a major role in the decision whether to digitize or not." This is a profoundly accurate statement, and it means that the semiconductor industry now offers electronic logic essentially for free, or bearing Gelbach's Law in mind, for five dollars a chip unless it sells for less. Electronic logic, as an aid to human intelligence, is no longer the domain of the large institution and the large computer.

While the basic building blocks of electronic logic may be essentially free on a per-bit or per-function basis, the additional circuitry and hardware required to implement that logic is certainly not. Nor is the software that is needed for programming it. Indeed, software now has become the costliest aspect of participating in the microchip business, and the semiconductor industry now finds itself in the position of giving away the razor (the microprocessor) in order to sell the blades (everything else required to make the microprocessor work). In the end, however, though the overall costs of implementing a microprocessor-based system can be steep, and the short-term start-up problems a major aggravation, the long-term economic logic of doing so remains indisputable in application after application. As a single, trivial example, consider that a few dozen microchips can replace sixty to eighty pounds of electromechanical switches and wiring in the average vending machine. As for more advanced applications, the software problem looms as a major brake on the unfolding of the microelectronics revolution, "free" electronic logic notwithstanding. Software, which computer scientist Douglas Hofstadter succinctly defines as "anything which you could send over the telephone lines," has not kept pace with the development of electronic hardware. In the field of programming, there is no such thing as a shrinking process, a learning curve, or a doubling of complexity each year. While this account is concerned mainly with hardware developments, it is the highly esoteric product called software which will pace the rate at which sophisticated new uses of microelectronics are realized. Finally, and most importantly from the hardware point of view, the semiconductor scaling process and associated cost/performance benefits quite obviously cannot go on forever. There must come a point, as the microchip continues to shrink, at which one simply can no longer *do* electronics in the conventional sense. But defining those limits is another matter, much like setting the limit on the ultimate mile run. Technological limitations on the future of the microchip revolution are hotly debated among industry scientists, engineers and executives. As the power of the electron is harnessed ever more subtly, as the work of electronic "compunication" is made possible by subatomic events lasting a few nanoseconds, by electrical pulses traveling a few thousand angstroms, the outcome of the debate is sure to disrupt the historical pattern of the semiconductor industry, and the electronics industry as a whole, in several important ways.

Future Technologies and the VLSI Era: Will the Shrinking Ever Stop?

There are obvious pitfalls in assuming that the semiconductor shrinking process can continue forever. A straightforward projection based on past experience yields an integration level of a million elements per chip by the end of the century. The problem is that such levels of complexity very likely will not be achievable with the traditional tools of the semiconductor trade.

The seventies, in industry parlance, were the years of LSI, or large-scale integration, symbolized by Intel's first memory and microprocessor chips. However, with the eighties began the era of VLSI, for very large scale integration, symbolized by 64K (65,536-bit) memory chips and microprocessors approaching the complexity of a mainframe computer's central processing unit reduced to three chips. At the level of complexity represented by VLSI, chips may contain as many as a hundred thousand active elements connected by lines a few millionths of an inch wide, and their threshold of sensitivity to electrical signals is so low as to plunge VLSI circuit designers into the problematic realm of quantum physics. To more than one researcher, "the dominant feature of VLSI chips is that they are simply too hard to design." For no sooner had the age of VLSI been announced in an atmosphere of general optimism than a number of technical hurdles began to crop up rather more dramatically than many in the industry had expected.

To begin with, cramming VLSI numbers of circuits on a single fingernail-sized chip calls for connecting line widths of ten microns, for starters, with an ultimate goal of one micron (a micron is one millionth of a meter). Conventional photolithography, bounded by the physical dimensions of the wavelength of light, cannot produce such fine lines on silicon without "blurring" the exposure. Some alternative to the mask-and-exposure system of making chips will have to be found, and some already exist. The most promising approach is to "write" the circuit pattern directly on the silicon wafer with a concentrated, high-energy beam of electrons, thus doing away with the masking procedure altogether. Other forms of direct writing are in the production stage, and while they offer better resolution, they are extremely costly — $2 million and up, or four times the cost of conventional optical machines, in the case of the so-called E-beam machines.

The VLSI challenge runs deeper, however, than the obvious limitations of line width and pattern resolution on silicon. On a memory chip containing a hundred thousand or more microscopic transistors, all of them switching on and off in a few nanoseconds along interconnecting lines a few microns wide, very small numbers of electrons suddenly begin to loom very *large* in the semiconductor design process. At the VLSI level, some eerie quantum effects begin to pop up.

Transistors on a chip, as two-state switches triggered by an input of electrical energy, are becoming so small and the amount of energy required to drive them is becoming so negligible that even the tiny burst of energy produced when a single subatomic alpha particle strikes silicon can be enough to cause a malfunction. The alpha effect is a telling example of how delicately powerful the newer microchips have become as researchers seek to push back the physical boundaries of miniaturized information storage and retrieval.

In the past few years, computer users have become familiar with an infrequent but troublesome glitch called a "soft fail." Suddenly, and for no readily apparent reason, a computer drops or garbles a binary bit stored in its memory, triggering an error. In extreme cases the computer simply stops cold. Unlike "hard fails," the error cannot be traced to any obvious circuit failure. It is a temporary form of computer amnesia, and as the newer, higher-density 16K memory chips found their way into computer design cycles in the late seventies, it got worse.

In 1978 two engineers at Intel pinpointed a probable cause of soft fails: alpha particles emitted by the spontaneous decay of tiny amounts of radium and thorium in the package of the memory chips. If the memory chip is sensitive enough (and the more bits it can handle, the more sensitive it is), the tiny burst of electrical charge from a single alpha is enough to "confuse" a transistor into flipping a bit, from zero to one, or vice versa. The result: a computer error.

And that isn't all. Since cosmic rays sometimes produce alpha particles when they strike silicon, other researchers began to wonder whether soft fails could be caused by the normal flux of cosmic rays continually bombarding the earth. Unhappily, the answer was yes. J. F. Ziegler of IBM and W. A. Lanford of the State University of New York calculated the electrical energy produced by a variety of cosmic ray–silicon interactions and found that computer memory chips had breached a critical threshold of sensitivity to cosmic rays. They predicted "dramatic increases in soft fails" at airplane altitudes, adding that a computer in Albuquerque, New Mexico, is four times as prone to cosmic rays as a similar one operating at sea level in L.A. Major solar events may triple the potential for such errors, and solar wind may have the same effect on computers in space.

"It's like a genetic mutation," explains Tim May, the Intel physicist who first brought industry-wide attention to the problem with a series of papers in 1978. The alpha's electrical charge "can mutate a binary zero into a one and vice versa, and that can cause data loss or even shut down a system completely." By 1980 May was convinced that the alpha effect's correlation with altitude was a finding that was sure to have an effect on the design of computers intended for airborne use in space and defense satellite projects. "The most severe implications are for weapons systems," he claims; adding: "Soft fails might explain some reports of data loss in military satellites." For lack of security clearance, May was excluded from a Defense Department meeting on the subject that year.

While far less prone to the alpha effect, even home computers here on earth are not immune. May calculates that the typical hobbyist microcomputer experiences a soft fail once every three weeks or so, but concludes that "you'll cause a failure more often than that by tripping over the power cord."

However, "smart" cash registers and other remote terminals such as automatic bank tellers "have been hit rather severely," claims May. One large department store in Europe scrapped its computerized inventory-control system when soft fails began to appear as errors in the sales records.

May's estimates can be taken only as informed guesses, since the overall rate of soft fails is difficult to quantify. But there is no doubt that the rate is rising as chip designers achieve higher and higher levels of complexity. To defend microchips and computer systems from the unwelcome effects of the alpha, designers are experimenting with new packaging and shielding techniques. Another promising approach is a programmed error-correction scheme that enables a computer to test itself for soft fails and make the required corrections automatically. The drawback is that error-correction programs take up coveted space on the silicon chip, further increasing the headaches, and the cost. With VLSI, the strict cost/performance efficiencies of the past become subject to new considerations.

At the energy levels and physical dimensions represented by the microcircuits of the eighties, the normal rules of the solid-state world begin to break down, and the alpha effect is only one example. However, another quantum mechanical effect — superconductivity — holds out great promise as a future way of mitigating the effects of energy confusion at the micro level. Superconductivity is a phenomenon that occurs when certain materials are cooled to a temperature very close to absolute zero (-460 degrees F.). At that point, the electrical resistance of certain metals and compounds begins to approach zero; that is, they become almost perfect conductors. This fact was discovered early in the century, but there was no sound understanding of it until 1957, when John Bardeen of the Bell transistor trio, then at the University of Illinois, propounded with two colleagues the first quantum mechanical explanation of superconductivity (winning for Bardeen his second Nobel Prize). Further research has provided a firm foundation for investigating the phenomenon. In the supercooled, superconducting state, electrons of lead, tin and other elements execute an abrupt transition, giving rise to a mysterious quantum behavior called tunneling. The explanation of it rests on the fact that electrons are not really discrete particles as they generally are referred to for convenience, but rather puzzling entities that behave sometimes as a particle and sometimes as a wave and are best pictured as a fuzzy statistical combination of both. In the superconducting state, electron particle-waves have the ability to tunnel through energy barriers they do not normally possess the energy to penetrate, and in doing so they carry electrical current without heat loss — more or less for free.

The growing understanding of superconductivity led to the prospect of both ultra-efficient transmission of electricity and a new class of powerful superconducting computers. Those prospects brightened appreciably in 1962 with several new theories by twenty-two-year-old Brian Josephson, a physicist then with Cambridge University. Josephson's work led to the Josephson junction, the fastest solid-state electronic component ever built, and one which may hold the key to future computers, if IBM's vote on the matter is taken into account. The Josephson junction, essentially a solid-state sandwich of two metals separated by a thin film, all connected to a control line and cooled to superconducting temperature, permits superconductivity to perform the work of a two-state switching device like a transistor. It uses only one ten-thousandth the energy required to drive a conventional transistor, with none of the thermal problems of VLSI circuits at room temperature, and its astonishing switching speed suggests hitherto undreamed-of computing power. For the past fifteen years, one of IBM's largest research projects has been aimed at designing just such an experimental supercomputer. If supercomputers come to pass, they will be very small indeed — about the size of a softball, for optimum results, cooled in a refrigerator-sized bath of liquid helium, and performing perhaps as many as a billion binary operations per second.

This vision of twenty-first-century supercomputers is still highly theoretical. Levels of integration are still low, and the commercial outline is unclear. But there are many other promising if somewhat less exotic room-temperature alternatives already in the works. One strong contender for computer memory chips is "bubble" technology, in which an area in a substance derived from gallium is magnetized and demagnetized to stand for zero and one. Another approach involves the use of "III-V" substances, so called because they are combinations of elements from the third and fifth rows of the periodic table, as substitutes for silicon. Other man-made "synterials" are also under investigation or in limited use, and still other breakthroughs of one sort or another are announced almost weekly, or so it seems.

Before venturing a look at what passes for the definitive word on the physical limits of *conventional* chip making as it exists in 1981, there is one other related technology deserving of brief mention because of the promise it holds as a source of cheap and efficient solar cells for the direct conversion of sunlight into electrical current. Photovoltaic technology exploits the fact that silicon wafers, properly configured, trap a portion of the sun's radiant energy and convert it into electricity. Arrays of silicon solar cells powered Skylab and other space projects, leading to the futurist vision of orbiting solar energy stations — Tesla's grand plan in spirit if not in practice. On earth, solar cells already are used at remote or rural sites where a generator ordinarily would be employed.

There are several methods of producing solar cells in large numbers at reasonable cost. Some companies are experimenting with long ribbons of silicon, rather than conventional wafers. Texas Instruments, under the leadership of Jack Kilby and with $14 million from the Department of Energy, has pioneered a "wet cell" technology that may lead to greater storage capacity. The most controversial approach has been touted by Stanford Ovshinsky, a self-taught maverick inventor from Ohio who has bedeviled the semiconductor industry for years with his theories of "amorphous" semiconductors — silicon in which the atoms are randomly arranged, rather than locked into the rigid crystalline structure of the relatively pure (and relatively expensive) silicon normally used. With his flair for promotion and intriguing demonstrations, Ovshinsky operates as an industrial gadfly in the Tesla tradition of lone-wolf engineering. "Amorphous" is precisely how some industry observers have viewed Mr. Ovshinsky's theories since he first propounded them in the sixties. Undaunted, he insists that amorphous semiconductors and solar cells can be produced far more cheaply than conventional semiconductor methods will allow, and recently he has scored some successes in enlisting support, including a development contract between Atlantic Richfield and his Energy Conversion Devices of Troy, Michigan, for the production of amorphous solar cells.

Solar cells last for years, and it may be possible to design them as shingles for domestic use. Certainly one can envision the possibility of solar cell arrays providing the energy to produce more solar cell arrays. However, solar cells capture only a fraction of the sun's available energy. Precisely what the maximum fraction is remains in doubt, but few estimates range much above 20 percent, and most commercially available solar cells range in efficiency from about 5 to 15 percent. Therefore, it takes a lot of solar cells to do the job. At present, the cost per kilowatt hour of solar cell–produced electricity is still several times higher than conventional electrical power. Costs are falling, but to budget-minded congressmen the promise of photovoltaics is a bit too good to be true, and past federal funding of the embryonic industry can best be described as erratic. And yet, the future cost reductions to be expected of any hardware adjunct to semiconductor technology makes photovoltaics a strong contender as an energy alternative. It is unreasonable to expect solar cells to decline in price as rapidly as microchips. However, in an era marked by the skyrocketing cost of oil and nuclear power, any energy technology blessed by falling costs and increasing efficiency of conversion deserves serious consideration.

That would seem to be the opinion of America's major oil companies — Atlantic Richfield, Mobil, Exxon, Standard, Shell and others. According to the Small Business Administration, almost 90 percent of the infant industry's sales in 1979 were made by affiliates of major oil companies, while fully two-thirds of the top fifty solar cell firms were subsidiaries of major corporations, including GE, Westinghouse, Motorola, Union Carbide, Texas Instruments, Honeywell and IBM. Critics charge that small, independent and innovative start-ups in the solar cell business are being forced to sell out or go broke, and that the oil industry is rounding up solar cell companies for the purpose of locking an alternative energy source in the closet. It seems far more likely that the motivation is an expectation of future profits when such systems are employed. Given the precarious nature of federal funding, the government's unwillingness to serve as a first test market, and the range of solar cell technologies yet to be explored, major corporate interest in photovoltaics may be its only short-term route to survival. What is needed in the future, if small company innovation is to survive and if future cost declines are to be realized, is just the sort of helpful federal nudge the U.S. government bestowed upon the semiconductor, nuclear and aerospace industries, among others, when they were in need of a market for relatively untested products at premium prices. In the case of semiconductors, the government provided research funds and served as first customer, thus assuring the industry's survival. Even though the raison d'être was primarily national defense, and the funding often represented a misguided emphasis on major research institutions at the expense of small innovators, federal support of what was, in the beginning, an "alternative" technology proved essential to the industry's success. Sadly, seed funding of new, nondefense-related technologies appears to be anathema in the current climate of deregulation aimed at unfettering the powers of corporate capitalism. The history of high-technology development shows that the "private sector" is not always so private after all. Federal largesse, and not just corporate zeal, powered the growth of post-war corporate high technology in California and the Sun Belt. It makes far more sense to fund promising new start-ups at the outset, rather than to rescue ailing companies, such as Chrysler, in their dotage.

All of these present and future technologies, moving at various speeds from research to production and with various prospects for commercial success, illustrate that the microelectronics revolution has yet to run its course. As for the ultimate limits of conventional semiconductor technology — scaling the chip down to the quantum world — Robert Noyce offers a prediction shared by others in the semiconductor industry itself, if not necessarily by all university scientists or other researchers: "There have been a lot of attempts to define that limit, and we've already surpassed quite a few of them. But it's pretty clear that there are limits to what we can do. It really comes down to the energy dissipated by each switching element on the chip. That energy has to be large compared to thermal energies. Now you can conceivably go down to low temperatures and go beyond what that imposes, but at room temperature the limits start to become effective at about a tenth of the dimensions that we're working with now. So overall, I think the limit is on the order of a thousand times more complex than where we are now, for circuits working at room temperature. That's another decade, at least. Again, that's at room temperature, so conceivably there are other ways around it."

A thousand times more complex than where we are now. Yet even if the evolution of the microchip stopped cold tomorrow, the victim of some unforeseen quantum limit, the engine of silicon chip production already in place would assure continuing cost and performance improvements in existing chips throughout the rest of the century. The shrinking process seems destined to continue on course for another decade or two at the least. What has changed in the VLSI era, however, is the *cost* of the shrinking. Noyce: "This business has become very capital-intensive, and the time when you could start up a business here in a garage with only a small amount of money and a lot of bright people is past. Now, you still have to have the brains, but you also need a massive supply of sophisticated and expensive tools. I don't think this industry is any different than the automobile industry in that sense. Those guys all started in their garages too, and there was intense competition, and then some consolidation of the industry. You don't go into that business now without massive, sophisticated tools, and you can't start by building an automobile in your garage. So we have the same kind of change going on in this business as well. In the entrepreneurial phase, companies were springing up everywhere and there was intense competition. Now there has been some consolidation. There are still 100 or 200 companies in the business, so it's not like the Big Three in the U.S. auto industry. It will continue to be intensively competitive for a long time to come."

As the American semiconductor industry began grappling with the technical demands and the spiraling costs of VLSI at the close of the seventies, the notion became common that the age of Silicon Valley entrepreneurship had come to an end. The technical challenges of VLSI, rising capital costs, a troubled economy, a less than venturesome venture capital community, debilitating competition from the Japanese, incursion by the multinationals — all of it had conspired to create a form of market hardball in which there was no room for a few talented engineers with a few good ideas and a few thousand dollars. Instead, the established players, many of them in partnership with capital-rich foreign firms, would contest among themselves for the spoils of the microelectronics market. In short, the ante had gone too high. In the eighties it would take some $50 million in serious institutional backing just to launch a new enterprise, and even that would be no guarantee of success.

But in 1980 and 1981, a half-dozen new chip makers sprang to life in California as if to disprove the conventional wisdom that the entrepreneurial fires had been banked completely. Thanks to a new round of high-technology fever among venture capitalists in the midst of wildly successful stock offerings by home-computer maker Apple and gene-splicer Genentech, plus a growing market for customized microchips, these new companies found backing in a hurry. As it turned out, the entry fee to the semiconductor game was considerably less than $50 million but a great deal more than a garage and a promise — $10 to $15 million on the average; a far cry from the old days.

Wilfred Corrigan, who presided over Fairchild as CEO during the dark days of its disastrous foray into digital watches and video games, announced the formation of LSI Logic Corporation, and secured financing for the new Fairchild spin-out within twenty-four hours. Jack Balletto and a few colleagues from Silicon Valley's Synertek, where Balletto served as a vice president, formed VLSI Technology Inc. with funding from smart-money venture capitalists Hambrecht and Quist of San Francisco and a Salt Lake City computer company. A group of marketers and engineers slipped from Intel's memory-chip operation to form Seeq, Inc., the firm's name a testimony to the fact that the confident group had not yet even landed its backers. Seeq's Larry Jordan, echoing the reason why his former boss, Robert Noyce, left Fairchild to form Intel, declared: "It appeared to us, when we looked at our career opportunities, that we'd like to go off and try to do it on our own."

This time around, however, Intel was not impressed with that time-tested logic, and quickly filed suit for violation of trade secret laws and employee-nondisclosure agreements. As a final example, there is Howard Bobb, the founder of American Microsystems back in 1970, who brought forth Applied Micro Circuits Corporation of San Diego to pursue the growing market for custom-made chips. "I'm too old to be doing this," the fifty-eight-year-old semiconductor veteran told *Business Week,* "but the technology simply brought me back."

These new companies have been formed to exploit the technical *disadvantages* of being an Intel or a National, and the constraints, from a user's point of view, of the McDonald's approach to chip making. Since the usual goal has been to produce as many standardized chips as possible in order to bring costs down and penetrate as many markets as possible, customers have been left by and large on their own as far as specific applications are concerned. In practice, however, the chip that can control a traffic light or steer a satellite may work very well in one application and not so well at all in the other. In many cases, producers of electronic equipment and systems would be better served with custom chips, made to order and tailored precisely for the intended use. Large companies attempt to solve this problem by making some custom chips of their own, but now other users have recourse to the new "custom houses" for small-volume custom projects discouraged by the industry at large. The custom market shows signs of growing even faster than the mainstream market, as customers clamor for more individual attention to their chip needs, while offering better profit margins than head-to-head competition with the majors at giveaway prices.

Such are the technology-driven complexities of a fast-moving industry in the throes of major change. In a practical sense, it does not matter whether or not the industry is fast approaching the limits of the solid-state paradigm. "Very likely before that," as Noyce points out, "we will run up against other, more pressing considerations. How do you design a piece of equipment in which a single chip is more complex than anything man has ever built? What is it that you design, and for what use? The point is to do something that is purposeful."

In fact, the microchip already has evolved well beyond the human ability to fully exploit what it can do. Even so, microelectronics in its present form has become an essential worldwide resource. In the late seventies, the fact that the world had come to recognize this became graphically evident. It was then that the U.S. government, various state governments, major universities and a large slice of corporations on the Fortune 500 list all conducted a blitz on Silicon Valley, seeking a valuable share of the commercial wonders being worked there. They were joined in this mad scramble by almost every other developed or developing nation in the world, and by a new breed of international corporate criminal. The rush to pry loose some of Silicon Valley's microelectronic secrets, so essential for such enterprises as computer networks, telecommunication systems and national defense, manifested itself as a wave of corporate takeovers, and when the smoke began to clear the industry emerged with a new and distinctly international flavor.

Some of the world's most profitable scientific and industrial trade secrets are found in Silicon Valley. Lately, anybody who's anybody has come charging in for a piece of the action.

CHAPTER SEVEN

Silicon Valley International

It is common knowledge in the electronics industry that the components people are a special breed of gamesman.
— MICHAEL MACCOBY, *"The Gamesman,"* 1976

Every place has its time. Ours is now.
Join Advanced Micro Devices.
CATCH THE WAVE.
— SILICON VALLEY RECRUITMENT AD, 1980

The Last of the Cowboy Capitalists

"Up periscope," says D.C. as he scans the lunch crowd at a Santa Clara Chinese restaurant. In dozens of restaurants from Palo Alto to San Jose, much the same scenario is taking place as engineers and managers from Silicon Valley's two hundred–odd electronics firms gather for lunch, a drink or two and the casual exchange of information, gossip and job offers. D.C., a marketing manager with one of Silicon Valley's largest semiconductor companies, is both recruiting and being recruited — a not altogether unusual situation — and he means to discover whether any of his hottest prospects are present here today. "This industry is desperate for top talent," he explains, digging a spoon into his bowl of wonton. In some other industry D.C.'s hair might be considered a touch overlong for his management level. But here in Silicon Valley, where technical élan is considered more vital than rigid adherence to a Corporate Look, nobody much cares, least of all his superiors. Just the slightest hint of a bulge is beginning to show beneath his belt, and he has been attacking that problem with a tougher schedule of tennis matches. D.C. loves tennis and chess, good solid one-on-one competition. He hates golf. D.C. is a fierce competitor, and in Silicon Valley that makes him a very valuable commodity.

"The big thing in recruiting right now [1980] is cash bon-

157

uses. We're giving good people a four- or five-thousand-dollar bounty just for walking in the door. This place has gained the reputation of being a business where management will cut you in on the action, all down the line. You take an electronics engineer with a master's degree, a little relevant experience, just starting out, and he'll come in at about $25,000. In just a couple of years and maybe another employer, he'll boost that to over $50,000 with stock options alone. Silicon Valley, as you know, is Porschland."

D.C. himself drives a Mercedes, and as for his salary, "it would be listed at about $120,000." That, however, is not the total yearly package. "Stock options are a wonderful thing." D.C., who is ten years out of college, has not yet hit a million on paper. But he is getting there.

"In the chip business you have to have a kind of creative madness throughout the ranks, and that means having a lot of highly talented and very egocentric individuals. If an employee doesn't have that kind of technical creativity, or can't sustain it, he gets sidelined. The competition in this business is unbelievable."

D.C. pours himself a beer and nods at a couple of acquaintances. "It's so preposterous the way we do things here," he says with a wry smile. "It's like the Wild West, the way we knock guys off. All that's lacking is pistols at high noon. Swords, maybe. Crossed swords at sunrise."

D.C. is short for Deep Circuit, which is how he leaves phone messages when he is feeling whimsical. At a semiconductor company half the size of his present one he would be a vice-president. As it is, he works for one, and dozens of engineers and technical people work for him. In addition to being a successful and aggressive young manager, he is a crack electronics engineer. Like many of his colleagues, he came up through the engineering ranks, making a name for himself in the development of high-tech circuits.

D.C. considers Silicon Valley the most challenging and prestigious high-technology playing field in the world. "People don't come to Silicon Valley for the pension plans. This is where the winners are. Job security and lifelong loyalty to a single company don't exist here, for the most part. You still see those attitudes in Europe and Japan, and even back East. It's fine for the steel industry, but it won't wash here." D.C. pronounces "steel industry" with scorn, the way some generals in Vietnam referred to the "Oriental mind." "Silicon Valley," he concludes, "is a curiosity that most people just don't understand yet."

Take D.C.'s friend "Harold," as a case in point. "Harold came to work for me out of the insurance business, which is very unusual. But he was a good manager and we had what was considered a fairly nontechnical slot for him to fill. When you've been in this business for ten years you tend to forget that in a semiconductor company people can carry on a conversation for hours without resorting to English. It's just one long string of acronyms, numbers, computer mnemonics, other bits of computerese. Schmoo plots, piggyback cerdips, ion implantation, response time in picoseconds . . . it's unintelligible. Even the top technical gurus don't understand all of it. Harold was completely lost. Nothing in MBA school had prepared him for this."

Nor was Harold prepared for corporate mobility, Silicon Valley style, the essence of which has never been better expressed than by Jerry Sanders, president of Sunnyvale's high-flying Advanced Micro Devices. In contrast to D.C., with his tennis shoes and casually knotted tie, Sanders is everybody's idea of what the successful California executive should look like — tall, tanned, elegant clothes, Rolls-Royce, designer accessories. "All a guy has to do here if he wants to change jobs," Sanders told a *Time* magazine reporter, "is drive down the same street in the morning and turn in a different driveway."

Naturally, Silicon Valley is a fertile ground for executive recruiters, and D.C. is popular with many of them because he specializes in keeping his options open. Three years with the same company, he feels, is playing it pretty conservatively at his management level. You have to gamble and you have to tap into that all-important corporate fuel, momentum. He is also popular with recruiters because, in industry parlance, he is wired. It has nothing to do with reading the *Wall Street Journal* every day. When a rival company holds secret marketing seminars to discuss the design of an upcoming microchip, D.C. is not only likely to hear about it but to lay hands on a copy of the presentation. When somebody is about to jump ship, he knows who, when and why. If there is an acquisition in the wind, he usually hears about it. "Headhunters can get pretty creative. A lot of companies try to protect against predation by instructing secretaries to screen out their calls. One of them got to me by saying he was the president of the firm I was trying to do business with. When I got on the line he said there was this great opportunity at that company, and did I know anybody who might be interested? Now I knew and he knew that he was talking about me, but he never said so. The recruiting wasn't obvious."

It doesn't need to be. Bob Harrington, an investment vice-president with Dean Witter Reynolds in Palo Alto, explained that "The dynamics of this industry are very tricky. When the momentum shifts, it can shift in a big way. The defection of a single key employee can trigger an erosion of other employees, and that can cause you to slip behind in the technology. At times, companies that buy into the valley have a lot of trouble operating according to the way we do things here."

In general, D.C. does not use headhunters in his own talent searches. "I just hired one guy from a competitor and I'm using him as my personal recruiting agency. He's nosing around a little at his former company." D.C. smiles. "And I think he just might bring me a few of his friends."

A noble valley tradition, that, but it can make for trouble in an industry as competitive as semiconductors. Winking the corporate eye at suspected bootlegging is not always the way of things in microelectronics.

One spring day in 1979 Howard Raphael, then microprocessor chief at National Semiconductor, walked into San Francisco International Airport with a few minutes to kill before catching a flight. Raphael had been with National for a couple of years, and before that held a similar job with Intel. He was hard at work on National's upcoming entry in the microprocessor sweepstakes, a yet-unannounced chip known inside the company as the 16000. "The way I hear it, there was a tremendous technical argument over the design of the chip," according to an insider at National. "Both sides had put together an army of consultants, industry experts, Cal-Tech scientists, whomever they could find. You have to allow for that kind of controversy, but in this case it got very emotional. It got personal." Shortly thereafter, a total of six National employees left the firm to join Zilog of Cupertino.

In the airport, Raphael spotted Ken McKenzie, an old friend and rival from the days the two had worked together at Intel. McKenzie, a tall, handsome engineer who spent his spare time racing cars or skiing, was now working for Zilog, and he was involved with Zilog's new microprocessor chip, the Z8000. That put him in direct competition with Raphael. The two men sat down for a few minutes of conversation, and McKenzie started kidding his friend about delays on National's chip. Then McKenzie smiled and said a Zilog engineer had seen a copy of National's confidential design specifications for the chip.

When Raphael returned to work after his trip he reported the conversation to National's vice-president and technical director. Scarcely had Raphael returned to his desk when a squadron of company lawyers arrived, asking some very pointed questions. National lodged a $5 million trade-secret suit against Zilog, claiming that copies of the following items were missing from company files: design specifications for the 16000, the proprietary "Thor" report on the status of the project, a confidential cost analysis, and other evaluation and review documents. In addition to the money, National asked the court for a ruling that would bar its former employees from working on Zilog's microcomputer efforts for two years.

In papers filed in court, McKenzie claimed he had only been

"baiting" Raphael, hoping to draw him out on the 16000 project. Raphael, he said, "is a very proud man and becomes extremely defensive when one challenges him." On court order Zilog produced six cartons of material from National — including the "Thor" report — but no 16000 design specifications. Zilog attorneys argued that the "Thor" report had been taken innocently, and that it was "entirely unintelligible" without the accompanying design information.

As with earlier situations of this kind, including the Fairchild–Motorola lawsuit of 1968, the legal action met with mixed reviews from the semiconductor community. Some see them as a healthy restraint on talent-raiding companies, others as an unfair infringement on the individual's right to market his talent at will. "That issue comes up every time there's a case like this," according to Roger Borovoy, vice-president and general counsel for Intel. "I tried the Motorola–Fairchild case when I was with Fairchild, and I think engineers generally want to do the right thing. They don't want to sell trade secrets to competitors. Maybe one engineer in a thousand might bring a whole process back with him to a new employer, whereas maybe a hundred out of a thousand, if they knew from previous experience that lowering the temperature a little might cure their new employer's processing problems, would find it very hard not to do it."

Two weeks before the trial was due to begin in Santa Clara, National agreed to submit the case to an arbitrator. The ruling was that Zilog did not use any of National's trade secrets in the design of its own products. The two companies settled the case out of court, quietly, with no further official mention of the missing specifications.

As D.C. explains it, "Design specs are covered under the standard nondisclosure agreements everybody signs when he goes to work for a Silicon Valley company. The legally binding agreement says you can't disclose the company's trade secrets to any future employers, but they're almost impossible to enforce — real paper tigers. Companies know this. If the project you're working on is sensitive enough or if they are unhappy with you for some reason they'll just escort you right to the door as soon as they find out you're planning to leave. I know of one case where a manager who was leaving came to work and found that all the locks on his file cabinets had been changed."

And that is not to mention, among other preventive measures, the widespread use of infrared cameras, paper shredders, armed guards and former FBI men as security personnel. D.C. thinks it is all rather amusing and futile. All that is really involved in stealing a trade secret is sticking a computer tape or a file folder under your jacket and hustling out the door with it. Trade secrets stored in the brains of engineers move from company to company every day. D.C. calls it "technological cross-fertilization, and it is what made this industry great in the first place." D.C. adds that "It's hard to keep secrets in this business, and that keeps the technology leapfrogging ahead. Companies are forced to wink at a lot of this because it goes on all the time and they'd be buried in lawsuits forever if they really tried to stop it."

While all this sounds rather cold-blooded, D.C. says it is precisely the kind of competition that made Silicon Valley possible. But it is not for the timid, and there are hazards and casualties. "The competition takes its toll sometimes. There's a very high degree of stress. It's amazing how many people in this business are divorced. Most of my friends, as a matter of fact." D.C. also refers to a "burnout syndrome. I don't really know how to describe it, but you know it when you see it. A guy puts in twenty years in this very hectic, go-go atmosphere, and psychologically he just starts to fall off the treadmill. He can't keep up with the technology any more. He stares out the window. He only stirs himself for routine presentations and meetings. It's just something I've seen firsthand. It's like falling off the edge. He either quits or gets fired." (One long-time denizen of the valley was even offered a substantial sum by a group of disgruntled Silicon Valley ex-wives if he would write a book that included the story of what the valley's Golden Age had done to a number of marriages.)

A new type of man is taking over leadership of the most technically advanced companies in America. In contrast to the jungle-fighter industrialists of the past, he is driven not to build or to preside over empires, but to organize winning teams. Unlike the security-seeking organization man, he is excited by the chance to cut deals and to gamble. Although more cooperative and less hardened than the autocratic empire builder and less dependent than the organization man, he is more detached and emotionally inaccessible than either. And he is troubled by it: the new industrial leader can recognize that his work develops his head but not his heart.

So wrote Michael Maccoby in 1976. And yet, for all this, D.C. offers a final and familiar observation about such matters. "There's no point in dwelling on this intramural stuff anyway. There's the Japanese question. And the Intel trade secrets that supposedly got to the Russians. Foreign competition is going to eat us up if we don't do something. The question is, who really owns Silicon Valley?"

To the first-time visitor arriving on the San Francisco Peninsula, there are few outward signs to suggest that the valley is anything other than a typical collection of industrial parks and well-groomed suburbs; a form of postwar industrial development which dots the outskirts of dozens of Sun Belt cities. Modern glass-and-concrete corporate centers dominate the landscape. Trucks and railroad cars load and unload at sprawling, low-slung manufacturing facilities. The affluent towns of the valley — Palo Alto, Mountain View, Cupertino, Sunnyvale, Santa Clara, the outskirts of San Jose, all linked by expressways — grade effortlessly into one another in a cityscape more suggestive of Los Angeles than nearby San Francisco. The car is king here, and growth is horizontal rather than vertical.

But a closer inspection reveals the valley as more than the ordinary industrial enclave. The profusion of Mercedes, Porsches, Peugeots and Ferraris zipping from one town to another are obvious evidence of a prosperity level more akin to, say, Beverly Hills than to most industrial cities. The arcane logos and futuristic company titles affixed to the buildings make clear that whatever profitable products are manufactured here, they are not shoes or steel. The all but unfathomable lexicon spoken in the valley is a language which describes science and technology in the service of profit.

It is commonly said here that there is more gold in Palo Alto's sewage — some thirty parts per million, a by-product of imperfect recovery methods in electronic processes where gold and other precious metals are used — than the amount that touched off the gold rush at Sutter's Mill. It is just as commonly said that more millionaires have been created per square mile in Silicon Valley than in any other manufacturing center on earth, and there is no reason to doubt it. Of all the states which benefited so handsomely from the postwar transformation of American science and industry, the California explosion was unparalleled. What began in Silicon Valley with Terman and Shockley had its counterpart in southern California in the form of the aerospace and defense industry — McDonnell Douglas, Rockwell, Northrop, Lockheed and others. During the golden years from 1941 to 1945, the federal government pumped some $35 billion into California, and the state has garnered some 30 to 40 percent of all Department of Defense research and development contracts since then. As a whole, California claimed 750 semiconductor companies, 200 computer firms and 400 electronic equipment manufacturers as of 1980 — roughly a quarter of all such enterprises in the country. California electronics firms account for about 25 percent of the state's manufacturing work force. Throughout the seventies the most spectacular manufacturing growth was centered right in Silicon Valley's Santa Clara County, where one worker in every three is employed by the electronics industry and where as many as forty thousand new jobs have been created in a single year. The valley's employees have resisted sporadic efforts at unionization, such as the failed effort at Raytheon in 1971 and again in 1980. Profit-sharing plans and a shortage of qualified labor have kept the industry one step ahead of the Brotherhood of Electrical Workers.

Indeed, the perennial cloud of smog perched like a brown felt bowler over nearby San Jose attests to the fact that Silicon Valley is suffering the effects of *too* much growth. The traffic jams, the soaring cost of housing, the dwindling availability of land and the never-ending shortage of experienced engineers and production workers have cramped Silicon Valley's expansion of late, forcing companies to make future plans outside the state. The current recession has taken its toll as well.

In truth, there is much more to Silicon Valley than just the chip-making companies that form its collective core. However pervasive its innovations, the semiconductor industry represents only a single, concentrated slice of Silicon Valley high technology. It is an even smaller slice of California electronics, and only a fraction, though growing, of the nation's vast microelectronics and compunications complex.

To begin with, the industry is linked intimately to several major research centers such as Stanford and SRI International (formerly Stanford Research Institute), as well as the University of California at Berkeley and Lawrence Livermore Laboratories across the San Francisco Bay. Near Silicon Valley are the "Steroid Hills," home of Syntex, the first producer of oral contraceptives, and other pharmaceutical companies. Sprinkled about the Bay Area are many of the new genetic engineering enterprises such as Cetus and Genentech. Every form of computer manufacturing is found here, from the large IBM-style mainframe systems to personal computers to the rainbow of small computers which fill every conceivable computing application between the two. There are makers of electronic testing and measurement equipment. There are companies which sell electronic subsystems to OEMs (original equipment manufacturers) and there are companies which do all of the above. There are manufacturers of lasers, missiles, video games and digital watches. Electronic manufacturing firms of various kinds — Amdahl, Hewlett–Packard, Memorex, the larger semiconductor companies — comprise the inner circle of the

Silicon Valley landscape and they are surrounded on all sides by production equipment makers, materials and packaging firms, distribution companies, software companies, consultants, recruiters, brokers, investors, black marketeers and high-technology thieves.

A brief and random list of the products produced by this hyperactive technological community would include mainframe computers, minicomputers, microcomputers, small computers, personal computers, hand-held computers, central processing units, office computers, hobbyist computers, business computers, computer memory systems, video games, high-stress environment bipolar programmable read-only-memories and shift registers, flip-flop gate arrays, guidance and tracking systems for the Defense Department, analog-to-digital converters, digital-to-analog converters, magnetic strip card readers, three-terminal adjustable voltage regulators, electrolytic capacitors, Schottky rectifiers, OEM cartridge disk drives, laser printers, modem dial hookups, multitasking attached processors, daisywheel printers, universal line multiplexers, floppy disk drives, add-on memories, add-in memories, bubble memories, charge-coupled-device memories, encryption sets, spectrometers, electron-beam micropattern generators, printed circuit boards, BIFET operational amplifiers, tuner circuits, in-circuit emulators, and bench-top IC testers.

They are all profitable machines and devices, dependent to one degree or another on the evolution of microchip technology. Silicon Valley, and the semiconductor industry in particular, is no bucolic haven for high-minded scientists and absentminded professors. Despite the striking atmosphere of informality for which these companies are known — the gold chains and open shirts, the casual office environments, the upper-management executives cheerily competing with production workers for unmarked parking spaces in communal lots — there is a carefully orchestrated structure designed to "maximize" technological innovation. Intel, for example, "measures absolutely everything," including post–eight A.M. arrivals, for an atmosphere Noyce has described as "casual, but not relaxed." It appears to work: In 1978 Intel threw a gala tenth-anniversary party for seven thousand employees at the San Francisco Cow Palace to celebrate the fact that while Intel's trio of original founders had hoped to grow a $100 million company in ten years, they actually had grown a $300 million high-technology company. That year, IBM ordered $25 million worth of Intel memory chips, the computer maker's largest outside purchase of memory chips ever, and a deal which had at least one Intel manager crowing that IBM now stood for "I Buy Memories." National Semiconductor, located only about a mile from Intel headquarters, has grown even larger under the irascible, cigar-smoking Charlie Sporck. National has demonstrated a canny commercial knack for producing every circuit imaginable at bone-cutting prices. A little farther up the road is Advanced Micro Devices, Intel's "leading follower" in state-of-the-art microprocessor circuitry and a pioneer in high-reliability chips. Helmed by the globe-trotting Jerry Sanders, AMD spends lavishly on advertising and public relations to reinforce its reputation as a young technology company on the move. Sanders's carefully cultivated image as a stylish California entrepreneur is more than just personal whimsy. It is intended as a message to employees, to Wall Street, and to industry at large, that Sanders is a winner and AMD is a winning company. Company programs have included such displays as a $350,000 Christmas party and drawings for cars or cash. In one memorable case, a lucky AMD employee was awarded $1000 a month for twenty years for the purchase of a new house. Aspiring engineers need look no farther than Sanders for a glimpse of the riches awaiting those who excel in Silicon Valley.

These sundry efforts to create a winning corporate style on the strength of a space-age product have combined nicely with the renewed public interest in science and technology. Increasingly, popular journalists and TV crews, both here and abroad, have trooped to Silicon Valley for the story. They come to the valley primed with facts about the spectacular growth of the microprocessor, its range of applications, its surgery-on-the-head-of-a-pin manufacturing process, and they begin to stalk the familiar scenario — the paperless office, the electronic cottage, the thinking computer, the Wired Life, the whole pop philosophy of high-tech electronics. When at last they are ushered in for an interview at a major semiconductor company, they commonly find a rather sober and conventional-looking executive who prefers to discuss, in most animated terms, such topics as the capital gains tax, Japanese tariff inequities and current book-to-bill ratios. For the journalist who sees Silicon Valley as one part science fiction, one part California iconoclasm, this can be a shock. The trappings of the California life-style and the uniqueness of the microchip often obscure the fact that Silicon Valley is awash in old-school boosterism. There is fierce loyalty here, not to a company but to a technology and to the concept of a free market. There is demanding discipline, Maseratis or no. Environmentalists, consumerists, wild-eyed futurists, friends of disarmament and foes of big business will find scant comfort here. Most prominent executives in the semiconductor industry hold economic and political views quite similar to those expressed by the National Association of Manufacturers and Chambers of Commerce everywhere.

Silicon Valley semiconductor companies want nothing so much as to continue excelling, innovating and growing under a clearly defined set of rules, which are, for the most part, the traditional rules of industrial capitalism — with a few notable subversions necessitated by the driving nature of the technology and the transcendental nature of the product line. In Silicon Valley, Horatio Alger and the American dream still live. Says Robert Noyce, "In the factory, we put in mechanical aids, all this sort of thing, so that we could produce more with fewer people, and we're going to have to do that in the service industries as well, so that we can produce more or we just simply are not going to have this American dream of everybody having more continuously." Perhaps it is not surprising, in light of this attitude, that a growing number of outside parties have chosen to adopt Silicon Valley methods to their own ends.

The selling of Silicon Valley began several years ago, as the No Vacancy sign went up after twenty years of solid growth. Up against local building restrictions, skyrocketing land costs and a pinched labor pool, the semiconductor industry stepped up its expansion into other parts of the country. Seeking the basic amenities to which they have become accustomed — a good university, a good airport, a good labor pool and plenty of energy, plus attractive surroundings and pleasant weather — companies have expanded mainly into Arizona and Texas (the Silicon Ranch), and portions of the Pacific Northwest (the Silicon Forest), plus numerous offshore sites such as Japan, Ireland and Hong Kong (the Silicon Islands).

Several states, anxious to establish or add to budding Silicon Valleys of their own, have not been content simply to compete for the outflow. Arizona's two largest industrial employers, Motorola and Honeywell, have been notably successful at luring away Silicon Valley engineers. In addition, the state has landed divisions from IBM, Digital Equipment Corporation, Intel, National Semiconductor and others. Texas has shaken loose more talent, though the traditional flow has been in the other direction. Massachusetts, with its tradition of high-tech employment and a planned $15 million VLSI graduate center at MIT, has trumpeted studies showing that the state will add sixty-four to one hundred and twenty thousand new employees to the roster from 1980 to 1983. (Such studies invariably go on to point out that California's Silicon Valley has become one of the nation's most expensive places to live, with modest tract homes selling for $200,000 and up.)

North Carolina, a recent entry in the semiconductor sweepstakes, has gone so far as to declare open war on Silicon Valley; in a battle for any companies or bodies not firmly nailed down, recruiting teams were dispatched after North Carolina's governor complained that his whole state was creating fewer new jobs each year than the county of Santa Clara. In order to sweeten the pot in this zero-sum game against California, North Carolina established a microelectronics center at the Research Triangle Industrial Park, within easy reach of Raleigh and three large universities. However, its initial success came not from Silicon Valley, but from General Electric, when the company announced that it planned to grace Raleigh with a new $55 million, fifty-five-acre microelectronics complex for production of its own chips.

The State of Minnesota and the University of Minnesota's Microelectronics and Information Sciences Center have sought to build upon the historical base of Twin Cities electronics begun by Sperry, Honeywell, Control Data and others. Florida, with roots in the space program and existing production from Harris Corporation and others, recently landed a $400 million Western Electric microchip plant. Maryland state planners have high hopes for a high technology corridor running from Washington, D.C., to Baltimore. In the Silicon Valley tradition, they have dubbed it "SciCom."

And so it goes, as a host of states seek to create the conditions which proved so lucrative for Santa Clara County. Perhaps in reaction to this civil war, Silicon Valley semiconductor and computer companies recently pledged about $16 million toward the creation of a new VLSI research lab at Stanford, while Governor Brown has called for a smaller joint Microelectronics Research Center at Berkeley.

Major American corporations have had the luxury of taking the direct route to microelectronics, via merger or acquisition. General Electric has acquired chip maker Intersil and Calma Company, a specialist in computer-aided-design. Westinghouse owns an interest in Siliconix, after beating out a rival bid from Honeywell. Mostek of Texas, a rival chip maker, was gobbled up by United Technologies, an aggressive conglomerate that was willing to pay a whopping $385 million for a company with 1979 earnings of $15 million.

There are many other examples, but the most telling one of all is Exxon. For years now Exxon has been positioning itself in high-technology electronics, electronic office equipment in particular. One of the linchpins of the Exxon strategy is Zilog of Cupertino, which began in the usual way — with a defection, this time from Intel. Intel engineers Federico Faggin and Ralph Ungermann founded Zilog, with eventual backing from Exxon Enterprises, Inc., for the purpose of producing microprocessors and other advanced microchips. Zilog, however, was not Exxon's only electronics ploy in the seventies. In all, the oil company spent $500 million to start or acquire a total of fifteen electronics firms. In addition to Zilog, the largest are Vydec, a maker of word-processing equipment; Qwip, a manufacturer of telephone facsimile machines; and Qyx, an electronic typewriter maker. In addition, there are research subsidiaries Kylex, Epid and Summit, all three located in Silicon Valley. The pattern is clear: Exxon, the world's largest oil company, is pursuing information, and information-processing technology, as a resource of the future. In 1980 Exxon made this manuevering official by consolidating its clutch of electronics firms under a new umbrella group, Exxon Information Systems (EIS), to bolster its attack on IBM, Xerox and others in the electronic office-equipment market. It also took options on two hundred acres in the rolling foothills of San Jose for a planned $200 million industrial campus for the Silicon Valley wing of EIS. As the eighties began, Exxon pushed still deeper into electronics and signaled an eventual move on AT&T with a controversial bid for Reliance Electronic Company, a maker of "nuts-and-bolts" telecommunications equipment. The oil industry at large has been diversifying into coal, solar energy, minerals and other areas as an antidote to the long-term prospects of depending upon a finite resource for growth, but Exxon's moves seem destined to place it squarely in competition with IBM, AT&T and other electronics industry giants as the decade of the eighties progresses. Still, the prospects for Exxon are far from clear. Zilog, its major microelectronics subsidiary, has had a rough-and-tumble history. Technologically sound but not always profitable, Zilog has been plagued with the management feuds and strained relations which often occur when an out-of-state company tries to run a Silicon Valley start-up. (Co-founder Ralph Ungermann subsequently left Zilog, citing a lack of the necessary independence under parent Exxon.)

Domestic efforts to emulate or acquire some of Silicon Valley's success continue unabated, but as the U.S. dollar declined in international markets through the mid to late seventies, these domestic developments paled in comparison to events on the international front. Silicon Valley's second-tier semiconductor companies, inveterately strapped for cash, became tempting targets for offshore companies seeking a foothold in advanced microcircuit technology. Semiconductor executives are increasingly fearful that the valley's homegrown and ever more costly electronics technology is being siphoned away, not just by rival companies down the street, but by the Kremlin, the Japanese government and major European multinationals. There are a variety of ways of going about this. Some methods are legal, some questionable, and some downright illegal, but they are all very popular, and competition in Silicon Valley is no longer primarily an intramural affair. In the past few years this battle for the latest microelectronic technology has transformed the valley into an international technological battleground.

With some 90 percent of the European market for the most advanced LSI microchips in the hands of U.S. producers in 1976, a counterattack from across the Atlantic made good sense. That year, a study of the European semiconductor industry by Mackintosh Consultants noted that "The prospects for indigenous European manufacturers getting a worthwhile slice of the cake look very bleak indeed . . . unless governments and semiconductor companies can agree on far-reaching radical changes in the present structure of the European semiconductor industry." These radical changes have taken two forms: acquisition of U.S. firms, and working partnerships with leading American semiconductor companies who have remained independent thus far. Britain and France have placed great emphasis on homegrown microcircuits and computers for national telecommunications systems.

Moreover, there are budding Silicon Valleys in Ireland, Italy, East Germany, West Germany, Yugoslavia, Poland, China and the Soviet Union. "Most knowledgeable analysts," says Bob Harrington of Dean Witter Reynolds of Palo Alto, "see the semiconductor industry emerging as one of the world's major industries in the twenty-first century. Our $6 billion semiconductor industry of 1979 may be a $30 billion semiconductor industry by 1989. Foreign governments do not want to be left out. We have the technology and the world wants it."

And increasingly, the world is getting it. Semiconductors may be a $100 billion market by the end of the century, and by the late seventies the roster of Silicon Valley investors read like a Who's Who of the Western world's industrial titans. Philips of The Netherlands, the fifth largest non-U.S. industrial conglomerate in the world, has long owned Sunnyvale's Signetics Corporation through a U.S. subsidiary. Siemans A.G., a $13 billion West German multinational, snatched Silicon Valley's Litronix away from rival bidder Honeywell and picked up a 20 percent interest in Advanced Micro Devices. Robert Bosch *GmbH,* another large West German firm, checked into the American market with several substantial investments, among them a 25 percent interest in American Microsystems of Santa Clara. Northern Telecom of Canada took a minority interest in two more valley firms (Intersil and Monolithic Memories), while Nippon Electric, one of Japan's largest producers of electronic products, brushed aside several interested American firms for total ownership of Electronic Arrays, for $8.5 million in cash.

In the summer of 1980 the Commission of the European Economic Community called upon its nine member governments to cooperate in a joint funding venture to further reduce European dependence on American microtechnology. Individual governments have pursued the same approach. The British government, in league with Richard Petritz, a seasoned veteran of the Texas microelectronic scene, launched a new company called Inmos International. To staff it, Petritz lured away enough Mostek engineers to prompt a lawsuit. The French government's Centre National d'Etudes des Télécommunications (CNET), an agency of the French Telecommunications Authority, plans to double its investment in VLSI circuit research by 1983. To do so, France went right to the source, buying $1.4 billion worth of basic technology from National Semiconductor. Meanwhile, Matra Harris, a joint venture of Harris Corporation and the French Matra group, struck a deal with Intel for the transfer of still more basic technology in return for future royalties. The same pattern can be seen in Italy, West Germany and other European nations.

For the most part, this invasion by cash-rich and semiconductor-hungry Western nations, the depth of which has only been hinted at here, has been welcomed by Silicon Valley as a troop of financial white knights coming to the rescue of an industry battered on all sides by relentless competition from the true foe, the Japanese. (See "Japan, Inc." at the end of this chapter.) The Japanese have engaged in outright buy-ins, and they have established their own U.S.-based engineering subsidiaries, such as Matshushita's R&D facility in Palo Alto, while selling aggressively into the American market. What particularly rankles Silicon Valley executives about these legal entities, or "listening posts," as they are known, is the opportunity they present for gaining access to hard-won U.S. technology, either by copying American chip designs or hiring away American engineers. Companies like Nippon, Toshiba, Fujitsu, Hitachi and others, some of which are backed by financial subsidies from the Japanese government's Ministry of International Trade and Industry, have cut a large path through the American market and can now claim almost half of the U.S. market for the most technologically advanced memory chips now widely available.

Seeking relief in the form of tariff revisions, Dr. Andrew Grove of Intel, testifying before a hearing of the U.S. International Trade Commission, pointed to the fate of the American television industry, all but blown apart by Japanese competition. Lest it be noted that America has, by and large, survived the beating taken by its television industry, semiconductor executives are quick to point out that televisions do not normally end up in the guts of missiles and intelligence-gathering satellites. Finally, as if all this were not enough, the long-standing American dominance in microelectronics has been threatened by the Soviet Union and communist bloc nations. Through industrial espionage, chip theft, black market transactions and other means, the Soviets have shown that they do not intend to be left out of the scramble for a share of Silicon Valley's secrets. The competitive milieu that is Silicon Valley has changed considerably since the days when Fairchild Semiconductor was American owned and the premier microelectronics laboratory in the world.

Fear of Spying

In 1978, Larry Worth, a purchasing manager for National Semiconductor, had a rather unusual phone conversation with Andrew Moore, owner of a small import-export business specializing in medical and electronic products. Moore let it be known that Intel trade secrets, including computer tapes and glass "masks" used in the process of manufacturing Intel's lucrative 2114 high-speed computer memory chip, as well as information on the company's tightly guarded "HMOS" chip-building process, were available for a price. The 2114 could be had for a couple hundred thousand, but the total package would be far more costly. Would National be interested?

Unfortunately for the caller, National was not. After the talk, Worth dutifully beelined straight for the office of National's president, Charlie Sporck, and recounted the conversation. Sporck alerted Intel and the Santa Clara police, while Worth called back to arrange a meeting. According to subsequent court testimony, Moore told Worth that a friend of his was in Europe peddling the Intel material to manufacturers there, but was expected back in a week.

A week later, at the behest of the police, Worth met with Moore and his associate, Peter Gopal, president of a Sunnyvale consulting firm. Gopal "kept stating [the materials] were Intel's," Worth later testified. "And then I asked him how and he said that he had inside people that made those things available to him." Worth added, "He then turned to me and said that if I would get him any current revision masks out of National, he would pay me $10,000 for every one I could get out."

Worth arranged a second meeting and told the two men that he would bring along a National engineer for further negotiations. On September 25, 1978, the four met for lunch at the Pruneyard in San Jose. Unknown to the would-be sellers, but not to Worth or the police, the man posing as a National engineer was Tom Dunlap, then Intel's administrator of technology exchange. Dunlap, wired with a transmitter, recorded the conversation and arranged for a purchase of the Intel 2114 memory data for $100,000. Two days later, with the police outside eavesdropping on his transmitter, Dunlap, posing as a prospective buyer, showed up at a Santa Clara apartment carrying a briefcase containing $25,000 in traveler's checks as the initial payment.

DUNLAP (*studying material*): And these are all supposed to be Intel's numbers?

SELLER: If you follow all these numbers you'll get the exact device.

DUNLAP: This is what you use or this is what Intel uses?

SELLER: This is what Intel uses and that's what I did to it — it's exact. . . .

DUNLAP: For the 2114?

SELLER: Yes.

DUNLAP: This is really hard to say.

SELLER: Well, when I deliver the process I will deliver you also some working units.

. . .

DUNLAP: Okay, you're supposed to call your Intel [contact].

SELLER: He doesn't want to give his number because there's only a very small percentage of people at Intel that know the number . . . so Intel security can immediately eliminate a certain group of people and just concentrate on one group only. He doesn't want that to happen. I think I've shown good faith so far. . . .

At a prearranged signal (Dunlap: "So we have a deal?"), the police entered the apartment and arrested the two sellers on charges that included receiving stolen property and theft of trade secrets. That afternoon police seized documents, glass plates and process specifications in possession of the two men from Intel, National, and several other electronics firms.

The case turned out to be of interest not just to Intel and the other companies, but to the Commerce Department as well. Given that the United States is not exactly cozy with the Russians of late, and that from computer memory chips like Intel's 2114 come high-speed computers, and from high-speed computers come high-speed computer systems which serve as the brains of sophisticated defense weaponry, the Intel theft was one of the cases cited in a confidential Commerce Department report leaked to the press in February of 1980 on the subject of illegal high-technology sales to the Soviets. The report stated that technical data relating to Intel's microelectronic circuits allegedly had been hand-carried to Austria from 1976 to 1978 and then "trans-shipped" to Poland, East Germany, the Soviet Union and possibly the People's Republic of China.

"That appears to be true," said Intel's Roger Borovoy, as the case progressed. "There is some suspicion that the designs stolen from Intel got to the Eastern European bloc. The accused had a number of Eastern European sales of various things, to a source the Commerce Department was familiar with. While the evidence I've seen does not show sales of any Intel masks to that source, I would be very surprised if some of them did not go. If the facts I have become aware of are proven true, this guy was not your basic honest engineer." (Gopal was later convicted of certain charges related to the theft, while Moore and a third man pleaded guilty to associated charges. Notices of appeal have been filed in the case.)

Your basic honest engineer — and your basic honest scientist, salesman and process technologist — began to come in for a good deal of scrutiny in Silicon Valley. By 1981 fear of industrial spying by offshore interlopers had grown so keen that Fairchild was accused of turning away a tour bus sponsored by the American Association for the Advancement of Science. Fairchild said the bus was running late and could not be accommodated in the allotted time. But some tour bus members thought otherwise, charging that the real reason was the threat of industrial espionage by foreign nationals aboard the bus. A year earlier the U.S. government had imposed a nearly total ban on high-technology sales to the Soviets, and in light of the potential pathways to the Eastern bloc suggested by dozens of cases which have surfaced in recent years, the U.S. Commerce Department had taken to reminding high-technology companies that even "oral exchanges of information with foreign nationals constitutes the export of technical data." Curiously enough, at the time of the tour bus incident, Fairchild's very halls were crawling with foreign nationals, but in that case the flag was French, and friendly. In 1979 Schlumberger Ltd. of France, a $2.6 billion multinational, purchased the progenitor of Silicon Valley outright for about $350 million in cash. Foreign nationals *own* Fairchild, a tidy irony which serves to point out the extent of the offshore invasion.

Acquisition, of course, is a legal means of gaining access to Silicon Valley technology, but it is not an option open to the Soviets, and there are a variety of other ways to go about it. Chips, chip design data, chip processes, chip production equipment and other assorted trade secrets can be stolen, copied or counterfeited, and then distributed through various clandestine black market networks. In most cases, where they ultimately end up is impossible to determine, but there is no longer any doubt that some of the trade secrets are ending up in Russia.

Since the goal of semiconductor espionage, by the Russians or anyone else, is to acquire the design of America's most advanced microchips, buying stolen masks and process secrets is the most cost-effective route. The most popular method, however, is to copy the chips themselves, since chips are easier to acquire. When the Russians copy American chips, it is considered a threat to national security. When the Japanese do it, it is considered a highly questionable trade practice. When U.S. semiconductor companies do it to each other, it is often called "reverse engineering," winked at, and in some cases even encouraged. The problem results from the exceedingly fine line the semiconductor industry attempts to draw between building a similar chip and building a circuit-by-circuit copy. Reverse engineering, the former case, is the euphemism applied to the industry-wide practice of buying, photographing and studying a competitor's commercially available microchip, thereby coming up with the design of it in reverse. It requires more engineering time and talent than copying a chip from masks and data tapes such as those allegedly stolen from Intel. And it is tolerated in the semiconductor industry because it results in an "informal second source" — a company offering a functional equivalent, if not an exact copy, of a competitor's chip — and the more companies producing a chip, the more likely the chip will become an industry-wide standard in its class. Normally, this is done by formal second-sourcing under license, but as long as a reverse-engineered copy is slightly different from the original — slightly bigger or slightly smaller is enough — few lawsuits result. (Advanced Micro Device's reverse engineering of the Intel 8080 was what got its microprocessor line off to a flying start.) For years the industry even tolerated reverse engineering on the part of the Japanese. When American engineers showed slides of new chip layouts at trade shows, no one doubted the source of the flashbulb explosion that generally ensued. It was more a cause of amusement than concern, and a clear indication of America's superiority.

But in the face of growing Japanese competition and increasing acquisitiveness by the Soviets, all this has changed. Chip copying of various kinds is now known as "chip piracy" — especially when it is practiced by foreign competitors. According to Roger Borovoy, Intel's legal counsel, "All we're saying is that people who want to make photographic copies ought to pay their dues. They shouldn't get it free. The Intels of the world can't afford to spend millions of dollars designing a complex chip when somebody else can spend a hundred thousand copying it."

In testimony before a House Judiciary Subcommittee on a bill which would extend copyright protection to the design "masks" used to manufacture microchips, Dr. Grove of Intel displayed photos of two Intel memory circuits along with what he said were two pirated copies from Russia and from Toshiba Corporation of Japan. Clearly, said Grove, these were straight copies of the Intel device and as things stood, there was nothing Intel could do about it.

The semiconductor industry is a substantial exporter, Grove testified, and if pirated chips begin to flood back into the American market, or turn up in Soviet defense systems, "We would suffer in balance of payments, stability of the dollar, and even in superiority of our military equipment as a result of losing our semiconductor technology leadership position."

Strong words. So it was with some surprise that the committee considered testimony *against* the bill from National Semiconductor and Fairchild. In a prepared statement signed by John Finch, vice-president and general manager for semiconductor components, National claimed that "The true beneficiaries of this law would be the foreign competitors of the U.S. semiconductor industry." As evidence, National pointed to a 1977 Federal Trade Commission staff report on the semiconductor industry, which said, in effect, that copying each other's chips is what made the American semiconductor industry the world leader in the first place. Add to that the tendency on the part of talented, highly paid engineers to hop from company to company, and the result is technological innovation, healthy competition and growth. What had started out as an industry plea for protection against foreign chip piracy had come down to one Silicon Valley company arguing with another over the practice of reverse engineering here at home. (To further muddy the waters, the Toshiba chip later turned out to be not a copy, but a reverse-engineered design that only *looked* like a copy.) To the committee, it was all a bit confusing. As one congressman politely concluded, "There is a very fine line between reverse engineering and copying, a line that I as a lawyer have some problem defining."

In the end, it is uncertain whether copyright protection would do much toward thwarting the chip pirates anyway, even if thwarting them was unanimously seen as desirable. Microcircuit designs — the "topography" of the chip — traditionally have not been held to be copyrightable, any more than the mass-produced products of industrial machine tools are copyrightable. The additional argument can be made that chip designs, like computer software, are the creative products of a human mind and deserving of the kind of copyright protection extended to books, works of music and, lately, new microorganisms. However, copyright or patent protection for semiconductor trade secrets would be relatively weak and difficult to enforce. The industry may be better off in the long run with what it already has — trade secret protection, violations of which can be litigated at the state level. This may prove even more true in the future, as some legal experts argue that a company cannot legally copyright what is already a trade secret in the first place. Moreover, while trade secret laws vary from state to state, a trade secret generally is considered to be whatever a company says it is, and once covered, the protection never expires.

Added legal protection would do little to stem chip copying and chip espionage, and even less to thwart another form of micro theft — chip counterfeiting. Compared to copying chips and selling purloined trade secrets, stealing and counterfeiting chips is a crude approach, but it can be just as profitable a way of benefiting from someone else's research and development investment, and stolen chips are likely to end up almost anywhere. Unfortunately for unsuspecting purchasers, what begins as an exercise in gray market greed can lead to unexpected ramifications, as the following case attests.

In the last few years, one of the hottest parts coming out of Silicon Valley has been a memory chip known as an ep/rom, for erasable programmable read-only memory. Demand for the device has been keen; a condition which is the primary requirement for the birth of a flourishing "gray" market. There is always room for some fine tuning of a fast-moving marketplace by enterprising third parties. Surplus distribution — the practice of brokering chips between a customer who has more than he needs and a customer who has fewer than he wants — is a perfectly legal business practice. But it is also an ideal pipeline for passing stolen or counterfeit chips.

In 1978, the Medical Products Division of Avco Corporation purchased 2,600 Advanced Micro Devices ep/rom chips through Cramer Electronics, a franchised distributor of AMD products. Avco needed the chips for its Model 10 intra-aortic balloon pumps, a sophisticated line of medical equipment used in hospital cardiac-care wards. The need for stringent quality control in the manufacture of such life-support products is obvious, so it was with considerable alarm that Avco discovered, after some 300 units of the Model 10 had been shipped, that several of the machines had failed mysteriously while in operation. For Avco, it meant a potential whirlwind of product liability suits and countersuits. When the company's field team returned with the burned-out circuit boards, the culprit appeared to be the memory chips from AMD. Avco, it seemed, had been sold a bill of goods — bad parts, rejects destined for the scrap heap.

Meanwhile, Monroe Calculator, a division of Litton Industries, had purchased 18,000 AMD ep/rom chips for use in a line of accounting machines, and the same failures were cropping up. While Monroe and Avco descended angrily on AMD and Cramer, demanding an explanation, Avco sent telegrams to hospitals warning them not to use the Model 10s and its field team feverishly swapped bad circuit boards for good. AMD, which had no idea what was going on, quickly discovered three salient facts: A check of its inventory lists showed more parts in Cramer's inventory than AMD had shipped them. After retrieving a handful of the bogus circuits for testing, microscopic examination of the AMD trademark embossed on the circuit packages revealed that the AMD logo had been counterfeited. And further testing confirmed that the circuits had been rejected during AMD's normal testing program for a variety of defects. At some point between AMD's scrap bin and the metal reclaimers, the failed parts had been stolen. Someone was counterfeiting AMD's trademark and selling the parts as genuine. And it was not too long before the parts began surfacing at British and German firms as well.

The scent of impending lawsuits hung over the affair. And there was the nasty upcoming business of tracing the counterfeit pipeline, tracking down the international connections, and putting an end to it, with the possibility of the trail leading straight to an inside man at AMD. For its part, Cramer Electronics said it had purchased the parts in good faith from small surplus distributors. "Cramer management never at any time had any knowledge these were other than bona fide parts," Cramer's president told the trade weekly *Electronic News.* "We don't know whether they were counterfeited, whether they were stolen from AMD, or what."

After Cramer revealed the source of the surplus parts, AMD dropped Cramer as its distributor and filed a $1 million trademark-infringement suit against two California surplus distributors, Gentronix Corporation of Hawthorne, California, and A-OK Electronics of Los Angeles. In an industry where "administrative handling" is often the preferred approach to such affairs, AMD laudably went public with the whole mess, but the search for the source of the rejected parts fizzled out completely in the court proceedings that followed. According to Tom Skornia, AMD's vice-president and legal counsel, "We were forced to settle out of court after one of the defendants repeatedly took the fifth as to how he came by the bogus devices. Our own investigation is continuing."

For Silicon Valley veterans, all this has a distinctly familiar ring to it. In the past few years, reported thefts of chips and chip designs have risen markedly, as have incidents involving counterfeit chips. In case after case, the discovery of a theft leads to a search for the illicit pipeline. The discovery may take the form of an inventory discrepancy or an inside tip or, in the case of untested chips, a complaint from a customer about abnormally high failure rates on chips it has purchased at bargain-basement prices. Once again, state and federal investigators undertake the torturous process of tracing the path of the stolen goods through the murky channels of the industrial espionage world. In the end, very few court cases produce a definitive answer to the question of where the material turned up, or who stole it in the first place. Out-of-court settlements, bargained pleas and lengthy appeals are commonplace. The twilight nature of gray- and black-market distribution, coupled with a general corporate reluctance to divulge the intimate details of such incidents, renders the formal prosecution of chip crimes into an uphill battle at best. And yet, since the trail so often leads to European countries believed by government officials to be hotbeds of high-technology espionage, there is usually the suspicion that some of the circuits, once again, may have gotten to the Russians.

In some cases, stolen and counterfeited circuits have turned up in the American defense community as well. In one documented case of semiconductor counterfeiting, stolen circuits were marked with a false military testing designation, indicating that the chips had passed the rigorous testing program required of manufacturers who sell high-reliability devices to the military. Some of the falsely labeled circuits were the kind being used by the Defense Department in such programs as the F-4 fighter plane and the Chaparral and Lance missile systems.

However, prosecutors made little headway, after three years of scrutinizing shipping documents, in proving that defense weapons systems had failed because of the faulty circuits. "It's not likely you're going to find out," observed the presiding judge. "When a missile is over the water and it goes down, you can't determine the cause of the failure." The judge added that "This is one of the worst white collar crimes. In wartime, it would be sabotage, which carries the death penalty. We don't know where the components have gone."

AMD's Tom Skornia provides the coda. "It's been very tough to get the authorities aroused on technology crimes. And if the case does go to trial, you put the jury to sleep. Nobody was raped, nobody had a gun, nobody was murdered."

With a smile, Skornia adds that "the lesson seems to be, never counterfeit silicon chips — during wartime."

By late 1980, there was no longer any doubt that American chips and chip designs were somehow getting to the Russians. Up until then it had been held by many that the U.S. maintained a commanding ten-year lead over the Russians in microelectronics technology. But a sampling of Soviet microprocessor chips, obtained by the government of Hungary and given over to Control Data Corp. for analysis in the U.S., quickly narrowed official estimates of the "circuit gap" to three years and gaining. Control Data dissected the chips in minute technical detail and reported to the U.S. defense community that the Soviet K80IK80.77 chip was a reverse-engineered design based on the Intel 8080A MPU — American industry's standard until quite recently. "While the [Russian] choice of design rules, materials and processes is conservative and probably expensive by our standards," said the Control Data report, "there can be no doubt that Soviet semiconductor processors can provide them with just about any of the off-the-shelf devices used in this country."

In light of this discovery, and others like it, federal law-enforcement officials awakened to the fact that high-technology trade embargoes are flouted by the Soviets with extraordinary ease. FBI Director William Webster decried the fact that Silicon Valley had become a watering hole for "hostile intelligence gatherers" bent on stealing "industrial technology that transcends mere military secrets." An assistant U.S. Attorney in Los Angeles heading a grand jury probe of high-tech espionage told the *Wall Street Journal* that "The Silicon Valley and Southern California are the cradles of the illegal and clandestine shipment of strategic goods to the Soviet Bloc." William Perry, former Undersecretary of Defense for research and engineering, told a House Armed Services Subcommittee that the Soviet Ryad I and Ryad II computers were copies of the IBM 360 and 370 respectively, and that copies of small computers from Digital Equipment Corporation were in the offing. The American versions came to Russia by way of diverted shipments and in some cases, "stealing them off trains in Poland." Dr. Perry added that the Soviets "plan to base their computer technology on Western technology as directly as possible, even to the extent of copying the circuits — circuit-by-circuit."

There are now almost as many keenly interested federal agencies as there are suspected cases of espionage — the Commerce Department, the State Department, the Customs Service, the Department of Defense, the CIA, the FBI, and so on. At times this swarm of federal investigatory enthusiasm tends to overwhelm the yeoman efforts of the beleaguered Santa Clara County Sheriff's Department, which to its credit has evolved a special task force on high-technology espionage to deal with a form of crime not normally encountered by local law-enforcement officers. None of this is likely to have much effect in the long run, however. "No wonder the Soviet Union is able to produce microprocessors equivalent to the Intel 8080, and Robotron of East Germany and Tesla of Czechoslovakia are said to have prototype microprocessors and 16K RAMS," writes Jack Robertson, Washington correspondent for *Electronic News*. Robertson goes on to argue that "Continued

U.S. intransigent controls on exports of microprocessors and LSI devices are ridiculous, considering the ease with which Communist customers can buy such devices in the West. A recent official disclosure by Hungary confirms that engineers of its Videoton electronics firm openly purchased Intel 8080 microprocessors in Munich and carried them in luggage into the Communist country. An incredulous U.S. embassy in Budapest refused to believe this — until U.S. attachés were able to repeat the exercise in a test trip to Munich." Perhaps, as has been wryly suggested, the United States should legalize high-technology trade with the Soviets, so that the American electronics industry can at least profit from the inevitable. Certainly the current ban is one of the least effective embargoes ever erected.

It has been pointed out by CIA director William Casey and others that the American semiconductor industry may have brought much of this upon themselves, eager as they have been to sell technology internationally in the "naked" form of technology transfer agreements, patent rights, licensing arrangements, and a widespread tolerance of reverse engineering. U.S. semiconductor producers sold off their birthright, runs the criticism, and now complain about debilitating foreign competition and a deteriorating balance of trade. Despite the extent of the foreign invasion thus far discussed, the primary backdrop against which all such fears for the future of U.S. chip makers are raised is the rising tide of competition from the Japanese microelectronics industry. The Japanese didn't steal the technology except in the ambiguous sense of reverse engineering, and they did not buy it either. Instead, they developed it through an unprecedented joint effort between private companies and the Japanese government, an effort which pumped massive government funds into the Japanese program to overtake the U.S. in the production of advanced VLSI circuits. And they recently have brought the fruits of this effort to the U.S. market by engaging in a form of competition Silicon Valley well understands — price-cutting —

and by placing an abiding emphasis on stringent quality control procedures. So successful has the Japanese thrust proven that many Silicon Valley executives now picture themselves as a distinctly endangered species.

Japan, Inc.

About the time that the flag of the Rising Sun first rose over Electronic Arrays, Japan's first major Silicon Valley acquisition, Jerry Sanders of Advanced Micro Devices met privately with then Prime Minister Fukuda to discuss worsening trade relations between their respective countries. After the meeting, a reporter phoned up to ask how it had gone. The executive paused for a moment. "Well," said Sanders at last, "he didn't tell me to fuck off."

As it stood, that sentiment passed for optimism, and there has been little improvement in the intervening years. The problem began in the mid-seventies with the Japanese VLSI project, a joint venture the funding for which was split 40–60 between Japan's Ministry of International Trade and Industry (MITI) and five private firms — Hitachi, Fujitsu, Mitsubishi, Nippon and Toshiba. By the end of the five-year program the Japanese had spent almost as much on VLSI research as the American semiconductor industry received as direct government aid since 1958. MITI further bolstered this effort by nurturing its microelectronics industry through tax breaks, attractive bank loans and accelerated depreciation rules. In order to protect the home market while it grew, the government pushed a "Buy Japanese" policy, brushed aside American calls for more equitable import tariffs, and discouraged the establishment of U.S. subsidiaries and marketing arms. Various forms of protectionism allowed the Japanese increasing penetration of the U.S. semiconductor market — upwards of 40 percent for advanced memory chips — while holding the Americans to about 15 percent of the Japanese market. Japan, in the eyes of many semiconductor executives, does not play by the same rules that everyone else does in the international market.

To answer the challenge, thirty-three American semiconductor firms, most of them headquartered in Silicon Valley, banded together to form the Semiconductor Industry Association and began taking the case against the Japanese to Washington. Texas Instruments, having somehow found its way into Japan with wholly-owned subsidiaries as early as 1968, was conspicuously absent from the SIA roster, if not from the growing anti-Japanese chorus. The SIA asked for redress in the form of tariff reductions, better tax breaks and more attention to the problems of rising capital costs. In a hearing before the U.S. International Trade Commission one commissioner wondered aloud why one of America's most robust private industries was having such a time of it against a government-funded "planned economy," AMD's Jerry Sanders replied: "What we are talking about is thirty-three companies taking on the sovereign nation of Japan. That's not a question of capitalism versus a planned economy. That's a sovereign nation against thirty-three companies." Beyond that, Sanders admitted, "We have genuinely not developed the remedies."

The commission remained unimpressed, and later issued a report suggesting that the Americans were losing market share to the Japanese because of sagging productivity levels rather than unfair trade practices. Some executives began urging a "Buy American" policy on the part of SIA members and customers to offset the "Buy Japanese" policy they perceived in Japan. This was a somewhat curious pitch for the industry to be making, since Silicon Valley itself buys Japanese circuits from time to time to offset spot shortages.

Then in 1980 Hewlett–Packard dropped a bombshell that markedly altered the course of the debate. In 1977 Hewlett–Packard began to turn to the Japanese for 16K RAM chips when domestic suppliers ran short. Three years later, after extensive testing, the company issued a report stating without equivocation that Japanese semiconductor chips were of a higher quality than equivalent U.S. brands. Failure and rejection rates were far lower, meaning less problems for customers, and testing procedures were far more stringent. Rather than concentrating on detecting bad chips after manufacture, the Japanese had been concentrating on building chips that didn't fail in the first place, or so ran the argument. Purchasing managers from Honeywell and other American firms doing business with the Japanese tended to agree. This of course is what the Japanese had been contending all along, and there wasn't much that American chip makers could offer by way of rebuttal except to reiterate complaints about government subsidies and unfair trade practices, and to contend that the quality had been exaggerated.

How can this be? How can a tiny trove of islands rival the best American industrial efforts time after time, from cars to steel to TVs and microchips? And, in light of suggestions that the situation is as urgent as the Sputnik scare was in its day, what does the Japanese challenge portend for the future?

Noyce, an ardent fan of conservative economist Milton Friedman, sees it as a question of who will dominate the post-industrial age, and puts the question in social, rather than simply economic terms: "Tariffs and the other obvious issues aren't really the problem. It is perhaps more like the mechanisms of the Industrial Revolution. Britain had control of that, because they started the movement early. They clearly rose to a pinnacle of power and standard of living in Britain as a result of it, and then just as clearly screwed it up — by immediate consumption philosophies that crept into their social and political structure.

"The character of *this* industry, this industrial revolution — innovation intensive, rapidly growing, intensely competitive — really played into America's hands. Because America is an enterprise where the pioneer is still admissible. We won that game. Other societies not organized to promote innovation and entrepreneurial activity got left behind. But as the business becomes more mature, in the sense that it's becoming more capital intensive, the elements of success are changing, too. And several of the elements are playing into the hands of the Japanese winning the next round."

In many cases, these elements are simply American practices magnified — a zeal for marketing, standardization as a means of cutting costs, and obsession with productivity and market share. Competitively, the Japanese have learned much from observing the practices of IBM, Intel and the rest. And yet there are very real differences, particularly in terms of corporate management and overall social structure. Japan has emphasized export, spends very little on national defense and has a higher personal savings rate than the U.S. Company loyalty and lifelong employment are still quite common, as is the subordination of corporate goals to national goals. Japan has almost as many engineers as the U.S. — but far fewer lawyers, and hence, less corporate litigation. It has emphasized close cooperation between business and government in order to execute extensive research and development projects. Through government subsidy, Japanese manufacturers enjoy an assured source of capital and thus can tolerate thinner profit margins and lower prices than can earnings-obsessed American counterparts. In short, a willingness to view government as partner rather than adversary or misguided referee is a major distinguishing feature between Japan, Inc. and thirty-three American semiconductor companies. And the payoffs have been many: state-of-the-art LSI circuits, bubble technology, electron-beam machines, Josephson junctions, assorted IBM-style computers, and rapid penetration of world markets at the expense of America's share.

Denied the presence of an all-important first market in the form of an expanding defense establishment, perhaps the Japanese may be forgiven for protecting and subsidizing the home market while it grew. Federal support has been essential to the American semiconductor industry — at least in the beginning. In a world market, however, obvious problems arise when one government continues the practice of such fruitful cooperation, while the other does not. If equitable world competition is to be established, either the Japanese government will have to cut back on the nourishment it extends to the native electronics garden — an unlikely proposition, since MITI plans to follow the VLSI joint project with a new five-year advanced computer systems research program — or the American government will have to come back into the game in a major way — equally doubtful, in light of Silicon Valley's proud entrepreneurial stance. U.S. chip makers have gone to Washington not to ask for money, but to ask for changes in the rules so that they can continue to make money on their own. That is the well-known American tradition, and in the current political climate of enthusiasm for deregulation and untrammeled private competition, it is not likely to change for a while. Even with the press of the Japanese, calls for large-scale joint efforts between industry and government tend to meet with a lukewarm reception in Silicon Valley, where engineering managers are generally quite confident they can spend the money more wisely all by themselves.

An interim funding approach, midway between state planning and the free market free-for-all, has been proposed by Control Data Corporation, a prominent computer innovator concerned about the wave of Japanese VLSI-based products now breaking on American shores: a national research and development cooperative of sorts, open to any American computer or semiconductor company. Control Data's concern was with the economies of scale operating in Japan's VLSI effort and the feeling that only IBM and Bell Labs are big enough to compete effectively. As for the question of why semiconductor companies would want to share their secrets with customers and sometimes competitors in the computer business, Control Data president Robert Price suggested that the incentive may be "survival. Most of the smaller firms have been 'conglomerated' or integrated with someone else. They still exist, but their survival now belongs to someone else." He characterized the semiconductor industry as "struggling with long-term business strategy" and added: "Either the U.S. computer industry will adopt a strategy of technological cooperation on a broad basis . . . or there will be isolation and sickness." It is not clear, however, where small, innovative start-up companies would fit into this scheme.

The Japanese story is all too familiar to Americans, in the form of cars, radios, cameras, televisions and other products. Commonly, the fears this engenders take the form of questions such as, "What can we learn from the Japanese, and how can we go about doing what they do?" One answer is that they are simply doing what we do, only better. But this is not altogether true, and there is another way of looking at it. What would we have to give up?

Corporate mobility for one, and highly paid labor for another. And also a long-standing reluctance to intertwine private pursuit of profit with state-directed planning and control. And "immediate consumption" philosophies, if Noyce's assessment proves true. As for government support, U.S. lawmakers must come to realize that any industrial nation built upon microelectronics now depends upon microelectronics; that as a technology and as an industry, microelectronics has much to do with the allocation of world resources, the economics of developed and developing countries, national defense strategy and so on. An unfettered, untended, unaided and unregulated free market should not be the sole locus of decision-making in such matters. Moreover, there is a need for a greater realization that the present competitive structure often breeds short-range profit at the expense of long-term vision. Government funding may not be needed. Government-industry cooperation clearly is.

And further, the industry might try to become a bit more receptive to joint research efforts. The government, in turn, might realize that the semiconductor and computer industry rarely does anything remotely deserving of a Golden Fleece Award, and try not to bury participating companies in the usual blizzard of qualifications procedures and paperwork. The Japanese would be well advised to play fairer on tariffs and to relax their internal discipline, as they have begun to do, to allow American companies in, as joint ventures and as wholly-owned subsidiaries. For their part, in return for these concessions, American executives might do well to accept the Japanese as a legitimate and wholly justifiable presence in the U.S. market, profit from those Japanese quality-control attitudes which can reasonably be incorporated into American manufacturing, and get on with what they do best — innovating and competing.

All of these problematic relationships with the Europeans, with the Soviets and with the Japanese are painful symptoms of a new world economic order, tied together by microelectronics-based transnational communication of information, and one which is no longer totally dependent on the U.S. for the basic technology that makes it go. U.S. industry will play a changed role now that microelectronics technology has at once diffused and consolidated internationally. Just as the microprocessor was a way of decentralizing the power of computers — electronic logic for free — so the industry is decentralizing, its intelligence now distributed throughout the developed world. As for matters of innovation, production, market share and future profits, the outlook is mixed at best. As producers, the U.S. may well be forced to settle for a diminished role in the age of VLSI.

It would be tragic indeed if these concerns boil down, in the end, to nothing more than a them-or-us, one winner, one loser–style battle for market share against the Japanese. Cooperation, not just competition, is needed. For there is nothing so disrespectful of national boundaries as microelectronics.

CHAPTER EIGHT

Consumer Electronics and Tales of the Home Computer

... The coming decade will, one hopes, give us sufficient time to prepare for the impact of what may well turn out to be the most powerful technology to be introduced in this century, one that could profoundly affect our lives both as individuals and as members of families.
— JOEL MOSES, *professor of computer science at MIT*

Enthusiasts for the home computer struggle with problems that could arise only as consequences of the triumph of the kind of mass-marketing techniques that gave us, for example, the multimillion-dollar deodorant industry. ...
— JOSEPH WEIZENBAUM, *professor of computer science at MIT*

The Digital Watch Disaster

Most American consumers first encountered the microchip in the form of the hand-held or pocket calculator. The personal calculator for home or office was a natural use for the microprocessor as a commercial consumer product. Almost any simple MPU chip would do, for basic arithmetic, algebra, even calculus and trigonometry. The required circuitry for such calculators fit into a space no bigger than the rectangular display window, and the calculator's actual size is limited only by the size of the human finger and the resolution of the eye. It made obvious sense for semiconductor companies to view the pocket calculator in terms of "added value" — the modest cost of a calculator was still several times the cost of producing the chips and packaging them in plastic calculator cases. Most of the cost was in the plastic itself. It looked like an excellent way to sell about $10 worth of chips for $200, in the early days, as well as a lucrative route to vertical integration — selling not just building blocks but finished products themselves. Throughout the first half of the seventies, scores of companies in America and Japan flooded consumer markets with a wide variety of small calculators at an even wider variety of prices. For consumers, it was a bit confusing. If someone bought a calculator at Christmas for $149.95, someone else was sure to buy the same model next Christmas for $69.95, and soon after that, for $29.95, at which point equivalent calculators on the same shelf would be selling at all three prices. Without giving the matter a great deal of thought, semiconductor companies that entered the business simply priced their consumer calculators the same way they priced everything else — according to the dictates of the semiconductor learning curve. Of course calculators got cheaper every year, and by a considerable margin. That was the way of microchips, and how could it be anything but a boon to the buyer? Every year, the consumer gets more for less and everybody makes out nicely all around.

Semiconductor companies pursued this same value-added philosophy into digital watches. The digital watch was an even purer consumer play than the calculator, because it put chip makers in direct competition with consumer product companies like Timex and the Swiss watchmaking firms. In the early seventies chip makers also began to dabble in more indirect consumer markets, such as selling to appliance makers for microwave ovens, washing machines and various "white goods," but the digital watch market looked especially hot. Almost everyone owns a timepiece, and as for established competition, the semiconductor people presumably would have price on their side, as they always did. Once they increased the manufacturing volume on this new chip product — in this case a consumer "end product" like the calculator — they stood to make a good deal of money, provided that consumers were persuaded to trade in their dial-and-sweep-hand watches for the new "wrist instruments" that displayed time as Arabic numerals composed of deep red light-emitting-diodes (LEDs) or cool green-gray liquid-crystal-displays (LCDs).

As it turned out, customer resistance was not much of a problem. Digital watches sold well, as calculators had before them. They came in stripped-down, low-priced plastic models, and in higher-priced versions with added features like alarm buzz and stopwatch mode and even a little built-in calculator which the wearer punched up with a tiny stylus. Everybody owned one. The premier of China wore one. And as always, prices fell inexorably, except for those manufacturers who shrewdly ignored the learning curve and stabilized higher prices by piling on extra "bells and whistles." In all, more than twenty semiconductor companies plunged into the market during the seventies, either with finished watches under their own brand names, or with semifinished watch modules sold to other suppliers. Timex and the other mainstream watch makers, both here and abroad, went digital as well.

Then something very odd began to happen. Semiconductor companies, whose chips made calculators and digital watches possible, began losing money in those very markets — disastrous amounts, in some cases. And the digital watch market was the worst money loser of all. One by one, throughout the late seventies, chip makers bailed out of the watch business, licking their wounds, drawing down earnings and rewriting annual reports to reflect their losses. A few companies that didn't get out fast enough ended up chasing the digital watch market all the way to bankruptcy court. How could such a sure bet have gone so badly awry?

There was more to the digital watch debacle than fierce competition. To begin with, the semiconductor people were not retail merchandisers. They were engineers for the most part, and not being merchandisers at heart they never really saw the digital watch for what it was — a piece of jewelry. Rather, they saw it as a nicely engineered chip set with good added value — an "end product" with healthy sales potential. And they set about selling digital watches to consumer retailers and distributors very much like they sold microprocessors to the Army, by cranking out huge batches year-round, bombing the price and waiting for the money to roll in. The problem was that if one wanted to sell watches through traditional retail outlets one would have to know something about the jewelry market; and if one wanted to learn something about the jewelry market one would have to bone up on the retail fashion business and the apparel business and the cosmetics trade, plus consumer distribution systems, seasonal inventory adjustments, Madison Avenue–style advertising . . . in short, all kinds of things the semiconductor people knew nothing about. It did not even occur to most of them that the digital watch (like any other watch) would prove to be a highly seasonal item, prone to the traditional retail cycle of a robust Christmas quarter and a thin summer. Chip makers stubbornly produced digital watches — and calculators, and the early video games — in a continuous manufacturing flow; whereas the market called for batch processing to fit the ups and downs of the buying cycle. Inventories were a shambles, prices were almost whimsically malleable, and as for matters of styling, packaging design, shelf placement, and TV spots, chip makers proved to be true babes in the woods.

In the chip business, the cost of marketing a product through the usual engineering sale rarely ran much more than 10 or 15 percent of projected revenues. But in consumer retailing, marketing costs often ran as high as 50 percent. Fifty percent! Just to market the thing!

For Silicon Valley and other chip makers, the digital watch gambit was a disaster, and by 1977 all but the three largest had bailed out, or been squeezed out, or otherwise fumbled the ball. Fairchild, which had confidently erected a new multimillion-dollar complex for its consumer products division, never even managed to occupy it before throwing in the towel. The building stood empty for years as a mute testament to the potential hazards of the retail world. Even Intel, which deviated from its strict industrial strategy long enough to lose a few million with its Microma digital watch subsidiary, ended up selling the operation to Timex.

Bruce Blakkan, who as company president saw Silicon Valley's Litronix through a nearly fatal plunge into digital watches, once offered this terse summation of the problem: "We found the consumer business to be vastly different from the electronic components business. In terms of marketing and product design, they don't mix." In the words of a former manager of a now-defunct digital watch subsidiary, "You would think it would have occurred to these companies that you can't run a railroad the same way you run a fishery. I can see making mistakes the first time out, but over and over again? Calculators, digital watches, video games — you keep seeing the same errors. The consumer makes out like a bandit over the short term, but if the company doesn't stay in business, the buyer ends up with a white elephant."

For an industry widely touted as one which would be selling home microcomputers to families in the space of a few years, it was not an auspicious beginning.

King Pong

Back in 1972, as chip makers dove into calculators, digital watches, microwave ovens and chip sets for vending machines, a young Silicon Valley research engineer invented a new electronic game. He called it Pong. Pong was a small black box with two plastic joysticks, and when it was hooked to an ordinary television set it turned the TV screen into an electronic Ping-Pong table. Two people could compete by controlling the motion of a phosphorescent dot with joystick-controlled "paddles." It was an extremely simple game, and yet, as inconsequential as it might seem, Pong proved to be a watershed product in the history of consumer microelectronics. It led more or less directly to the commercial home computer, and it earned for its inventor, Nolan Bushnell, a personal fortune of $15 million in four years.

Pong was actually a rudimentary version of a popular after-hours campus computer game known as Space War. To the consternation of university officials, student programmers, electrical engineers, mathematicians, artificial intelligence researchers, and assorted computer freaks — the "hackers," as they were known — were crazy about Space War. Hackers were the students who could be seen trickling into university computer centers late at night, carrying a candy bar, a pack of cigarettes and a bedroll. They were not there to do their homework. For hackers, computers were not just a field of professional study, but an ongoing hobby and, at times, a fierce personal obsession. Hackers loved to invent games that could be played on computers, and Space War is said to have started at MIT around 1960. The basic game was a matter of programming graphic representations of rocket ships on a computer display terminal. The object of the game was to shoot down enemy rockets with missiles that could be fired at the touch of a button. Space War combined new methods of programming with new forms of computer-generated visual displays, and as time passed the game grew more varied and complex. Realistic pitch, thrust and yaw could all be controlled via buttons, and when the little blip of a rocket chugged off the upper right-hand corner of the computer screen, it reappeared instantly, missiles blazing, at the lower left-hand corner of the screen. Clever programmers introduced new options. Under attack, a beleaguered rocket could be made to simply disappear, popping up later in some other space-time dimension. The gravitational influence of a nearby planet could pull a rocket into a fatal tailspin. Hackers who were keen on computer graphics learned to program dramatic explosions, even sound effects. Sometimes there was running commentary in the form of messages across the screen: YOU ARE HITTING THE MOON AT A SPEED OF EXACTLY 0276.20 MILES PER HOUR. BLOOD, GUTS, TWISTED METAL.

Among confirmed players, Space War was as much a cult as a hobby, with its own jargon, its own rules, and its own superstars. And when hackers joined the ranks of the electronics and computer companies after graduation, they did not always lose their taste for the game. Early on, universities and corporations made an effort to stamp out Space War. It was a waste of time, it distracted students and employees from more serious work and, worst of all, it was an unauthorized use of large, expensive computer systems. Hackers were finding all sorts of ingenious ways to steal computer time in order to play Space War, and efforts to thwart them only lent to the game an aura of romantic outlawry. As Space War spread and the tournaments grew, players often competed anonymously, adopting science-fiction-style monikers like Tovar and Rem.

As he studied for an electrical engineering degree at the University of Utah during the mid-sixties, Nolan Bushnell played a great deal of Space War on the college's $4 million computer system. Bushnell, however, did not view the game quite the way his fellow students did. Bushnell spent his college summers working at a large Salt Lake City amusement park. Having been promoted from a pitchman for hit-the-bottle games on the midway to manager of the park's entire games division, he made it his specialty to study the behavior, and the spending habits, of parkgoers. After several seasons of this, Bushnell had come to a number of conclusions about the leisure mentality of games customers. The entertainment they sought, judging by the most popular games, wasn't very cerebral. They wanted simple, stimulus-response challenges, a few basic rules, and a test of manual dexterity. Bushnell also noticed that the most popular games were the ones at which parents were willing to park their children so that they could go off on their own for a while, family outing or no.

In the course of the school-year Space War fests, Bushnell sat at the computer punching buttons and firing missiles and thinking about what he had learned at the park. During one of these bouts, it came to him: if there was a coin slot on the computer they used for Space War, students would be lining up ten deep, their pockets bulging with quarters, willing to pay for the privilege of blowing each other up on the video display terminal.

The rest, as they say, is history. Nolan Bushnell took a job in Silicon Valley and began to pare down the Space War concept, aiming at a simpler video game that would appeal to game players in general, and not just campus computer freaks. He also needed a computer that was small enough and cheap enough to make good on the coin-slot idea — a computer that did nothing but accept coins and play a simple electronic game. Along came the microprocessor. In 1972 Bushnell rounded up enough backing to launch Silicon Valley's Atari, the name taken from a term used in the ancient Chinese game of Go. Atari bought microprocessors and assorted chips from other suppliers and simply made games out of them.

The microprocessor-controlled game of Pong was Atari's first product, and it proved astonishingly successful, both as a coin-operated arcade computer and as a home game for use with television screens. Kids loved it. What Bushnell, the former amusement-park manager, had invented was really an electronic babysitter, a device that used a TV screen but was not a television itself. And it really didn't matter if people tired of it. A sale was a sale. Pong was only a starting point.

The basic problem with Pong, from a sales standpoint, stemmed from the fact that Pong was *too* simple. The chips and the instruction set were easy to duplicate, and before long more than two dozen other manufacturers, including some major Silicon Valley chip makers, were in the video games business. Bushnell couldn't do anything about Pong pirates. All they had to do was change a few computer commands, juggle the chip layout, alter the playing field and offer Pong as Video Tennis or Electronic Field Hockey or dozens of other variations. Many semiconductor firms that began manufacturing video games found themselves recapitulating the sorry marketing history of calculators and digital watches, but Atari, whose only business was consumer games, fared better. To combat the boredom factor, Bushnell followed Pong with a slew of programmed cartridges which changed the basic Pong set into other simple games — race track, poker, simple space battle games, word games like Hangman and Scrabble. This had the additional effect of creating new learning curves for each product and corresponding price advantages for Atari.

In 1974 Atari struck a deal with Sears, Roebuck, and Pong games began turning up on Sears' shelves. By 1976 Atari was a

$40-million-a-year leisure-time industry. Companies like Mattel and Warner Communications and Bally, the largest manufacturer of pinball machines, were trooping to Silicon Valley to find out what was going on in this new adjunct of the traditional toys and games business. Bushnell ultimately sold Atari to Warner Communications for $30 million, and by 1980 Atari had broken the $100 million mark in annual sales.

Pong may not have been the first video game, and it may have been viewed by many as a one-shot electronic gimcrack, but in reality it was the first solid salvo in the home computer revolution. By the mid-seventies, the average consumer already was enveloped in microelectronics technology. At some point, almost every daily activity intersected the grid. People told time with digital watches and carried calculators in their pockets. Nearly every use of a Bell System telephone was in reality the use of computers as well. Anyone who owned a late-model luxury car or a microwave oven was growing accustomed to seeing simple measurements like time and temperature expressed digitally, as an LED readout rather than a needle sweeping across a meter. At the grocery store or the department store, a computer tallied purchases as the cash register of old gave way to the microprocessor-based point-of-sale terminal. At the bank, customers made after-hours deposits or withdrawals automatically, using simple computer terminals. In the office, the typewriter and stack of file folders on a secretary's desk were being supplanted by electronic word-processing systems consisting of microprocessors stuffed into remote computer terminals.

The computer at the checkout counter made funny noises and produced a sales slip that looked as if it had been printed in a foreign language. The computer terminal as bank teller broke down periodically. The word-processing computer in the office was confusing and unfamiliar. But the first tiny computer to arrive in many American living rooms, other than calculators and high-priced digital watches, was just a game — an entertaining toy. Pong, with its clever graphics display projected on an ordinary TV screen, rendered the first living room computers about as threatening as going to the movies. Pong was the wedge that opened the door to Space Invaders machines in every bar and shopping center; electronic Christmas toys like Simon and video football; microprocessor-based educational toys for children such as Texas Instrument's Speak and Spell, and home computers like the Radio Shack TRS-80 and the Apple II. While it was possible to lose money in electronic games just as in any other consumer foray, Silicon Valley's relationship with the consumer was never quite the same after Pong. A host of middle-and upper-class shoppers had graduated from the calculator to the video game, and it was a major step, because the video game was a rudimentary form of computer programming involving the same type of cathode-ray tubes used in standard small computer terminals.

Though there was hardly a conspiracy by design in the matter, in retrospect video games were the perfect means of introducing the home computer concept to consumers at large. To realize that the home computer revolution indeed will come to pass, one has only to watch a group of youngsters feeding quarters into a Space Invaders machine, or gazing at computer-generated special effects in movies like *Star Wars,* or punching up displays on microprocessor-based toys. A generation growing up on such computerized entertainment is not likely to view a small computer in the living room as an alien intrusion.

Defining the Home Computer

The first microprocessor-based home computers offered directly as commercial products did not originate in Silicon Valley, but in New Mexico at a small electronics firm run by a talented group of hackers. First built in early 1975, using an Intel 8080 microprocessor chip as the central processing unit, the MITS Altair 8800, as it was known, didn't stir up any immediate interest in the mainstream electronics world. For years, a small, informal spare parts market had existed among computer enthusiasts who built their own systems, and within this limited arena the Altair 8800 met with its initial success. The computer hobbyist and hacker market was mostly mail order and mostly in the form of classified ads at the back of engineering trade journals. Used circuit boards packed with microchips were the most popular items for sale, and trade was brisk since it was the rare hacker or hobbyist who could afford to spend thousands of dollars of his own money for a finished computer system. The Altair 8800 sold for a few hundred dollars. It was aimed at computer freaks who already knew something about programming, and who in many cases would go on to customize the machine to suit their own needs. It wasn't really very powerful, and a computer neophyte couldn't do much with it at all, but the Altair 8800 sold by the thousands. Evidently, a market existed for a cheap do-it-yourself home microcomputer system.

Since it consisted simply of an 8080 chip, memory chips and interconnections, the Altair was easy to copy, and soon a few more small firms were offering knockoffs of the system. Computing, as a hobby, began to spread, and computer clubs composed of seasoned hackers, off-hours engineers and eager high school students grew up in California and Boston. *Byte* magazine, a journal for computer hobbyists and hackers, began publication, and the first computer stores, similar to those radio shops which catered to ham operators earlier in the century, opened their doors to the public. Small, inexpensive computers were catching on among the technically inclined, and in 1977 several new home computer manufacturers broke open the market for good.

One of the first new entries was the PET home computer from Commodore International, an established electronics and adding machine company. It was followed shortly by offerings from two nontraditional sources — Heath Company, a Benton Harbor, Michigan, maker of build-it-yourself electronic kits for the hobbyist or homeowner, and Radio Shack, a chain of discount electronics supply outlets owned by Tandy Corporation.

The Radio Shack TRS-80 home microcomputer was based on a microprocessor chip developed by Zilog, Exxon's Silicon Valley affiliate. The TRS-80 looked like a combination television and typewriter in a molded plastic housing. In the Radio Shack tradition, it was offered at bargain-basement prices — as little as $499. It had less memory than some other versions on the market, but it was the cheapest commercial home computer of all. With several thousand Radio Shack stores sprinkled across the country, Tandy Corporation was in an excellent position to promote it. The TRS-80 line performed a number of easily programmed operations: figuring taxes, storing family financial information, even computing horoscopes. Radio Shack salespeople, though far from expert with computers, were squarely in the mainstream retail world and knew enough about customer "hand-holding" to emphasize service after sale. The TRS-80 and other early home computers, with a host of amusing games to be played on the terminal, and with salespeople eager to assist to the best of their ability in troubleshooting the process of getting the computer "up," entered the consumer market as a means of family entertainment and financial bookkeeping.

Meanwhile, in Silicon Valley, two young engineers who may rightly be called true children of the microprocessor had gotten together to form a new home computer company. Steven Jobs and Stephen Wozniak grew up in Silicon Valley, met in the eighth grade, and attended high school together in Santa Clara. They were teenagers when the microprocessor was invented. Jobs was born the year William Shockley brought the transistor to Palo Alto. Wozniak, whose father worked for Lockheed Missiles and Space Company, started tinkering with computers in the fourth grade. After high school Stephen Wozniak went on to the University of Colorado and Steven Jobs knocked around for a while overseas. Eventually, they both ended up back in Silicon Valley, Wozniak with Hewlett–Packard and Jobs with Atari.

In 1976 the two got together again, fell in with a local computer club and indulged in the ever-popular California pastime of garage shop tinkering. They built a few basic microcomputer circuit boards and started selling them. In the best hacker tradition, they built a few finished home computers for themselves as well. Fellow computer freaks took a look and were interested. From then on, Jobs and Wozniak were in business. To bankroll their new enterprise, Jobs sold his Volkswagen bus and Wozniak his Hewlett–Packard H-P 65 calculator. They managed to secure thirty days' worth of credit and a few thousand dollars from an electronics distributor, and finally talked Intel's advertising and public relations firm, Regis McKenna, Inc., into promoting them with only a promise of future payment. (Since Intel did not make home computers and the two young men did not plan to make chips, there was no competitive conflict.) Finally, recognizing their own lack of marketing expertise, "the two Steves" talked former Intel marketing manager Mike Markkula into joining the uncertain venture. Markkula, a thirty-four-year-old valley veteran at the time, gave an aura of corporate authenticity and some personal financing to the new company, which was incorporated in early 1977. They called it Apple Computer, in commemoration of Steven Jobs's apple-picking summers in the Northwest. They began setting up distributorships and shipping the Apple I and Apple II home computers. Apple Computer immediately caught the attention of venture capitalists. Ultimately, Bank of America provided seed money, as did Arthur Rock, venture capitalist extraordinaire and prime backer of Intel. Venrock Associates, which ventures with Rockefeller money, chipped in $3 million.

Working at Apple in the early days was like riding a rocket. Sales zoomed from essentially zero in 1976 to $100 million in 1980. Jobs and Wozniak, during the same four years, went from part-time hackers assembling computers to the blare of rock music in Silicon Valley garages, to the microcomputer darlings of Wall Street. In late 1980, Apple Computer went public in one of the most successful high-technology stock offerings ever staged. The happy underwriters were Hambrecht and Quist of San Francisco and Morgan Stanley of New York.

When it was over, Steven Jobs's block of shares was worth, at the public offering price, roughly $165 million. The stock owned by Stephen Wozniak was valued at about $88 million. Jobs was twenty-five years old. Wozniak was twenty-eight. Still more silicon, in the hands of the young, had turned to gold.

Nineteen eighty was also the year that overall sales of home computers broke the billion-dollar mark. By then, the three major suppliers — Radio Shack, Apple and Commodore, in that order — had been joined by Atari, Texas Instruments and a few smaller suppliers. Amid that kind of growth, no future sales estimate for home computers seemed too outlandish. But the truth of the matter was that home computer suppliers had managed to sell a billion dollars' worth of home computers without landing very many of them in American living rooms at all. Other than hobbyists and hackers, the home computer market of the late seventies was actually composed of small businesspeople and upper-income, self-employed professionals. Owners of small businesses, like their larger counterparts, were turning to computers for recordkeeping, payroll, budgeting and inventory control. Lawyers and accountants used them for billing. Scientists and technicians used them to do math and program experiments. Writers and editors used them as word-processing machines for editing text on the display terminal. However, for the "average" consumer who did not own a small business or work at home, the basic hook was still game playing, and $500 to $1,500 and up seemed like a lot for an electronic toy. The average consumer didn't have a computer-sized tax problem, other than amount due, and wasn't immediately convinced of the need for a four-color bar graph display of the family's monthly finances. Home computers could do much more than this, of course, but fully exploiting the machine meant learning the rudiments of computer programming, and programming requirements that seemed childishly simple to a programmer did not always appear so simple to a first-time user.

In order to bring the product more in line with the actual customer base, suppliers simply stopped calling it a home computer. It became "the personal computer for home or office," emphasis on office. This smooth semantic shift had the additional advantage of allowing suppliers to bow out of the price-conscious low end of the consumer market, where so many manufacturers had met their Waterloo in calculators, watches and games. Suppliers could now stabilize their offerings in a higher price range and concentrate on memory capacity and performance, since the bulk of the buyers were professionals who in some cases already were accustomed to using the so-called minis: small computers in the $10,000 to $20,000 range. By 1980 the typical home computer system, redefined as the personal computer system, consisted of a microcomputer, an attachment for disk or cassette memory, a keyboard and a video display terminal (or attachments by which an ordinary television could be turned into the display). It sold for anywhere from $500 to $5,000, and it sold well.

But if 1980 was the year in which the personal computer industry surpassed the billion-dollar mark, it was also the year that the infant industry became fully enmeshed in a widespread controversy that had been brewing ever since the midseventies. At issue was the amount of harmful radiation emitted by video display terminals, or VDTs, the small, TV-like screens which flash the results of the computer's work in the form of numbers, words and pictures, and which make up a crucial part of almost every commercial computer system.

Are Personal Computers Hazardous to Your Health?

The great VDT radiation scare began in the mid-seventies as major newspapers converted from printer's ink and lead type to computerized editing and printing systems. Reporters and other staffers started to spend long hours hunched over electronic keyboards attached to individual desk-top VDTs. The newsroom VDTs, in turn, were linked to a central memory bank. Stories could be written, edited, filed, recalled and passed on to editors without ever appearing on paper. It was not an easy switch for journalists to make, and in the early days newspaper computer systems seemed to have a malicious knack for going "down" at precisely the wrong moment, causing many a story to vanish forever into the unfathomable maw of digital circuitry created by IBM and other major suppliers of such systems. The people in the newsroom or the advertising department or the production room would call in the computer technicians, and the technicians would coolly announce, nine times out of ten, that the trouble had resulted from "operator error."

But as employees mastered the new system, however grudgingly, some far more troubling reports began to surface. VDT operators complained of blurred vision, eye strain, headaches, backaches, dizziness, irritability. In 1977, two copyeditors at the *New York Times* charged that constant exposure to VDTs had given them cataracts. There were several other reports of cataracts among VDT operators, and the suspected culprit was excessive radiation from the cathode-ray tubes in VDTs. Before long the Newspaper Guild, a collective bargaining unit of journalists, began looking into the matter. Other unions joined in, as did three federal agencies — the Food and Drug Administration's Bureau of Radiological Health, the National Institute for Occupational Safety and Health (NIOSH), and the Occupational Safety and Health Administration (OSHA). In early 1980 the VDT radiation controversy culminated in the announcement by the *Toronto Star* that four pregnant women who worked with VDTs at that newspaper had given birth to deformed babies.

Personal computers have VDTs too, or use the cathode-ray tube of a television set as a VDT, and as the health studies progressed another government agency awakened to the fact that a whole new class of radiation-emitting devices was appearing in American homes and businesses. Any device that hooks to a television set, or that emits radiation of a frequency that might interfere with TV or radio reception, must pass muster with the Federal Communications Commission (FCC).

The FCC's concern was not with health, but with broadcast interference. The commission well remembered the nightmare that ensued in the wake of the CB radio craze, when irate homeowners complained of strange CB jargon issuing from televisions and radios, and policemen charged that CB owners were jamming up emergency radio channels. The FCC had no wish to see the same kind of mess repeated with personal computers, and since it knew very little about them, it embarked on a radiation testing program in 1979. On first pass, all but Atari's offerings exceeded existing standards for radio frequency (RF) radiation, meaning that the potential for interference did exist. Subsequently, Commodore and Texas Instruments personal computers passed the testing cycle as well, amid considerable rancor over a proposed relaxation of RF emission standards, much haggling over rules for classifying personal computers, and several petitions for the extension of compliance deadlines. In the end, Apple, Radio Shack and Heath had no choice but to begin redesigning their personal computer offerings to lower the levels of RF radiation.

This form of radiation is not a major health concern, but other forms of radiation are not so benign. Radiation is classified as either ionizing — the so-called hard radiation such as x-rays and gamma rays — or non-ionizing, "soft" radiation such as microwaves and infrared rays. Prolonged exposure to high levels of ionizing radiation can be lethal. High levels of non-ionizing radiation are absorbed by human tissue and have been linked experimentally to brain wave alterations, cataracts and testicular malformities. The question was whether the health complaints voiced by VDT operators were caused by excessive radiation, or whether, as some suggested, they were attributable to a textbook case of mass computer paranoia. Many of these same radiation fears had been raised earlier when it was discovered that color television sets gave off x-rays. The solution in that case was to suggest that viewers sit no closer than six feet away from the screen, but in the case of VDTs, several million of which were in use in 1980, that was clearly impractical advice.

By mid-1981 the results of several testing programs were in. VDTs had been studied for x-rays, microwaves, high-frequency radio waves and other forms of radiation. Bearing in mind the highly subjective nature of setting allowable radiation standards, and the fact that so little is known about the effects of prolonged exposure to low-level, non-ionizing radiation, the computer industry's VDTs emerged with a reasonably clean bill of health. According to the FDA, NIOSH and other federal investigators, radiation from computer terminals does not pose any verifiable biological hazards. A number of unions and independent health specialists pronounced themselves dissatisfied with the results, maintaining that even extremely low levels of non-ionizing radiation present a significant long-term health hazard. Several new studies are now in progress.

As for the specific health complaints with which the matter began, none of the studies found any strong statistical support for the contention that VDTs caused cataracts, and the Canadian government was unable to detect any x-rays or microwaves emanating from the VDT terminals used by the women who gave birth to deformed infants. Still, the controversy over VDT radiation is far from over, and many VDT operators have been left wondering whether they might become the asbestos cases of the 1990s.

Unfortunately, the furor over VDT radiation has obscured some of the verifiable and correctable health problems associated with VDTs. Many of the complaints attributed to VDT radiation, such as eye strain and muscle aches, may in fact be caused by environmental factors — the improper deployment of computer terminals. The New York Committee for Occupational Safety and Health (NYCOSH), an organization of workers, unions, and health and legal professionals in the New York City area, has suggested a number of ways to mitigate the chronic eye strain and fatigue often associated with prolonged use of computer terminals. Bad lighting, very small VDTs and screen glare are major culprits. The ideal VDT should be equipped with a nonreflective glass screen, and the bigger the better. Indirect lighting, which further cuts glare, is preferable to direct sunlight or fluorescent lighting. NYCOSH proposes that the optimum screen-to-eye distance is two feet or more, and favors VDT systems with detached keyboards so that the user has more latitude in adjusting the viewing distance. Characters on the screen should be at least 3/16 of an inch high, and there should be some provision for brightness adjustment. People who wear corrective lenses or contacts may encounter special problems, and NYCOSH advises them to let their doctors know that they work with VDTs.

In addition, NYCOSH calls for union contract language which guarantees periodic eye examinations and rest periods for VDT workers. "One good job design feature (work rule) for V.D.T. operators provides a fifteen minute break every hour (or a half-hour every two hours) so that operators have a chance to rest their eyes by viewing at greater distances. . . . The key element of good work rules for V.D.T. operators is substantial time away from the machine. Two hours is the maximum time that should be spent doing continuous screen work."

Naturally, as the computerization of the workplace continues, such suggestions are not calculated to win the hearts of management negotiators at contract time. The Newspaper Guild has scored several notable successes in its efforts to use eye exams, rest periods and radiation testing as potent bargaining chips. According to the *Wall Street Journal,* seventeen major newspapers now pay for VDT operator eye exams, and another seven pay for new or improved eyeglass prescriptions. Four Guild newspapers in the Minneapolis–St. Paul area have won extra rest breaks for VDT operators.

The Guild efforts have been watched closely by the 625,000-member Communications Workers of America, and by other unions whose workers are apt to meet with VDTs in due course, if they have not done so already. VDT safeguards are shaping up as a major union bargaining issue in the eighties, and while there is no union for those who labor over personal computers in their homes, the same concerns, and the same rules for minimizing eyestrain, will likely apply to domestic use of VDTs.

Dividing up the Spoils:
A Roster of Interested Parties

The VDT radiation issue, directed as it was toward computer terminals in the workplace, did not have any effect on the personal computer market, other than forcing personal computer designers to pay more attention to shielding techniques for reducing emissions. As the eighties began, new small-business markets continued to open up, and sales to professionals, the self-employed and the merely curious continued to increase. The personal computer system, a direct descendant of the mighty microprocessor chip, was here to stay, and the billion-dollar industry that grew up around it had scratched only the surface of its potential customer base. In a single decade the microprocessor had become the microcomputer, and the microcomputer had become the personal computer, and in the process what was once primarily an industrial market had blossomed to include consumers of all kinds.

As the electronics industry largely viewed it, the personal computer was poised on the brink of mass commercial acceptance. Coupled with ongoing advances in communications technologies, the personal computer meant that the saga of electricity which began with Edison's incandescent light was entering a novel and wholly unpredictable phase. Digital data transmission and electronic logic were no longer futuristic concepts of interest to an elite corps of corporations and technologists. Personal computer enthusiasts, computer suppliers, corporate planners, hackers, consultants and researchers at think tanks all had a long list of answers to the question of what the computer could do for the American family, other than play games and estimate next month's utility bill. It was Nikola Tesla's grand list, and then some — electronic newspapers, electronic mail, electronic reproduction of documents and pictures, electronic banking, electronic credit, electronic shopping, even electronic grocery buying. Access to libraries, consumer bureaus, government agencies, offices, events calendars, weather reports, and traffic updates. Electronic voting. Two-way, interactive participation in government, from traffic court to Congress. Services like message centers, answering centers, referrals and ticket reservations. Immediate emergency medical advice. Foolproof burglar and fire alarm systems. As computer scientist Joel Moses has written:

> A visitor to an American home in the last decade of this century might note several scenes not present in today's homes. For example, a six-year-old child might be seen playing with toys. . . . One toy is tracing a figure on a piece of paper spread on the floor. It is doing this without human intervention. . . . In another part of the house two teenagers are seen playing Space-War, a game played on a TV-like screen. . . . Later one of the teenagers is seen reading a book. The pages of the book are displayed on the face of a hand-held screen, and are turned by pressing buttons on the console attached to the screen. . . . The father appears to be reading the newspaper on yet another screen. . . . The mother is seen paying this month's telephone bill. No checks are visible. Rather, the bill is viewed on the screen, and various keys are punched on the console informing the bank to pay the telephone company the full amount.

Moreover, the average home contains dozens and dozens of devices which in turn contain little electric motors. Soon, they would all contain microprocessors hooked to, and controlled by, domestic computer systems. The stereo, the coffee pot, the garage door, the thermostat — all could be linked to the home information-energy-management-entertainment system of the future. The concept of the "smart" house had ample technical precedent. Russell Schweickart, former astronaut and now chairman of California's State Energy Commission, recalled: "My smart house was Apollo 9. In terms of resource planning, allocation of resources, efficiency and safety of operation — it couldn't have existed without those computers. Well, the homes we live in today, the buildings we work in, are primitive in terms of intelligence and information. A particular light bulb may save a little more electricity than one designed five years ago, and there may be a sun film on the window, but in terms of interactive environmental control systems, we just haven't gotten there. Almost as a by-product, because they're so powerful, home computers can be environmental control centers as well as information and entertainment centers."

About the only thing the personal computer of the future would not be able to do was generate its own electricity, and with solar cells on the roof, perhaps that could be arranged as well.

There was nothing technologically askew about these predictions at all. Indeed, much of Tesla's list had been repromised in the late fifties and early sixties, with the introduction of cable television. Many of the proposed services were technically feasible without computers. The fact that few of these consumer services were much in evidence by the late seventies did not deter the personal computer enthusiasts from renewing the pledge. And to bolster it, proponents of the wired life could point to several small-scale or experimental examples. In many locales, personal computer owners could have the daily newspaper and the *Wall Street Journal* delivered electronically to a home terminal, though the cost was steep. Hackers, hobbyists and assorted corporations were pioneering computer networks that offered subscribers a wide assortment of digital services.

It was astounding to contemplate what the personal computer could do, and once on the track, it was hard to resist letting the ball roll. Like storytellers eager to skip over the details and get to the happy ending, personal computer enthusiasts and suppliers and the press all trumpeted potential services without going into much detail about either the actual means of implementation or the parties most likely to prosper therefrom. As Joseph Weizenbaum argues:

> What and whose needs will be satisfied by the functions described here and by the ongoing proliferation of computers and computer controlled systems? . . . We may recall the euphoric dreams articulated by then Secretary of Commerce Herbert Hoover at the dawn of commercial radio broadcasting and again by others when mass television broadcasting was about to

become a reality. . . . This magnificent technology, more than Wagnerian in its proportions, combining as it does the technology of precise guidance of rockets, of space flight, of the cleverest and most intricate electronics, of photography, and so on, this exquisitely refined combination of some of the human species' highest intellectual achievements, what does it deliver to the masses? An occasional gem buried in immense avalanches of the ordure of everything that is most banal and insipid or pathological in our civilization.

We are beginning to see this same calamitous script reenacted in terms of the home computer.

If homes and offices are to become electronic information centers in the broadest sense, personal computers must be linked to the rest of the world, primarily by means of the telephone and television. This was the early weak point in the home computer sales pitch — the question of linking up the computer, the telephone and the television, the holy triangle of electronic information systems. When some respected scientists blithely predicted, at the close of the seventies, that the book and other forms of the printed word would be obsolete by 1990, it was less a case of overenthusiasm for personal computer technology than a case of political and economic naiveté. As for when the full rainbow of computerized services will truly arrive, in the mainstream sense of a personal computer system in a majority of American homes and offices — estimated time of arrival, usually considered to be any day now, is due for a slight revision. It now appears that the eighties, commonly thought to be the decade during which personal computers will reach the masses, will be marked instead by massive corporate turf wars *in anticipation* of the wired life. In 1980, the University of California released a study predicting that the $1 billion personal computer market of 1980 will become a $21.5 billion market by 1990. However, in breaking down the estimates, the study forecast that the growth of personal computers in the home will be quite modest. Of the total estimate, only $3.5 billion or so is expected to come from the sale of true home computers. The rest will come from the same quarters as in 1980 — offices, small businesses and self-employed professionals. The average consumer is far more likely to be confronted with a computer terminal at work before one arrives in the home.

In general, it appears to take about twenty years for a major technological invention to go from inception to mass commercial acceptance. This has been true of the telephone, the television and the larger computer, and if it proves true of the personal computer as well, then the real home computer revolution is still a decade or so away. Robert Noyce has put it another way: "You have to remember that the effect of the printing press was not felt immediately because most people didn't know how to read. Today we have the developing effect of the small computer, and it can't be as immediate or widespread as some people predict because you're not a good programmer." With a smile, he adds, "But your kids will be. Oh yes, they'll be computer literate. The electronic calculator caught on very quickly because everybody had learned in school that there was a sequence of symbols you used to program a mathematical operation. But with the computer, you have things like, 'if A, do loop B' or whatever, and it's like suddenly being thrown into having all the literature around you in Greek. And until you learn Greek it's all sort of meaningless, and you can't use any of the books in the library. Designing computers that communicate in the same language humans use is going to simplify that problem a great deal. Even now you don't have to know how a small computer works to use it. Ask the average person how a telephone works and he or she will say, well, you pick up the instrument and push these buttons and then you get to talk to whoever you want to talk to. And that's the only level of understanding you have to have in order to make the telephone a useful tool."

If it is the children who are to inherit the new keys to the kingdom — personal microcomputers, and the entire range of capabilities a thorough knowledge of programming can bring to them — then the eighties can be viewed as the stage for a monumental battle over the marketplace for digital transmission systems. The concept of the home linked to every other home, office, business, agency and institution, and even to pocket-sized personal computers in every pocket, is either the prescription for an electronic utopia or a totalitarian nightmare, depending upon one's point of view. But in a practical sense it means a hugely lucrative market, however quickly it comes to pass. In the sixties, "silicon" was the password to success. In the seventies, the word was "microprocessor." In the eighties, through a combination of microelectronics, computers and communications technologies the magic word is "telecommunications." Broadly defined, it simply means the communication of information by any electronic means. There has never been another market like it, and companies large and small all over the world are scrambling to gain a foothold in it.

While young hackers, hobbyists and computer mavericks will play a part in this developing, innovation-intensive market, they are not likely to be the ones who chart its direction. The same is true of the major semiconductor companies, none of which, except Texas Instruments, had shown any signs of moving into personal computer products by 1980. Perhaps they had been burned once too often with consumer products. Or perhaps, as hackers were quick to suggest, for all their vaunted innovation over the years the semiconductor people simply didn't see the personal computer coming. In fact, some hackers and hobbyists tended to view Intel and the rest of the chip makers, those youthful risk takers of the sixties and seventies, as the old guard, too deeply mired in the industrial mindset to catch the next big wave they had made possible. More and more, the major semiconductor companies were coming to resemble giant, foreign-owned silicon factories with huge capital requirements. With the personal computer, a new learning-curve slide had been created, and very few semiconductor companies were on it. They would benefit from the personal computer revolution in the form of ever-increasing chip sales, but they would not direct it.

Who would? Now that personal computers were a smart

Wall Street play rather than a promise, a lot of companies with strange names like Apple, Umtech and Video Brain figured that *they* would. Hackers in the computer underground who kept the outlaw faith figured that they would too. Computers simply would become too cheap and too pervasive to monopolize. IBM and AT&T were outmoded dinosaurs — Intel, too, perhaps. Undergrounders like Bob ("The Dragon") Albrecht of the People's Computer Store and Ted ("Computer Lib") Nelson rode forth to refute the myths about computers — that they had to be big; that they weren't fun and exciting; that IBM controlled them. Alan Kay, then a Xerox researcher of independent mind, pushed forward his concept of the Dynabook, a combination electronic book and three-dimensional, multicolored sketch pad with capabilities well beyond current performance levels of personal computers.

It all boiled down to roughly three opposing camps — a counterculture that believed in "computer power to the people," an established electronics culture that believed, as the Bell System advertises, that "The System is the Solution," and companies like Apple that fell somewhere in between. The idea that IBM and AT&T and other large electronics companies had had their day, and that "the people" would be reshaping the grid any way they wished, was an exciting argument — *if* one knew something about computers already, and *if* one were willing to sustain the touchingly naive doctrine that major corporations somehow were going to be frozen out of the personal computer revolution altogether.

It isn't going to happen that way. As of early 1981, in addition to existing suppliers, the following corporations had either offered their own personal computing and word-processing systems or else had announced plans to do so: IBM, Exxon, Xerox, Digital Equipment, Burroughs, Sperry Univac, NCR, Hewlett–Packard, Data General, Zenith, Mattel, Ohio Scientific, Vector Graphics and General Telephone — plus Nippon Electric, Sharp and Hitachi of Japan. Other corporations intimately involved in the developing personal computer and telecommunications age include, as a sampling, Merrill Lynch,

American Express, Time–Life, McGraw–Hill, United Technologies, United Artists, Westinghouse, General Electric, Sears, the Associated Press, NBC, CBS, ABC and assorted advertisers everywhere. Also keenly interested are such bodies as the FBI, the CIA, the National Security Agency (NSA) and the Department of Defense.

In the end, however, the two most salient facts about upheavals to come are these: IBM, which sells well over half the large computer systems in use today, has only recently entered the market with its version of the personal computer. And AT&T, the major purveyor of hardware for the communications portion of the existing electronic grid, is now emerging from a regulatory thicket as IBM's principal competitor. The likely results of this unprecedented clash are the subject of the following chapter.

CHAPTER NINE

Telecommunications: The Grid Rewired

Information is power. Control over communications services is a source of power. Access to communication is a condition of freedom.
— DANIEL BELL

Goliath vs. Goliath

American Telephone and Telegraph, known to millions as AT&T, Ma Bell, or simply the phone company, will emerge in a few years as a major vendor — perhaps *the* major vendor — of personal computer systems for the home and the office. This very fact calls for a wholesale redefinition of the personal computer market, and as the corporate drive to spearhead this lucrative market unfolds, Ma Bell's unprecedented participation in it bears directly on the fortunes of electronics companies from IBM to Intel to Apple, and on the consumer products and services they offer. An immense power struggle has commenced, over the digital information traffic that is the coin and commerce of the electronic grid. Very little about the industrial landscape, domestic or international, will look the same when it has run its course.

The subject of this chapter is the broad field known as telecommunications, and the term means a good deal more than just simple communication by telephone. It means telephones acting like computers, and it means computers "talking" to each other over telephone lines. It means a corporate battle over electronic *systems* and the information they process and transmit, rather than over the invention and sale of discrete pieces of electronic equipment.

223

For purposes of this discussion, telecommunications can be defined as the synthesis that results when telephones, televisions and computers are linked together in vast digital networks. Two factors distinguish modern telecommunications from historical means of electronic communication: the microchip, which makes the synergistic three-way interplay possible, and the technology of digital data transmission. Digitized, all information looks the same in mid-transmission — a stream of electronic pulses representing ones and zeroes, ons and offs, yeses and nos. As information specialist John McHale wrote, "Implicit within the new convergence of information and communication technology is the reduction, where required, of the many differences in methods of transmission of voice, print, picture, telegraph, etc., to one possible channel through which they may be transmitted simultaneously — as identical electronic pulses for reception in any preferred form." The vocal message of the telephone call, the visual signal of the television set, the bits and bytes of the computer system — all these forms of electronic information are becoming the same. The nub of the telecommunications issue is the battle for the right to originate, carry, process, allocate and sell that digitized information.

It becomes readily apparent that the twin developments of computerized telephone systems and phone-linked computer systems make it difficult to decide what is or is not a data-processing service. The normal operation of distributed processing (communication from computer to computer) involves sending electronic messages unaltered from one site to another — Bell's business. The normal operation of phone systems involves the processing of data at centralized computer centers — IBM's business. And, since there are fewer and fewer functional distinctions between telephones (data transmission) and computers (data processing), how is the regulatory line between these industries to be drawn? What sense does it make to regulate the one and not the other? At issue is the question of legal access to AT&T's vast system of existing telephone lines — or legal alternatives to it. Under what conditions can

AT&T's huge, hard-wired portion of the grid be dispensed with altogether, using new technological alternatives?

In a nutshell, the battle over systems of telecommunication is the result of dramatic changes the microchip has worked on both IBM's and AT&T's basic lines of business. By the end of the seventies, microcomputers had become an essential ingredient in modern telephone systems, just as telephone systems themselves were becoming a vital channel for computer-to-computer communication. This dual trend — telephones behaving like computers and computers behaving like telephones — had the effect of blurring the functional differences between, and the markets for, these two electronic products, while vastly increasing the capabilities of both.

Consider, for example, the relatively straightforward and entirely plausible task of fitting conventional telephones with microprocessor chips. Conceivably, this could be accomplished in the industrialized nations by the year 2000, if the myriad legal, political and regulatory obstacles, none of which can be taken lightly, are overcome. A phone with a microprocessor in it, or a phone coupled to a separate microcomputer, becomes a hybrid electronic instrument, neither wholly computer nor wholly telephone. A kind of technological synergism takes hold, and the combination results in a new instrument with capabilities far exceeding those of its two components.

In this light, even the term "personal computer" is not as precise as it may seem. A microprocessor-controlled push-button telephone can be programmed to act as a simple computer terminal of sorts, with the user simply sending instructions to a central computer by dialing in various number sequences. If the "smart" telephone in turn is hooked to a TV screen, an electronic typewriter or a printer, the user theoretically can call up several computerized services, such as stock tickers, airline schedules, or even a list of the day's specials at the A&P. Note that the usual video display terminal and keyboard are not necessarily required.

What this means is that the traditional distinctions between the *communication* of information by telephone and the *pro-*

cessing of information by computer have all but vanished. Each giant corporation fears the other is engaged in a wholesale invasion of its domain — and they are both right. Two previously discrete industrial arenas have merged into one, a combined market of immense proportions. As AT&T now threatens IBM's traditional computer business, so IBM finds itself competing directly with AT&T in what was once the staunchly regulated field of communications. Technological evolution, court decisions, the force of the free market and a changing federal regulatory climate are unshackling these two corporate giants and, at the same time, unleashing new waves of competition, as AT&T's former monopoly over electronic communication crumbles away. The so-called electronic office of the future is shaping up as the crucial battleground, and since personal computer systems in the office may well migrate to the home (along with the job itself), the telecommunications war is the story of what is really at stake economically in the personal computer revolution. Personal computer entrepreneurs will be competing directly in the marketplace with two of the largest industrial opponents of all time.

Until recently, the distinction between AT&T's business and IBM's business was quite clear. Early on, electronic communication became largely AT&T's domain, by federal fiat. Consisting mainly of the regional Bell companies, Western Electric and Bell Labs, AT&T became a national communications company more akin to a public utility than a free market corporation. Its status stemmed from the belief that electronic communication constituted a "natural" monopoly — an essential public service most efficiently supplied, due to certain economies of scale, by a large, centralized "common carrier" under government regulation. In adopting this view early in the century, the U.S. government looked to its recent history of regulating interstate transportation, the railroads in particular. The railroads were a service vital to the health and growth of the country, and to assure that rail transportation was available on an equitable basis to anyone who could pay for it, the government classified railroad companies as "common carriers" subject to federal regulation and rate-setting. The railroads carried goods and passengers, but they also carried messages in written form, as mail.

At the same time, the new telephone and telegraph companies were busy crossing state boundaries as well. The government chose to view these companies as a transportation industry hauling a different sort of freight — voice and electronic telegraph messages. Theodore Vail, AT&T's first president, saw quite early that his fast-growing company, the leader in the field, was destined to be drawn into the regulatory net the government had cast over interstate transportation. Rather than fight it, Vail welcomed it, in return for official federal recognition of AT&T as a de jure monopoly over domestic telephone service. Hence, in 1910, the government amended the Interstate Commerce Act to include a new breed of common carrier, the telephone company. The price of telephone service then had to be approved, or "tariffed" by the federal government. Radio companies, when they arrived, were simply added to the list of licensed common carriers in the communications field.

In 1934 Congress passed the Communications Act, which split out AT&T and smaller communications common carriers as a separate regulatory field under the purview of a new agency, the Federal Communications Commission. The FCC's job was to police AT&T's behavior as a natural monopoly over telephone service, and to allocate frequencies of the electromagnetic spectrum to radio and television broadcasters. Today, almost fifty years and a major technological paradigm shift later, the Communications Act of 1934 is being rewritten. Yet it remains the fundamental statute of communications law in America. "For this reason," as Anthony Oettinger has written, "the FCC has often found itself with a regulatory structure that pretends that communications channels are railroad tracks."

Starting in the 1960s, electronic advances made that questionable analogy even more suspect as a sound basis for regulation. And, as technological alternatives to the basic two-wire telephone loop proliferated, the concept of a natural communications monopoly began to erode as well. Companies seeking to compete with AT&T on the basis of advancing technologies, such as microwave transmissions, charged the phone company with attempting to stifle new, innovative communications services. This was a long-standing, if previously unsuccessful, attack on AT&T's natural monopoly. In the absence of competition, ran the argument, there is no compelling pressure on the Bell system to innovate technologically, since such innovation renders its own equipment obsolete — a costly prospect in a company the size of Bell.

The first crack in the Bell monopoly — and a major hint of things to come — was a landmark FCC ruling known as the *Carterfone* decision of 1968. Until then, Ma Bell's monopoly over communications hardware could best be described as impregnable. "No equipment, apparatus, circuit, or device not furnished by the Telephone Company shall be attached to or connected with the facilities furnished by the Telephone Company . . ." according to the pertinent tariff. This edict covered every conceivable attachment, from computers to the plastic dialing disks on telephones themselves. "Foreign attachments," Bell called these outlawed interconnections, arguing the case against them on the grounds of possible "technical harm" to the phone system. If Bell didn't make it or approve it, it couldn't be used on Bell's lines. For telephone hardware, Ma Bell was the only store in town.

There were, however, certain FCC-sanctioned alternative phone services, called private line transmission. One such alternative was the radio telephone, which provided local mobile phone service through the airwaves rather than through the wires. Radio telephones are popular in the building and construction trades, in aviation, and for police, fire and other emergency services. Commonly, private mobile phones in trucks and other vehicles were linked via radio waves to a central base station. Ideally, a mobile phone is most useful when it is connected to the telephone system at large; that is, when the base station is connected to AT&T's phone lines, so that the mobile caller can reach any desired telephone number, and not just the base station. In fact, this connection is easily made, and quite common today. All it requires is a simple acoustic coupling device that patches the mobile caller into the Bell System phone lines. The same such device, it is important to note, also could connect computer terminals to the phone lines. But in 1968, such devices, one of which was the "Carterfone" supplied by Carter Electronics, were in apparent violation of the "foreign attachment" rule. When AT&T and Carter Electronics took their differences to court, the judge tossed the question to the FCC for a ruling under the Communications Act. After considerable haggling, the seven FCC commissioners threw out the blanket ban against the practice of connecting devices like the Carterfone to Bell's lines, and the action created a novel category of AT&T competitors known as the interconnect industry.

The ruling also meant that other suppliers could sell telephones too. From the consumer's point of view, as so often happens, the immediate result seemed rather frivolous: the Mickey Mouse telephone, soon followed by other "decorator" telephones. But for Ma Bell, even the Mickey Mouse telephone, purchased outright from another supplier rather than leased in perpetuity from the phone company, was a shattering precedent and a first incursion into its natural monopoly. The interconnect industry followed with other foreign attachments — telephone answering machines, paging devices, and equipment for linking telephones to computers and televisions. Case after case ended up in court, where the hopeful hardware suppliers claimed the status of innovative underdogs seeking to squirm out from under the heavy hand of AT&T. Ma Bell, faced with true competition, fought back bitterly, but the *Carterfone* decision stood, and the unique competitive note it injected into the telecommunications market quickly rose to a chorus.

In 1969 another chunk of Bell's natural monopoly began to

fall away when the FCC approved a plan by MCI Corporation for a private microwave telephone system between St. Louis and Chicago. MCI planned to build a series of microwave stations along that route and sell wireless phone service to corporate clients in the two cities as a cheaper alternative to the Bell System. Rather than "piggybacking" its service on AT&T lines, MCI wanted to offer a clear-cut, competitive alternative to a select business market. After another long battle, the FCC affirmed the right of "specialized" common carriers like MCI to compete with AT&T in certain select markets. Scores of other applications followed, many of them from new companies proposing to service the communications needs of business customers by digitizing their phone calls and sending them via microwave. Again, AT&T fought bitterly against these specialized services, since they often paralleled some of the phone company's most lucrative intercity routes. AT&T charged its would-be competitors with "cream-skimming" — providing service only along high-traffic routes, and offering no service at all where it is costly to do so, whereas Bell is mandated to provide service even where it is not highly profitable. Nonetheless, the FCC allowed the growth of specialized alternatives to the Bell system, and new carriers sprang up on the strength of new technologies, offering interoffice and interplant data transmission services to the business community.

Having paved the way for a full-scale assault on the phone company's natural monopoly, the FCC later carried the trend to its logical conclusion. While the *Carterfone* decision poked a first hole in Bell's monopoly over hardware connected to the phone lines, the FCC in early 1980 opened the mobile phone market to all comers on the strength of a technological advancement called cellular radio, which greatly expands the number of mobile calls that can be packed into a single radio frequency. AT&T, other telephone companies and radio common carriers now all compete openly for mobile telephone customers, and the customer list is growing. "Dick Tracy," said acting FCC chairman Robert E. Lee, "comes true." Similarly, the end result of the *MCI* decision to allow long-distance alternatives was a 1980 edict by the FCC which dissolved Bell's monopoly over long-distance service. The specialized common carriers became less and less specialized, and more and more obviously in direct competition with Bell for long-distance service everywhere. (Moreover, MCI later capped its thrust into communications by winning a massive antitrust case against AT&T.)

These competitive developments in the seventies helped set the stage for an incursion from yet another quarter, the data-processing industry. Ironically, the invasion of the computer makers, and AT&T's efforts to compete right back, also set the stage for Ma Bell's entry into the free market. What happened in the seventies was that the computer industry discovered distributed data processing, and the full growth of telephone-linked computer communication demanded a complete re-thinking of the boundaries between regulated and unregulated electronics.

The solid-state computer, an outgrowth of the transistor invented at Bell Labs, found a natural home in AT&T's telephone switching centers, where many calls must be routed simultaneously, efficiently and automatically. Up until roughly a decade ago, the telephone wasn't considered very "sexy," in engineering parlance. Nor was there much that was sexy or exciting about Ma Bell itself, a great, gray leviathan protected by the government from anything amounting to serious competition in basic telephone service. But the computer changed that picture much more fundamentally than individual decisions like *Carterfone* and *MCI* ever could.

As a regulated monopoly over telephone service, AT&T was barred quite specifically from anything having to do with the computer market under the terms of a 1956 Justice Department consent decree which ended an antitrust action against the phone company. However, this did not prevent Bell and lesser common carriers from using computers in their *own* telephone systems. Many large office and corporate communications systems incorporate on-site telephone switching centers known as private branch exchanges, or PBXs. A PBX controls the flow of telephone traffic through the institution itself, and as these PBXs inevitably went solid-state, they came to resemble computers, or rather lots of little computers. With computerized PBXs, all sorts of novel services were possible. Individual callers could store calls, stack calls, leave recorded messages and dial direct anywhere in the world. There were automatic call back and dialing and paging systems, and a potent little feature known as least-cost routing, which sorted through the maze of corporate phone rates and put the calls through along the cheapest possible route.

Bell offered many computerized office products during the seventies, such as the popular Dataspeed 40. To any casual observer, this machine appeared to be a computer terminal tailored specifically for word-processing tasks. Ostensibly barred from selling such products, Bell slipped this and other offerings past the FCC as legally tariffed services.

While computerized PBXs, Dataspeed 40s and other systems didn't put Bell in the business of selling computers, they did seem to move the phone company squarely into the business of selling computer *services*. Moreover, IBM began selling computerized telephone switching systems to corporate customers in Europe, a move which put that company squarely in the communications business.

As the microchip streamlined corporate communications systems and computerized the branch exchanges, more and more of Bell's voice traffic came to be carried in digital form. For example, through a technique called pulse code modulation, sound can be coded into the same form of digital electronic bits that computer instructions are made of. There is a remarkable microchip called a coder-decoder circuit, or Codec chip, which has been tailored specifically for this purpose. The advantages of digital voice transmission are the usual advantages of low cost and high efficiency. If it were possible somehow to seize and examine a digital voice transmission as it coursed through the phone lines, or along microwaves, it would "look" no different from a stream of computer data moving from one computer terminal to another.

This computer-driven convergence of electronic media forced the FCC to promulgate Computer Inquiry II, a lengthy investigation into what the computer had done to the field of regulated communications. Quite obviously, computers had made a sorry hash of the boundaries. AT&T, smarting under the press of competition from several sources, argued that the FCC couldn't very well carve up its old monopoly over "pure" communication while at the same time refusing to allow it to offer computer services, a market into which it was tumbling already by virtue of the blending of computers and communications into "compunications." The anti-Bell forces argued that allowing Bell to sell computer systems outright would be high folly, tantamount to handing Bell a new monopoly over computers for the one it had lost over electronic communication. Bell would have an insurmountable advantage in selling or leasing computer systems, they argued, because it owned most of the existing communications channels of the grid along which computer communication takes place. It also owned Western Electric, a huge manufacturing subsidiary that would give it an equally strong head start in lowering production costs. Moreover, what would prevent Bell from seeding its foray into the computer market with a large chunk of the regulated profits it reaped from telephone rate payers everywhere? This concern, called "cross-subsidization," was a frightening prospect for the computer industry. Conceivably, it meant that if Bell were allowed into the computer market, it would have at its disposal enough capital to underprice competitors and drive established computer vendors out of the market. As it stood, it was tough enough for newly allowed competitors to carve their way into Bell's communications businesses — "Like a competition between you and God," as one executive lamented in the *Wall Street Journal*. What would happen if Bell was free to turn its vast resources loose on the computer business?

It was the most far-reaching quandary the FCC had ever

faced. Finally, in April 1980, the FCC promulgated a sweeping and bitterly contested decision: it would let AT&T loose in the free market at last. For the first time in seventy years, AT&T was given the go-ahead to compete in unregulated markets — data-processing services and computer hardware — provided that it established an arm's length, unsubsidized and unregulated subsidiary for that purpose. The proposed subsidiary, quickly christened "Baby Bell," is to be completely distinct from AT&T's phone business. And it is not likely to remain a baby for long.

It was an historic decision, and it meant that only Bell's most basic regulated telephone service would remain subject to close federal scrutiny. Baby Bell would be permitted to slug it out freely in the open market for "compunications" services. At the same time, the FCC would look more leniently upon forays by IBM and other computer makers into the market for communications services. "We have today removed the barricades from the door to the information age," grandly proclaimed then-FCC chairman Charles Ferris. "Government will no longer be a barrier that prevents or delays the introduction of innovations in technology."

Immediately, though the end result is still several years away, AT&T began laying the groundwork for what it called "the most massive reorganization in modern American corporate history," the cleaving of the Bell System into two separate halves, the one regulated, the other unregulated. The FCC unshackled AT&T in the computer field and broke open its former monopoly over communications in the spirit of innovative competition, but as one unnamed FCC official confided to *Science* magazine: "Who knows what's going to happen when you take a $120 billion company (AT&T) and deregulate it, or when you let IBM into the communications market on an unregulated basis. Nobody knows."

Various parties to the dispute pronounced themselves dissatisfied with the FCC's decision to allow the creation of the Baby Bell computer subsidiary. For Bell competitors and computer vendors, Baby Bell was not just a contradiction of the

1956 consent decree, and further proof of Bell's ability to lead the FCC around by the nose — it was quite possibly their death knell as well. By the end of this decade, Baby Bell could be selling computer terminals to consumers and corporate customers at large, and would the restrictions placed on it be sufficient to prevent AT&T from funding its computer adventures with regulated assets exceeding $100 billion?

Competitors thought not, and Congress had a few qualms of its own concerning the FCC's plans. It wasn't so much that Congress disagreed with the commission's intent to facilitate Bell's entry into the computer business, but that Congress wished to do the job itself, and do it better. Some congressmen, in the throes of tortuously rewriting the Communications Act of 1934, argued that the FCC had overstepped its boundaries, since the act they were attempting to rewrite didn't give the FCC any say about computers in the first place. At the outset of the Reagan administration, deregulatory fever struck Congress, and thus did a measure of political one-upmanship enter the deregulation debate, as Congress vied with the FCC for the right to open telecommunications and "compunications" to equitable competition. As House Communications Subcommittee chairman Lionel Van Deerlin put it prior to the FCC's Baby Bell decision, "Why should any corporation invest millions to develop sophisticated telecommunications hardware when the return on that investment may be affected more by seven commissioners in Washington than by the firm's own technical, managerial or marketing teams?" Presumably, this wouldn't be a problem if Congress broke the regulatory hold over telecommunications legislatively, but Congress itself was squabbling badly over what restrictions to place on Bell's participation in the computer market. Much of the debate focused on the relationship between Baby Bell and AT&T's giant manufacturing subsidiary, Western Electric. At one extreme, AT&T competitors pushed for a complete divestiture of Western Electric, in order to lessen the chances of cross-subsidization. At the other, AT&T pushed for what chairman Charles L. Brown termed a "less radical" approach, requiring a clear separation of Baby Bell from an accounting point of view, but no major surgery on the neat symmetry of the AT&T–Bell Labs–Western Electric triangle.

The question of Baby Bell's future relationship to the Bell System at large brought to light another governmental party deeply involved in the reshaping of AT&T — the U.S. Justice Department. As it happened, while Congress and the FCC vied with each other for the privilege of unleashing the phone company, Justice was deeply enmeshed in a long-standing antitrust case aimed at breaking AT&T apart. To the Justice Department prosecuters, it seemed only proper that the details of Bell's deregulation, and the rules for its entry into the computer market, should await the outcome of the antitrust case. But the growing sentiment in the Reagan administration was that Justice's seven-year-long suit was becoming something of a nuisance; one that threatened to put the Communications Act rewrite, and Baby Bell, on ice indefinitely. Congress faced the difficulty of writing the rules for AT&T's conduct in the free market when at any moment the corporation might be radically rent asunder by a guilty verdict. And, in light of the Japanese electronics invasion and endemic electronics espionage on the part of the Russians, was this any time to be breaking up the world's most efficient communications system?

The Reagan administration wanted it both ways — open competition in telecommunications but the continuation of a strong, centralized Bell System — and congressional efforts to rewrite the Communications Act came to be seen as a way of preempting the tangle of antitrust litigation now surrounding AT&T. As the quarreling between Congress, Justice and the FCC heated up, officials from the Pentagon stepped into the fray, venturing that the breakup of the Bell System, the military's favorite contractor, would lead to severe consequences for military communications and national security. At first, Justice Department antitrust chief William Baxter stood fast, vowing to litigate the AT&T case "to the eyeballs." He added,

"I don't intend to fold up my tent and go away because the Department of Defense has expressed concern."

They were brave words, and quickly eaten. As pressure from the Pentagon increased, Justice found itself more and more alone on the antitrust question. A few months later, Baxter reported to Congress that he now "wholly support[ed]" the idea that less radical legislative restrictions on AT&T were an adequate substitute for the divestiture sought by Justice. At this writing, the antitrust trial has ground more or less to a halt, in the wake of a controversial Defense Department report asserting that "divestiture as currently proposed by the Justice Department . . . would cause substantial harm to national defense and security and emergency preparedness telecommunications capability." However awkwardly worded, the report was a bombshell, and not just because of its assertions. Presiding Judge Harold Green interrupted the trial when he learned that Defense officials had prepared the report only after a round of helpful consultation with planners from AT&T itself. As reported in *Electronic News:*

> "Didn't you think it was odd to ask the supposed victim of such divestiture?" asked Judge Green.
> "No sir, I did not," the [Defense Department] witness replied, explaining the AT&T briefings were needed to describe network planning and management so that DOD officials "could understand it."

As it stands now (1981), the most likely outcome is that Justice will drop the suit if Congress makes sure that Western Electric sells as much equipment to outside competitors as it sells internally to Bell itself. In any event, the Justice Department antitrust suit is clearly in jeopardy. "After a generation or more of littering the American industrial scene with the corpses of its competitors," raged William McGowan, the outspoken chairman of MCI and the leading hound at the heels of AT&T, "and after the Department of Justice and the courts are finally in a position to structure the telecommunications industry so as to foreclose continuation of this wanton misconduct, it would be ironic if the Congress were to succeed in immunizing AT&T from the consequences of its misdeeds." *

So much for Justice. As for IBM, the company with the most to lose if Baby Bell clears all the legal hurdles in its path, there were fears that all the bureaucratic infighting over telecommunications might lead to "creeping regulation" of the computer field. Having recently entered the market for personal computers with a product built around an Intel microprocessor chip, and facing the prospect of competitive personal computer terminals from AT&T by the end of the decade, if not sooner, IBM had a vision of the future it is tempting to call the Dire Scenario. It goes like this: The government and the courts unshackle AT&T. Its supposedly arm's-length subsidiary, Baby Bell, begins selling computer systems in direct competition with IBM. Suppose, however, that the net effect of this historic move proves to be a classic free market brawl in which smaller innovative competitors are eliminated rather than encouraged. If that happens, there might come a point in the grand telecommunications experiment when the government decides that it made a mistake. It comes lurching back onto the field, not necessarily to boot Bell out of the computer business, but to *regulate* the computer business as a vital public service, just as it had once chosen to regulate the telephone field. At this point, the government offers IBM two equally unpalatable choices: submit to regulation as some sort of computer common carrier, or stop making and selling computers altogether.

Given the historical twists and turns of the government's efforts at regulating electronic communication, this outcome is not nearly as farfetched as it sounds. Furthermore, AT&T, which one might assume would be wholly satisfied with the deregulatory efforts thus far, has its own version of the Dire

---

* On January 8, 1982, the Justice Department dropped the AT&T case, in return for Bell's promise to sell off its twenty-three local operating companies. On the same day, the Justice Department dropped the thirteen-year-old IBM antitrust case as well.

Scenario — the Invasion of the Market Snatchers. This time out, a misguided government interprets deregulation, in the long run, as the unleashing of Bell's competitors and the checkmating of Bell's rightful attempts to compete back. IBM is allowed to take on the added mantle of telephone company, while the government hamstrings Bell so severely that it loses its play for a piece of the computer market, as well as its former monopoly over communications. The nightmare ends with AT&T falling to pieces, as the cost of telephone and computer services soar, while the reliability of communications channels plummets. The GNP sinks, and the U.S. defense capability dwindles. And even if IBM becomes the new centralized heir to the Bell System, the Japanese march in and finish off the victor. The high-technology end of the American economy goes into a deadly tailspin, and all is lost.

As evidence that its future in the computer world was much less clear-cut than the Baby Bell decision might indicate, there was AT&T's aborted attempt to provide electronic Yellow Pages via computer terminals. Shortly after the Baby Bell decision, AT&T announced plans for a test project in Texas. The object was to supply a few subscribers with computer terminals, send them an electronic version of the advertising making up Bell's Yellow Pages, and see how it went. The plan was quite modest, compared to ongoing "video text" experiments elsewhere. Warner Communications' Qube project in Ohio, for example, allowed test subscribers to indulge in a number of futuristic electronic services via two-way, interactive cable television, while allowing advertisers to indulge in several interesting experiments of their own — primarily the test-marketing of new products. The British, the French and the Canadians had even grander video text experiments under way, but when AT&T revealed its plans for the pilot project in Texas, this seemingly logical first step into the computer field was met with enough howls of outrage to kill the idea even before it got off the ground. Predictably, many of the complaints came from the computer makers, but the clincher was heated opposition from newspaper publishers who were deep in their own sundry test efforts at providing home computer owners with electronic newspapers, and who feared that the Yellow Pages project was nothing but a blatant attempt to siphon away advertising dollars.

"It's the basic AT&T question," said one supplier of personal computers. "That is, should a monopoly with tariffs and rates regulated by the government be able to use its funds to compete with non-regulated companies who are investing their funds into computers and videotext?" It is the same question that continues to plague the government's efforts to let AT&T into the computer market; namely, the phone company's dominant marketing position, crumbling monopoly or not, amounting to a government-sanctioned entry into some four out of five American homes and businesses. Computer companies and newspaper publishers portrayed the Bell experiment as an affront to the First Amendment as well, a charge AT&T read as "specious." In the end, however, both the Texas State Public Utilities Commission and a Texas state district court barred AT&T from offering its video Yellow Pages as planned. At that point, AT&T withdrew from the field to lick its wounds and plot a less controversial opening gambit.

It should be apparent from this brief discussion of regulatory issues, and the number of combatants and claimants involved, that in telecommunications all manner of confusing and contradictory outcomes are possible. The future of Baby Bell is by no means assured, no more so than the future of IBM's leap into personal computers. IBM has yet to demonstrate that it can transfer its industrial marketing savvy to the retail world of consumer electronics, where so many corporate efforts have misfired in the past. Electronics companies have been better at selling to other companies than they are at selling to individual consumers, especially when the "what" being sold is access to digitized information. Lurking behind the upheavals in telecommunications, and the fight for "market share," are more basic questions having to do with digitized information as a resource — how to price it, how to sell it, how to structure and regulate the systems that deliver it. In short, how to decide who has access to which information, and at what price.

Telecommunications and compunications are nothing more than terms for describing the portion of the grid along which electronic information flows from place to place. The question of which companies will come to dominate this market remains open, dependent in part on new technologies and in part on less spectacular matters such as court decisions. (Almost every move into telecommunications will be litigated "to the eyeballs" by somebody.)

The future look of telecommunications, and the rewiring of the grid required to allow for the information services the telephone-television-computer makes possible, are made even more cloudy by a wild-card technology not yet discussed. It is the last major technological advance to be discussed in this book, precisely because it has the potential of becoming the most readily accessible means of tapping into the worldwide flow of digitized information. It is satellite communication, and if the satellite connection takes hold in a major way, the radical restructuring of the grid thus far may turn out to be nothing more than an interesting historical interregnum, a minor skirmishing before the storm. Access to existing communications channels, and all the telephones, televisions and computers connected to them, may well hinge on access to invisible transmissions from space. With the satellite connection, the future known as the wired life may have very little wiring in it at all.

The Satellite Connection: The Grid **De**wired?

If telecommunications is what results when computers, telephones and televisions are joined together in systems that simultaneously transmit and process digitized information along diverse pathways of wire, cable and radio waves, satellite communications is what happens when a growing portion of that information traffic is carried some twenty-three thousand miles above the earth.

Communication satellites, or comsats for short, represent the great unknown in the telecommunications equation. As integrated circuits did away with much of the internal wiring in modern electronic machines and systems, so satellites and new methods of digital data transmission may do away with the outer wiring and switching hardware of the grid itself. Comsats call into question every conceivable form of land-based communication, and the future of the companies that profit from them. Anyone who benefits from the laying of cable and the stringing of wires, from cable-TV maven Ted Turner to Ma Bell's Wichita lineman, might do well to ponder what the satellite connection bodes for the future. As telecommunications specialist James Martin has written, "AT&T alone is spending $9 to $10 billion *per year* on capital improvements of the Bell System. AT&T top management has indicated that they intend this level of expenditure to continue. The annual revenue from telecommunications in the United States is around $35 billion and is growing at about $4 billion per year. Much of the capital expenditure in the telecommunications industry is going into the trunks and trunk switching that satellites and [related] equipment could replace today." And, as Martin further points out, "To a traditional common carrier a satellite is a means to *augment* its existing network. To a new entrant, a satellite is a means to *bypass* the established common carrier facilities."

The promise of satellite communication is actually the combined promise of several advancing technologies — microcomputers, digital data transmission, radio, television, space science, and others. Comsats work very much like land-based radio systems. Electronic signals representing voice, pictures or computer data are beamed via radio waves from a terrestrial transmitting station to an orbiting satellite. Essentially a collection of sophisticated integrated circuitry connected to a solar power source, the comsat processes the signals it receives and then retransmits them earthward on another radio frequency. The signals can be picked up by any properly tuned receiving station. An earth station, as these receivers are called, is nothing more than a concave dish with a short antenna in the middle of it.

As with any application of solid-state technology, the driving force in satellite communications is the falling cost and increasing performance of the requisite integrated circuitry. This is particularly true of earth stations, which are rapidly becoming smaller and cheaper, and it is the reason why the satellite connection is so tantalizing, and so potentially inimical to certain entrenched interests. As improbable as it sounds, when the freight is electronic information the cheapest distance between any two points — New York to Los Angeles, say, or Des Moines to Djarkarta, or even Boston to Pittsburgh — may be the distance from earth to satellite and back, or about fifty thousand miles. Conventional communication between any two such points requires costly miles of land wires or undersea cables, while as many as 150 transmission towers are required to pass signals cross-country in land-based microwave transmission systems. Satellites can do it in one bounce. They are "distance-insensitive." As an official of the Bonneville Satellite Corporation told the *San Francisco Chronicle,* a satellite transmission costs "the same regardless of how far you go. With AT&T you pay by the mile."

The satellite connection poses a direct economic threat to the dominance of the major television networks, cable TV operators, radio broadcasters, communications common carriers, and vendors of distributed computing services. Corporations like IBM, AT&T and RCA, all well aware of this fact, are struggling for position in a new space race of sorts, as telecommunications escalates into what has been called the "corporate Star Wars." While ownership of the orbital "birds" themselves is largely in the hands of the military and major American multinationals, and will likely remain so, the market for affordable earth stations here at home shows every sign of becoming a new haven for the garage-shop entrepreneur and the small, innovation-intensive company. Obviously, this suggests a certain clash of interests. Large corporations and interests may decide to favor a future satellite network which depends upon small numbers of large and relatively costly earth stations. Not coincidentally, this approach would serve to protect corporate investments in existing wire and cable transmission schemes, since they would still be required to connect the centralized earth station with the homes and offices of subscribers. Smaller companies, however, are venturing forth with a more radical approach — sending electronic signals directly from comsats to small, affordable, individually owned earth stations on rooftops or in backyards. Known as DBS, for direct broadcast satellite transmission, this system conceivably eliminates traditional common carrier functions entirely, since it eliminates the need for land-based information traffic and complex, centralized switching centers.

For this reason, the satellite connection could become a dramatic new way of making good on all the individual electronic services promised on behalf of the personal computer revolution — provided that the environmental and health effects of microwave transmissions and other forms of "electronic smog" do not prove to be major limiting factors. If cheap earth stations become as common in the future as rooftop TV antennas are today, satellites will offer a connecting link that potentially puts every home or office electronic information center in touch with every other such system, anytime, anywhere, without wires. Satellites will assure that Dick Tracy not only will live, but that his wrist radio-telephone will become the wrist or pocket computer terminal. Mobile computer terminals, which already exist, could be linked via satellite with one's own home computer system, or with any other computer or telephone owner.

Any technology tends to precede and continually outrun society's ability to envision its applications and write the laws that will govern them. It is always amusing to recall the fumbling forecasts that accompanied the early days of electrical power, the computer, the transistor and the microcomputer.

No doubt this chapter contains a few mispredictions as well, but the satellite connection opens so many new doors to the world information order now unfolding, that specific predictions about the wired life are just so much educated guessing. Almost anything anyone chooses to forecast about the future of the microelectronics revolution has at least a chance of coming true. The satellite connection very nearly ushers in Nikola Tesla's great Wardencliff vision entire. Tesla, it will be remembered, predicted that wires would have no place at all in the future transmission of "intelligence and power." The grid and all the things it could do would be "teleautomatic," invisible, instantaneous, global. Information and energy would be "drawn off" by anyone, anywhere, with a suitable antenna.

With the satellite connection, every bit of it is true. Children of the future may laugh when they learn of a time when phone calls, TV programs, computer data and electrical energy all traveled along miles and miles of crude copper wire or undersea cable. Even without satellites, wires and cables will play a greatly diminished role in future telecommunications systems. In recognition of this fact, Bell has simply stopped laying any new copper wire at all in high-traffic locations like Los Angeles. Light waves, with frequencies many thousand times higher than radio waves, are a nearly perfect medium for digital data transmission. Sending information by light wave is not a new technology but rather, under the influence of microelectronics, a vastly improved one. The most promising current approach is called fiber optics, wherein data is transmitted along light waves coursing through tiny, hair-thin glass fibers. These optical fibers carry many times the information traffic copper wires or conventional cables can carry, and thanks to massive research investment, fiber optics has become a growing adjunct to conventional transmission lines.

As the power of the electron yields to the power of the photon, there are even more radical alternatives in the wind. Since optical fibers cannot be strung into space, and since there are only so many frequencies available in the radio spectrum, much current work concerns ways of beaming information to satellites on "unguided" beams of light, rather like shining a flashlight on a target. Also called "free-space" optics, these laserlike techniques, if successful, will free satellite communication from both the constraints of land-based wire and cable, and the traffic jams in radio frequencies now used for satellite communication.

The first true communications satellite was TELSTAR, designed by AT&T in 1962. AT&T did considerable planning in the 1960s for handling telephone traffic via satellite, and satellites might have helped make an initial success of "Picturephone," AT&T's early stab at corporate teleconferencing, offered as a vision of the future but perceived, more often than not, as a balky gimmick. AT&T had the skills, the facilities and the most to gain from the satellite connection, but the U.S. government blocked its full-scale entry into satellite communications, just as it was barred until recently from entering the computer market. AT&T's inability to exploit the satellite market in its formative stages very likely was the factor that allowed the subsequent birth of private corporate satellite networks and the infant earth station industry.

Gradually, comsats came to be seen as a less-costly alternative to undersea cables for international telecommunications traffic. Having denied AT&T a priority position in the satellite field, the FCC handed the satellite business to a quasi-public company known as Comsat General. The FCC said that only Comsat could operate satellites, and that the satellites could only be used for international communications traffic. Comsat, in turn, leased satellite channels to various parties, including a consortium of more than one hundred nations — Intelsat — which negotiated operating agreements and provided satellite communication services to other nations of the world.

In 1972, however, Canada turned to satellites for *domestic* telecommunications traffic, and the results were spectacular. Canada's ANIK satellites bought telecommunications and television service to remote regions of its sparsely populated north country, but they also helped to prove that the satellite connection could mean keen competition for established common carriers. According to James Martin, ". . . for their first two years in orbit these satellites earned a return on capital investment that was virtually unprecedented in the telecommunications industry."

When antennas for receiving ANIK broadcasts began appearing on the American side of the border, Congress and the FCC moved to open up the satellite market to free competition, just as it was beginning to do for telecommunications at large. The result was the FCC's Open Skies Policy, which encouraged private industry to submit proposals for launching and operating their own communication satellites. The first to do so was Western Union, and its WESTAR satellites of 1974 offered a new mode of competition against land-based common carriers. Soon, company after company petitioned the FCC for the privilege of building, buying, leasing or launching comsats.

One of the first private industries to grasp the potential of the satellite connection was the cable-TV industry. To the alarm of the three major television networks, cable-TV operators could compete very effectively by leasing satellite channels and beaming programs to a system of earth stations scattered throughout its broadcast area. From the regional earth stations, programming went out to individual subscribers through a feeder system of cables. This was the origin of Home Box Office and other pay-TV offerings. Ironically, or so it may prove, the rosy predictions issuing from cable-TV executives made little mention of the likely next step in the satellite connection — individual earth stations on every rooftop, meaning direct broadcast from satellite to home or office, with no intermediary cables at all.

Various large corporations were interested in satellite communication for two-way business teleconferencing, while computer makers and users were interested in comsats for the same reasons they were interested in phone lines and microwave bands — as channels over which computers could "talk." In 1980 the FCC's deregulatory enthusiasm culminated in the approval of proposals for more than twenty new satellites from major American corporations, representing roughly a threefold increase in the existing communications capacity of the satellite connection. One of the petitioners was AT&T, for just as with computers, the FCC had decided to allow the phone company fully into the satellite business at last.

Beyond AT&T, the roster of successful petitioners thus far adds up to a rather familiar family of established interests. IBM has entered the satellite business through Satellite Business Systems (SBS), a joint venture with Comsat General and Aetna Life and Casualty. RCA Corporation is in the air with its SATCOM family of birds, and now entering the market are satellites from Southern Pacific, Hughes Communication, General Telephone and Electronics, and others. Also investing heavily in various aspects of the satellite connection are TRW, General Electric, Rockwell International, and Ford Motor Company's wholly-owned subsidiary, Ford Aerospace and Communications Corporation. In light of the current automobile market, Ford's investment in the satellite connection may represent as shrewd a ploy as George Westinghouse's leap from railroad air brakes to AC electrical power. And it would be remiss not to mention whopping investments by other familiar parties, among them the U.S. Department of Defense, Japan and Russia.

These satellite owners and investors will be leasing communication channels to a host of clients. Western Union's WESTAR 1, for example, provides satellite service to Dow Jones, Muzak, and National Public Radio among others. There are lesser entrants in the field as well, but so far, while embracing the concept of open competition, the FCC has given great weight to the needs of large, established communications companies in allocating orbital space for satellites. This is a problem, because there are only so many choice orbital slots to go around. Like players in a game of musical chairs, large and small competitors in the satellite market must vie for permission to occupy the precious orbital slots available.

The preferred allocations are "geosynchronous" orbits about

twenty-three thousand miles up. At that distance, satellites orbit the earth in twenty-four hours, which means that they remain in a stationary position with respect to the earth. They are "parked" permanently, over a fixed point on earth. To a ground observer, they do not appear to be moving at all. With only so many optimum parking spaces for the picking, the international competition for them is growing fierce.

A finite number of orbital slots is only one of the limitations the laws of physics impose upon the growth of the satellite connection. Traffic jams in space are a novel development, but there is nothing new about traffic jams in the radio frequency spectrum. Radio frequencies are those wavelengths of the electromagnetic spectrum over which most electronic communication takes place. Radio, TV, mobile telephones, microwave systems and communications satellites all depend upon these wavelengths, and, once again, there are only so many of them to go around. Until recently, this wasn't such a pressing problem. Since radio and TV were developed, scientists have learned how to use higher and higher frequencies for electronic communication, meaning that the number of broadcast channels available for use has increased as much as a millionfold since the early days of the century. However, the greater the information freight on a given wavelength, the greater the potential for interference — a scrambled or obliterated signal. Interference can be as mundane as the wavy lines on a television screen caused by the operation of a nearby power saw, or as serious as the breakdown of communications between the Pentagon and a military information satellite. The problem of interference, and the anarchy in communications that would result if it becomes widespread, imposes a special need for cooperative international efforts to coordinate the complicated process of "spectrum management."

There are ways out of these twin traffic jams, the physical one in space over orbital slots, and the invisible one over communication frequencies in the spectrum. In space, some structure akin to an orbital space station occupying only a single orbital slot might serve in the future as a platform for many comsats, all sharing common equipment and a common power source. As for frequency shortages, there is the obvious promise of light wave communication as a way of opening up new reaches of the spectrum. New forms of digital circuitry might serve as frequency-control chips to alleviate interference. For the near term, however, the physical limitations now extant will make satellite ownership a costly and hotly contested business, accessible only to a limited number of well-heeled players.

Even so, the limitations on satellite ownership do not necessarily restrict the number of people who can make *use* of the satellite connection. The question of who stands to gain, and who to lose, from comsats depends in large part upon the nature of the earth station industry on the ground below. It isn't necessary to own a $30 million satellite, or even to lease its available communications channels, to benefit from the satellite connection. In fairness, it should be noted that the $30 million price tag for a satellite launch will soon fall dramatically. Comsat enthusiasts were buoyed by the success of the space shuttle Columbia, and its future cargoes will contain many comsats. It is far cheaper to kick satellites out the door of a reusable shuttle in orbit, than to launch them one at a time, one comsat per rocket. Direct broadcast satellite transmission to affordable earth stations means that, potentially, any earth station owner can pull in any transmission on the satellite connection.

Private earth stations first appeared in the parking lots of businesses for teleconferencing or, in the case of cable-TV companies, for broadcasting programming to subscribers. As the cost and size of earth stations fell, other businesses and institutions, particularly newspapers, joined in. Regional editions of the *Wall Street Journal* and the *New York Times* are transmitted via satellite. Gannett Company, the nation's largest newspaper chain, is laying plans for its own comsat network. Hotel chains, led by Holiday Inn, are looking to earth stations for teleconferencing as a way of bolstering the convention trade. The Mormon Church has considered buying some eight hundred earth stations as vehicles for offering electronic church services to its three million members across the country.

But today's $10,000 to $20,000 satellite dish, with a diameter of ten feet or more, is becoming tomorrow's $300 to $3,000 backyard earth station, with a diameter of three feet or less. Homeowner earth stations first appeared in remote areas where TV reception previously was unavailable. Now earth stations have reached the point where any affluent consumer can own one. The 1979 Neiman-Marcus Christmas catalogue offered a deluxe dish from Scientific–Atlanta for $36,500, including installation. Heath Company has applied for FCC approval to sell a $7,000 do-it-yourself earth station kit. Dozens of other companies are moving into the market, and the emergent earth station industry has reached that rather frenzied, evangelical stage that marks the beginning of a new solid-state invasion. This consumer market in the making has some intriguing ramifications. A small company called Microdyne, advertising its new $12,500 "Megastar" home earth station, blithely promises "your choice of all the best programs this hemisphere has to offer."

But for free? Why would anyone pay Home Box Office, for example, when a backyard earth station can bring in all of HBO's movie offerings without benefit of subscription? Video piracy, the reception of satellite signals intended for a paying audience, requires only an earth station and, in some cases, an associated "descrambling" device. The up-front costs of the equipment are falling enough that a $300 to $500 investment for the total package is foreseeable. "Poaching" broadcasts in this fashion is a development that threatens to draw advertising revenue away from the networks and subscribers away from the pay cable channels. Earth station owners and suppliers, at this writing, are still awaiting a definite court test relating to this matter, but the television industry was shaken considerably when a large company, Comsat General, announced that it planned to seek FCC approval for offering direct satellite-to-home TV transmission to viewers willing to purchase cheap earth stations. While the initial offerings would likely be familiar ones like movies, sports and news, a system like the one Comsat envisions could be expanded in the future to include the reception of electronic mail and newspapers. In addition, if present receive-only dishes give way to equally affordable two-way earth stations for reception *and* transmission, personal computer owners as well as TV viewers ultimately could take advantage of the communications lines such direct broadcast satellite systems provide. Any electronic information service at all can be carried on the satellite connection, and any company that offers such services could find its share of future information traffic greatly diminished if it fails to plan for a comsat in its future.

While companies large and small are seeking to profit legally from direct broadcast satellite transmission, there may be little anyone can do to prevent outright piracy. An aura of outlawry almost certainly will be a part of the satellite future, similar to that which pervaded the formative stages of the personal computer industry. And the same question of access to electronic transmissions is raised. The argument over direct broadcast satellite transmission is similar in many respects to the recording industry debate over the practice of "bootlegging" newly released albums on home tape cassette decks. The recording industry has pressured radio stations to stop showcasing new releases in their entirety, while exerting similar pressure on the recording tape industry to boost the price of blank cassettes. Little of this is likely to have much effect on the tape pirates, however, since an easier avenue is simply to borrow a new album for taping from someone who already owns it. Satellite piracy may prove equally difficult to fend off, and the reception of TV broadcasts is only the beginning. The FCC has predicted that, regardless of the regulatory stance it chooses to take toward the satellite connection, small earth stations will be in widespread use by 1990. The endemic piracy — legal or illegal — made possible by this growth calls up a related question that plagues the satellite connection: what will the widespread availability of communication and personal computer services do to the cherished American notion of personal privacy?

"When my children's homes are wired," reflected former FCC chairman Charles Ferris, a few months after the "barricades from the door to the information age," had been removed by his commission, "a computer will have a record of what they buy and how much they spend. It will know whether they pay bills quickly, slowly or not at all, and it will know where their money comes from. It will know whether they watched the debates, or the football game or a controversial movie. In other words, it will know more about them than anyone should."

Perhaps so. Already, computerized information about people's credit records, criminal records, medical records, driving records, financial data, and other information from which personal habits can be deduced, is easily available to anyone who asks for it in the absence of specific restrictions against it. But the question cuts both ways. The prospect of millions of personal computer owners tapping into various private corporate computer networks, perhaps even military networks, led a major business research institute to conclude: "The reason [distributed processing] computer networks will not be available to the general public at an earlier date is primarily one of security. At present, fraudulent input or access to a data base management system cannot be prevented." Questions of security, privacy and unauthorized access, as they relate to compunications services, will only become more ticklish as the satellite connection flourishes.

It took telecommunications, radios and televisions about two decades to saturate the households of the developed world. Personal computers appear to be speeding along roughly the same course, and there are no convincing reasons to assume that earth stations will deviate markedly from this timeline. In the industrialized West, the struggle over telecommunications and satellites is being waged for profit. In the so-called Third World, access to these services is an urgent matter of survival.

Third World Airwaves

When the new government in Iran seized American citizens and held them hostage a few years ago, one of the sanctions the Carter administration considered in retaliation was a cut-off of Iran's access to the Intelsat fleet of communication satellites. More than 70 percent of Iran's international telecommunications traffic travels by satellite, and had this threat been carried out, Iran's international computerized financial transactions, its airline service, and its radio and television reception would have been thrown into utter disarray. Its economy would have been disrupted severely, perhaps fatally. Though this action was never taken (partly because Intelsat officials saw it as a bad precedent), the incident underscores the fact that access to telecommunications and the satellite connection is a highly charged political issue for the lesser-developed nations known collectively as the Third World.

If the age of wires is coming to an end, to be replaced by optical glass fibers, satellites and earth stations, then there is no reason for developing nations to recapitulate it. Satellite communication offers them a low-impact, high-efficiency, potentially affordable alternative. It is a lesson the Third World has learned. Because laying wires is so costly and so difficult in formidable terrain, many nations have turned to shortwave radio telecommunications systems for communication. This makes the leap to satellite communication even more logical, since there is less existing investment in land wires to be lost. What the Third World needs, and is beginning to demand, is room in space and in the electromagnetic spectrum for independently owned domestic comsat systems. Third World nations want their own satellites, and they want changes in international law that will prevent them from being frozen out of the world electronic information order. Otherwise, they face the future prospect of finding that all of the orbital slots and usable frequencies have been taken.

From the viewpoint of the developed West, the growth of telecommunications in the Third World has represented both a market for American corporations and an obvious boon to the underprivileged. Yet often in the Third World itself, as Vietnamese scholar Tran Van Dinh has written, "Telecommunications were first perceived by colonized peoples as a visible instrument of colonial power." Telecommunications points to global unification and the free flow of international information, but developing nations often fear it will also mean the undermining of efforts to achieve national sovereignty due to ever-increasing economic dependence on major powers. Compounding the problem is the fact that the needs of the world's peoples have been given short shrift in the overall allocation of telecommunications services. Comsats could make widely available a host of vital services at low cost. As John McHale wrote in *The Changing Information Environment:*

> For example, in the provision of expert medical diagnostic service, the advice of any specialist anywhere in the world could be available in any of its remotest hamlets; complex physiological analysis requiring the most advanced equipment could be on hand via telemetering devices. The highest application of human knowledge, via libraries, computer banks and 'live' human specialists could be within the reach of any small community.

So far, however, the satellite connection more often has meant a steady avalanche of *Starsky and Hutch* reruns. The U.S., having pioneered the field of telecommunications, also established the long-standing "first-come, first-served" method of allocating rights to the airwaves, a cornerstone of U.S. communications policy now under heavy fire from the Third World. There is an international body, the World Administrative Radio Conference, charged with sorting out matters of this kind. WARC, as it is known, has convened periodically throughout the century, but for most of its history it has functioned as little more than a rubber-stamp agency, routinely approving requests by the U.S. and other developed nations for more and more international telecommunications frequencies. Now under the auspices of a United Nations agency, the International Telecommunications Union, WARC has no enforcement powers, and compliance with its resolutions is strictly voluntary. Nonetheless, it is the only international forum of its kind, and since it operates on a one-nation, one-vote basis, the U.S. must listen, if not necessarily bow, to the case for change developing nations are now making.

Of the many issues addressed at the 1979 conference in Geneva, the first full-scale meeting of WARC since 1959, the allocation of satellite orbits and frequencies was perhaps the most far-reaching. A special mini-WARC held in 1971 on the subject of space telecommunications had adopted a resolution stating "That all countries have equal rights in the use of both the radio frequencies allocated to various space radiocommunications services and the geostationary satellite orbit for these services. . . ."

But it was one thing to resolve it, and quite another to make it come true when the full 1979 WARC came around. This time out, twice as many Third World nations showed up as did for the last full meeting in 1959. By and large, U.S. interests got what they wanted out of WARC once again. But on the significant issue of increasing the number of orbital slots and spectrum frequencies available to existing satellite owners, the Third World chose to stand fast. Opposing business as usual under the first-come, first-served doctrine, Third World leaders called for a policy of reserving orbital positions for future use. Some countries have even suggested that a nation's territorial airspace rightly extends twenty-three thousand miles into space, a doctrine that would yield a reserved orbital slot for every nation on earth. The U.S. wasn't about to buy the idea of leaving precious slots fallow under some vague priority system of reservations for the future, but so adamant were

Third Worlders on the matter that the issue ended in a stalemate. The question of Third World satellites was put off, to be resolved at a special mini-WARC to be held on the subject in the prophetic year 1984.

The Third World also demanded, and got, a 1982 mini-WARC on another issue left unresolved: the request by several industrialized nations, including the U.S., for more shortwave frequencies used in international broadcasting. Fearful that the 1982 session would lead to a curtailment of its available shortwave frequencies, the U.S. took the rare step of refusing to pledge compliance with the outcome. If WARC does not grant the U.S. the new frequencies it wants, the chairman of the U.S. delegation told *Business Week,* "we might want to operate in the adjacent bands anyway."

The hows and whys of the electronic age are being patched together in the courts, in Congress, in corporate boardrooms and various other official arenas. In the U.S., the salient question is the amount of concentration and standardization of the electronic industry that will result. In his survey of global telecommunications issues, *The Geopolitics of Information,* Anthony Smith offers as an example the potential ramifications of IBM's participation in Satellite Business Systems, the comsat venture known as SBS.

> The new system will offer large corporations the chance to send all of their messages — letters, invoices, filing systems, computer data and telex and telephone services — by way of the satellite to small ground stations situated on the premises of the companies concerned. From these local points telephone calls can be sent through AT&T's normal system. SBS is capable of transmitting an enormous volume of traffic, all of which, in effect, would be business taken away from the US postal system and AT&T. . . . SBS is not only, however, a blow for communications cheapness, instantaneity and corporate autonomy. It is also a blow against all the new competitors of IBM which have sprung up in Europe, Japan and the developing countries. All companies using the new internal communications system

based on SBS would have to use IBM's computer installations. The new mini-computer movement might even be crippled, since it will become cheaper to use the capacity of a distant mainframe computer of the kind IBM specializes in, once the heavy cost of normal telecommunications links (as previously provided through AT&T) are eliminated.

The point is that an undue concentration of technological prowess or market clout in the hands of a very few large corporations goes against the grain of how technological innovation occurs. With thirty-five years of solid-state electronics as evidence, it is clear that the major wellspring of technological innovation — and new jobs — is the small, rapidly mutating new start-up company. If telecommunications becomes an all-or-nothing battle for market share between a handful of giants, the real loser could be the individual consumer everywhere, whose freedom of choice could be drastically curtailed.

CHAPTER TEN

The Hidden Costs of Automation

Remember: You can be replaced by a silicon chip.
— SIGN ABOVE THE DESK OF AN OFFICE WORKER
IN A 1981 MAGAZINE CARTOON

Automating Jobs

Automation is the term normally used to describe the technology-driven displacement of labor by capital, meaning the displacement of men and women by machines in the workplace. "Structural" unemployment is the term used to describe the results. While microelectronics and telecommunications links, the triumphs of the machine age, tend to accelerate this process, automation has been intensely debated ever since a frustrated worker named Ned Ludd destroyed stocking frames in a quixotic attempt to keep machinery out of the textile business in early nineteenth-century Britain. Those who fear technology and automation have been labeled "Luddites" ever since, while those who embrace these entertwined forces are just as commonly known as "technocrats."

Automation, made possible by new technologies, is the motive power behind several hallmarks of the industrial age — the rise of the large corporation, the specialization of labor, the standardization of goods and services, and the growth of the market economy made possible by mass-production. What began in the United States with Frederick Taylor's turn-of-the-century Scientific Management movement — an attempt at bringing the principles of engineering to bear on the matter of increasing worker productivity in factories — has culminated in the fully automated factory and the electronic office of

259

today. With microprocessors providing the links between intelligent robotic equipment and computerized information and control centers, industrial society begins to resemble an automated nervous system, an organism, a collective metabolism which transcends the mere mechanical. More and more workers become living links in a feedback system of automated electronic logic.

Traditionally, economists view automation as a means of increasing productivity. Automation means that output per worker goes up for the simple reason that there are fewer workers and more production. Increased productivity (and not just increased production) lowers labor costs and hikes sales. This, in turn, increases profits, but these profits must be offset to an increasing degree by a major investment in the innovative technologies that make automation possible. One of the basic arguments over the long-term effects of automation is the fate of the workers who are displaced by machines in the pursuit of the production efficiencies automation affords. Corporate managers commonly argue that the structurally unemployed, meaning those workers whose job skills have been rendered obsolete by technology, are "reabsorbed" into the new sectors of the economy that new wealth creates. Moreover, it is held that the jobs lost are usually menial (read manual), while those created are usually meaningful (read white collar). As Fairchild's C. Lester Hogan tersely put it in *Science* magazine, "Advancing technology never reduces employment in the long run." The semiconductor industry itself is a prime piece of evidence in behalf of this assertion. Certainly the jobs lost when the integrated circuit put an end to the manual wiring of circuits were more than offset by the explosive employment growth of a completely new industry.

And yet, for all this, automation historically has been blamed for labor unrest, the breakdown of the family, suicide, mental illness, and the systematic exclusion of women and ethnic minorities from the workplace. In addition, the spiraling capital costs that automation implies, and the increasing economic growth rate required to sustain it, have drawn the wrath of environmentalists and foes of big business. Thus, concerns about automation lead directly back to larger concerns over the desirable growth rate of the consumer economy.

So far, the effects of automation have been addressed far more critically in Europe than in the U.S., partly because current unemployment levels are correspondingly higher. In the West German press, microprocessors have been assailed as "job killers," and sundry studies have been produced in various nations to bolster this claim. However, as one automation researcher put the dilemma: "European industries face a stark choice — adopt new technology and lose some jobs, or fail to remain competitive and lose most or all of your jobs." For the faltering economy of Great Britain, wracked by record levels of joblessness, automation by microprocessor is a particularly acute question. A 1978 BBC documentary on the microchip stated it this way: "Can we all live on the wealth of automatic factories and the earnings of an elite band of 60,000 software engineers?"

No one really knows. Though studies of these questions do exist, most of them originating outside the U.S., the nature of structural unemployment is a far more subtle matter than outright layoffs, and it frustrates attempts to quantify accurately the effect of the microchip on employment patterns. At present, the range of predictions is so varied as to suggest that economists, analysts and policymakers have yet to reach a consensus on the basic issue — whether the microchip creates jobs or destroys them. However, one salient point is beyond dispute — a growing percentage of the work force will be involved in the ongoing experiment of finding out. Regardless of the microchip's impact on the *quantity* of jobs in the future, there is no doubting that the *quality* of such jobs as exist will be altered drastically. The following examples of the changing labor market are not intended as an exhaustive survey of microelectronics-induced disruptions in the workplace, but rather as a glimpse of the wholesale upheavals in store for workers as the microelectronics revolution proceeds apace. Very few vocations will prove immune. As a sampling, consider what the microchip portends for the factory shift foreman, the secretary, the mail carrier, the automobile mechanic, and the farmer.

In 1980, the Joint Economic Committee (JEC) of the U.S. Congress assembled a report on the changing face of the American workplace. As reported in *Electronic News:*

> Robots, aided by computers and microprocessors, already are being used in the automotive, aerospace, appliance, metalworking, glass, rubber, and machinery industries. They weld, paint, cut, assemble and machine-load. Worldwide robot sales last year totaled $279 million and are expected to expand to $4.6 billion by 1980. . . . By 1984, the Japanese government plans to have an unmanned metalworking plant on line, producing machinery components ranging from hydraulic pumps to heavy duty transmitters. The JEC said every operation, from casting to final inspection, would be handled by flexible automatic systems and robots, all supervised by a central computer and a handful of engineers and technicians.

As an idealized case in point, how will this trend affect a shift foreman at a small production plant? When his factory becomes computerized, the shift foreman won't necessarily lose his job. Nor will he necessarily leave it. The job, in a sense, will leave him.

For thirty-five years, the shift foreman has worked at a battery manufacturing plant owned by a large corporation in another state. His job is to supervise battery production during his shift run in order to meet predetermined production goals sent down by management. He functions as an intermediary between corporate management and the plant labor force of roughly 150 line workers. His job, in essence, is communication, and computers have nothing to do with it. The only computerized aspect of the plant is the accounting, personnel and other recordkeeping functions of the front office. He spends the majority of his shift on the plant floor, talking to workers and troubleshooting. The rest of his time is spent in his plant-side office, writing and filing production reports. He has an excellent job record, he relates well to his fellow workers up and down the human chain of command, and he is five years from retirement.

Soon, however, squadrons of management information specialists, dispatched from the parent corporation, descend upon the factory. They scrutinize plant records, design computer flow charts, and study the various tasks that the workers on the assembly line perform. Their conclusion: The installation of some robotic equipment and a computerized management information system (MIS) would shave the factory work force by 20 percent at the outset, and 50 percent within about five years. A master computer network hooked directly to "intelligent" equipment on the line would automatically adjust production levels in accordance with preprogrammed instructions while simultaneously managing and correlating the flow of written records. The result: A decline in labor costs, and a lift for productivity and profits.

Fearful of being left behind as competing battery manufacturers announce plans to begin automating their factories, management gives the green light to the major overhaul, and awards a lucrative contract to a leading computer company. While line workers brace for a round of pink slips, the shift foreman and his immediate boss, the plant manager, are whisked away to corporate headquarters for crash seminars in the series of steps required to implement the new MIS. Meanwhile, computer consultants and software engineers arrive at the plant to supervise the changeover.

Someone once suggested that the genius of experts is their ability to take a solution and divide it neatly into two problems, and at times, the introduction of a computerized information network serves only to prove the point. If all the information is simply loaded into the computer system, without a detailed analysis of ways to cut down on redundant recordkeeping and other forms of "information pollution," the introduction of such a system simply adds a new problem — unfamiliar computer procedures — to the existing and costly problem of time-consuming paperwork.

Assume, however, that management has had the foresight to restructure, rather than simply transfer, its information traffic. When the shift foreman returns from the first phase of his retraining, he now spends most of his working day seated before a computer terminal, in the company of software consultants. He spends very little time out among the dwindling number of employees on the plant floor. His job requires new programming skills, and less and less face-to-face contact. The changeover is arduous and confusing. He is a programmer trainee on his way to becoming a data-base manager. To government manpower statisticians, nothing has really happened — the shift foreman is still the shift foreman. In reality, however, he has lost his job and been given a new one, provided the retraining goes well. He is no longer a shift foreman in the sense of what that title has meant to him all of his working life. Furthermore, if he is unwilling or unable to retrain, and if his employer has no provision for early retirement or priority relocation to cushion the effects of job obsolescence, he may find himself out of luck altogether, replaced by a computer-literate successor.

While factories are obvious targets for automation, this tends to obscure the fact that women workers will number prominently among the early victims of computerization, particularly in those fields where women are in the majority — secretaries, receptionists and nurses, for example. Secretaries in particular also will be drawn into the controversy surrounding the health effects of on-the-job VDT use.

Word processors and related electronic office equipment have been widely hailed as a way of taking the drudge work out of the secretary's day. Electronic work stations reduce the amount of typing, transcription and filing in the secretary's job, thus freeing her for more challenging, management-oriented responsibilities. Corporate managers maintain that office automation provides talented secretaries with a clear pathway to entry-level management positions and higher salaries, as the need for analytical skills replaces the need for routinized, essentially manual ones.

This view, however, is not always shared by secretaries with firsthand knowledge of the evolving electronic office and the unemployment it can create. In an article entitled "Word Processors and the Oppression of Women," a former British secretary charged that office automation is tantamount to a "deskilling process. Once trained to operate the word processor, in the words of [one company]: 'A less experienced typist is able to produce the same quality of work as a really skilled girl and almost as quickly' — thus enabling cheaper labour to be employed. . . . The repetitive, standardized typing will go to the word processing centres and the cream of the secretarial workforce will hang on to those few jobs at the top — the two extremes of the structure becoming increasingly polarized. The loss of skills which word processing effects will make it almost impossible to bridge the gap between the two extremes." Thus, a large number of women will be denied access to a profession which traditionally has provided ease of entry and exit.

The "gap" in the work force referred to here is also known as "taking out the middle" of the job market. Evidence suggests that office automation has a tendency to aggregate workers into two clumps — the very skilled and the barely skilled. Or, "those who tend the computers and those who sweep out the building," as one cynic capsulized it. Since one of the prime goals of computerization is a reduction in labor costs, it is highly likely that the introduction of electronic office information systems will lead to mass attrition in the secretarial ranks. For every secretary promoted to information manager, many others will be out of work. A certain amount of attrition probably is in store for the nursing profession too, if automatic monitoring and diagnostic equipment proliferates in hospitals and medical centers.

For mail carriers and other employees of the U.S. Postal Service, widespread structural unemployment is a certainty. Seven-tenths of the mail handled by the post office is business mail, which begins and ends in corporate offices. Since American corporations are in the forefront of the move from paper to electronic pulses, the computerization of the post office would seem to be inevitable. And considering that the Postal Service and its hundreds of thousands of employees have generated a running billion-dollar deficit over the past few years, it is hard to imagine how computerizing the mail could possibly make things any worse from a financial point of view. But the coming of electronic computer-originated mail (Ecom) service may be the end of the line for many mail carriers and handlers. Unlike the shift foreman and the secretary, there is little possibility of transferring related skills, unless the National Association of Letter Carriers immediately begins to foster a massive computer retraining program. The mail carrier's intimate knowledge of his or her delivery route will be of no use if Ecom is carried to its natural conclusion. (The same will be true of paperboys and papergirls if electronic newspapers take hold.) Again, those nearing retirement age are likely to be the hardest hit during the automation of the post office.

The Postal Service slated January 1982 as the proposed date for inaugurating a limited electronic mail service for business customers. It was to be an interim step, during which bills and other business mail would be transmitted electronically from post office to post office, then printed on paper and delivered by mail carriers in the usual way. Even so, the decision was met with a surprising flurry of protests, most notably from AT&T and from IBM's satellite joint venture, SBS. Maintaining that the Postal Service's plans posed ''grave implications'' for private industry and communications common carriers like itself, AT&T argued for a "judgment by the court that the Postal Service is not empowered to offer the proposed Ecom service." The Departments of Justice and Commerce joined with private companies to urge a full-scale investigation of whether the government-subsidized Postal Service should be allowed into the increasingly unregulated business of electronic communication at all.

Who will carry the electronic mail of the future, if not the post office? AT&T, IBM and other communications and computer companies, of course. Whether private corporations will succeed in keeping the post office out of the electronic mail business remains to be seen, but in any event, today's mail carrier stands a very real chance of losing his or her job to a VDT operator in the future.

The automobile mechanic, indeed any repair person, faces a similar future — retrain or retire. The automobile industry's increasing reliance on microprocessors for engine control represents a major growth market for chip manufacturers. As the eighties began, Ford, Chrysler and General Motors were incorporating millions of microchips in new car models. Delco Electronics, a subsidiary of GM, cranks out its own microprocessors at the rate of some twenty thousand a day. Designed as control and sensing devices, the chips monitor electrical systems, cooling systems, and the optimum mix of gas and air in the carburetor. They also time the firing of the spark plugs for maximum fuel efficiency. Future systems may include a miniature dashboard VDT that not only flashes the automobile's vital signs, but connects the car's computer system to the home or office computer system as well.

This being the case, it is clear that the future of car repair includes some drastic changes, as the mechanic becomes, in effect, a computer systems analyst. Where once a car owner or an independent garage mechanic could adjust an automobile's performance with a set of socket wrenches and a few screwdrivers, soon such tinkering will involve the replacement of circuit boards and complex computer diagnostics. Microprocessor-controlled cars point to a future of sealed engine systems, and perhaps sealed engine hoods as well. "We may have passed the day some time ago," a Ford Motor Company executive told the *Wall Street Journal,* "when an individual could work on his own car."

Mechanics will be compelled to master computer flow charts as a way of tracking down balky microchips for replacement. For repair garages, this will mean a stiff up-front investment in new computerized troubleshooting equipment, and the end of the rebuilt carburetor. Expensive and extensive retraining will be the only option. For car owners, the computerized automobile will mean higher repair bills. "We don't make service calls on late-model cars anymore because of all the electronics," a California garage owner remarked in the same *Journal* article. "If they can't get their cars started, they just have to call a tow truck." As the *Journal* points out, this development "adds $25 to $30 to the tab before the real work begins."

Finally, there is the case of the American farmer. While it might seem that farming is as far removed from the world of computers and electronic communication as any vocation can be, this observation is true no longer. "I believe the personal computer will become, if not common, at least fairly plentiful on the larger, better managed farms," asserts Dick Hanson, editor of *Successful Farming* magazine, a major U.S. farm journal. "Few industries have as many input factors as farming. The computer can be a great help in this area, and I see farm magazines educating readers on how and why computers can save time, money and effort."

Hanson also sees farm publications and agricultural extension services moving heavily into the business of writing and selling the customized software programs farmers will need, if the computer is to become a common tool of farm management. To that end, *Successful Farming* magazine has launched a new publication, *Farm Computer News*, as a means of bringing the computer revolution to American agriculture. The question — and a similar one plagues almost every application of the computer — is whether the effect will be to enhance the dominant position of huge agri-business concerns (where the automation of agriculture is already well under way) or whether the small computer will be a money-saving key to the future survival of the small family-owned farm.

A U.S. Department of Agriculture report notes that "the typical family farm operation will find it difficult to make effective and successful use of stand-alone microcomputers" without extensive hand-holding in the form of one-to-one tutorial assistance between small farmers and computer-trained field administrators from agricultural extension services. Moreover, the emphasis must be on overall "management assistance rather than simply on the mechanics of record-keeping."

In other words, every aspect of the farmer's daily routine — the optimum mix of livestock feed and crop fertilizer, the investment in a new tractor or a new piece of land, the timing of insect-and disease-control procedures, and assorted cash-flow projections — must be scrutinized minutely, and altered, where necessary, to fit the dictates of existing agricultural computer software. Whether any of this will truly aid the small farmer in the battle for survival remains to be seen, but a number of major computer companies, sensing a new market, have leaped into the fray. Tandy Corporation is involved in a federally funded effort, Project Green Thumb, to install interactive TV-telephone information systems in the homes of Kentucky farmers. Control Data Corporation, convinced that the technical know-how available to farmers through interactive computer systems will assure the profitability of smaller farmers, has kicked off Rural Venture, an experimental, computerized community of small farms near its Minneapolis headquarters.

If the family farmer is becoming a microcomputer customer,

who can be considered exempt? Not even the Hell's Angels, it seems. When the court transcripts of a massive government racketeering case against the Angels threatened to bury them in their San Francisco jail cells, members of the outlaw motorcycle gang asked for — and got — a Radio Shack personal computer system for streamlining the preparation of their defense.

What is suggested by these examples, and others to follow, is that a growing portion of the work force will be required (some might say forced) to become computer-literate, by acquiring a working knowledge of rudimentary computer programming skills. As the job goes, so goes the worker, meaning a huge investment in retraining programs. Moreover, more and better computer software is needed. Software is the bottleneck, the fundamental brake on the spread of the microelectronics revolution. This fact raises another job-related question, and a disturbing one: Where is all this needed software going to come from?

Software generally denotes the set of printed instructions that tells a computer how to go about performing a given task, and a set of microchips is only as useful as the software that goes with it. The semiconductor industry has passed the point of being able to satisfy customers by simply flinging new chips at them. Users are demanding that suppliers assume more and more of the costly software burden themselves. Writing software, unlike producing hardware, is a labor-intensive task, more a matter of individual creativity than mass-production. Chip makers have discovered that it takes several hundred thousand dollars to create the software needed to realize the built-in capabilities of a five-dollar microchip. A General Accounting Office (GAO) study predicts that by 1985, 90 percent of the federal government's data-processing expenditures will be software-related.

It is common knowledge in the electronics industry that the

software bottleneck has created a "programmer catastrophe." According to Intel's Andrew Grove, the U.S. will need more than one million software engineers by 1990, or about three times the number of software engineers now working. Sounding an urgent note in *Electronics* magazine, Grove warned that "If we do not have a million software engineers, and do not change the way we do things, the growing pervasiveness of electronics will stop."

This urgent plea translates into a hot job market for software engineers and computer programmers, as well as an expected surge in the number of students enrolling in electrical engineering and the computer sciences. Engineering schools are already cramped, and more students may mean less enrollment in other departments. The result will be a continued decline in liberal arts majors and social science graduates — fewer sociologists, fewer teachers, and so on. The question this raises for the future is whether a nation of software engineers is a desirable prospect, however urgent the concerns of the electronics industry, and whether other, equally urgent human needs will go unaddressed as this technical shift is played out.

Automating Money

The automation of banking, finance and credit means structural unemployment for many workers in those fields, such as bank tellers, but it has other major ramifications as well. Electronic banking calls into question commonly accepted definitions of money as a tangible, countable asset, and it allows insurance companies, brokerage firms and other businesses to compete with banks in the money business.

The introduction of credit cards can be taken as the first step in the process, followed some years later by the introduction of automatic teller machines in those states where branch banking is allowed. Every time a bank customer inserts a plastic bank card into an automatic teller machine and punches in an identification number, the customer is programming a computer, and the transaction that results is telecommunicated to the bank's central data file. On the back of every credit card is a magnetic stripe encoded with information identifying the owner and the account. On the horizon is the "smart" credit card, in which the magnetic stripe gives way to a tiny embedded microchip. This cuts back on the need for accessing the bank's central computer each time, since the smart card already "knows" the customer's current account balance and automatically adjusts the record of the balance at the close of each transaction at the automatic teller.

Electronic funds transfer, or EFT, is the term used to describe any financial transaction handled electronically, rather than by the manual transfer of written records, such as paper checks. Banks and other financial institutions plan to rely heavily on EFT as a way of alleviating the labor costs associated with processing paper checks and other written records of money transfers. As a step in this direction, the day is fast approaching when the checks written by a bank's customers will no longer be returned to customers in the mail at all, replaced instead by a computer printout. Various forms of EFT via computer terminal are also the basis for the bulk of securities transactions on Wall Street. The paper stock certificate of old moves from seller to buyer almost as an afterthought, when it is transferred at all.

Considering the high cost of check handling, the savings that accrue from substituting automatic teller machines for fully staffed branch banks, and the ease with which telecommunications expertise can be brought to bear on EFT, why aren't paper checks already a relic of the past? There are several reasons, one of which may be the impact of EFT on "floating" currency. In simplest terms, the "float" represents financial transactions recorded on paper but not yet tallied at the bank. As Martin Mayer explained it in *The Bankers,* one of the most common forms of float "is created every time someone writes a check to pay a bill and puts it in the mail. He deducts the amount of that check from his working balance in his checkbook, but his bank does not see it until it has passed through the hands of the person whose bill is being paid, that person's bank, and the [Federal Reserve System] clearing mechanism. During that time, the customer's bank continues to have the unrestricted use of customer money to which the customer no longer has a claim." Moreover, if the check is drawn on one of the newer interest-bearing checking accounts, the resulting float is "free money," in that the bank pays nothing for its use, investing it overnight or longer as the bank sees fit. The float is the reason why Karl Malden advises TV viewers to hang onto their traveler's checks after they return from their vacations. Until the traveler's checks are redeemed, they represent a profitable addition to the float. The float is a hugely valuable asset for banks, and the lightning speed with which EFT transactions are tallied will vastly reduce the amount of it available.

Another aspect of EFT widely touted by banks is automatic check paying. However, as Mayer rightly points out, the growth of this service has been stymied by "the inability of consumers to see why they should give up control of their checking accounts, and authorize automatic first-of-the-month deductions for payments they could otherwise make pretty much at their own convenience."

For institutional investors, rather than individual bank customers, EFT means that more and more money will be kept in constant motion, as the owners of that money seek to place it wherever it will earn the best return, even if that placement is only on a one-day or overnight basis. With EFT, it becomes virtually impossible to freeze the international monetary system long enough to make an accurate count of who owns the money, where the money is, and how much there is of it at any given time. With so much money changing hands so quickly through electronic means, the "dismal science" of economics faces a dismal future as a predictive tool. The Eurodollar market, for example, operates essentially by transatlantic computer data transfer. By most accounts, it is already impossible to quantify it. It can only be estimated, and the estimates vary widely.

EFT calls into question the accuracy, and the worth, of all the familiar statistics and indices — the growth of the money supply, the distinction between demand accounts and time accounts, even the universal yardstick known as the Gross National Product. If economists can no longer know for certain where the money is, or how much there is of it, the practice of economics takes on a new and disturbing twist. Predictably, economists have turned to computers and computer modeling as a way of attempting to organize the constantly mutating input-output chart of computerized money flow. However, the switch to computerized economic forecasting does not seem to have improved the predictions spectacularly.

To grasp the extent of the problem, picture the world's brokers, bankers, investors and assorted money men, all huddled over computer terminals, ears glued to the phone, as players in a very high-stakes game of computer Space War, even though the object of the game more closely resembles Monopoly. Charged with refereeing the game and tallying the results on the American side are various institutions like the Federal Reserve Bank, the Securities and Exchange Commission and other bodies. Unless the referees are as zealous and as skilled as the players themselves, a good deal of rough-and-tumble play will ensue, because the referees simultaneously must enforce and rewrite the rules of the game, so as to conform to the dictates of the new all-electronic playing field. It is interesting to note that young stockbrokers, by many accounts, are second only to teenagers in their fierce love of computerized video arcade games like Space Invaders. To some young money mavens, EFT is simply another computer game, played with other people's money.

Electronic money leads to another, rather obvious game that can be played. Automate money, and the automation of crime cannot be far behind.

Automating Crime

A team of computer scientists at the Naval Research Laboratory conducts an experimental attack on a Sperry Univac 1108 computer system used for security purposes by the military. It takes the team exactly thirteen seconds of computer time to extract classified data.

Police link the sabotage of a Rome computer facility to a series of planned attacks on Italian computer centers, allegedly organized by a terrorist group known as Unit Combattenti Communiste.

A talented computer analyst, awaiting trial in Los Angeles on charges of using a computer to steal $10 million from Security Pacific National Bank, is arrested again in Marina del Rey and charged with attempting to steal $50 million from Union Bank.

Striking British civil servants pull the plug on vital national computer systems, costing the government undetermined millions. The action temporarily shuts down the Royal Mint, the National Savings Lottery, the collection of taxes, and computerized payments to workers.

Officials of Telenet, a telecommunications network based in Virginia, lose control of one of their computers to unknown interlopers, who proceed to keep legitimate users off the system while garbling millions of bits of stored computer data. The perpetrators prove to be four precocious thirteen-year-old boys.

The computer outlaws are here. And they are very difficult to catch. Computer abuses take many forms — bank embezzlement by computer, fraud by computer, the theft of valuable assets stored in computer systems, the quasi-legal theft of computer operating time, even outright computer vandalism. Reported cases of computer crime and computer abuse represent the tip of the proverbial iceberg. "Nobody seems to know exactly what computer crime is, how much of it there is, and whether it is increasing or decreasing," according to SRI International's Donn Parker, the dean of computer abuse specialists. "The only thing we do know about computer crime is that computers are changing the nature of business crime so significantly that new forms of protection, investigation, prosecution, and legislation are needed to deal with it."

When a computer outlaw *is* caught, the owners of the system he penetrated often opt for "administrative handling" rather than prosecution, in order to avoid adverse publicity. Corporations are reluctant to admit it, but to meet the demands of the Information Age, large distributed computer systems have become much more flexible — and much more difficult to secure.

"Every large computer operating system is a Swiss Cheese," writes Parker, in *Crime By Computer.* "We've got to design and build them without holes, but we are still only starting to learn how to do that." Members of the business community are only too aware of this fact. In the banking industry, the grim truth has been formalized in the concept of Maximum Time to Belly Up, or MTBU: If a bank's computer system is sabotaged seriously, how much time could elapse before the bank is forced to declare a default?

The problem is compounded by the fact that many forms of crime by computer are not anticipated under existing criminal statutes. Furthermore, auditors untrained in the technical details of computer operation have little chance of assuring adequate controls. In a study of computer-related crimes undertaken by Parker at SRI, an intriguing profile of the typical computer crook emerged, based on interviews with thirty of the more sophisticated ones. They are bright, highly motivated, and, so far, almost exclusively male. They often have a grudge against a former employer, and they often view their actions as an intellectual challenge to "the system." Many defend themselves as modern electronic Robin Hoods.

In *Computer Capers,* reporter Thomas Whiteside calls computer crime "a form of breaking and entering in which the burglar's tools are essentially an understanding of the logical structure of and logical flaws inherent in particular programming and processing systems." Beyond a thorough knowledge of programming, the only other tools the outlaw requires are a computer terminal and a telephone. He need venture nowhere near the "scene of the crime" to do his work. Whiteside theorizes that "The attenuation of money into digital impulses has probably contributed to the increasing evidence of waywardness among people who continually process so much of it in such a form."

Obviously, calculating the economic loss attributable to computer crime is a guessing game, but there is good reason to consider those losses substantial. According to Parker, "Assets tend to be more highly concentrated in computer systems than in equivalent manual systems. The automation of crime required in automated systems means that it is just as easy to steal a million dollars as it is one dollar."

Strengthening the laws against computer crime will be a difficult task, for it will require a precise definition of the legal status of invisible electronic pulses. This is already a problem at tax time. "What really amuses me," offered one Silicon Valley executive, "is the government's attempt to tax computer software as a tangible asset. What I'll do is, I'll just put all the software on the line and send it to Timbuktu or just keep it bouncing from computer memory to computer memory somewhere outside the country. Now I don't have it anymore. What are you taxing?"

Another approach to combating computer crime — and the related matter of international intelligence espionage by computer — is to devise new encryption (coding) schemes that require computer systems users to know a secret key or coded password. Most of the data entered into commercial computer systems is not encrypted at all, because it is a costly extra step, and far from foolproof. So far, for every clever encryption technique, there is an equally clever programmer out there somewhere who can crack it. More sophisticated methods of encryption are in the offing, including one devised by Martin Hellman and others at Stanford University. Said Hellman, in an interview with the Stanford University News Service,

"Most authorities now agree that sensitive information is much more vulnerable than was realized until recently. The urgent need has been to work out a system of preserving the privacy of messages transmitted over insecure channels. That means we have to produce a means of encryption which can be used easily in a typical commercial environment. We believe that we have managed that."

But even if Hellman's assertion proves true, it will not put an end to the host of problems related to computer security. In the same interview, Hellman addressed the matter of personal privacy:

> There are all sorts of social issues which are going to surface as part of the revolution in communications which is now beginning. It has already been learned that one government agency had monitored international Telex traffic in order to get hold of messages to or from persons on a "watch" list. This list grew until it included antiwar activists and other "undesirables." The possibility of widespread, inexpensive invasion of citizen's privacy is ominous, and poses the threat of police-state operations. Care must be taken to ensure that technological advances are not used in a detrimental manner. For example, a user's secret [encryption] key will probably be stored on a magnetic card that will be needed to transact any business on the system. The system may become all-pervasive in our daily lives. If so, it is possible that people will be expected to carry their magnetic cards with them constantly, to transact even minor purchases, much as most people carry their bank charge-cards with them now. It could be only a small step from this to allowing the police to demand the magnetic card as a form of universal identifier, without which a person becomes a nonperson. Proponents of electronic funds transfer in banking argue that cash will always be acceptable, but that is already not true for certain purchases such as car rentals to people less than 25 years old and gas purchases late at night. Legal issues may also arise. For example, if an accused criminal has encrypted his business records, a subpoena can force him to hand over the physical records. But can he be forced to give the key that makes the records intelligible? Or can he invoke the Fifth Amendment? We are on the verge of a communications revolu-

tion which can alter all our lives for the good. But unless we plan ahead to ensure the privacy and security of those communications we may find a whole new world of problems.

Automating Education and Politics

Almost every human activity can be automated to one extent or another by the introduction of systems of electronic logic. Two other areas of endeavor — education and politics — deserve brief mention; the former because it represents a field in which the trend toward automation suffered something of an early reversal, and the latter because it points out what can happen when some members of a profession automate, and others do not.

The ubiquitous classroom use of the hand-held electronic calculator and the increasing use of computers as an educational tool tend to obscure the fact that educators and textbook publishers have gone over a portion of this ground before. The automation of the American classroom was announced back in the sixties, but the thrust was greatly muted in the face of one of the back-to-basics movements that periodically arises in the educational establishment. In *America Revised*, her excellent study of American history textbooks in the public schools, Frances FitzGerald writes:

> In the mid-sixties. . . . Sitting at the feet of Marshall McLuhan, the [textbook] publishers decided that the era of mass production was over — along with the era of literacy and linear reasoning — and that they should at once prepare to deliver instant all-around audiovisual programming with individualized feedback for every child. The era of software had come — the era of total communication and perfect customization. Not only — or even principally — the textbook publishers but a lot of high-rolling communications-industry executives dreamed of equipping every classroom in America with television sets, video cameras, holography sets, and computer terminals. As a first step toward this post-industrial future, the executives built

conglomerates designed to put all kinds of software components and communications capability under one roof. Xerox acquired Ginn and Company; RCA bought Random House; C.B.S. acquired Holt, Reinhart & Winston; Raytheon bought D.C. Heath; and Time Inc. acquired Little, Brown and Company and Silver Burdett and, with General Electric, formed the General Learning Corporation.

The bubble, however, burst quickly:

And then, with great speed, fashions changed, and education theory turned conservative. Parents and school boards complained that children couldn't read or write anymore — that what they needed was textbook drill. Publishers, up to their ears in machinery, began to look on textbooks as the basic winter coat. While they continued to produce some of the cheapest of the new materials — such things as magazines and filmstrips — they put their money back into books: both the hardbacks and a new generation of paperbacks; which allowed teachers a choice of supplementary material. "It began to dawn on them," one trade-book editor says, "that the book is finally the most efficient retrieval system we possess."

Today, the automation movement is making a comeback, in the form of the personal computer. This time, it is the computer makers, rather than the textbook publishers, who are leading the charge. Summer computer camps for kids have appeared in California, and students everywhere are being introduced to programming. While the trend toward computer-literacy among schoolchildren will only increase, this does not mean the death of the printed word, as so many have claimed. Books are, and will remain, one of the most efficient information retrieval systems in existence. Computers in the classroom do not mean the end of books, anymore than the automobile meant the end of the bicycle, or the telephone meant the end of letter writing. Books, bicycles and letters have several unique advantages, and it is highly misleading to suggest that the evolution of electronic technology simply means the wholesale replacement of old forms by new ones. Often, it means instead that the advantages of older ways of doing things are rediscovered anew, even when all the economic factors seem to mitigate against them.

As for politics, computers and electronic communication have turned political campaigning into a technocrat's delight. The influence of television on the course of American politics has been much discussed. The influence of computers is less apparent, but no less troublesome, the more so since one end of the political spectrum seems to have taken to them much more markedly than the other. The New Right, a loose coalition of ultraconservative Republicans and religious fundamentalists, which organized heavily for Ronald Reagan in the 1980 presidential campaign, sees little contradiction between God, Family and the Computer Age, as the following excerpt from a *Wall Street Journal* article attests:

> Richard Viguerie, the New Right's chief fund-raiser, strides jauntily down the hallway of his Falls Church, Va., headquarters, past a watching security man, through two doors with special locks and into the nerve center of the Viguerie direct-mail operation. It is a room stacked, floor to ceiling, with shiny black computer tapes. They contain the cross-indexed names and addresses of 20 million voters, including 4.5 million conservatives.
>
> Nearby, a laser-powered printer spits out conservative form letters with machine-gun rapidity. "We're organized, we're structured, we're on the offensive," Mr. Viguerie says. "Organized labor and the liberal organizations are way behind us technically. They're still trying to fight this war with the weapons of the last war. There's no way they're going to stand up to our young Turks."

If Mr. Viguerie is correct, a growing number of liberal politicians may find themselves caught out of position for the sin of simply not knowing where the action is.

There is one final area of activity subject to automation, and it merits a chapter of itself. It is a field that has undergone increasing automation ever since World War II, and more than any other, there is no warranty or possibility of redress if things go dreadfully awry. It is the automation of warfare, and if it proves to be a fatal mistake, the microelectronics revolution will be the last revolution anyone is privileged to witness.

CHAPTER ELEVEN

The Electronic Warriors: Which Way to the Front?

Electricity — The high priest of false security.
— BASIL RATHBONE,
in *Sherlock Holmes and the Pearl of Death*

PGWs and ECMs: The Weapons

Electronics, as it is used in military weapons and communications, accounts for nearly 50 cents of every dollar spent by the U.S. Department of Defense. Once considered a rather exotic and specialized branch of the military, electronics today forms the underpinning of modern national security systems. The microelectronics revolution has meant a steady, inexorable increase in the complexity of national defense, and the military's increasing reliance on the microprocessor has prompted a rancorous debate over defense strategy, between those who view the new technologies and the automated battlefield as the only secure course for the future, and those who see electronic warfare as a dangerous means of transferring military decision-making from humans to computers.

Today, regardless of differing stances on the matter, electronics is what war is all about. The Cybernetic Cold War, as it has been called, is being fought in the invisible reaches of the electromagnetic spectrum, between competing arsenals of "intelligent" electronic equipment. Since microelectronics and computers are widely viewed as two segments of defense policy over which the U.S. holds a commanding lead, military officials are determined to milk that lead for all it is worth. To this end, the Pentagon plans a rapid escalation of its investment in microelectronics research, development and procurement.

283

The steady growth of electronic warfare translates into boom times for defense contractors, especially the smaller specialty subcontractors in Silicon Valley whose forte is "black box" electronic wizardry for military applications. The role of the modern soldier in all this bears almost no resemblance to the rifle-toting G.I. and the dogfighting combat pilot of yore. Precision-guided weapons, or PGWs, have taken the conduct of warfare out of the hands of officers and noncoms alike.

The deadly effectiveness of precision-guided weapons was demonstrated for all the world to see in the 1973 Arab–Israeli war, when Egyptian soldiers carrying portable, wire-guided antitank missiles scored heavily against Israeli tanks on the Egyptian and Syrian fronts. Electronic information transmitted along the trailing wires guided the course of the missiles as they sped toward the targets. Early PGWs were used with less publicity in the Vietnam war as well. Soviet wire-guided "Sagger" missiles scored hits on American tanks, while "smart" heat-seeking American missiles were used against Russian MiGs.

The war in Vietnam also was the site of an early and controversial experiment at automating the battlefield itself, as well as the weapons. "McNamara's Wall," the brainchild of physicists in the JASON division of the Institute of Defense Analysis, was to be an impenetrable barrier forming a lethal no-man's-land between North and South Vietnam. Essentially a string of electronic sensors, computers and explosive devices aimed at thwarting guerrilla movements from the North, McNamara's Wall didn't distinguish very effectively between civilian and military traffic, and for this and other reasons it caught heavy flak from antiwar activists. In practice, it failed miserably.

This was manifestly untrue, however, of the new precision-guided weapons. The deadly, automated accuracy of wire-guided PGWs led to a new military motto: If you can see the target, you can blow up the target. Wire-guided missiles represented only the first generation of precision-guided weaponry, followed quickly by the enhanced destructive capability of laser-guided PGWs. And, since laser beams suffer a decrease in performance under certain weather conditions, a third generation of PGWs, relying on microwaves, millimeter waves and other forms of radiation for guidance control, is in the offing. These newer PGWs, known as "fire and forget" weapons, are also less susceptible to enemy "jamming" and other countermeasures. The revised motto for PGW deployment might well be: Even if you can't see the target, you can blow it up anyway. Moreover, the new PGWs are much more dependent upon microprocessor and memory chips than earlier systems, meaning that the Department of Defense is becoming even more heavily reliant on the evolution of the microchip and computers as the guiding principles behind the evolution of war strategy.

For starters, precision-guided weapons radically alter the nature of ground warfare, particularly the tank-oriented strategies that characterize much of the deployment of NATO and Warsaw Pact forces in Europe. The foot soldier of the future, if indeed there are any, will carry a complex microcomputer system in his or her backpack. With it, the soldier is a walking electronic sensing system, seeking out and pinpointing the location of hidden enemy rocket launchers, gun emplacements, or moving tanks. In the blink of an eye, the microcomputer translates the coordinates of the target into digital format and telecommunicates them to the nearest firing station. From there, a precision-guided missile rises with a roar, following the spoor of a laser beam, a radar pulse, or a microwave frequency on an automated journey to the target. The PGW rarely misses, because its microchip sensors constantly monitor the underlying terrain, comparing what they "see" with maps of the area stored in computer memory, and preventing the missile from detonating until it locates the target it seeks. A precision-guided missile packed with microchips can hover about like an electronic bloodhound, waiting for its microcomputers to locate and identify a moving target. (Heat-seeking missiles can do the same, but they are more easily fooled into mistaking one warm object for another.) The U.S. Army's 9th Infantry Division, which has been called the Army's high-technology division, is being equipped with a system of this kind, based on laser-guided Copperhead missiles. In short, the microprocessor has become an awesome weapon.

In the air, precision-guided missiles launched from fighter planes perform the same feats. Electronic warfare adds another occupation to the list of automation-prone professions — that of fighter pilot. In the newer Air Force F-15s and F-16s, for example, the pilot's role has evolved, or perhaps devolved, into a curious blend of computer operator/programmer and fail-safe backup technician. The planes are packed with dozens of microcomputers and microprocessors, which process digital data from radar and infrared sensors at nanosecond speed. If the microelectronic sensors tell the aircraft's computer system that a squadron of enemy aircraft is approaching, the computers instantly correlate the information with programmed instructions, select an optimum firing strategy based on which enemy planes present the most immediate threat, and ask the pilot for permission to fire. If the pilot punches in "yes," the computer system releases the missiles, timing the firings so that the most effective kill pattern will be achieved.

Even though the pilot has been reduced to caretaker, his senses have been electronically extended in dramatic fashion. For navigation, pilots of the most advanced planes have recourse to a futuristic system known as HUD, for head-up display. No need for a pilot to glance down at computer displays in the cockpit — HUD projects computer data onto the transparent canopy of the jet itself. Through a blend of mirrors, lenses and sophisticated optical tricks, the data appear directly before the pilot's eyes. In addition, HUD can display tiny white blips representing the location of other aircraft or ground targets, and at night, a computerized infrared map of the ground below is superimposed over the pilot's own, more limited view of the world.

Other means of automating air warfare may reduce the role of the pilot to an even greater degree. Remotely Piloted Vehicles (RPVs) are lethal drones that allow navigators to orchestrate an attack or a surveillance mission from computer terminals located miles away. Alternately, work is proceeding on the completely computerized RPV, programmed for a mission that requires no human intervention or monitoring at all.

For all the futuristic gadgetry involved, military electronics is far from foolproof. One of the perceived virtues of electronic warfare is also its Achilles' heel. Since PGWs depend upon frequencies of the electromagnetic spectrum for remote sensing, guidance and communications, they are vulnerable to what are called electronics countermeasures. In the acronym-laden world of military electronics, ECMs. The most common ECM is chaff, the strips of aluminum foil that pilots drop to confuse enemy radar. While chaff is still in the U.S. arsenal, it is a primitive form of ECM compared to the newer forms of electronic deception. ECMs are designed to enable aircraft or guided weapons to reach their targets without detection by enemy radar and weapons systems. Devices called detection jammers accomplish this by giving off spurious electronic signals, creating, in effect, a phantom target. The Airborne Self Protection Jammer, now under development, is a microcomputerized ECM system only slightly larger than a toaster. It is programmable, meaning that fighter pilots will be able to change ECMs on the spot, or throw out several at once.

With ECMs, one of electronic warfare's major drawbacks comes sharply into focus. The very existence of electronics countermeasures insures the existence of counter-countermeasures on the part of the enemy, and then counter-counter-countermeasures in response to that, and so on, ad infinitum. The never-ending technological spiral this implies takes the form of never-ending requests for higher and higher defense budgets. If there is any way out of this self-protection trap — and it assures a handsome future for companies in the ECM business — Pentagon officials haven't discovered it yet. Instead, they have concentrated on even more advanced electronics countermeasures.

Satellite war is one of those advances, though "advance" may not prove to be the word for it, if space war is the result. U.S. military spy satellites can snap rapid-fire pictures of a Soviet intercontinental ballistic missile complex and beam the heat-sensitive images to CIA headquarters in Langley, Virginia, where analysts feed the data into computer systems. If the temperature of the earth at the Soviet site is suspiciously warm, computers deduce that a new underground missile silo is in the process of construction. Almost as a by-product, these satellites offer a phenomenal level of navigational accuracy. The NAVSTAR satellite system, for example, allows computerized military vehicles to plot their positions on or near the planet with an error rate of only a few yards.

Not much farther down the road are "hunter-killer" satellites, which seek out and destroy other satellites. Finally, there is the possibility that to America's and Russia's arsenal of thousands of nuclear warheads will be added the prospect of warfare conducted by pure energy — particle beam weapons, wherein a focused, high-energy stream of satellite-launched protons instantly performs the task of destruction.

Even without space war, electronic weapons nullify all the historical rules of warfare. In an account of precision-guided weaponry for *Scientific American*, Paul F. Walker suggests that "As small missiles become more accurate and deadlier, the major capital pieces of equipment — the tank, the combat-support aircraft and the large surface ship — will ultimately become obsolete for virtually all war-fighting tasks. They will then be relegated to a largely ceremonial role, being put on display in Russian May Day and American Memorial Day celebrations."

Walker goes on to suggest the disturbing corollary: "Small, accurate guided missiles, carried in a suitcase or a small vehicle, capable of penetrating all but the heaviest battle armor, may become the weapon of choice for the terrorist of the 1980's and 1990's."

Whenever a new electronic weapon issues forth from the defense electronics establishment, the sheer complexity of the miniaturized internal workings of the equipment invariably prompts two questions: Do we really need it? And, if so, will it work? The military's reliance on electronic hardware leaves it open to the failures that can result from the inadvertent use of defective or substandard chips. The level of quality control in electronic warfare depends utterly upon the quality of micro-chips spewing forth from the semiconductor industry. So far, the record has been good, but not great. Not long ago, Fairchild Semiconductor discovered, to its misfortune, that some thir-teen million transistors sold to military and government con-tractors over a three-year period had not been tested to military specifications. The components already were being used in radar, missile and air-traffic-control systems. Fairchild hastily instituted a recall; and there have been others, including a re-cent incident at National Semiconductor.

Incessant technological obsolescence, a fact of life for semi-conductor users, further compromises the reliability of elec-tronic warfare. Advances in the art of chip making often render new equipment out-of-date even before it is installed. To make matters worse, the game of technological leapfrog makes chip companies notoriously reluctant to produce the small batches of obsolete components the military need for servicing aging equipment still in place. Commonly, this takes the form of refusing to bid on contracts involving chips for which a major commercial market no longer exists. Often, when the military is the only buyer, there simply isn't enough money in it. Once an older line of semiconductor components has been discontinued commercially, it is difficult and costly for chip makers to reinstitute production. And, since today's chip sales to the military add up to only about 10 to 20 percent of total semiconductor industry sales, large semiconductor companies no longer need the military as desperately as they once did. The reverse, however, is far from true.

Government officials fear that if U.S. semiconductor suppli-ers won't stock the needed replacement parts, the Department of Defense will have no way of repairing and maintaining the equipment it already has. An electronic weapon isn't worth the silicon it is made of if it cannot be kept in working order. Defense contractors and chip makers retort that spare parts would not be a problem if the military got out of the habit of designing new equipment with obsolete components. As examples, they cite Army combat radios designed around long-forgotten germanium transistors, older mechanical printers in battlefield computer terminals, and vacuum tubes in the radar systems of B-52 bombers. "It's incredible," an Army colonel in charge of procurement confessed to *Electronic News,* "but I'm still trying to scout up vacuum tube suppliers for much Army field communications equipment."

The situation is no better for the large computer systems used by the government as a whole. The General Accounting Office reported that at the end of fiscal 1979, only 45 of the 1,366 computer systems in use were modern generation systems. As reported by Jack Robertson in *Electronic News:* "The Feds still had nearly 300 Xerox computers, although that firm has been out of the computer business since 1975. More than 115 General Electric computers were still clunking along, despite GE's abdication 10 years ago from the computer field. Some 90 RCA Spectra 70 computers were still running 9 years after RCA gave up on computers. Agencies still have 181 IBM Model 1401 computers installed, although IBM stopped making that system more than a decade ago."

It is an alarming situation. Older, simpler equipment has become unreliable for lack of spare parts, while the bewildering, untested complexities of newer equipment is equally suspect. The computerized F-15, as a case in point, can only be field-repaired with the aid of even more complex computers, some of which require air-conditioning. And more often than not, the repairs can only be accomplished by cannibalizing the needed parts from other F-15s. Certain critics have suggested that the Air Force ought to admit defeat and return to the old F-4 Phantom, whose combat-ready record exceeds that of its sophisticated electronic successor. Military brass, while acknowledging the occasional instance of "maldesign" have no plans to end the love affair with high technology by turning back the clock.

Microelectronic weaponry, however awe-inspiring, and however prone to failure, is only one aspect of electronic warfare. Beyond discrete weaponry and equipment, the conduct of the modern military rests upon a complex telecommunications network connecting thousands of large computer systems. In the United States, this network is known as C^3, for command, control and communications (also known as C^3I, when electronic intelligence-gathering activities are added to the mix). It is at once the most vital and the most fragile link in both American and Soviet defense systems; so vital, in the end, that the numbers game by which comparative military strength is usually assessed may add up to nothing.

C^3 and Wimex: The Failures

C^3 is the military's portion of the electronic grid. It consists of the computers, the satellites, the telephones and the telecommunications links that tie together the Pentagon's twenty-seven major military command centers worldwide. C^3, in turn, puts those centers in constant touch with the rest of the military network, including missile silos in North Dakota, submarines cruising beneath the seas, the Strategic Air Command (SAC) headquarters in Omaha, Nebraska, and the North American Air Defense Command (NORAD) hidden in a hollowed-out mountain near Colorado Springs, Colorado.

C^3 is also the conduit for communicating the results of the military's vast electronic intelligence-gathering operations. This intelligence work is constant and all-pervasive. "It is hard to grasp the sheer bulk and constant flow of all these intercepted messages and the ceaseless images," notes the Boston Study Group in *The Price of Defense*. "Tens of millions of documents, thousands of miles of recorder tape, millions of video images are made, often never to be translated, transcribed, or examined. The tactical material is frequently redundant with similar efforts by NATO allies in the same sector, several national services carefully picking up and recording one and the same Soviet transmission, of transient interest. The prodigious ability to collect and to store drives the system to excesses of commission; nothing is left undone, because any scrap *might* prove worthwhile!''

As the study group concludes, ''The present surveillance seems closer to a state of actual war than to one of prudent preparation in a world seeking peace by design.''

Ultimately, C^3 is the controlling grid for the nation's entire defense system; the information network that connects the parts. Without it, early-warning radar systems could not warn anybody. The signal to launch a missile would never reach the silo. The split-second timing required to warn the President of an attack and relay his orders to military commanders would be impossible, and the ''hot line'' from Washington to Moscow would be wiped out. Knock out the C^3 network, and the left hand of the military has no chance of knowing what the right hand is doing.

This being the case, the reliability of C^3 channels is of paramount importance in any modern military strategy, and the Pentagon has spent a great deal of money to assure ''system redundancy,'' meaning that if one channel goes out, another can take its place. The system *must* work, for in the event of an attack it is the means by which the military arsenal is set in motion. And it must be failsafe, or else a random glitch could trigger an all-out response to an attack that only exists as a set of erroneous signals deep in the circuitry of a defective computer. C^3 stands as the most convincing demonstration of the trend toward cybernetic warfare first set in motion during World War II. The problem, as any computer systems analyst well knows, is that in a computer network as complicated as this, any number of things can go wrong, however many failsafe features and ''redundant'' channels are built into it. And, as the case of Wimex makes clear, the computers upon which the military depends are not necessarily state-of-the-art specimens.

Wimex is a double acronym, derived from WWMCCS by way of the official title, the World Wide Military Command

and Control System. It is vital to the Pentagon's global command structure and one of the crucial linchpins of C^3 operations. Valued at about $15 billion, the Wimex system represents an average investment of roughly $160 per American taxpaying family, and if it does what it is supposed to do, no taxpayer could rightfully complain.

But it doesn't. Or at least, not often enough. Computers represent only about $1 of that per-family investment, but the computers are the problem. The Wimex system is built around the Honeywell 6000 computer series, a line first introduced back in 1964 — two computer generations ago, and about six years before the microprocessor was invented. To say that the Wimex computers are obsolete is to be charitable; the Honeywell 6000 series operates in "batch mode," an ancient method of data processing which means, in effect, that the Wimex computers plod through problems one step at a time, rather than performing many problem-solving steps simultaneously, as modern "real-time mode" computers do. To lessen that drawback, military planners at major command centers have been forced to patch on other, more modern, computers and expensive new software to speed things up.

Still, the Wimex computers are hard pressed to keep up with the ordinary, day-to-day flow of data processing tasks. In fact, Wimex is said to be operating dangerously near full capacity already. "They really have no wartime or crisis surge capacity left to send the right planes to the right places and load the right stuff," according to one researcher.

Word of the Wimex deficiencies reached the public in late 1979, when a panel of independent computer experts completed work on an eighteen-month review of Defense Department computer systems. (Some months earlier, the House Appropriations Committee cut funding for Wimex, citing major shortcomings and deficiencies, but the move went largely unnoticed.) The review panel concluded that Wimex was "operationally vulnerable as a consequence of obsolescent equipment and systems and underdeveloped technical personnel." Moreover, a General Accounting Office (GAO) investigation, prompted by congressional concern, reached the same general conclusion. According to the GAO study, the Wimex system was unable to pinpoint the target of an incoming missile with anything approaching the necessary degree of accuracy. "If the president can't tell where the warheads are going to land between New York and San Francisco," said a GAO director involved in the study, "I think we've got a problem."

Another crucial responsibility of the C³ system is to assure that the thousands of worldwide computers in the network can "talk" to each other reliably. In 1977 the military tested some of these links in an exercise known as PRIME TARGET.

As reported by *Science* magazine, "This exercise linked computers in the Atlantic Command (LANTCOM), European Command (EUCOM), Readiness Command (REDCOM), Tactical Air Command (TAC), and the National Military Command Center in the Pentagon. During the test, EUCOM attempted to obtain or send information through the computer network 124 times. It failed 54 times as the result of 'abnormal' shutdowns of the computer. LANTCOM tried 295 times and failed 132 times. TAC went 19 for 63, a failure rate of 70 percent. And REDCOM found itself able to receive and send instructions in only 43 of 290 attempts — a failure rate of 85 percent."

Pentagon officials deny most of the charges leveled at Wimex, labeling critics of the system as "alarmists." But the Wimex computers are not the only substandard ones in the military arsenal. The same House panel that cut funding for Wimex also called for deleting the entire $94 million fiscal 1980 outlay for TACFIRE, the Army's Tactical Fire Detection System, which links field observers with artillary units. According to the panel's report, the AN/GYK-12 computer, "the heart of the TACFIRE system, was designed in the 1960s and is technically obsolete. The AN/GYK-12 also uses an obsolete type of integrated circuit. Long term supply of these circuits, without which the system cannot be supported, is uncertain."

There are no end of examples, and the Defense Department's primary response has been that more money, not less, is the answer. However, more money, by itself, does not necessarily guarantee better computer systems. Career officers do not come up through the ranks of the military on the basis of their computer expertise. Only six Air Force generals are reported to have a solid academic background in computer technology, and in the words of one admiral, "There are three ways to make a career in the Navy: under the water, on the water, and in the air. I'd really wonder about an officer who wanted to make a career in computers."

An additional problem, as William J. Broad points out, again in *Science* magazine, "is that the electronic network that ties intelligence and weapons together is undoubtedly critical, but not very glamorous compared to the systems it services. Guns, tanks, satellites, and missiles are much easier to understand and manage than the transnational flow of electrons, and this fact determines in part the limited time and attention devoted to worldwide computer networks."

These complaints about inadequate military computers might have remained academic if not for a series of three fiascos that leaked to the press in late 1979 and 1980. In the first incident, on November 9, 1979, computers at NORAD flashed the message that a Soviet submarine off the West Coast of the United States had launched a missile attack. Military command posts were alerted, fighter planes were scrambled, and personnel at missile silos across the country got ready to retaliate. Federal Aviation Agency officials were instructed to prepare for the grounding of all commercial air traffic. The U.S. military was preparing for nuclear war.

As it turned out, the alert lasted for six full minutes — the amount of time it took for military commanders to realize that there had actually been no attack at all. Somehow, a data tape used in a computerized war game had been fed into the NORAD computers accidentally. Having discovered the problem, military officials declared a false alarm and went back to business as usual.

On June 3, 1980, it happened again. Computers indicated

an attack by Russian ICBMs, missile silos were prepared once more, and B-52 bomber crews ran to their planes and started the engines. Within three minutes, it was over. The culprit this time was a faulty microchip in the telecommunications network that links NORAD computers to the Pentagon.

Three days later, on June 6, another Soviet attack was declared, found to be false, and blamed on similar circuitry.

Pentagon officials stressed that the central NORAD computer operated without error throughout the two June alerts, adding that there was no cause for alarm because the attack warnings were not taken very seriously in the first place. Neither Defense Secretary Brown nor President Carter was alerted. One reason military commanders were skeptical of the alerts was that computer-related false alarms had happened before — raising the question of what might have transpired if the attacks had proven to be real after all. In the November 9 incident, six precious minutes passed while the military ascertained what had happened. Had the attack been genuine, it is doubtful that President Carter would have had the time to order retaliatory measures before the missiles reached their targets, a fact that does not greatly bolster confidence in the American defense system and ''launch-on-warning'' strategies.

While there is considerable doubt about the operating reliability of C^3 channels, that is far from the end of the story. Missile bases and major cities are commonly considered to be the priority targets in the military plans of both the United States and the Soviet Union. And yet, the most damaging target may be neither of these. Over the past few years, there has been growing interest in the idea of targeting C^3 centers in the event of war. The advantages of this approach, on the surface at least, would appear to be obvious, for without operating communications channels there is little chance that either an attacking or defending nation would be able to maintain an orchestrated war effort. No doubt the thinking is the same on the Soviet side — cutting communications lines is a long-standing battle tactic.

Therefore, the destruction of Soviet C^3 centers, and greater protection for American ones, has taken on the look of a very attractive strategy. Several years ago, the Carter administration promulgated Presidential Directive 59, which, among other things, called for targeting Soviet C^3 centers, sparing some of the cities, and shoring up the defenses surrounding the American counterparts as a means of waging a "limited" nuclear war. This was seen as a way of adding an extra deterrent to all-out nuclear war.

The sad truth is that marking Soviet C^3 centers for destruction is likely to have exactly the opposite effect, and may in fact represent the single most damaging shift in military policy since the beginning of the arms race. Horrified scientists quickly pointed out that, in the first place, there is absolutely no guarantee that American C^3 centers can be rendered attack-proof, and in the second place, knocking out each other's communications capability leaves little chance of ceasing hostilities once they have started. And finally, if one nation knows the other is planning to make priority attacks on C^3 capability, one logical strategy is to fire first, and fire everything, before it becomes impossible to fire anything at all.

Even if this advice is taken to heart, the utter dependence of the military on C^3 systems and channels strongly favors the "fire everything" option. As Nigel Calder observed in *Nuclear Nightmares,* "The built-in dynamics of command and control make it very likely that any low-level conflict between the United States and the Soviet Union will lead to all-out nuclear war."

Another major problem is that the hundred thousand or so large and mid-range computers employed by the three branches of the military speak hundreds of different computer languages, as might be expected, necessitating several billion dollars' worth of contradictory software. As William Broad has aptly observed, this is "similar to having speakers of French and Farsi struggling to communicate with one another on the telephone." Some of this confusion of tongues is unavoidable, but some of it occurs as a result of the traditional rivalry between the Army, the Navy, and the Air Force. However, when the Pentagon proposed to streamline things by adopting a single language, called Ada, for communication between military computers, many researchers who do work for the Pentagon immediately announced that locking all systems into one format would stifle software creativity and cause more problems than it solved. Some military commanders felt that the adoption of a single language would amount to handing the Russians the key to American C^3 on a silver platter.

And so it goes, as every attempt to end communication chaos in the military simply seems to open the door to a new set of difficulties. The sheer complexity of all modern computer networks mitigates against the quick fix. Once such systems have been put in place, it is far easier to make them grow than to trim them back for efficiency's sake. Large computers take on a life of their own, in a sense; they are not so much run as steered. Using the automobile as an analogy, it is often easier to add a new carburetor than to fix an ailing one.

What can be done to make military computer systems work together as they should? So far, a definitive answer to the question has eluded the best efforts of Pentagon planners, outside consultants, and academicians. "There is not much chance for the formulation of a command and control concept," one consultant concluded, "so long as the dominant paradigm persists in emphasizing things over relationships, hardware over the concepts needed to use it effectively." In other words, as long as the military remains mesmerized by high technology for its own sake, the long-term problems of implementing it effectively in the field will remain unresolved. Both the U.S. and the Soviet Union have come to an extremely problematic pass: computers and other electronics, as the backbone of military planning for the past thirty-five years, seem to have escalated rather than lessened the tensions caused by massive nuclear arsenals. No amount of new weaponry, however advanced, can guarantee the security of national defense systems, when the weapons are only as dependable as the complex electronics that controls and connects them. And increasing the sophistication of the electronics is no absolute guarantee against fatal error, a false alarm, a computer glitch that triggers a holocaust.

However, there is still one last weakness in C^3 to be discussed, and it is perhaps the most troubling one of all. It is a weakness that the possession of thousands of nuclear bombs cannot diminish, because the bombs themselves are the problem.

EMP: The Last Acronym

In the 1951 science fiction movie, *The Day the Earth Stood Still*, a flying saucer lands in Washington, D.C., and an alien named Klaatu emerges to warn earthlings about the dangers of meddling with nuclear weaponry. When his attempts at communication meet with failure, Klaatu commands his giant robot helper, Gort, to make the earth stand still. Gort does this by neutralizing all electrical power and communication on the planet for one hour. Everything stops, and all is chaos and confusion. Having gotten everyone's attention at last, Klaatu delivers his message and heads back whence he came.

About a decade after this movie appeared, the atmospheric testing of atomic bombs was at its height. American scientists were then puzzling mightily over a series of odd disturbances in radio communication and electrical power apparently caused by those high-altitude fireballs. One such explosion over the Pacific tripped circuit breakers, knocked out streetlights, and triggered electronic burglar alarms all over Hawaii. A growing body of evidence now suggests that the high-altitude detonation of powerful nuclear bombs is all it might take to make a modern, electronics-dependent nation stand still. In an irony far too alarming to be very amusing, the capacity to neutralize the electronic grid resides in nuclear weapons themselves.

The reason for this, long known but little remarked upon, is a phenomenon called electromagnetic pulse, or EMP. It looms as the ultimate threat to the security of modern defense systems, the reliability of C^3 channels, and the safety of the civilian population. One of the many additional ironies surrounding the EMP issue is that without the microelectronics revolution, EMP would hardly be a threat at all. When the Pentagon took to microchips, it opened a frightening Pandora's Box, and it is difficult to say when, or if, the lid will ever be nailed securely shut again.

Through a complex reaction between gamma rays and electrons in the upper atmosphere, a nuclear explosion many miles above the earth produces a high-energy tidal wave of electromagnetic forces. While any nuclear explosion touches it off, the EMP effect is far more powerful when that explosion takes place about one hundred miles above the earth. Some scientists believe that the EMP burst associated with high-altitude explosions over the central United States would pack enough wallop to black out today's electrical power and communications systems from coast to coast. Like a massive lightning bolt, though many times more powerful, EMP has an affinity for metal, and it can streak through antennas, wires or cables, wreaking havoc on whatever solid-state equipment is connected to them. One self-defeating scenario has it that a nuclear counterstrike against incoming missiles would be an excellent way for the U.S. military to knock out its *own* C^3 system.

Physicists have known about EMP ever since the nuclear testing programs of the late 1950s and early 1960s. Senator Barry Goldwater even touched upon the question of EMP in his 1964 presidential campaign. However, the nature of the electronic grid back then was such that the effects of EMP were minimal. This is true no longer, and we have the microchip to thank for it. Experts have learned that solid-state electronic equipment and systems are millions of times more susceptible to EMP than older versions. One of the least susceptible electronic devices of all, as it turns out, is the outmoded, much-scorned vacuum tube. America's vaunted lead in microelectronics, as it applies to military hardware, telecommunications systems and commercial electrical power, simply renders American equipment that much more vulnerable to the effects of EMP.

The phenomenon of EMP also is well known in the Soviet Union. One Soviet discussion of EMP induced by high-altitude nuclear explosions makes reference to "impulsive electrical currents and stress in aerial and ground conductors and cables, and in radio station antennae. . . . Burnout of the elements of electrical and radio apparatus or massive damage of protection devices. . . . Destruction of insulation on electrical and radio technical installations. . . . Confusion of military staff." For military planners, this raises the question of whether an EMP gap might be just as disturbing, if not more so, than the so-called missile gap. Given the potential magnitude of the EMP problem, and the Kremlin's awareness of it, Soviet reliance on older, only slightly less lethal electronic technologies can be seen as an advantage for the Russians.

The primary defense against the possibility of EMP-induced disruptions is called radiation "hardening." The Pentagon has spent billions shielding its electronic systems and links from the effects of electromagnetic pulse. But even if it is assumed that military C^3 channels can be rendered completely immune to the effects of electromagnetic pulse, few experts seem willing to suggest that nonmilitary electronic systems could withstand such a catastrophe. The commercial electronic grid remains almost completely vulnerable. The massive investment required to shield it mainly would fall to the Bell System and the utilities, and hence, rate-paying phone and electricity customers.

The vulnerability of the commercial electronic grid — radios, telephones, televisions, and various computer-linked telecommunications systems — suggests the possibility that open warfare may not be necessary to create an EMP nightmare. Electrical power systems and generating stations, better known as the power grid, are no less susceptible to electromagnetic pulse. A study of energy security compiled for the Federal Emergency Management Agency, quoted in *Science* magazine, asserted that "one or two well-placed nuclear warheads detonated in the upper atmosphere could cause failure in the entire national power grid, including destroying the sensitive control facilities at modern electric power plants." Presumably, by extension, this destructive scenario could include the sensitive control facilities at modern nuclear power plants as well. There is no way to rule out the possibility that for terrorists who are politically motivated, technologically adroit and in possession of plutonium, EMP could prove to be a dream come true. For innocent civilians, and quite possibly portions of military C³ as well, EMP could mean blackout and chaos; the nation at a standstill. Indeed, terrorists need not accomplish anything so exotic as a high-altitude nuclear detonation and EMP in order to knock out selected portions of the electronic grid, military or commercial. Technically sophisticated saboteurs could attack military computers, while economic chaos could reign in the commercial world after well-planned attacks on government and corporate computer systems. Computer guerrillas are not so much a threat as a certainty, and several dozen well-documented attacks on corporate computers already have taken place in Europe.

Gloomy predictions about EMP are still conjecture, largely because so little is known for certain, and most of it is classified. "It has a 'Star Wars,' Armageddon quality that captures public fancy. An invisible bolt out of the blue that causes our computers to glitch and planes to fall out of the sky," a Defense Department science adviser said in the *Wall Street Journal*. "But the military is aware of the potential problem and has spent a great deal of money protecting against it."

Nonetheless, the military is also clearly worried about the level of protection it has got at the moment. A Joint Chiefs of Staff report arrived at the point rather obliquely, but no less tellingly: "A C³ deficiency today is the widespread loss of connectivity which would be caused by a high-altitude nuclear explosion and its resulting electromagnetic pulse. . . . Some C³ hardware has been EMP-hardened; however, full systems analysis and fixes are required." If the Soviets detonated two or three nuclear bombs high over the U.S. as a prelude to a full-scale attack, the same EMP that knocks out C^3 channels simultaneously would lessen the possibility of halting the conflict anywhere short of "mutually assured destruction," or MAD-ness. The Pentagon, and the rest of the nation, could be plunged, quite literally, and quite possibly eternally, into darkness.

There are several ways to attack the EMP problem in order to shield the electronic grid from its effects once and for all. Here the satellite connection comes into play again, for satellite communication and optical methods of information transmission, such as fiber optics, virtually eliminate vulnerability to EMP. Conceivably, replacing all of the wire in military telecommunications systems would end the matter. It would represent a huge investment in fiber optics, and implementing the switch would be entirely in the hands of the Bell System, the military's contractor of choice. But EMP-proofing every piece of the commercial electronic grid, by optical means or any other, is hardly a realistic option. And considering the treaties prohibiting atmospheric nuclear testing and the health effects of radioactive explosions, pinning down EMP effects and workable countermeasures through extensive field research isn't very likely either. A piece of EMP-proof equipment is like an earthquake-proof building: no one really knows whether it will stand until it is put to the test.

As for satellites, which can be hardened quite easily, this form of electronic communication is more of a vulnerability trade-off than a clear way out of the fix. Satellites are easy prey for other killer satellites, or for lethal weapons directed from enemy ground stations. For this reason, the military is reluctant to put all of its telecommunications eggs in the satellite basket.

The EMP debate only serves to illuminate the uncertainties that surround today's high-technology military gambles. It suggests, as well, other costly versions of the countermeasures vs. counter-countermeasures syndrome: the military increasingly hardens its C^3 system against EMP, only to find that the Soviets have hardened theirs better, and so on. At the bottom of it is the unending growth in defense budgets, the recipients of which are only rarely the small, innovative start-up companies responsible for so many electronic innovations, and needful of the help. In the end, it may matter very little who gets the money, and what innovations are fueled by it, if war is the result. National security and the future health and well-being of the populace are not things that can be purchased, nor measured in terms of numbers of sophisticated weapons and computers, nor manufactured in the research and development labs of electronics companies.

The Federation of American Scientists, in a newsletter devoted to C^3 and EMP, pleaded that "We ought not talk of attacking Soviet command and control lest we simply encourage the Soviet Union to devolve nuclear authority in advance on ever more junior officers. Further, we ought not, in fact, launch such attacks, unless *our* command and control is attacked, lest we lose all chance of war-termination. . . . We ought not to kid ourselves that we are prepared to fight a protracted nuclear war when no plausible improvement in C^3 is likely to permit it; countervailing strategies with numerous complicated options that cannot, in fact, be carried out could become an expensive kind of self-delusion."

EMP and the vulnerability of C^3 means that deterrence, in the raw sense of fire power, may not be much of a deterrence at all. And EMP is a further impetus to "fire first, fire everything" strategies. EMP, combined with all the other dangers posed by electronic and nuclear warfare in general, only means what the arms race has always meant: more arms translates into less security. Any nuclear exchange between the two powers, any suggestion that such an exchange can be "prolonged" or "limited," is an insane, no-win prospect. The microelectronics revolution comes to nothing unless it leads to a realization that mutual arms limitation leading to eventual disarmament is the only life-affirming foreign policy left to choose.

If nuclear war is allowed to happen, what a final mockery of all the promise electronics holds, whatever its perils; a last laugh that no one, perhaps, would be around to appreciate.

CHAPTER TWELVE

Toward the Silicon Future

*Planet implodes! Everything is changed! Few
notice!*

— STEWART BRAND

Artificial Intelligence: Automating the Mind

In the space of one hundred years, the United States has moved from the first tentative experiments with the electric light bulb and electrical power, to the computer on a silicon chip and the automated network of military electronics. It has not been an altogether smooth and simple ride. Anyone who was born near the beginning of this century has witnessed more technological and scientific change, more constant alteration in the daily patterns of life, than any single generation in history. And that record will almost surely be surpassed by anyone born near the beginning of the next century.

Microelectronics and computers have given new meaning to the definition of machines, and have imbued them with previously unimagined capabilities. New technologies and scientific breakthroughs, once discovered, are almost always applied. That is part of the nature of man's intellectual quest, and now man has begun to consider hurling sensate machines made of silicon beyond the solar system, toward the stars.

With the computer, man has striven to create an image of himself; not of his body, but of his intelligence. The quest for the thinking machine has deep roots in history, and today it has a scientific discipline, a cachet and a promise all its own. Artificial intelligence is the name for the field that concerns itself with the parallels between mind and computer. Its primary goal is to push back the limits on what computers can do; to make man's premier machine his intellectual equal. The science of artificial intelligence got formally underway when Alan Turing, of Bletchley and ULTRA fame, first posed the question, "Can Machines Think?" A number of prominent artificial intelligence researchers no longer feel that the question even admits of debate.

The "artificial intelligentsia" is a term popularized by Joseph Weizenbaum, a computer scientist, and most artificial intelligence researchers are no doubt thoroughly sick of it by now. What makes the nickname even more galling to that community is the fact that it came from within the ranks. In 1966 Weizenbaum composed a computer program called ELIZA (after Pygmalion). Mimicking the role of a psychiatrist interviewing a patient, the program produced dialogues such as this:

HUMAN PATIENT: Men are all alike
COMPUTER: IN WHAT WAY
HUMAN: They're always bugging us about something or
     other
COMPUTER: CAN YOU THINK OF A SPECIFIC EXAM-
     PLE
HUMAN: Well, my boyfriend made me come here
COMPUTER: YOUR BOYFRIEND MADE YOU COME
     HERE
HUMAN: He says I'm depressed much of the time
COMPUTER: I AM SORRY TO HEAR YOU ARE DE-
     PRESSED

And so on. Weizenbaum had intended his program, which grew into a program call DOCTOR, as a parody of psychotherapy in order to point out some of the problems inherent in attempting to make computers understand natural language. Imagine his surprise, then, when he discovered that "A number of practicing psychiatrists seriously believed the DOCTOR computer program could grow into a nearly completely automatic form of psychotherapy." Weizenbaum was aghast.

"What must a psychiatrist who makes such a suggestion think he is doing while treating a patient, that he can view the simplest mechanical parody of a single interviewing technique as having captured anything of the essence of a human encounter?" This reaction prompted Weizenbaum to begin questioning the basic tenet guiding research in the field: namely, that computers can be made to "think" in the same way that humans think. And even if they can, Weizenbaum concluded, perhaps we ought not let them do it, for our own sake.

Indeed, the thinking computer has been announced many times in the popular press. "New Machines That Are As Smart As People," proclaimed the headline of a recent article in the *San Francisco Examiner.* "PAM, The Computer, Can Think Like A Human." *Life* magazine announced the thinking computer more than a decade ago, in an article entitled, "Meet Shakey, The First Electronic Person."

Despite these glowing pronouncements, the thinking computer does not yet exist, and the general optimism of the AI community is being tempered by dissenters like Weizenbaum, as well as others outside the field. In *What Computers Can't Do: The Limits to Artificial Intelligence,* the philosopher Hubert Dreyfus dissected twenty years of artificial intelligence research and concluded: "The answer to the question whether man can make [an intelligent machine] must rest on the evidence of work being done. And on the basis of actual achievements and current stagnation, the most plausible answer seems to be, No."

Needless to say, most artificial intelligence researchers do not think much of Hubert Dreyfus.

The early days of the research in the 1950s and 1960s were marked by an amazing amount of optimism, most of which proved misguided. Workers in the field bubbled over with predictions which, in light of the actual progress since then, look rather ridiculous now. Artificial intelligence researchers often frame their views on the computer future so glibly, indeed so shockingly, that it is tempting to see this predilection as a deliberate attempt to jolt readers and listeners out of their complacency about man the dominant.

In 1965, a prominent researcher stated flatly that machines would be capable, within twenty years, of doing any work that a man can do. And here is another, slightly later prediction, offered by another researcher: "In three to eight years we will have a machine with the general intelligence of an average human being. I mean a machine that will be able to read Shakespeare, grease a car, play office politics, tell a joke, have a fight."

Missed predictions such as these have not deterred the reigning stars in the artificial intelligence galaxy from making new, equally rosy ones.

Robert Jastrow, director of NASA's Goddard Institute for Space Studies, stated the case for the thinking computer anew in a 1978 essay for *Time* magazine:

> Four generations of computer evolution — vacuum tubes, transistors, simple integrated circuits, and today's miracle chips — followed one another in rapid succession, and the fifth generation, built out of such esoteric devices as bubble memories and Josephson junctions, will be on the market in the 1980s. In the 1990s, when the sixth generation appears, the compactness and reasoning power of an intelligence built out of silicon will begin to match that of the human brain. By that time, ultra-intelligent machines will be working in partnership with our best minds on all the serious problems of the day, in an unbeatable combination of brute reasoning power and human intuition. What happens after that? Dartmouth President John Kemeny, a pioneer in computer usage, sees the ultimate relation between man and computer as a symbiotic union of two living species, each completely dependent on the other for survival. The computer — a new form of life dedicated to pure thought — will be taken care of by its human partners, who will minister to its bodily needs with electricity and spare parts. Man will also provide for computer reproduction, as he does today. In return, the computer will minister to our social and economic needs. Child of man's brain rather than his loins, it will become his salvation in a world of crushing complexity.

That is Dr. Jastrow's opinion, to which he is quite rightly entitled. The history of artificial intelligence is strewn with such predictions, and given the breakthroughs required to make good on this one, Dr. Jastrow would be wise to omit any mention of a date.

Marvin Minsky, a pioneer of AI research, sounded a similar note in a 1980 edition of *Newsweek* magazine: "At some point people may even prefer to convert themselves into machines, because if they can transfer their intelligence into another embodiment, they might be able to live forever and continue developing." Here is mind-body dualism in the extreme. "Many people get angry at this suggestion," Minsky added, "because they are carbon chauvinistic. Quite possibly, other forms of carbon life in the universe that had a million years of development ahead of them might consider such a conversion — and might have already done it."

This cry of carbon chauvinism is central to the artificial intelligence theme, because it allows for higher forms of intelligence that are not embodied in cellular form. If there are other forms of highly intelligent life not dependent upon the carbon-solar cycles of life on earth, this allows for various speculations about "other kinds of computational structures." Specifically, it allows for the possibility of a silicon species.

"We're getting very good at making small computer circuits," Minsky continued. "I should think that in less than 500 years we will be able to make machines that are very much like us and represent our views and thoughts. If we can make a miniaturized human mind or brain, perhaps 1 gram or 1 cubic centimeter in size, we can place it in an interstellar spaceship and send it off at nearly the speed of light. It would be hard to make a spaceship big enough to carry an Apollo astronaut and all his food for 10,000 years. But I would be surprised if a Saturn V rocket with a few more stages couldn't spring a 1-gram payload across the galaxy."

Minsky is suggesting that silicon is the vehicle by which intelligent life will endure, long after man in his present form has shuffled off into the sunset along with the dinosaurs. But note that the time of arrival for silicon intelligence (five hundred years) has been stretched considerably since the early days (six, or ten, or twenty years).

A popular real-life testing ground for computer intelligence traditionally has been the game board. In 1976 artificial intelligence researchers cheered when a Northwestern University chess program, CHESS 4.5, won the Class B section of the Paul Masson American Chess Championship — five wins, no losses. Three years later at a professional backgammon championship in Monte Carlo, the BK69.8 computer program designed at Carnegie–Mellon University snatched the world crown in backgammon away from an angry Luigi Villa of Milan, taking four out of five games in a seven-point match. The program, running on a computer at Carnegie–Mellon, was linked by satellite to a three-foot robot in Monte Carlo. The ability of computers to play winning chess or backgammon, however, may reveal more about the nature of chess and backgammon than it does about the intelligence of computers. That they can calculate is no secret.

Another controversial part of the artificial intelligence debate concerns the matter of defining intelligence itself. Despite the common use of various IQ tests, and the ready acceptance of their results, measuring intelligence, let alone defining it, is an inexact, elusive pursuit, and highly prone to misinterpretation. In 1912, the U.S. Public Health Service at New York's Ellis Island gave a version of the famous Binet IQ test to a sampling of newly arrived immigrants, and the conclusion was reached that 83 percent of the Jews, 80 percent of the Hungarians, 67 percent of the Russians and 79 percent of the Italians tested were feebleminded. Today's intelligence tests are under attack for much the same reason — that cultural biases built into the tests render them unreliable as a method of measuring innate thinking ability. Since human intelligence is an elusive concept to measure, it is that much more difficult to endow a computer with it.

And yet, some of the more tempered predictions begin to look far more plausible as the microelectronics revolution proceeds and as the microchip grows more powerful. "Smart" machinery and "intelligent" robotic equipment are referred to as such because of their ability to process instructions, solve problems, and do work through the wonders of electronic logic. To perform the work it is instructed to do, and monitor the results, a piece of intelligent equipment also must have some way of sensing changes in its environment; some way of "seeing" what it is doing. Through microelectronics, researchers are finding better and better ways of doing just that.

Plenty of economic reasons exist for making computers and computerized equipment more and more intelligent, in this limited industrial sense. Oil and mining interests are eager to put such advances to use in harvesting precious resources on the sea floor and in outer space. Intelligent mobile equipment could do hazardous duty, saving the lives of firemen, for example, by rescuing people from burning buildings. And there is DENDRAL, a program that acts as an automated organic chemist, impressively deducing the molecular structures of various complex substances. The driving force of automation assures a ready market for machine intelligence as a way of performing *certain* kinds of physical and mental work.

To many who are skeptical or uncomfortable about the prospects of silicon intelligence, the current limits and the failed predictions are seen as a reaffirmation of the unique nature of human intelligence, and the impossibility of totally recreating it in machine form. Few serious computer scientists would argue that programs like DOCTOR, designed to parody psychotherapy, and a similar one called PARRY, designed to mimick a paranoid psychiatric patient, have proven the case for the thinking computer, though Weizenbaum's psychiatrists came close to asserting just that. It is far easier to make a computer mimic the evasive responses of a clinical paranoid than the straightforward responses of a well-adjusted human being.

The short excerpt below is a portion of the historic conversation that resulted when two of the most famous "intelligent" computer programs ever written, DOCTOR and PARRY, got together for a chat over the telephone:

> PARRY: I don't understand your motives.
> DOCTOR: Why don't you understand my motives?
> PARRY: Shouldn't I be?
> DOCTOR: Why do you say that just now?
> PARRY: That's just the way it is.
> DOCTOR: Suppose that's just the way it were not.
> PARRY: So?
> DOCTOR: I am not sure I understand you fully.
> PARRY: You harp on the same questions too much.
> DOCTOR: What does that similarity suggest to you?
> PARRY: I don't get you.
> DOCTOR: Do you wish that you did get I?
> PARRY: It's about time you showed some interest in my feelings.
> DOCTOR: Oh? I showed some interest in your feelings?

What little intelligence there is in this exchange does not result from an understanding of the words involved. DOCTOR and PARRY select preprogrammed responses stored in computer memory, and vary them on the basis of word clues in the question or statement that is posed to them. Alan Turing suggested that the best experiment to prove computer intelligence would consist of a human interrogator in one room typing test questions to a hidden subject in another. If the interrogator was unable to distinguish between the typed response of a computer and those of a fellow human being, Turing held, then that computer has proven its ability to think. PARRY already can pass carefully circumscribed versions of the Turing Test. PARRY is an impressive feat of programming, to be sure, but no computer in existence today can win in a truly open-ended encounter of the Turing kind.

According to philosopher Yehoshua Bar-Hillel: "The step from not being able to do something at all to being able to do it a little bit is very much smaller than the next step — being able to do it well. In artificial intelligence, this fallacious thinking seems to be all pervasive." Support for the thinking machine rests on the theory that in principle, the human mind is knowable; that intelligence can be formalized in such a way that its structure can be represented in digital format. But can human intelligence, in truth, somehow be "lifted" out of the human brain and body and installed in the circuitry of a computer?

Robert Noyce of Intel, whose company's microchips have done so much to fuel the promise of artificial intelligence, remains unconvinced: "While microelectronics has already surpassed the human brain in terms of logical operations performed per second, the idea of computers running around controlling things and reproducing themselves, as some have suggested, is totally ridiculous. If you want a computer to recognize handwriting, it can do that. If you want it to read a book out loud or write music, it can do that too. Not very well yet, but it can do it. It's clear to me that the organization of the brain is quite different from that of the computer. One of the things I speculate on is that the human brain, operating normally, occasionally makes mistakes at the cellular level. It doesn't go according to the pre-programmed routine. And that may be where human creativity comes in. I don't think you can program that in any real sense. I continue to think of man as a tool-making animal, and of the computer as his tool."

When artificial intelligence workers first ran up against the idea that the ability to err might be a fundamental attribute of brain circuitry, they set about teaching computers to do things wrong occasionally, by deliberately introducing the capacity for random error. Language would seem to be a perfect arena for this, because when people talk they routinely make grammatical errors. Yet they are understood. If a computer was programmed to understand language too literally, or to throw out a sentence as incomprehensible when it contained minor errors in a structure, causing a bad bit string the computer couldn't accept, then the computer was going to have a very hard time of it with human speech or written language. Computers *did* have a hard time with human speech and written English — and they still do today.

Computers are very good at game playing, and at solving other problems the solution of which can be arrived at unambiguously through a precise, finite and step-by-step set of computer instructions. Computers are becoming better at various forms of pattern recognition and optical sensing. Computers can even plausibly mimic the responses of a clinical paranoid. But the living complexities of language, and all the marvelously subtle ways people communicate and make themselves understood, are formidable stumbling blocks in the path toward the thinking computer. Nothing like Hal, the conversational computer in *2001: A Space Odyssey*, will be available by that year.

Computer speech recognition and its opposite, synthesized computer speech, are ways of cutting back on the amount of programming knowledge required to communicate with computers. Reading systems, though still quite expensive, can convert written words into synthesized speech for the blind. Speech recognition systems can transcribe simple, carefully articulated sentences, and respond verbally to a verbal question, if the speaker stays within a limited vocabulary of a few hundred words or so. Inexpensive speech chips have been developed in Silicon Valley and at Texas Instruments. The ability of microcomputers to listen and recognize a relatively small set of words, and to speak an equally limited vocabulary, will be spurred by commercial applications. For example, speech recognition computers, linked to corporate telephone systems, are able to record credit card transactions when the caller simply reads the numbers aloud. Voice-activated controls for televisions, ovens, hospital beds, toys, and other products are at hand.

But again, the fallacy of the successful first step must be borne in mind. Adults commonly possess a working vocabulary of as many as a hundred thousand words or more, and in everyday speech the words are slurred together, contracted, clipped off, and pronounced in innumerable ways. The same word can be used in many different ways, and have many different meanings, as in the case of homonyms, and yet sound alike in each case. A shrug or a smile can alter the usual meaning of a word or a phrase entirely. A human listener can follow two or three conversations at once. A computer that understands language, as humans understand it in the form of continuous speech at normal speed, remains only a vision.

A computer must digitize the sound waves representing spoken words and then compare them with its stored vocabulary until it finds a match. Currently, about a thousand words is all a computer can handle, and to manage even that it first must be "trained" to the voices of individual speakers, by having them speak the words over and over until the computer is familiar with individual voice patterns. Only a few dozen words currently can be recognized without this preconditioning process. The job of dictation secretary will likely remain impervious to large-scale automation for some time to come.

One other famous artificial intelligence program is called SHRDLU, written by Terry Winograd, then of MIT. One way of looking at SHRDLU is to say that it knows a lot about a little. SHRDLU's arena is a table upon which have been placed objects like children's blocks, a box, a pyramid and other simple geometrical forms. An associated robotic device, rather like a computer-controlled "hand-eye" machine, can pick up the objects and move them around, when the appropriate instructions are typed in:

> HUMAN: Find a block which is taller than the one you are holding and put it into the box.
> ROBOT: By "it" I assume you mean the block which is taller than the one I am holding.
> HUMAN: OK.
> ROBOT: (*The hand sets down the block it is holding and picks up a taller one.*)
> HUMAN: What does the box contain?
> ROBOT: The blue pyramid and the blue box.
> HUMAN: What is the pyramid supported by?
> ROBOT: The box.

SHRDLU is a remarkable work, and it has obvious applications in the field of industrial automation and control, and it seems to understand language. Winograd is one of the most talented programmers in the artificial intelligence community. But SHRDLU exhibits a certain level of intelligence only in a drastically narrowed world. It knows the meaning of certain spatial relationships and certain words, and it is sensate after a fashion, but it cannot think as humans do.

In order to understand language, computers must master an enormous amount of information about the world, and about the meaning of the words used to describe it. As one programmer observed, "It takes a page of instructions to tell the machine that when Mary had a little lamb, she didn't have it for lunch." Automating intelligence in the full sense — creating programs and inventing chips that allow computers to become man's intellectual equal, or even his superior — would require of the artificial intelligentsia an astounding insight into the workings of the human mind, from its neurons and molecules to its capacity for language and emotion. Uttering synthesized speech, responding to simple vocal commands, and answering questions about a severely limited environment do not prove that computers understand language. Much like humans themselves, computers are better at talking than at listening or understanding. In fact, the possibility that computers might turn out to be *too* much like humans — contentious, uncompromising, prone to misunderstanding and error — makes the future of artificial intelligence all the more intriguing and unsettling. Thought and language are at times fragile and easily disrupted processes. A highly creative computer might also be a highly unreliable one.

No method of simply dumping huge numbers of words and sentences into computer memory will bring true language comprehension to computers, and artificial intelligence researchers are well aware of this. Such "brute force" methods work up to a point, but a computer needs shortcuts, and shortcuts, so far, have been hard to come by. Competing theories about language abound, but the explicit rules of language, if such exist, remain hidden to computers — and to their human builders as well. Artificial intelligence, in the most meaningful sense, would require a deep understanding of how the brain is coded for grammar, semantics and syntax. In other words, a deep understanding of language's structure, arrangement and meaning. As yet, that understanding is not nearly deep enough, and the thinking computer must await it.

Despite the obstacles to computer understanding of language, written or spoken, the basic question still exists: Will computers ever be able to think like people? Douglas R. Hofstadter plumbed that debate in a most challenging, unusual and much acclaimed book, *Gödel, Escher, Bach: An Eternal Golden Braid*. Hofstadter explored the nature of intelligence and the prospects of transferring it to machines, and in doing so, he revealed a profound and witty intelligence of his own, reflected in the book's subtitle, "A metaphorical fugue on minds and machines in the spirit of Lewis Carroll." Hofstadter often used imaginary dialogues between colorful characters to put his points across. In a column written for *Scientific American*, he provided a playful summation of the artificial intelligence debate through a conversation held by "Sandy," a philosophy student with views suspiciously like the author's own; "Chris," a physics student unconvinced by the claims made for artificial intelligence; and "Pat," an equally skeptical biology student. In the midst of the discussion, selectively excerpted below, the subject of chess-playing computer programs arises.

SANDY: . . . As for chess programs, it so happens I know how they work, and I can tell you for sure that they aren't conscious. No way.

PAT: Why not?

SANDY: They incorporate only the barest knowledge about the goals of chess. The notion of playing is turned into the mechanical act of comparing a lot of numbers and choosing the bigger one over and over again. A chess program has no sense of shame about losing or pride in winning. Its self-model is very crude. It gets away with doing the least it can, just enough to play a game of chess and nothing more. . . .

This observation eventually leads Sandy to expound further on the subject of "feelingless calculation."

SANDY: . . . Sure, that exists — in a cash register, a pocket calculator. I'd say it's even true of all today's computer programs. But eventually when you put enough feelingless calculations together in a huge coordinated structure, you'll get something that has properties on another level. You can see it — in fact, you *have* to see it — not as a bunch of little calculations but as a system of tendencies and desires and beliefs and so on. When things get complicated enough, you're forced to change your level of description. To some extent that's already happening, which is why we use words such as "want", "think", "try", and "hope" to describe chess programs and other attempts at mechanical thought. . . .

PAT: How can you think of a computer as a conscious being? I apologize if this sounds like a stereotype, but when I think of conscious beings, I just can't connect that thought with machines. To me consciousness is connected with soft, warm bodies, silly though it may sound. . . .

CHRIS: . . . So tell us — *do* you believe in the idea of an intelligent computer or don't you?

SANDY: It all depends on what you mean. We've all heard the question, "Can computers think?" There are several possible interpretations of this (apart from the many interpretations of the word "think"). They revolve around different meanings of the words "can" and "computer."

PAT: Back to word games again.

SANDY: That's right. First of all, the question might mean, "Does some present-day computer think, right now?" To that I would immediately answer with a loud no. Then it could be taken to mean, "Could some present-day computer, if it was suitably programmed, potentially think?" That would be more like it, but I would still answer, "Probably not." The real difficulty hinges on the word "computer." The way I see it, "computer" calls up an image of just what I described earlier: An air-conditioned room with rectangular metal boxes in it. . . . I see no reason for [computers designed for the study of intelligence] staying fixed in the traditional image. They will probably soon acquire as standard features some rudimentary sensory systems, at first mostly for vision and hearing. They will need to be able to move around, to explore. They will have to be physically flexible. In short, they will have to become more self-reliant, more animal-like. . . . I do think it is necessary, if people are realistically going to try to imagine an artificial intelligence, to go beyond the limited, hard-edged picture of computers that comes from seeing what we have today. The only thing all machines will always have in common is their underlying mechanicalness. That may sound cold and inflexible, but what could be more mechanical — in a wonderful way — than the working of the DNA and enzymes in our cells?

PAT: To me what goes on inside cells has a wet, slippery feel to it and what goes on inside machines is dry and rigid. It's connected with the fact that computers don't make mistakes, that computers do only what you tell them to do. At least that's my image of computers. . . .

SANDY: . . . But your image of computers is stuck in a rut. Computers certainly can make mistakes — and I don't mean on the hardware level. Think of any present-day computer's predicting the weather. It can make wrong predictions, even though its program runs flawlessly.

PAT: But that's only because you've fed it the wrong data.

SANDY: Not so. It's because weather prediction is too complex. . . .

PAT: So you do think computers will be making fewer mistakes as they get smarter?

SANDY: Actually it's the other way around. The smarter they get, the more they'll be in a position to tackle messy real-life domains, so they'll be more and more likely to have inaccurate models. To me mistake making is a sign of high intelligence. . . .

PAT: I once heard a funny idea about what will happen when we eventually have intelligent machines. When we try to implant that intelligence into devices we'd like to control, their behavior won't be so predictable.

SANDY: They'll have a quirky little "flame" inside, maybe?

PAT: Maybe.

CHRIS: And what's so funny about that?

PAT: Well, think of military missiles. The more sophisticated their target-tracking computers get, according to this idea, the less predictably they will function. Eventually you'll have missiles that will decide they are pacifists and will turn around and go home and land quietly without blowing up. We could even have smart bullets that turn around in mid-flight because they don't want to commit suicide.

SANDY: A lovely thought.

CHRIS: I'm very skeptical about all this. Still, Sandy, I'd like to hear your predictions about when intelligent machines will come to be.

SANDY: It probably won't be for a long time that we'll see anything remotely resembling the level of human intelligence. It rests on too awesomely complicated a substrate — the brain — for us to be able to duplicate it in the foreseeable future. That's my opinion, anyway.

But as always — and who can really say in the end? — Hofstadter insists on leaving the door to the thinking computer slightly ajar. Sandy concludes:

If I were shown a machine that can do things I can — I mean pass the Turing test — then instead of feeling insulted or threatened, I'd want to chime in with the philosopher Raymond Smullyan and say, "How wonderful machines are!"

The Know-how and the Know-what

As Tzu-Gung was traveling through the regions north of the river Han, he saw an old man working in his vegetable garden. He had dug an irrigation ditch. The man would descend into a well, fetch up a vessel of water in his arms and pour it out into the ditch. While his efforts were tremendous the results appeared to be very meager.

Tzu-Gung said, "There is a way whereby you can irrigate a hundred ditches in one day, and whereby you can do much with little effort. Would you not like to hear of it?"

Then the gardener stood up, looked at him and said, "And what would that be?"

Tsu-Gung replied, "You take a wooden lever, weighted at the back and light in front. In this way you can bring up water so quickly that it just gushes out. This is called a draw-well."

Then anger rose in the old man's face, and he said, "I have heard my teacher say that whoever uses machines does all his work like a machine. He who does his work like a machine grows a heart like a machine, and he who carries the heart of a machine in his breast loses his simplicity. He who has lost his simplicity becomes unsure in the strivings of his soul. Uncertainty in the strivings of the soul is something which does not agree with honest sense. It is not that I do not know of such things; I am ashamed to use them."

There is no doubting it: machines *are* wonderful. Unlike the gardener along the river Han, most of us are unwilling to live without them, and for good reason. Standing before the machine, the technologist wonders at the workings, the scientist wonders at the structure, and the philosopher wonders at the principles. Everyone else, along with them, stands in awe of what machines designed by man can do *for* man, and what, as well, they can do *to* him.

The computer and the microchip represent today the highest examples of the machine maker's art. No other artifact on earth comes close to equaling the astonishing range of their capabilities. No other product of human workmanship has their kind of power, or their propensity for changing the ways that people go about their business. They have begun to change the way we think about ourselves and the world, and in the future, perhaps, if the artificial intelligence community wins its bet, they will even change how thinking occurs at all, by usurping the process of thought entirely; stealing it away from a frailer species for the greater good of the universe, one might say.

The artificial intelligence debate, taken to extremes, is a matter of philosophy — the mechanist versus the vitalist, the rationalist versus the romantic. But electronics and intelligence are immutably linked: as complementary systems of logic, as forces driving world change, and as elemental powers of nature. It seems, in fact, that we cannot have one without the other. The human brain is a maelstrom of electrical activity, and the electronic computer, product of man, is a system for expressing a kind of humanlike intelligence. The grid is where the two meet, and where the powers of both commingle.

Electricity, as we have seen, has been with us all along, everywhere. It was a symbol for power and intelligence long before Nikola Tesla and Thomas Edison first showed how to harness it effectively, and it will remain so after we who enjoy its benefits and endure its hazards have long since ceased to exist. In many ways, our minds *are* more suited to the electronic way of life than to the mechanical-industrial way of life, because systems of electronic logic aid the brain and not just the body. We cannot use a shovel to solve a complicated mathematical equation, for example, but we can teach a computer to dig.

There is no industrial precedent for what is happening today, no prior experience upon which to draw, no comforting historical rules of operation to fall back on. In this century, nothing can measure up to the impact of the microchip; not television, not the automobile, and, so far, not even gene-splicing. Microelectronics, a manufacturing process as technically exacting as brain surgery, as intellectually demanding as atomic physics, yields products that contain the power of logic; products that *reason*.

Today, there is no way to do electronics more cheaply and

effectively than semiconductors. If some revolutionary new development arrives to make that statement obsolete — and there is no reason to think that it won't — the experience and the momentum behind semiconductor electronics will propel it for at least another several decades on the strength of expected advances and falling prices alone. Today, the great railroads and steel conglomerates are gone, and the oil industry must face an uncertain future built upon a dwindling resource. The automobile industry is in the midst of dismemberment. Union Pacific, U.S. Steel and Ford are all shadows of their former selves, while mighty Exxon looks for ways to transform a portion of itself into an information company. Yet AT&T and IBM exist virtually unchanged, in terms of historical power and influence, and the next few years will see a steady extension of their global reach.

The electronics industry has played a role in every twist and turn of this technology-driven and often tragic century. "We are still wrestling, in much of our present thinking," wrote John McHale, in *The Changing Information Environment,* "with the difficulty of orienting ourselves towards this new knowledge of a world in which many of our physical transactions and manipulations are now conducted in the hitherto unknown reaches of the electromagnetic spectrum. . . . We have not yet evolved ways of socially or economically accounting for the kinds of power, energy and material value that accrues, for example, through the use of small transistors or the tiny components of micro-miniaturized circuits or the many other means with which we explore the invisible areas of electromagnetic energies."

The industry that created the computer and the microchip is built upon the most fundamentally indispensable resource of all — information. Information, as McHale pointed out, has a number of characteristics that set it apart from other resources. To begin with, all other resources depend upon it utterly. No other resource can be utilized without it. In a study of the radio spectrum and its uses, Harvey J. Levin observed that "insofar as it is free from depletion upon use, the spectrum has characteristics of a sustained yield (flow) resource of a unique sort, perhaps most similar to solar or water power. . . . In the spectrum, if equipment is maintained intact, then the same flow of information is possible, indefinitely, with no depletion of the resource itself."

However, this observation does not apply so readily to the electronics industry itself, where the soaring cost of building the devices that process and transmit the information resource is of major concern. The industry is gobbling up capital at a frightening rate, and it remains to be seen whether the new wealth and new jobs this creates will be sufficient to offset the price tag. The money the industry needs in order to grow must come from somewhere; the fierce rise in the demand for capital signals a rapidly growing, major industry increasingly capable of exercising more collective muscle, and more concerted influence, on national decision-making.

Perhaps the most cogent definition of the Post-Industrial Society which electronics has wrought comes from Daniel Bell, the man who popularized the term. "A Pre-Industrial Society," Bell told a panel of the U.S. House of Representatives, "is essentially based upon raw materials, as a game against nature in which there is diminishing returns. An Industrial Society is organized primarily around energy and the use of energy for the productivity of goods. A Post-Industrial Society is organized around information and the utilization of information on the basis of organizing the flow of knowledge; it is also a society uniquely dependent upon the compilation of theoretical knowledge."

In a Post-Industrial Society, as another information specialist warned, "Who *knows* what becomes more important than who *has* what."

This does not mean, of course, that agriculture and traditional industry simply disappear. McHale offered agriculture as an example. "In the United States the agricultural sector still remains a vitally productive component of the economy, but its relative importance has declined as a motivating force in the society. . . . Though *technically* innovative, it is no longer a major focus for *social* innovation, and it no longer plays such a prime role as hitherto in shaping the values, goals and ways of life in the society."

Today, for better or worse, electronics is the locus of social innovation. And the speed with which new electronic technologies arrive, the little that can be known for certain about how they will be used, and what will come of it, induces a certain amount of stress. The steady bombardment of electronic information threatens to overwhelm society, and numbness, or a retreat to the hills, seems at times to be the only way of shutting out the flood. "For the society and the political process there are enormous problems which arise from this communication overload," wrote Bell in *The Coming of Post-Industrial Society*. "At a time when, in our psychological values, we place a greater emphasis on individuation, where is the possibility of privacy . . . the finding of open spaces . . . and a relief from the stresses created by these incessant 'messages' out of the blue?"

The sheer amount of electronic information we must cope with, however, is not the only problem. One newcomer to Silicon Valley, after two years' hard labor at untangling the mysterious complexities of electronics, confided that, finally, he thought he had discovered the hidden secret of the *business* of electronics. He had mastered the lingo, and spoke RAMS, ROMS, and learning-curve pricing with the best of the inhabitants. Several speculative stock issues he had shrewdly seized upon, by virtue of his newfound insider's knowledge, had done quite nicely for him. In fact, he had managed to enter the industry with commendable ease, for an outsider. It was difficult work in a strange land, but he had come away from it with a ruling principle. "The only thing you have to know about the electronics industry," he revealed, marveling once again at the speed with which the technology outruns the ability to comprehend its applications, "*is that nobody's driving the bus.*"

Our utter dependence upon cheap and pervasive electronics

has its price, and part of that price is the feeling that we have lost control of our lives to technology. Someone, or some group, must be to blame for the fact that nothing is certain or simple anymore. We point the finger and look for scapegoats: How are we to orchestrate this giddy, headlong plunge into technological complexity? We lay the blame everywhere — on the technocrats, the environmentalists, the Luddites, the Russians or some unseen cabal of sinister politicians and power-hungry industrialists. *Someone* must be driving the bus, and we are not always happy with the road we are on.

Citizens have a right to be skeptical about any litany of electronic changes just around the proverbial corner. The cable television industry promised the Wired Life back in the 1950s, and the artificial intelligence community has been making extravagant claims for about as long. The pace of change is swift and becoming swifter, but there is a tendency to overlook the potent drag effect exerted by government, reluctant consumers, regulatory boards, endless court proceedings and a host of other social, political and economic factors. Personal computers and telecommunications are in a wildcat stage (and the outlook for energy, the means of powering the grid, is uncertain). We hear how our homes and our lives are being transformed by computers and software tailored just for us, and yet most of us come home each night to a house or an apartment in which the television is just a television, the telephone is just a telephone, and there are no computer terminals to be seen. Very few of us are directly involved in the decision-making and the ongoing maneuvers — corporate, political and legal — that are shaping both the look of the electronic home systems to come, and the quality, not to mention quantity, of the electronic services they will offer. Even fewer of us are involved in actually designing and implementing them. It may prove that the personal computer and the telecommunications links that connect it to the rest of the world are being designed, tested, honed, standardized and priced primarily in the offices of large corporations. There is nothing wrong with this, by itself, but it is not altogether clear whether the wants and needs of the average citizen at home will be fully addressed if this is so. If the result of the personal computer revolution is to bring a hundred new forms of electronic advertising and entertainment into the home, and precious little in the way of access to genuine information — libraries, medical and other public services, knowledge of all kinds stored in sundry places — then there may be little about it that we can call truly revolutionary at all.

In the end, some continuing form of government regulation and supervision, however benignly or lightly applied, will be inevitable and necessary. Business rightly decries the useless, duplicative and inconsequential forms of regulation that do exist, and government would do well to pay heed where it is warranted. But far too often we have seen a version of the environmental "Tragedy of the Commons" played out in the business pasture, where serious financial penalties accrue to those companies which deviate from the single-pointed, short-term march toward ever greater productivity, consumption, profits and growth. By itself, the play of the free market cannot assure that the full benefits of electronics are equitably dispersed. The government's interest in, and awareness of, the electronics industry's impact must go hand-in-hand with regulation. So far, the modern electronics industry remains for government a new and exotic adjunct to business as usual, its impact acknowledged but by no means deeply understood. And those who do recognize what is happening, inside government or outside it, are often viewed with suspicion when they speak of "the next industrial revolution," or, as filmmaker Francis Coppola once put it, "electronic reindustrialization." Much of it sounds too California, too trendy and hip, too tied in somehow with science fiction and space travel. It is comforting to dismiss the tentative attempts to articulate the direction of the coming changes; changes which anyone familiar with microelectronics knows to be possible, if not inevitable.

As to the specifics of the future these changes will bring, nothing is ordained. Electronics affords us the physical tools for remaking the culture, for rewiring everything — cities, industries, communication systems, jobs, schools and perhaps even our own thought processes. It would be comforting to pretend that the future can be clearly and rigidly delineated because computers have turned the speculations of futurism into an exacting science. But it is not so. Trends can be extrapolated with mathematical exactitude. The process of ongoing change, and the future it will bring, cannot.

If, as Wendell Berry has written, the only possible guarantee of the future is responsible behavior in the present, then predictions tell us less about the shape of things to come than about our perceptions of the troublesome world we live in now. Models of the future are not so much a divination of things to come (and such predictions are never really wrong, if the person doing the predicting takes care to set the time of arrival far enough in advance) as an encapsulization of the predictor's beliefs about what is important in the present. Take, for example, these three computer-related predictions of what the future holds, culled from a collection published by *Next* magazine in its November/December 1980 issue.

Isaac Asimov: "We are witnessing a fall in the world birthrate and a rise in world computerization. And if the latter overtakes the former, we may yet be able to solve the problems that face us, and in future decades look back on the 1980s as the turning point."

Timothy Leary: "The 1980s will be the most exciting, liberating, optimistic decade in human history because of space migration, intelligence increase, and life extension. . . . Human intelligence will be multiplied by the use of psychoactive drugs. . . . Science will become the new religion."

And David Packard, chairman of Hewlett–Packard Company and a former Deputy Secretary of Defense: "If U.S. industry does not keep a high commitment to quality and reliability, Japanese computers could be real competition in the decade ahead. The U.S. will be challenged by computer developments in several of the major European countries as well. In the face of this, I clearly see productivity improvement from computers continuing at an accelerated pace. I believe also that productivity within the industry will continue at a high rate. I am very bullish on the future of the computer industry."

These predictions reveal as much or more about those doing the predicting than they do about the likely course of events throughout the decade and into the next. These visions have been framed so that they validate the work of the speakers, and so that they appeal to their respective constituencies. The predictions are not necessarily *wrong*, because any or all of them may prove true. But the danger of acting *as if* we know what the future will hold lies in what has been left out, and in the implication that there is a single future out there, if only we could foretell it. This book contains a number of specific predictions as well, and the problem with them is the same. There are a wealth of alternative futures, and when we forget this we narrow the range of possibilities in the present.

It seems self-evident that the future is a complex matrix of unknown influences too subtle to be wholly foreseen. And yet it seems just as self-evident that the behavior of large bodies of men and equipment cannot be predicted in advance, or that no one can know the number of dogs that will bite humans in the city of New York next year. These things *have* been predicted, and with astonishing accuracy, through a mix of statistics, probability theory, and computer science. Computers cannot do everything, but, as Douglas Hofstadter has pointed out, computers do some things far better than anyone has a right to expect. It is not that the futures predicted will never come to pass, but that so many other futures, equally plausible or desirable, must be excluded from our thinking.

Highlighting the useful future applications of technology is not the same as designing for them today. The computer is slightly more than thirty-five years old, and we now know that computers can be a tool for every individual, not just institutions and specialists. Simply recognizing this to be so does not end the matter. For what purposes will everyone be using them?

The evolution of computers, it is commonly said, is a mighty

330 ◇ *THE NEW ALCHEMISTS*

engine of progress. But progress and evolution are elusive terms. There are scientists who say that progress consists of increasing our ability to capture and use ever-larger amounts of available energy, which is why, they say, we now have nuclear power plants instead of waterwheels, and five billion people instead of a few hundred million. Progress consists of creating and maintaining new pockets of negative entropy — pockets of energy order in a disordered universe. And, since this is progress, it follows that this ever-increasing energy and information curve will lead us to create pockets of order other than those which exist on the fragile skin of the fourth stone from the sun, and that perhaps those new pockets will be peopled, if that is the word, by a silicon species.

There are economists who say that progress is a mathematical function, an econometric measure of the available money supply and the goods and services produced and purchased by virtue of it. Progress, then, is a result of an increasing Gross National Product and other quantitative parameters.

Such linear definitions are out of place in the age of information. We must look beyond science and economics for an acceptable definition of progress. When we place our faith solely in science and in numbers, we have no right to expect answers to our problems, because we have not yet learned to put the right questions. True progress requires a careful distinction; one that is implied in Norbert Wiener's conception of the need to distinguish between the *know-how* and the *know-what*. We know *how* to do so much, and yet we know so little about *what* ought to be done. The know-how is primarily the business of the scientist, the engineer, the businessman and the machine. The know-what is everybody's business; a province without experts. "The solidest piece of scientific truth I know of," wrote the distinguished scientist Lewis Thomas, "the one thing about which I feel totally confident, is that we are profoundly ignorant about nature. . . . It is this sudden confrontation with the depth and scope of ignorance that represents the most significant contribution of 20th century science to the human intellect." True progress is that ineffable process whereby information, intelligence, knowledge and numbers — the know-how — is transformed into wisdom — the know-what. "Where is the wisdom we have lost in knowledge?" asked T. S. Eliot. "Where is the knowledge we have lost in information?"

Silicon chips are mere markers along the path of an intellectual journey that began long ago. The true keys to the kingdom are not microchips and computers. The keys to the kingdom can be found in the individual human heart, and no amount of sophisticated machinery can change that.

"The machine itself makes no demands and holds out no promises," in the words of Lewis Mumford. "It is the human spirit that makes demands and keeps promises."

We are all the new alchemists now.

Notes

INTRODUCTION:
The Grid

For a concise technical and economic introduction to microelectronics, see Robert N. Noyce, "Microelectronics," *Scientific American,* September, 1977. Reprinted in *Microelectronics,* A Scientific American Book (San Francisco: W.H. Freeman and Co., 1977), pp. 3–9.

xi Clarke quoted in *Omni* interview, March, 1979, p. 141.
xi Noyce from *Microelectronics,* A Scientific American Book, p. 3.
xi–xii Neil Postman, "The Information Environment," *Et Cetera,* Fall, 1979, pp. 234–245.
xiii Weizenbaum quoted in "Continuum," *Omni,* December, 1979.
xiii Jastrow quoted in Gene Bylinsky, "Life in Darwin's Universe," *Omni,* September, 1979, p. 116.
xiii Noyce, *Microelectronics,* p. 9.

CHAPTER ONE:
Why Is Thomas Edison Frying Dogs?

For a general introduction to Thomas Edison, see Robert Conot, *A Streak of Luck* (New York: Bantam Books, 1979) and Matthew Josephson, *Edison* (New York: McGraw-Hill Book Co., 1959). Two Nikola Tesla biographies of note are John J. O'Neill, *Prodigal Genius* (Hollywood: Angriff Press, 1981) and Margaret Cheney, *Tesla: Man Out of Time* (Englewood Cliffs, N.J.: Prentice-Hall, 1981). See also Marshal Eliot, "Seeking Redress for Nikola Tesla," *Science,* October 30, 1981, pp. 523–525.

For a detailed analysis of the rise of science-based industry and the engineering manager, see David Noble, *America by Design* (New York: Alfred A. Knopf, 1977). See also Lewis Mumford, *Technics and Civilization* (New

York: Harcourt, Brace and World, A Harbinger Book, 1934, 1963) and Daniel Kevles, *The Physicists* (New York: Random House, Vintage Books, 1979).

3-5 An account of Tesla's Colorado experiments appears in O'Neill, *Prodigal Genius,* pp. 183–187.

7-8 For the early history of electrical theory, see J. L. Heilbron, *Electricity in the 17th and 18th Centuries* (Berkeley: University of California Press, 1979).

8 See Thomas S. Kuhn, *The Structure of Scientific Revolutions* (Chicago: University of Chicago Press, second edition, 1970), pp. 17–22.

9 "I sell here, sir" — Jacob Bronowski, *The Ascent of Man* (Boston: Little, Brown and Co., 1973), p. 280.

10 Mumford discusses the "neotechnic" in *Technics and Civilization,* pp. 221–229.

10 Duchamp quoted in Samuel C. Florman, *The Existential Pleasures of Engineering* (New York: St. Martin's Press, 1976), p. 134.

10 Comte quoted in Mumford, p. 220.

11 See David Noble, *America By Design,* p. 6.

12 "a minor invention" — Noble, p. 8.

12 Edison's jibe at mathematicians is quoted in Daniel Kevles, *The Physicists,* p. 8.

12-13 "lusty, crusty, hard-driving" — Robert Conot, *A Streak of Luck,* p. xiv.

14 Edison's concept of distributing electricity is discussed in Matthew Josephson, *Edison,* p. 211.

15 The homage to Tesla appears in Noble, p. 98.

17 Tesla's sunset epiphany is described in O'Neill, *Prodigal Genius,* pp. 48–50. See also Bud Spurgeon, "Tesla," *CoEvolution Quarterly,* Winter 1977/78, p. 65.

18 "$75 a month" — Conot, p. 192.

18 "by the size of the silver dollar" — Josephson, p. 283.

18 Tesla on Edison's working methods — Alfred P. Morgan, *The Pageant of Electricity* (New York: Appleton-Century Co., 1939), p. 163.

19-21 The AC-DC rivalry is discussed in Conot, pp. 304–310. See also Josephson, p. 347, and Morgan, pp. 164–165.

21-24 For early patent warfare and the invention factory see Noble, pp. 10–100.

23 "Edison's greatest invention" — Norbert Wiener, *The Human Use of Human Beings* (New York: Houghton Mifflin Co., 1950; Avon Books, 1967), p. 157.

23 "sensitive, cheerful and profane" — Conot, p. 175.

23-24 Edison's quotes on patent litigation — Josephson, pp. 355–358.

25-26 Tesla's Wardencliff Vision is reprinted from O'Neill, pp. 210–211.

26 "We are automata" — O'Neill, p. 260.

28-30 For Lee De Forest's version of the vacuum tube, see his *Father of Radio* (Chicago: Wilcox and Follet, 1950). For a more objective appraisal, see Gerald Tyne, *Saga of the Vacuum Tube* (Indianapolis, Ind.: Howard W. Sams and Co., 1977). See also Rupert McLaurin, *Invention and Innovation in the Radio Industry* (New York: MacMillan Co., 1949).

30-31 For the early history of AT&T, see N. R. Danielian, *AT&T: The Story of Industrial Conquest* (New York: The Vanguard Press, 1939).

32 "In all the 3,400 miles of line" — Jane Morgan, *Electronics in the West* (Palo Alto, Calif.: National Press Books, 1967) pp. 63-64.

33 "War should mean research" — Kevles, *The Physicists*, p. 116.

33 "charging the sea with electricity" — Kevles, p. 138.

35 Jewett quoted in Noble, p. 130. For a discussion of the radio patent pool, see Noble, pp. 91-99.

36 *Saturday Evening Post* and *Nation* quoted in Kevles, pp. 173-174.

36 "John Doe isn't quite" — Kevles, p. 238.

36 "There is nothing wrong with electricity" — G. K. Chesterton, "A Plea That Science Now Halt," *New York Times Magazine*, October 5, 1930, p. 2.

37 "A father mourns his child" — De Forest, *Father of Radio*, p. 444.

CHAPTER TWO:
World War II and the Universal Machine

The origins of the electronic computer are discussed in several books, among them: Jeremy Bernstein, *The Analytical Engine* (New York: Random House, 1964); B. V. Bowden, ed., *Faster Than Thought* (London: Pitman Publishing, 1953); Herman H. Goldstine, *The Computer from Pascal to von Neumann* (Princeton, N.J.: Princeton University Press, 1972); Nigel Hawkes, *The Computer Revolution* (New York: E. P. Dutton and Co., 1972); and B. Randell, ed., *The Origins of Digital Computers* (New York: Springer-Verlag, 1973).

For an introduction to cybernetics and information theory, see Norbert Wiener's *The Human Use of Human Beings* and John von Neumann's *The Computer and the Brain* (New Haven: Yale University Press, 1958). Alan Turing and many other pioneers of artificial intelligence are discussed in Pamela McCorduck's *Machines Who Think* (San Francisco: W. H. Freeman and Co., 1979).

39-40 For more on Project Ultra and the Enigma cipher machines, see William Stevenson, *A Man Called Intrepid* (New York: Harcourt Brace Jovanovich, 1976) and F. W. Winterbotham, *The Ultra Secret* (New York: Harper and Row, 1974).

40 See Sara Turing, *Alan M. Turing* (Cambridge: W. Heffer and Sons, 1959).

41 "it is difficult today" — Glen Fleck, ed., *A Computer Perspective* (Cambridge, Mass.: Harvard University Press, 1973), p. 125.

41–42 "I won't say" — McCorduck, *Machines Who Think*, p. 53.

42–43 Boole and Leibnitz are quoted in Hubert L. Dreyfus, *What Computers Can't Do* (New York: Harper and Row, Harper Colophon, revised edition, 1979), pp. 67–71.

44 ". . . it is by no means hopeless" — Glen Fleck, *A Computer Perspective*, p. 33.

47 "it is unworthy of excellent men" — Herman Goldstine, *The Computer from Pascal to von Neumann*, p. 8.

47 For more on Babbage, see Philip and Emily Morrison, eds., *Charles Babbage and his Calculating Engines* (New York: Dover Publications, 1961).

49 "Think of that" — Fleck, *Computer Perspective*, p. 33.

50 "In a scientific war" — Kevles, p. 309.

51–54 Wiener's quotes are taken from *Human Use*. "Besides the electrical", p. 23; "At the beginning," pp. 84–86; "A series of operations," p. 207.

56 See Christopher Evans, *The Micro Millennium* (New York: The Viking Press, 1980), p. 35.

62 "It was time" — Herman Lukoff, *From Dits to Bits* (Portland, Ore.: Robotics Press, 1979), p. 64

63–64 "The Univac I was clearly" — Lukoff, pp. 117–118.

64 Mauchly's quote appears in N. Metropolis, et al., eds., *A History of Computing in the Twentieth Century* (New York: Academic Press, 1980), p. 549.

65 "It will be interesting" — Bowden, *Faster Than Thought*, pp. ix–x.

65–66 Wiener, *Human Use*, pp. 219–250.

67 Wiener, p. 90.

67 Turing's quote is from his article, "Computing Machinery and Intelligence," in A. R. Anderson, ed., *Minds and Machines* (Englewood Cliffs, N.J.: Prentice-Hall, 1964). See also Douglas R. Hofstadter, *Gödel, Escher, Bach* (New York: Basic Books, 1979), p. 597.

CHAPTER THREE:
The Solid State

For a scholarly account of solid state research and the early semiconductor industry, see Ernest Braun and Stuart MacDonald, *Revolution in Miniature* (Cambridge: Cambridge University Press, 1978), as well as John E. Tilton, *International Diffusion of Technology: The Case of Semiconductors* (Washington, D.C.: The Brookings Institution, 1971). See also *Electronics*

Magazine, Special 50th Anniversary Issue, April 17, 1980, for a technical view.

69 "The transistor in 1949" — Braun and MacDonald, *Revolution in Miniature,* p. 57.

69–70 "A device called a transistor" — *New York Times,* July 1, 1948.

71 "the old dream of a control valve" — Ralph Bown, "The Transistor as an Industrial Research Episode," *Scientific Monthly,* January, 1955, p. 42. Quoted in Braun and MacDonald, p. 53.

72 "The atomic bomb" — Kevles, *The Physicists,* p. 308.

72 Post-war science policy and funding is discussed in Kevles, pp. 342–359.

74 "the research carried out" — *Electronics,* April 17, 1980, p. 229.

76–77 The discovery of the point-contact transistor is related in *Electronics,* April 17, 1980, pp. 230–233.

78–79 For more on the Bell Seminars, see Braun and MacDonald, pp. 54–57.

79 "as a memorial" — Braun and MacDonald, pp. 54–55.

80 "As we enter the age of transistors" — reprinted in *Electronics,* April 17, 1980, p. 239.

80 "The transistor was not simply" — Braun and MacDonald, p. 60.

81 "Trouble with the big companies" — Braun and MacDonald, p. 55.

CHAPTER FOUR:
The Silicon Priesthood

In addition to sources cited for the previous chapter, see Michael F. Wolff, "The Genesis of the Integrated Circuit," *IEEE Spectrum,* August, 1976, pp. 45–53.

86 Noyce quoted from author interview, 1980.

87 Wickenden quoted in David Noble, *America by Design,* p. 167.

89–90 "The Shockley organization" — author interview, 1980.

91 Noyce quoted from author interview, 1980.

92 "traitorous eight" — *Electronics,* April 17, 1980, p. 249.

92 Noyce quoted from author interview, 1980.

93 Dummer quotes taken from Michael F. Wolff, "The Genesis of the Integrated Circuit," p. 45, p. 53.

93–94 Noyce quoted from author interview, 1980.

95 "In those days" and "gets a picture" — Wolff, "The Genesis of the Integrated Circuit."

95 "Three key features of the invention" — correspondence with the author, 1982.

97 Noyce quoted from author interview, 1980.

99 Cox quoted from author interview, 1980.

99 "The proposal was" — author interview, 1980.

99 Anixter quoted from author interview, 1980.

100–101 Noyce quoted from author interview, 1980.

102 "One company official" — *Electronics*, April 4, 1966, p. 46. Quoted in Tilton, p. 78.

102 Engineering employment figures taken from Daniel Bell, *The Coming of Post-Industrial Society* (New York: Basic Books, Harper Colophon Books, 1973).

103 "The Fairchild folks" — author interview, 1980.

104–105 Lloyd quoted from author interview, 1980.

106 Cox quoted from author interview, 1980.

106–107 Marren quoted from author interview, 1980.

107–108 Marren and Cox quoted from author interview, 1980.

109 "the power of commercial motivation" — Braun and MacDonald, *Revolution in Miniature*, p. 84.

109–110 Quotes pertaining to the 1950s electrical conspiracy appear in Richard Austin Smith, "The Incredible Electrical Conspiracy," *Fortune*, April–May, 1961 (reprinted February 11, 1980, pp. 174–186).

110–111 "No geniuses here" and "Why go to the moon?" — Kevles, *The Physicists*, p. 383, p. 387.

CHAPTER FIVE:
The Computer on a Chip

The bulk of this chapter is derived from author interviews. Magazine articles on the industrial genesis of the microprocessor include: Gene Bylinsky, "Here Comes the Second Computer Revolution," *Fortune*, November, 1975 (reprinted in Forester, *The Microelectronics Revolution*, pp. 3–15); Philip H. Abelson and Allen L. Hammond, "The Electronics Revolution," *Science*, March 18, 1977 (reprinted in Forester, pp. 16–28); Tom Forester, "The Jelly Bean People of Silicon Valley," *New Society*, July 27, 1978 (reprinted in Forester, pp. 65–71); "New Leaders in Semiconductors," *Business Week*, March 1, 1976.

113–115 Quotes taken from author interviews, 1980.

115 Noyce from "Creativity by the Numbers," *Harvard Business Review*, May–June 1980, p. 122ff.

116 Noyce quoted from author interview, 1980.

116–121 Hoff and Noyce quoted from author interviews, 1980.

122–123 "The future is obviously" — "Microcomputers Aim at Huge New Market," *Business Week*, May 12, 1973, p. 180.

123 Noyce quoted from author interview, 1980.

124 Lloyd quoted from author interview, 1980.

125 Grove's quotes taken from Victor K. McElheny, "High-Technology Jelly Bean Ace," *New York Times*, June 5, 1977.

126 Noyce quoted from author interview, 1980.

126 Hoff quoted from author interview, 1980.

126 Moore quoted in Intel press release, 1974.

127 "These systems will be sold" — "Microcomputers Aim at Huge New Market," *Business Week*, May 12, 1973, p. 181.

127 "All electric forms" — Marshall McLuhan, *Understanding Media*, (New York: McGraw-Hill, Mentor Books, Second Edition, 1964), p. 167.

129-130 Noyce quoted from author interviews, 1980.

130 "It would seem" — McLuhan, p. 148.

CHAPTER SIX:

Angstrom Economics

Microchip economics and production techniques are discussed in the following articles: Arthur L. Robinson, "New Ways to Make Microcircuits Smaller." *Science*, May 30, 1980, pp. 1019–1022; Robinson, "Problems with Ultraminiaturized Transistors," *Science*, June 13, 1980, pp. 1246–1249; Robinson, "Are VLSI Microcircuits Too Hard to Design?" *Science*, July 11, 1980, pp. 258–262; William Oldham, "The Fabrication of Microelectronic Circuits," *Scientific American*, September, 1977, reprinted in *Microelectronics*, pp. 40–53; Robert N. Noyce, "Hardware Prospects and Limitations," in Michael Dertouzous and Joel Moses, *The Computer Age: A Twenty-Year View* (Cambridge: MIT Press, 1979), pp. 321–337; R. W. Keyes, "Physical Limits in Digital Electronics," *Proceedings of the IEEE*, May, 1975, pp. 740–767. See also Ruth M. Davis, "Evolution of Computers and Computing," *Science*, March 18, 1977, pp. 1096–1101.

132-133 "The pure white gowns" — Arthur L. Robinson, "New Ways to Make Microcircuits Smaller," *Science*, May 30, 1980, p. 1019.

133 Grove quote from Intel press release, 1979.

133 "Don't worry about getting" — author interview, 1977.

136 "Today's microcomputer" — Robert N. Noyce, "Microelectronics," *Scientific American*, September, 1977, p. 65.

137 "It has been a long time" — "The Computer Society: Business — Thinking Small," *Time*, February 20, 1978, p. 51.

141 "From its earliest beginnings" — Charles J. Sippl and David A. Kidd, *Microcomputer Dictionary and Guide* (Champagne, Ill.: Matrix Publishers, first edition, 1976), p. 109.

142 "With microprocessors, the customers are potentially" — Ruth M. Davis, "Evolution of Computers and Computing," *Science*, March 18, 1977, p. 1099.

142 Quotes from "The Microprocessor/Microcomputer Industry," In-

dustry Analysis Service, Creative Strategies, Inc., San Jose, Calif., 1977.

144-145 "the dominant feature of VLSI" — Arthur L. Robinson, "Are VLSI Microcircuits Too Hard to Design?" *Science,* July 11, 1980, p. 258.

146 "dramatic increases in soft fails" — J. F. Ziegler and W. A. Lanford, "Effect of Cosmic Rays on Computer Memories," *Science,* November 16, 1979, p. 787.

146-147 May quoted from author interviews, 1980. For more on the alpha problem see also Timothy C. May and Murray H. Woods, "Alpha-Particle-Induced Soft Errors in Dynamic Memories," *Proceedings of the 1978 International Reliability Physics Symposium* (New York: Institute of Electrical and Electronics Engineers, 1978), reprinted in *IEEE Transactions On Electron Devices,* January, 1979; Steven Hershberger and Dirk Hanson, "Widen Effort to Control Alpha Particles in 16Ks," *Electronic News,* August 28, 1978, p. 58.

147-149 For more on superconductivity and Josephson junctions, see Juri Matisoo, "The Superconducting Computer," *Scientific American,* May, 1980, pp. 50-65.

149-152 For more on recent developments in photovoltaics, pertinent articles include: Tracy Kidder, "The Future of the Photovoltaic Cell," *Atlantic Monthly,* June, 1980, pp. 68-76; Charles G. Burck, "Solar Comes Out of the Shadows," *Fortune,* September 24, 1979, pp. 67-75; Jeffrey L. Smith, "Photovoltaics," *Science,* June 26, 1981, pp. 1472-1478; Amal Nag, "Big Oil's Push Into Solar Irks Independents," *Wall Street Journal,* December 8, 1980, p. 29.

152-153 Noyce quoted from author interview, 1980.

154 Jordan quoted in Sabin Russell, "Five Ex-Intel Staffers Form New Firm," *Electronic News,* February 2, 1981, p. 10.

155 Bobb quoted in "New Starters in Silicon Valley," *Business Week,* January 26, 1981, p. 68. See also "The Boom in Tailor-Made Chips," *Fortune,* March 9, 1981, pp. 122-126.

155-156 Noyce quoted from author interview, 1980.

CHAPTER SEVEN:
Silicon Valley International

A number of technical trade journals regularly cover events in Silicon Valley on an ongoing basis. Among them are *Electronic News, Electronics* magazine, *Computer World* and *Datamation.* See also the business section of the *San Jose Mercury.* For a sociological perspective on high technology managers, see Michael Maccoby, *The Gamesman* (New York: Simon and Schuster, Bantam Books, 1976).

Material on microchip espionage and the international invasion of Silicon Valley can be found in the following sampling of articles: Gene Bylinsky, "The Japanese Spies in Silicon Valley," *Fortune*, February 27, 1978, p. 74ff; Dirk Hanson, "Chips of War," *New West*, July 28, 1980, p. 51ff; Dirk Hanson, "Second-Tier Semicon Suppliers Target for Offshore Firms," *Electronic News*, June 13, 1977, p. 1ff; Kathleen K. Wiegner, "The Micro War Heats Up," *Forbes*, November 26, 1979, p. 49ff; Marilyn Chase and Jim Drinkhall, "The Silicon Spies: Semiconductor Firms Are Plagued by Thefts of 'Hi-Tech' Materials," *Wall Street Journal*, April 28, 1981, p. 1ff.

157 "It is common knowledge" — Maccoby, *The Gamesman*, p. 24.

157 AMD recruitment ad in *Electronic News*, October 29, 1979, p. 68.

157–163 "D.C." quoted from author interviews, 1979, 1980.

159 Sanders quoted in "The Computer Society: Down Silicon Valley," *Time*, February 20, 1978, p. 51.

160 Harrington quoted from author interview, 1979.

161 "The way I hear it" — author interview, 1980.

162 McKenzie quoted from court records in Jim Leeke, "National Gets Injunction in Secrets Suit Against Zilog," *Electronic News*, June 11, 1979, p. 6.

162 Borovoy quoted from author interview, 1980.

164 "A new type of man" — Maccoby, p. 24.

169 Noyce quoted from author interview, 1980.

171–173 For more on Exxon's push into electronics, see "Exxon's Next Prey: IBM and Xerox," *Business Week*, April 28, 1980, p. 92ff.

173 Mackintosh Consultants quoted in Dirk Hanson, "Second-Tier Semicon Suppliers Target for Offshore Firms," *Electronic News*, June 13, 1977, p. 1.

174 Harrington quoted from author interview, 1980.

177 Worth quoted from court records, Santa Clara County Superior Court, San Jose, Calif., 1980.

177–178 Dialogue between Dunlap and seller from court records, Santa Clara County Superior Court, San Jose, Calif., 1980.

178 For more on the Commerce Department's report, see Robert C. Toth and John H. Averill, "U.S. Investigating Sale to Soviets of Restricted Items," *Los Angeles Times*, February 14, 1980.

178–179 Borovoy quoted from author interview, 1980.

179 The Fairchild tour bus incident is described in William J. Broad, "Fear of Spies Cuts Short Industry Tour," *Science*, January 25, 1980, pp. 388–389.

179 "oral exchanges of information" — "U.S. Bars Reds at Computer Science Meet," *San Francisco Examiner*, February 22, 1980.

181 Borovoy quoted from author interview, 1980.

181–182 All quotes from testimony before the Subcommittee On Copyrights, House of Representatives, San Jose, Calif., April 16, 1979.

184 "Cramer management never had" — Dirk Hanson and Denny Mosier, "AMD files $1M Suit to Halt 'Bad' Ep/ROM Distribution," *Electronic News*, April 3, 1978, p. 1ff.

185 Skornia quoted from author interview, 1980.

186 Judge quoted in *Electronic News*, March 19, 1979, p. 54.

186 Skornia quoted from author interview, 1980.

186 "While the [Russian] choice" — Jack Robertson, "Soviets Develop 8-bit MPU Based on Early Intel Design," *Electronic News*, November 3, 1980, p. 42.

187 "hostile intelligence gatherers" — "Foreign Envoys Step Up High-Tech Thefts," *San Francisco Examiner*, December 17, 1980.

187 "The Silicon Valley and Southern California" — Marilyn Chase and Jim Drinkhall, "The Silicon Spies," *Wall Street Journal*, April 28, 1981, p. 1ff.

187 "stealing them off trains" — Mark Hosenball, "Say U.S. CPU Know-how Was Stolen by Soviets," *Electronic News*, November 3, 1980, p. 7.

187–188 "No wonder the Soviet Union" — Jack Robertson, "Government Closeup: Curiouser and Curiouser," *Electronic News*, December 8, 1980, p. 16.

189 Sanders quoted from author interview, 1978.

190 Sanders quoted in Jim Leeke, "Practices Abroad Unfair, SIA Says at ITC Hearing," *Electronic News*, June 4, 1979, p. 6.

190–191 See R. W. Anderson, "Quality and 16K RAMs: A Hewlett-Packard Case History," presented at Electronic Industries Association of Japan, Washington, D.C., March 25, 1980.

193 Price quoted in "Control Data Seeks to Form VLSI R&D, Production Cooperative," *Electronic News*, April 13, 1981, p. 1ff.

CHAPTER EIGHT
*Consumer Electronics and Tales
of the Home Computer*

Popular accounts of the wired life and the computer in the home include: Alvin Toffler, *The Third Wave* (New York: William Morrow and Co., 1980); Christopher Evans, *The Micro Millennium* (New York: The Viking Press, 1980): Adam Osborne, *Running Wild* (Berkeley: Osborne/McGraw Hill, 1979). See also Ted Nelson's self-published *The Home Computer Revolution*.

Two good collections of scholarly articles and papers are: Michael L. Dertouzos and Joel Moses, eds., *The Computer Age* (Cambridge, Mass.: MIT Press, 1979), and Tom Forester, ed., *The Microelectronics Revolution* (Cambridge, Mass.: MIT Press, 1981). Of special interest is Joseph Weizenbaum's dissenting view, which appears in both books. See also Alan C. Kay,

"Microelectronics and the Personal Computer," *Scientific American*, September, 1977 (reprinted in *Microelectronics: A Scientific American Book*, pp. 125–135).

196 Moses, "The Computer in the Home," in Dertouzos and Moses, *The Computer Age*, p. 20.

196 Weizenbaum, "Once More: The Computer Revolution," in Dertouzos and Moses, p. 441.

200 Quotes on the consumer business from Dirk Hanson, "Marketing Consumer Lines Is Tricky, Many Semiconductor Suppliers Find," *Electronic News*, April 18, 1977, p. 29.

200–205 The discussion of video games is derived in part from Nolan Bushnell's first-person account, with John Joss, "To Win the Business Game, Do What You Know," *INC.*, August, 1979, pp. 43–46. For more on hackers and Space War, see Stewart Brand, "Fanatic Life & Symbolic Death Among the Computer Bums," in *II Cybernetic Frontiers* (New York, Berkeley: Random House, Bookworks, 1974), pp. 35–90 and Joseph Weizenbaum, *Computer Power and Human Reason* (San Francisco: W. H. Freeman and Co., 1976), pp. 111–131. See also "The Hacker Papers," *Psychology Today*, August, 1980, p. 62ff.

207–209 For more on the Apple Computer story, see Susie Gharib Nazem, "The Folks Who Brought You Apple," *Fortune*, January 12, 1981, p. 66ff.

210–214 For more on VDT radiation, see "Health Protection for Operators of VDTs/CRTs," a pamphlet from the New York Committee for Occupational Safety and Health (NYCOSH), New York City, 1980. Articles of interest include: Eliot Marshall, "FDA Sees No Radiation Risk in VDT Screens," *Science*, June 5, 1981, pp. 1120–1121; Joann S. Lublin, "Health Fears on VDTs Spur Union Action," *Wall Street Journal*, October 27, 1980, p. 45; John Crudele, "Say FCC Finds Computers Exceed Radiation Levels," *Electronic News*, July 9, 1979, p. 45.

216 Moses quoted from *The Computer Age*, pp. 3–4.

216–217 Schweickart quoted from author interview, 1980.

217–218 Weizenbaum quoted from *The Computer Age*, p. 442.

218 University of California study quoted in *Electronic News*, December 29, 1980, p. 18.

219 Noyce quoted from author interview, 1980.

CHAPTER NINE:
Telecommunications: The Grid Rewired

An excellent introduction to telecommunications is James Martin, *Future Developments in Telecommunications* (Englewood Cliffs, N.J.: Prentice-

Hall, second edition, 1977). For the politics of telecommunications, see Anthony G. Oettinger, et. al., *High and Low Politics* (Cambridge, Mass.: Ballinger Publishing Co., 1977), and Anthony Smith, *The Geopolitics of Information* (New York: Oxford University Press, 1980). See also John McHale, *The Changing Information Environment* (Boulder, Co.: Westview Press, and London: John Elek, 1976).

Articles of interest include: M. J. Richter's coverage of AT&T regulatory issues, *Electronic News*, 1978–1981; William J. Broad's two-part series, "Ma Bell Eyes New Markets," *Science*, August 8, 1980, pp. 663–668, and "Ma Bell Losing Grip on Old Markets," *Science*, August 15, 1980, pp. 787–790; Vivienne Killingsworth, "Corporate Star Wars: AT&T vs. IBM," *Atlantic Monthly*, May, 1979, pp. 68–75; Charles G. Burck, "Getting to Know the Smart Phone," *Fortune*, February 25, 1980, p. 134ff.

224 McHale, *The Changing Information Environment,* p. 95.

227 Oettinger, *High and Low Politics,* p. 175.

228 Bell tariff quoted in Martin, *Future Developments in Telecommunications,* p. 351.

230 "Dick Tracy comes true" — quoted in Margaret Garrard Warner, "AT&T is Given Approval to Offer Portable Phones," *Wall Street Journal,* April 10, 1981, p. 2.

233 "Like a competition" — quoted in Susan Chace, "Tough Customer," *Wall Street Journal,* January 29, 1981, p. 1.

234 "We have today removed" and "Who knows what's going to happen" — quoted in William J. Broad, "Ma Bell Eyes New Markets," *Science,* August 8, 1980, pp. 663, 668.

235 "Why should any corporation" — M. J. Richter, "House Com Unit Chief: Break Hold of Regulation," *Electronic News,* October 15, 1979, p. 13ff.

236 "to the eyeballs" — Robert E. Taylor, "Antitrust Chief Won't Drop AT&T Case But May Adjust It for Pentagon Fears," *Wall Street Journal,* April 10, 1981, p. 2.

237 "wholly support[ed]" — M. J. Richter, "Justice: Drop Bell Suit, Allot WE Sales," *Electronic News,* August 3, 1981, p. 4.

237 Quotes on AT&T and the Defense Department report from M. J. Richter, "Judge Probes Bell Role in DOD Report," *Electronic News,* August 17, 1981, p. 1, p. 4.

237–238 McGowan quoted in M. J. Richter, "Bell, MCI Argue Effect of Pending Com Act Bill in House Hearing," *Electronic News,* September 15, 1980, p. 8.

240 "It's the basic AT&T question" — quoted in "Uphold Bar on Free AT&T Videotext," *Electronic News,* March 30, 1981, p. 55.

242 Martin, pp. 478–479.

247 Martin, p. 215.

251 "your choice of all the best" — quoted in Aimée L. Morner, "The Heavenly Prospects for Earth Stations," *Fortune,* February 9, 1981, p. 102.

253 "When my children's homes are wired" — quoted in "FCC Chief's Concern for Personal Privacy," *San Francisco Chronicle,* October 14, 1980.

253 "The reason [distributed processing]" — in "LSI Circuits," SRI International, Business Intelligence Program, Research Report 583, December, 1976, p. 10.

255 "Telecommunications were first perceived" — Tran Van Dinh, "WARC, the Third World, and the New International Information Order," *CoEvolution Quarterly,* Summer, 1979, p. 108.

255 "For example, in the provision of" — McHale, p. 95.

256 "That all countries have" — quoted in Robert Horvitz, "Tuning in to WARC," *CoEvolution Quarterly,* Summer, 1979, p. 100. See also Charles Lee Jackson, "The Allocation of the Radio Spectrum," *Scientific American,* February, 1980, pp. 34–39.

257 "we might want to operate" — in "Can the Third World Rule the Airwaves?" *Business Week,* December 17, 1979, p. 38.

257-258 Smith, p. 136.

CHAPTER TEN:
The Hidden Costs of Automation

Most studies of microprocessor-induced automation have been done in Europe, and tend to be pessimistic, compared to American studies. See, for example, "Technical Change and Economic Policy," by the Organization for Economic Cooperation and Development (OECD), Paris, Washington, D.C. (reviewed in *Science,* September 5, 1980, p. 1098). Several articles about automation are found in Forester, *The Microelectronics Revolution,* including a condensed version of the script for "Now the Chips are Down," an award-winning British documentary written by Ed Goldwyn, first screened on BBC 2 television in March, 1978. See also Daniel Bell, *The Coming of Post-Industrial Society* (New York: Basic Books, Harper Colophon Books, 1973).

For the automation of money and crime, see Donn B. Parker, *Crime by Computer* (New York: Charles Scribner's Sons, 1976) and Thomas Whiteside, *Computer Capers* (New York: Thomas Y. Crowell Co., 1978).

260 "Advancing technology never reduces" — quoted in Arthur L. Robinson, "Electronics and Employment: Displacement Effects," *Science,* March 18, 1977 (reprinted in Forester, pp. 318–333.)

261 "European industries face" — Philip Sadler, "Welcome Back to the 'Automation' Debate," in Forester, p. 295.

262 "Robots, aided by computers" — Lloyd Schwartz, "Predict Robots, CPUs to Change Face of U.S. Workplace," *Electronic News,* November 17, 1980, p. 80.

265 "deskilling process" — Hazel Downing, "Word Processors and the Oppression of Women," in Forester, pp. 283–287.

265 "those who tend the computers" — quoted from author interview, 1979.

267 See "AT&T Urges Court Uphold FCC Claim on Electr. Mail," *Electronic News,* June 30, 1980, p. 29.

268 "We may have passed" and "We don't make" — quoted in Robert L. Simison, "Is Repairing Your Car Frustrating? It Will Soon Be Worse," *Wall Street Journal,* January 13, 1981, p. 1ff. See also Clare E. Wise, "Cars and Computers Come Together," *Machine Design,* November 23, 1978, p. 24ff.

268 Hanson quoted in *Successful Farming,* December, 1980.

269 "the typical family farm" — Buel F. Lanpher, "A View of National Computer Development in Agriculture," SEA-Extension, U.S. Department of Agriculture, presented at Northeast Extension and Research Administration workshop, 1980.

271 Grove quoted in John G. Posa and Bruce LeBoss, "Intel takes aim at the 80's," *Electronics,* February 28, 1980, p. 89. See also "Missing Computer Software," *Business Week,* September 1, 1980, p. 64ff.

272–273 Martin Mayer, *The Bankers* (New York: Random House, Ballantine Books, 1976), pp. 138–142.

275 "Nobody seems to know" — Donn Parker, "The Future of Computer Security in a World of Increasing Risk," presented at Honeywell Information Systems Computer Security and Privacy Symposium, April, 1981.

276 "Every large computer" — Parker, *Crime by Computer,* p. 113.

276–277 Whiteside quoted in Thomas Whiteside, *Computer Capers,* pp. 8–9.

277 Parker, *Crime by Computer,* p. 33.

277 "What really amuses me" — quoted from author interview, 1980.

278–279 Hellman quoted from Stanford University News Service press release, March 20, 1979. See also Martin E. Hellman, "The Mathematics of Public-Key Cryptography," *Scientific American,* August, 1979, pp. 146–157.

279–280 Frances FitzGerald, *America Revised* (Boston: Atlantic/Little, Brown and Co., 1980), p. 44–46.

281 For computers and the New Right, see Dennis Farney, "Bloc Power," *Wall Street Journal,* September 11, 1980, p. 1ff.

CHAPTER ELEVEN:
The Electronic Warriors:
Which Way to the Front?

The business of electronic warfare is the subject of two main journals of the trade, *Defense Electronics* and *Countermeasures.* See also the relevant coverage in another trade journal, *Aviation Week.* A good technical introduction to the newer electronic weaponry is Paul F. Walker's "Precision-guided Weapons," *Scientific American,* August, 1981, pp. 37–45.

The definitive account of the dangers of electromagnetic pulse is William J. Broad's award-winning three-part *Science* series, "Nuclear Pulse": "Awakening to the Chaos Factor," *Science,* May 29, 1981, pp. 1009–1012; "Ensuring Delivery of the Doomsday Signal," *Science,* June 5, 1981, pp. 1116–1118; and "Playing a Wild Card," *Science,* June 12, 1981, pp. 1248–1251.

288 "As small missiles become" — Paul F. Walker, "Precision-guided Weapons," p. 45.

290 Jack Robertson, "Government Closeup: Garbage In, Garbage Out," *Electronic News,* January 19, 1981, p. 14.

291–292 Boston Study Group, *The Price of Defense* (New York: Times Books, 1979), pp. 228–229.

293 "They really have no wartime" — in William J. Broad, "Computers and the U.S. Military Don't Mix," *Science,* March 14, 1980, p. 1186.

293–294 "operationally vulnerable" and "If the president can't tell" — in Frank Greve, Knight News Service, "Pentagon calls its computer a 'disaster,'" *San Francisco Sunday Examiner and Chronicle,* November 4, 1979.

294 "This exercise linked" — Broad, "Computers and the U.S. Military," p. 1184.

294 "the heart of the Tacfire system" — "Panel: WWMCCS 'Deficient', Tacfire 'Obsolete'; Funds Cut," *Electronic News,* September 24, 1979, p. 6.

295 "There are three ways" and "is that the electronic network" — Broad, "Computers and the U.S. Military," p. 1187.

297 "similar to having speakers" — Broad, "Pentagon Orders End to Computer Babel," *Science,* January 2, 1981, p. 31.

298 "There is not much chance" — quoted in Broad, "Philosophers at the Pentagon," *Science,* October 24, 1980, p. 412.

301 "impulsive electrical currents" — quoted in Broad, "Nuclear Pulse (II): Ensuring Delivery of the Doomsday Signal," *Science,* June 5, 1981, p. 1117.

301–302 "one or two well-placed" — Constance Holden, "Energy, Security and War," *Science,* February 13, 1981, p. 683.

302 "It has a 'Star Wars'" — Quoted in Richard A. Shaffer, "Electronic Systems Vulnerable To High-Altitude Atomic Blast," *Wall Street Journal,* May 29, 1981, p. 29.

302 "A C^3 deficiency today" — Broad, "Nuclear Pulse (I): Awakening to the Chaos Factor," *Science,* May 29, 1981, p. 1009. See also W. J. Karzas, et al., "Detection of the electromagnetic radiation from nuclear explosions in space," *Physical Review,* March 8, 1965, pp. B1369–1378.

304 "We ought not talk of attacking" — "C^3," *Scientific American,* February, 1981, p. 66.

CHAPTER TWELVE:
Toward the Silicon Future

There are scores of books on artificial intelligence, not all of them intelligible to the layman. Some of the more accessible volumes include: Pamela McCorduck, *Machines Who Think* (San Francisco: W. H. Freeman and Co., 1979); Joseph Weizenbaum, *Computer Power and Human Reason* (San Francisco: W. H. Freeman and Co., 1976); Hubert L. Dreyfus, *What Computers Can't Do* (New York: Harper and Row, Harper Colophon Books, 1972, 1979); Alan Ross Anderson, *Minds and Machines* (New York: Prentice-Hall, 1964); Margaret Boden, *Artificial Intelligence and Natural Man* (New York: Basic Books, 1977). A most challenging approach to the artificial intelligence debate is Douglas R. Hofstadter's *Gödel, Escher, Bach: An Eternal Golden Braid* (New York: Basic Books, 1979).

For more on the sociological issues facing citizens of the computer age, see Daniel Bell, *The Coming of Post-Industrial Society* (New York: Basic Books, Harper Colophon Books, 1973), and John McHale, *The Changing Information Environment* (Boulder, Co.: Westview Press, 1976).

307–308 Weizenbaum's discussion of his DOCTOR program appears in Weizenbaum, *Computer Power and Human Reason*, pp. 1–16.
308 Dreyfus, *What Computers Can't Do*, p. 187.
309 "In three to eight years" — Carole McCauley, *Computers and Creativity* (New York: Praeger, 1974).
309 Jastrow, "Toward an Intelligence Beyond Man's," *Time*, February 20, 1978, p. 59.
310 Minsky quotes from "Looking for Life Out There," *Newsweek Focus*, June/July, 1980, pp. 72–76.
311 For more on computer game playing, see Hans Berliner, "Computer Backgammon," *Scientific American*, June, 1980, pp. 64–72.
313 The encounter between DOCTOR and PARRY appears in Hofstadter, *Gödel, Escher, Bach*, p. 599.
313–314 Bar-Hillel quoted in Dreyfus, p. 147.
314 Noyce quoted from author interview, 1980.
316 Excerpts from SHRDLU appear in Dreyfus, p. 6
317 "It takes a page of instructions" — McCauley, *Computers and Creativity* (New York: Praeger, 1974).
318–321 The conversation on the thinking computer is excerpted from Douglas R. Hofstadter, "Metamagical Themas: A coffeehouse conversation on the Turing Test to see if a machine can think," *Scientific American*, May, 1981, pp. 15–36.
322 "As Tzu-Gung was traveling" — quoted in McLuhan, *Understanding Media*, p. 69
324 McHale, *The Changing Information Environment*, pp. 107–108.
324–325 "Insofar as it is free" — quoted in McHale, p. 21.
325 "A Pre-Industrial Society" — quoted in McHale, p. 22.

325 "Who *knows* what" and "In the United States" McHale, pp. 25, 60.
326 Bell, p. 317.
326 "The only thing" — quoted from author interview, 1979.
329-330 Quotes from Asimov, Leary and Packard appeared in "Thinkers and Shakers," *Next,* November/December, 1980, p. 52.

Selected Bibliography

Bell, Daniel. *The Coming of Post-Industrial Society* (New York: Basic Books, Harper Colophon Books, 1973).

Berkeley, Edmund Callis. *Giant Brains* (New York: Science Editions, 1961).

Bernstein, Jeremy. *The Analytical Engine: Computers — Past, Present and Future* (New York: Random House, 1964).

Boston Study Group. *The Price of Defense: A New Strategy for Military Spending* (New York: New York Times Books, 1979).

Bowden, B.V., ed. *Faster Than Thought: A Symposium on Digital Computing Machines* (London: Pitman Publishing, 1953).

Brand, Stewart. *II Cybernetic Frontiers* (New York, Berkeley: Random House, Bookworks, 1974).

Braun, Ernest, and MacDonald, Stuart. *Revolution in Miniature: The History and Impact of Semiconductor Electronics* (Cambridge: Cambridge University Press, 1978).

Carneal, Georgett. *A Conqueror of Space: An Authorized Biography of the Life and Work of Lee De Forest* (New York: Horace Liveright, 1930).

Conot, Robert. *A Streak of Luck: The Life and Legend of Thomas Alva Edison* (New York: Seaview Books, Bantam Books, 1979).

Danielian, N. R. *AT&T: The Story of Industrial Conquest* (New York: The Vanguard Press, 1939).

De Forest, Lee. *Father of Radio* (Chicago: Wilcox and Follet, 1950).

Dertouzos, Michael L., and Moses, Joel, eds. *The Computer Age: A Twenty-Year View* (Cambridge, Mass.: MIT Press, 1979).

Dreyfus, Hubert L. *What Computers Can't Do: The Limits of Artificial Intelligence* (New York: Harper and Row, Harper Colophon Books, 1972, 1979).

Evans, Christopher. *The Micro Millennium* (New York: The Viking Press, 1980).

Fleck, Glen, ed. *A Computer Perspective* (Cambridge, Mass.: Harvard University Press, 1973).

Florman, Samuel C. *The Existential Pleasures of Engineering* (New York: St. Martin's Press, 1976).

Forester, Tom, ed. *The Microelectronics Revolution: The Complete Guide to the New Technology and its Impact on Society* (Cambridge, Mass.: MIT Press, 1981).

Goldstine, Herman H. *The Computer from Pascal to von Neumann* (Princeton: Princeton University Press, 1972).

Hawkes, Nigel. *The Computer Revolution* (New York: E. P. Dutton and Co., 1972).

Herrick, Clyde N. *Survey of Electronics* (New York: Macmillan and Co., 1973).

Hofstadter, Douglas R. *Gödel, Escher, Bach: An Eternal Golden Braid* (New York: Basic Books, 1979).

Josephson, Matthew. *Edison: A Biography* (New York: McGraw–Hill Book Co., 1959).

Kemeny, John G. *Man and the Computer* (New York: Charles Scribner's Sons, 1972).

Koenjian, Edward, ed. *Microelectronics: Theory, Design and Fabrication* (New York: McGraw–Hill Book Co., 1963).

Kevles, Daniel J. *The Physicists: The History of a Scientific Community in Modern America* (New York: Random House, Vintage Books, 1979).

Kuhn, Thomas S. *The Structure of Scientific Revolutions* (Chicago: University of Chicago Press, 1962).

Lukoff, Herman. *From Dits to Bits: A Personal History of the Electronic Computer* (Portland, Ore.: Robotics Press, 1979).

Maccoby, Michael. *The Gamesman* (New York: Simon and Schuster, Bantam Books, 1976).

Mann, Martin. *Revolution in Electricity* (New York: The Viking Press, 1962).

Martin, James. *Future Developments in Telecommunications* (Englewood Cliffs, N.J.: Prentice–Hall, second edition, 1977).

Mayer, Martin. *The Bankers* (New York: Random House, Ballantine Books, 1976).

McCauley, Carole Spearin. *Computers and Creativity* (New York: Praeger, 1974).

McCorduck, Pamela. *Machines Who Think: A Personal Inquiry into the History and Prospects of Artificial Intelligence* (San Francisco: W. H. Freeman and Co., 1979).

McHale, John. *The Changing Information Environment* (Boulder, Col.: Westview Press, and London: Paul Elek, 1976).

McLuhan, Marshall. *Understanding Media: The Extensions of Man* (New York: McGraw–Hill Book Co., Mentor Books, second edition, 1964).

Morgan, Alfred P. *The Pageant of Electricity* (New York: D. Appleton–Century Co., 1939).

Morgan, Jane. *Electronics in the West: The First Fifty Years* (Palo Alto, Calif.: National Press Books, 1967).

Morrison, Philip, and Morrison, Emily, eds. *Charles Babbage and his Calculating Engines* (New York: Dover Publications, 1961).

Mumford, Lewis. *Technics and Civilization* (New York: Harcourt, Brace and World, A Harbinger Book, 1934).

Nelson, Ted. *The Home Computer Revolution* (self-published, distributed by The Distributors, South Bend, Ind., 1977).

Noble, David. *America by Design: Science, Technology and the Rise of Corporate Capitalism* (New York: Alfred A. Knopf, 1977).

Oettinger, Anthony G., et. al. *High and Low Politics: Information Resources for the 80s* (Cambridge, Mass.: Ballinger Publishing Co., 1977).

O'Neill, John J. *Prodigal Genius: The Life of Nikola Tesla* (Hollywood, Calif.: Angriff Press, 1981).

Osborne, Adam. *Running Wild: The Next Industrial Revolution* (Berkeley: Osborne/McGraw–Hill, 1979).

Parker, Donn B. *Crime By Computer* (New York: Charles Scribner's Sons, 1976).

Randell, B., ed. *The Origins of Digital Computers: Selected Papers* (New York: Springer–Verlag, 1973).

Schneider, Ben Ross, Jr. *Travels in Computerland, or Incompatibilities and Interfaces* (Reading, Mass.: Addison–Wesley, 1974).

Seligman, Ben B. *The Potentates: Business and Businessmen in American History* (New York: Dial Press, 1971).

Sharlin, Harold F. *The Making of the Electrical Age: From the Telegraph to Automation* (London: Abelard–Schuman, 1963).

Sippl, Charles J., and Kidd, David A. *Microcomputer Dictionary and Guide* (Champaign, Ill.: Matrix Publishers, 1975).

Smith, Anthony. *The Geopolitics of Information: How Western Culture Dominates the World* (New York: Oxford University Press, 1980).

Stevenson, William. *A Man Called Intrepid: The Secret War* (New York: Harcourt, Brace Jovanovich, Ballantine Books, 1977).

Tilton, John E. *International Diffusion of Technology: The Case of Semiconductors* (Washington, D.C.: The Brookings Institution, 1971).

Toffler, Alvin. *The Third Wave* (New York: William Morrow and Co., 1980).

Turing, Sara. *Alan M. Turing* (Cambridge: W. Heffer and Sons, Ltd., 1959).

Tyne, Gerald F. *Saga of the Vacuum Tube* (Indianapolis, Ind.: Howard W. Sams and Co., 1977).

Von Foerster, Heinz, ed. *Cybernetics: Transactions of the Tenth Macy Conference* (New York: Josiah Macy, Jr., Foundation, 1955).

von Neumann, John. *The Computer and the Brain* (New Haven: Yale University Press, 1958).

Weizenbaum, Joseph. *Computer Power and Human Reason: From Judgement to Calculation* (San Francisco: W. H. Freeman and Co., 1976).

Wiener, Norbert. *The Human Use of Human Beings: Cybernetics and Society* (New York: Houghton Mifflin, Avon Books, 1967).

Whiteside, Thomas. *Computer Capers: Tales of Electronic Thievery, Embezzlement, and Fraud* (New York: Thomas Y. Crowell Co., 1978).

Acknowledgments

The author is grateful to the following publishers for permission to quote as follows:

Basic Books, Inc., Publishers for excerpts from *The Coming of the Post-Industrial Society: A Venture in Social Forecasting* by Daniel Bell. © 1973 by Daniel Bell. By permission of Basic Books, Inc., Publishers, New York.

Business Week for excerpts from: "Microcomputers Aim At a Huge New Market" May 12, 1973. © 1973 by McGraw-Hill, Inc. "Can the Third World Rule the Airwaves?' December 17, 1979. © 1979 by McGraw-Hill, Inc. "New Starters in Silicon Valley." February 26, 1981. © 1981 by McGraw-Hill, Inc. All rights reserved.

Cambridge University Press for excerpts from *Revolution in Miniature* by Ernest Braun and Stuart MacDonald.

Electronics Magazine for excerpts from the April 4, 1966, April 17, 1980 and February 28, 1980 issues. Copyright © by McGraw-Hill, Inc., 1966, 1980. All rights reserved.

Electronic News for excerpts from the April 18, 1977; April 3, 1978; May 1, 1978; March 19, 1979; June 4, 1979; June 11, 1979; September 24, 1979; October 15, 1979; June 30, 1980; September 15, 1980; November 3, 1980; November 17, 1980; December 8, 1980; January 19, 1981; February 2, 1981; March 30, 1981; April 13, 1981; August 3, 1981; August 17, 1981 issues.

Fortune for excerpts from articles by Austin Smith, February 11, 1980. © 1980 Time Inc. Aimee L. Morner, February 9, 1981. © 1981 Time Inc. Courtesy of Fortune Magazine.

W. H. Freeman and Company for excerpts from *Computer Power and Human Reason: From Judgment to Calculation* by Joseph Weizenbaum. W. H. Freeman and Company © 1976.

Houghton Mifflin Company for excerpts from *The Human Use of Human Beings* by Norbert Wiener. Copyright 1950, 1954 by Norbert Wiener. Reprinted by permission of Houghton Mifflin Company.

IEEE Spectrum for excerpts from *Genesis of the IC* by Michael Wolff. August 1976 edition.

McGraw-Hill Book Company for excerpts from *Understanding Media* by Marshall McLuhan. Copyright © 1964 by Marshall McLuhan. Used with the permission of McGraw-Hill Book Company.

The MIT Press for excerpts from: *The Computer Age*. Reprinted from *The Computer Age* by Michael Dertouzas and Joel Moses by permission of The MIT Press, Cambridge, Massachusetts. *The Microelectronics Revolution* by Tom Forrester. Reprinted from *The Microelectronics Revolution* by Tom Forrester by permission of The MIT Press, Cambridge, Massachusetts.

Newsweek for excerpts from "Looking for Life Out There" from Newsweek *Focus,* June/July 1980. © 1980 by Newsweek, Inc. All rights reserved. Reprinted by permission.

The New York Times for excerpts from "News of Radio" and "High Technology Jelly Bean Ace." © 1948, 1977 by The New York Times Company. Reprinted by permission.

OMNI for excerpts from the March 1979, September 1979, December 1979, and September 1980 issues. Copyright 1979, 1980 by Omni Publications International, Ltd. Reprinted by permission.

Alfred A. Knopf, Inc. for excerpts from *America by Design: Science, Technology and the Rise of Corporate Capitalism* by David Noble. Copyright © 1979. Reprinted by permission.

Vintage Books for excerpts from *The Physicists* by Daniel Kevles. Copyright © 1978. Reprinted by permission.

Howard W. Sams, Inc. for excerpts from *Microcomputer Dictionary and Guide* by Charles J. Sippl. Copyright © 1976. Used by permission.

Science for excerpts from: "New Ways to Make Microcircuits Smaller," "Evolution of Computers and Computing," "Effect of Cosmic Rays on Computer Memories," "Are VLSI Microcircuits Too Hard To Design?," "Ma Bell Eyes New Markets," "Electronics and Employment: Displacement Effects," "Computers and the U.S. Military Don't Mix," "Pentagon Orders End to Computers Babel," "Philosophers at the Pentagon," "Nuclear Pulse: Ensuring Delivery of the Doomsday Signal," "Energy, Security and War," "Nuclear Pulse: Awakening to the Chaos Factor." Copyright 1982 by the American Association for the Advancement of Science.

Scientific American for excerpts from "Metamagical Themas: A Coffeehouse Conversation on the Turing Test to See If a Machine Can Think" by Douglas R. Hofstadter from *Scientific American,* May 1981. "Microelectronics" by Robert F. Noyce, from *Scientific American,* September 1977. "50 and 100 Years Ago" from *Scientific American,* January 1980. "Precision-guided Weapons" by Paul F. Walker from *Scientific American,* August 1981. "Science and the Citizen: C³" from *Scientific American,* February 1981. Reprinted by permission.

Simon and Schuster, Inc. for excerpts from *The Gamesman* by Michael Maccoby. Copyright © 1978. Reprinted by permission.

SRI International for excerpts from "LSI Circuits," SRI Business Intelligence Program, Research Report 583, December 1976.

Time Inc. for excerpts from "Business: Thinking Small"; "Down Silicon Valley"; "Toward An Intelligence Beyond Man's." Copyright 1978 Time Inc. All rights reserved. Reprinted by permission from TIME.

The Wall Street Journal for excerpts from: "The Silicon Spies: Semiconductor Firms Are Plagued By Thefts of 'Hi-Tech Materials' "; "Tough Customer"; "Antitrust Chief Won't Drop AT&T Case But May Adjust it for Pentagon Fears"; "Is Repairing Your Car Frustrating? It Will Soon Be Worse"; "Electronic Systems Vulnerable to High-Altitude Atomic Blast." Reprinted by permission of The Wall Street Journal. © Dow Jones & Company 1981. All rights reserved.

Westview Press for excerpts from *The Changing Information Environment* by John McHale. Copyright © 1976 by Elek Books Ltd., London, England. Reprinted by permission.

Index

General Telephone and Electronics (GTE), 248
Gentronix, 184
Geosynchronous satellite orbits, 248–249
German Aircraft Research Institute, 56
Germanium, early research on, 74–77, 89, 91, 94–95, 97
Germanium Products, 81
Germany, electronics industry in, 174, 175
Glitches, 146–148
Goldstine, Adele, 63
Goldstine, Herman, 58, 63
Goldwater, Barry, 300
Good, I. J., 42
Gopal, Peter, 177, 179
Gramme machine, 16
"Gravity's Rainbow," 55
Great Depression, effects of electronics industry on, 36–37
Green, Harold, 236
Grove, Andrew, 114, 122, 125, 133, 175–176, 181, 271

Hackers, 201–202
Hale, George Ellery, 33
"Hard fails," 146
Harrington, Bob, 160, 174
Harris Corporation, 171, 175
Harvard Mark I, 63
Hayden Stone, 90
Head-up display (HUD), 286
Heath Company, 206, 212, 251
Hellman, Martin, 277–279
Henry, Joseph, 71
Heraclitus, 6
Hewlett, William, 87
Hewlett-Packard, 87, 88, 190–191
Hinkleman, Thomas, 110
Hitachi, 175, 189
Hoerni, Jean, 97, 101
Hoff, Ted, 117–121, 126
Hofstadter, Douglas, 143, 318–321, 330
Hogan, C. Lester, 115, 260
Holiday Inn, 250
Hollerith, Herman, 48
Home Box Office, 247, 251
Home computers. *See* Microcomputers
Honeywell Corporation, 64, 116, 151, 170, 171, 174, 191, 293
Hopper, Grace, 63
Hughes Communication, 248
Hugle, William, 101
Hybrid circuits, 104

IBM 360 computer, 103–104
IDEA Corporation, 82

Incandescent lamp, 10, 13–15, 21
Information sciences, 50–51, 55
Inmos International, 175
Integrated circuits, development of, 88–89, 92–111, 117, 127
Intel, 115–126, 154–155, 167–168, 170, 172, 176–178, 199, 208
Intelligence, artificial, 306–321
Intelligence gathering, electronic, 291–292
Intercontinental ballistic missile (ICBM) program, 99
International business Machine Company (IBM), 48, 84–85, 88, 103–105, 109, 128, 149, 151, 168, 170, 221–226, 232, 238, 240, 248, 257–258, 266–267, 290
International electronics industries, 173–195; espionage in, 176–182, 186–188; Third World, 254–258
Intersil, 171, 174
INTREPID, 39
Inventors, individual vs. multiple, 70–71
Iran, telecommunications in, 254
Ireland, electronics industry in, 174
Italy, electronics industry in, 174, 175

Japan, electronics industry in, 175, 181, 188–195, 248
Jastrow, Robert, 309–310
Jewett, Frank, 35
Jobs, changes in due to automation, 259–271; automobile mechanics, 267–268; farmers, 268–269; mail carriers, 266–267; secretaries, 264–265; shift foremen, 262–264
Jobs, Steven, 207–209
Joint Board of Patent Control, 22
Joint Committee on New Weapons and Equipment, 50
Jordan, Larry, 154
Josephson, Brian, 148
Josephson junction, 148–149
Junction transistor, 78, 82

Kay, Alan, 221
Kemmler, William, 20
Kennedy, John F., 111
Kilby, Jack, 94–97, 136, 150
Kuhn, Thomas, 8, 70
Kylex, 172

Labor market, changes in, 261–271
Lanford, W. A., 146
Lang, Fritz, 37
Large-scale integration (LSI), 116, 133, 144
Leary, Timothy, 329

Negative feedback, 29
Nelson, Ted, 221
"Neotechnic" period, 10
Netherlands, electronics industry in, 174
NIH (Not Invented Here), 80
Nippon Electric, 174, 175, 189
Nobel Prize: for explanation of super-conductivity, 148; for transistor effect, 70, 80–81
Noble, David, 11
North Carolina, electronics industry in, 170–171
Northern Telecom, 174
Noyce, Robert, 86, 90–94, 97, 100, 107, 112, 114–119, 122–123, 129–130, 136, 152–156, 167–169, 191–192, 219, 314
"n-type" doped semiconductors, 76
Nursing, changes due to automation, 266

Obsolescence, 289–290
Oettinger, Anthony, 227
Office automation, 264–265
Office of Scientific Research and Development (OSRD), 50, 72
Ovshinsky, Stanford, 150

Packard, David, 87, 329–330
"Paleotechnic" period, 10
Paradigm shift, 8, 71
Parker, Donn, 276, 277
PARRY program, 312–313
Pascal, Blaise, 46
Patent disputes: early computers, 64; early electrical inventions, 21–24, 30–31, 34–35; integrated circuit, 97–98
PBXs, computerized, 232
Pearl Street Power Station, 15
Perry, William, 187
Personal computers, 210–225; see also Microcomputers
Personnel recruitment in electronics industry, 157–163
PET computer, 206
Peter the Great, 47
Petritz, Richard, 174–175
Philco, 81, 101
Philips, 124, 174
Photolithography, 134, 145
Photovoltaic technology, 149–152
Pierce, Charles Sanders, 44
"Planar" process, 97–98, 101
"p-n-p junction" transistor, 78
Point-contact transistor, 77–80
Poland, electronics industry in, 174
Politics, automation of, 281
"Polyphase" AC-generating system, 17, 19

Pong, 200–205
Powers Tabulating Machine Company, 48
Precision-guided weapons (PGWs), 284–287
Price, Robert, 193
Price fixing, 109–110
PRIME TARGET, 294
Privacy, electronic invasion of, 253
Programming, 48, 60–61, 63, 104, 270–271
Project Green Thumb, 269
"Project Pigeon," 54
Project ULTRA, 39
"p-type" doped semiconductors, 76
Pulse code modulation, 232
Pynchon, Thomas, 55

Qube, 239
Qwip, 172
Qyx, 172

Radar, 33, 34, 72, 73, 92–93
Radiation, VDT, 211–214
Radiation hardening, 301
Radio, 27–29, 32–35, 37–38, 69–70
Radio Shack, 128, 205, 206–207, 209, 212, 270
Radio Telephone Company, 29
Radio telephones, 228–229, 231
Random access memory (RAM) micro-chip, 116, 139
Raphael, Howard, 160–162
Rathbone, Basil, 283
Raytheon Semiconductor, 81, 101, 165
RCA, 35, 81, 100, 110, 124, 248, 290
Regis McKenna, Inc., 208
Relay gates, 45
Relays, electromechanical, 44–45, 48, 56
Reliance Electronic Company, 172
Remington Rand, 48, 63, 64–65, 84
Remotely Piloted Vehicles (RPVs), 286–287
Resonance, electrical, 24
"Reverse engineering," 180
Rheem Semiconductor, 101
Robertson, Jack, 187–188, 290
Robots, 262
Rock, Arthur, 115–116, 208
Rockwell International, 124, 248
Route 128 (Boston), 87, 112
Rural Venture, 269

Safety, problems with, 211–214
"Sagger" missiles, 284
Salaries in electronics industry, 156–157
Sanders, Jerry, III, 103, 107, 115, 124,

Tesla, Nikola, 3–5, 15–19, 23, 24–26, 245
Tesla Coil, 4, 24–25
Texas, electronics industry in, 112, 170
Texas Instruments (TI), 81–82, 88, 93–98, 100, 107, 112, 113, 120, 124, 150, 151, 190, 209, 212
Third World, telecommunications in, 254–258
Thomas, Lewis, 331
Thomson-Houston, 21
"III–V" substances, 149
Time sharing, 104
Timex, 198, 199
Toshiba, 175, 181–182, 189
Trade secrets, violations of, 160–164, 176–188
Transistors: early research and development of, 69–85; miniaturization of, 94–97; silicon, 82, 88–90, 94
TRS-80, 205, 207
"Truth tables," 44
TRW, 248
Tunneling, 148
Turing, Alan, 39, 40–42, 46, 51, 56, 62, 67, 71, 307, 313
Turing Machine, 41
Twain, Mark, 24

UHF channels, 106–107
Umtech, 221
Unemployment, structural, 259
Ungermann, Ralph, 172–173
Union Carbide, 151
United States Postal Service, changes in due to automation, 266–267
United Technologies, 171
UNIVAC, 61–65
University of California at Berkeley, 166

Vacuum tube computers, 58–68, 81
Vacuum tubes, 28–32, 36, 69, 81
Vail, Theodore, 227
Van Deerlin, Lionel, 235
Van Dinh, Tran, 255
Varian Associates, 88
Venrock Associates, 208
Very large scale integration (VLSI), 133; economics of, 153–156; limitations of, 144–148
VHF channels, 106
Video Brain, 221

Video display terminal (VDT) radiation scare, 210–214
Videotext, 239–240
Videoton, 188
Viguerie, Richard, 281
Villa, Luigi, 311
VLSI Technology Inc., 154
von Neumann, John, 51, 60, 61, 71
Vydec, 172

Wafers, production of, 133–135
Walker, Paul F., 288
Wardencliff Project, 24–26, 245
Warfare, electronic, 283–305
Warner Communications, 204, 239
Watches, digital, 197–200
Watson, Thomas, 48–49
Watt, James, 9
Weaver, Warren, 51
Webster, William, 187
Weizenbaum, Joseph, 196, 217–218, 307–308
WESTAR, 247, 248
Western Electric Company, 35, 73, 79, 81, 171, 226, 233, 235, 237
Western Union, 20, 30, 247
Westinghouse, George, 19–20
Westinghouse Electric Company, 19–24, 26, 28, 30, 35, 151, 171
"Wet cell" technology, 150
Whiteside, Thomas, 276–277
Whitney, Willis, 33
Wickenden, William, 87
Wiener, Norbert, 23, 51–54, 55, 65–67, 331
Wimex, 292–294
Winograd, Terry, 316
Wireless transmission, 3, 27, 32–35
Word processors, 264–265
World Administrative Radio Conference (WARC), 255–257
Worth, Larry, 176–177
Wozniak, Stephen, 207–209

Xerox Corporation, 172

Yugoslavia, electronics industry in, 174

Ziegler, J. F., 146
Zilog, 161–162, 172–173, 207
Z3 and Z4 electronic computers, 56
Zuse, Conrad, 56–57, 62, 71